An Economic History
of Modern France

**The Columbia Economic History
of the Modern World
Stuart W. Bruchey, General Editor**

An Economic History
of Modern France

François Caron

Translated from the French by Barbara Bray

Columbia University Press / New York / 1979

Library of Congress Cataloging in Publication Data

Caron, François.
  An economic history of modern France.

  (The Columbia economic history of the modern world)
  Includes bibliographies and index.
  1. France—Economic conditions. I. Title.
II. Series.
HC273.C28 1979 330.9′44 78–15353
ISBN 0–231–03860–7

To the memory of Pierre Léon

Acknowledgments

THE BOOK WAS written in French and translated by Barbara Bray, whom I should like to thank for agreeing to tackle a highly technical vocabulary and for numerous observations which helped me to clarify the text. The book has a purely economic and historical purpose. It is not a textbook on French economics. It is not a work of social history. Many people may regard these as artificial frontiers. But it was not my intention to put forward a new general explanation of the facts about France. My only object was to present an account of the present state of the problem, taking into account past and recent academic research. The chapter bibliographies consist almost entirely of books and articles quoted or directly used. For a more complete bibliography the reader may consult volume VI of the *Cambridge Economic History of Europe (The Industrial Revolution and After)*. The present work owes a great deal to discussions with colleagues and students. Among the first I should like to cite the names of Jean Bouvier, François Crouzet (who kindly read over and commented on the text), Claude Fohlen, and Pierre Léon, whose death in October 1976 casts a cloud over the publication of a book I now dedicate to his memory.

F. CARON

Contents

An Economic History
of Modern France

Part One: The Nineteenth Century (1815–1914)

Introduction

THE NINETEENTH CENTURY in France was a subtle and ambiguous period. Some recent books, especially those concerned with social attitudes, have shown the pitfalls that may lie in wait for anyone taking too apriorist an approach. Intellectuals tend to reconstruct some imaginary nineteenth century and then project their own fantasies onto it. But it is a century that needs to be approached from within, and looked at in the first instance through contemporary eyes. True, the dangers of apriorism are less in economic than in social history; but they are nonetheless real. The view that emerges from some works on the subject is of an upper middle class of bosses meanly running the French economy by exploiting the labor of the workers and making use of the savings of the lower middle classes, both the latter sections of society allowing themselves to be manipulated in this way because they were "alienated" by a press dependent on the power of money. The upper-middle-class oppressors did not even have the excuse of efficiency, for they were only the representatives of an exhausted capitalism which preferred guaranteed profit to risk. An eminent American sociologist has even maintained that under the Third Republic there was a kind of tacit alliance between the Malthusian upper middle class and the conservative peasantry, opting for slow growth in order to limit the development of the working class and keep it within a "social ghetto." Such constructions may seem to present a daunting internal coherence, but though certain individual bricks may be sound, the building as a whole is precarious. To describe France's economy in the nineteenth century as a frozen economy is to extract certain elements, magnify them, and reject the overall complexity of a reality which can never be properly seized by a historian who is in too much of a hurry, or unduly preoccupied with ideology. Far be it from me to overlook the failings and horrors of the period; but it is not as easy as all that to understand. The nineteenth century was something else besides: above all a sustained and sincere effort to free people from the material constraints which weighed upon them. In this sense it was what P. Léon, speaking specifically of Lyons, has called a "glorious century." As I have said, it was ambiguous: liberal, but maintaining a tradition of bureaucratic interventionism; industrialist, but pursuing, and partly realizing, its dream of industrialization within a context of small units of production; centralist, but achieving prodigies in the area of local plants; production-oriented, but the preserver of France's forests; scientific, but empiricist, making use of technical know-how.

It seems to me that French growth in the nineteenth century is distinguished by four main features: (1) the population slump, (2) the special nature of its technical progress, (3) the peculiarities of its structure of production and finance, and (4) its agrarian structures.

1. By a process which began quite slowly but accelerated after 1870, the nineteenth century arrived in its last decade at zero population growth. This demographic slump produced a marked decrease in France's power in the world, and did much to help slow down the per capita growth rate by reducing the size of the market and by limiting the mobility of the factors of production (whereas stronger demographic pressure would have made greater mobility inevitable). So long as demographic pressure remained high and the mass of unemployed constituted a permanent threat to social order, the élites were bound to wish for rapid changes of economic structure: this attitude prevailed under the Second Empire, after the slump of 1848–52, which had revealed what many authors have called the "over-

loading" of the rural areas. But as soon as this pressure was relaxed, there were visions of a future based on a search for stability, and France saw itself as the country of equilibrium and the happy medium.

2. But another factor—technical progress—steadily undermined this longed-for equilibrium. France, which at the beginning of the nineteenth century had been obsessed by its "backwardness" vis-à-vis England, had learned and adopted British techniques and made them its own, developing, in terms of its own material circumstances (lack of sources of energy; high quality and, for a long time, abundant supply of labor; etc.), and also in terms of different technical traditions and scientific influences, an original technical system peculiar to France itself. This system produced a series of remarkable discoveries in various essential sectors of industry: very high quality textiles; the utilization of water power, leading to hydroelectricity; electrochemicals; the metallurgy of aluminum; automobile manufacture. The link between science and industry was certainly less "established" in France at the end of the nineteenth century than it was in Germany or the United States, but France's contributions to this new stage of the industrial revolution were not negligible.

3. The original features of French innovation were merely one factor in a system of production which we cannot attempt to judge. Industrialization in France was at once ancient and limited. When the liberal Empire expired in 1871, after the disaster of the Franco-Prussian war, France was a great industrial country only very partially industrialized. During the first two-thirds of the century its entrepreneurs had built up a "dualist" system of production. C. E. Labrousse has expressed this by saying that the economic Ancien Régime in France lasted up to the great watershed of the 1847–52 crisis. Means of production that were scarcely capitalistic continued to develop at the same time that the "Industrial Revolution" was spreading, culminating in the building of large factories using steam engines. This dualism never entirely vanished.

French business in the nineteenth century was not the closed world too often described. In a society where it was difficult to rise, and success always remained precarious, men imbued with the spirit of enterprise came from the most varied social backgrounds. Whether one is concerned with the creators of the engineering industry in the first half of the century, or those of the automobile industry toward its end, one sees them emerging from social origins of every kind; and there was also a stratum of small entrepreneurs always on the alert for something new. The image of the French saver (*rentier*) as one looking out for "safe investments," burying his savings in government bonds, then in railway stocks, then in foreign loans, is a true one; but it is not the only one. The French financial system, though modern from the outset in its monetary centralization and the power of a few big merchant banks, was also characterized by the survival of many pockets of anachronism. Their tardy but rapid disappearance facilitated the emergence in the 1860s of deposit banks, which was accompanied by a strengthening of the big merchant banks. All this made France the second greatest financial power in the world in the 1900s. Contemporaries all contrasted a Germany strong through its industries with a France strong through its banks. On the eve of the 1914–18 war, France was the second greatest exporter of capital in the world. But this power was not backed up by equivalent commercial successes. Up to the 1870s, France had followed world economic growth only with difficulty, and after that date had been left far behind. The income from France's large exports of capital made up the deficit in the trade balance. It was as if the accumulation of capital abroad took place through reinvestment of income from previous investment.

On the whole, French capitalism was neither entirely successful nor entirely played out on the eve of the First World War. It was the product of the slow and difficult development, within an open and dynamic world economy, of a system in which it was difficult to justify the erection of the huge units of production suited to the needs of the world economy. Such expansion encountered considerable obstacles both natural and sociological, for the domestic market could act as a "mass market" for only a limited number of products.

4. For nineteenth-century France was fundamentally a peasant country. Economists such as J. Marczewski and M.

Lévy-Leboyer have held French agriculture responsible for the deceleration of the economy in the second part of the nineteenth century. But this is to apply to the nineteenth century the a priori judgments of the twentieth. French agriculture in the nineteenth century developed rapidly within the framework of agrarian structures there could be no question of destroying. It makes no sense to compare the competition French agriculture had to meet from new countries after the 1870s with competition between industrial countries. France could not turn itself into the Far West or become another Denmark. Agricultural protectionism was unavoidable. But it was not absolute, and a certain level of competition was maintained. French agriculture's undoing was not protectionism but the weakness of the domestic market.

The first chapter in this part attempts to define and measure growth. The second, third, and fourth chapters analyze the developments—institutional, financial, and physical (formation of capital)—which lent a rigid and incoherent system more unity and flexibility, for despite the continually heavy weight represented by the state, the nineteenth century wanted to be regarded as liberal, and the mobility of men, capital, and goods was generally accepted as a special instrument of economic progress. The fifth chapter deals with the development of domestic and foreign trade, the first being less well known than the second. It is only in the three final chapters in this section that an attempt is made to describe agricultural, productive, and industrial structures.

Chapter One: Economic Growth in France in the Nineteenth Century: Problems of Method and Results

Population Growth and Growth of National Income

ECONOMIC GROWTH IN France in the nineteenth century took place against a demographic background which presented striking contrasts. In the first part of the century, although its dynamism as regards population was already less marked than that of other European countries, France, according to some observers, was on the brink of overpopulation. Yet from the 1870s onward, France's population growth was close to zero. In order to study the relation between the two factors, we shall define the pattern of population growth, try to evaluate the growth of national income, and then compare the two.

Population. Table 1.1 shows the main periods in the evolution of the population in France during the nineteenth century. Compared with that of other European countries, population growth in France between 1816 and 1846 is low. The population of France increased by 18 percent as against 50 percent in Great Britain. Between 1800 and 1850 the population of France increased by 0.5 percent per year, as against 0.74 percent in Germany. But this increase is high compared with later figures. Between 1846 and 1886 the increase was only about half what it had been in the first part of the century. From 1886 to the end of the century, France was close to stagnation.

This pattern is the result of facts which, as a whole, are quite well known. The slowness of population growth over the

Table 1.1 Population Growth in France in the Nineteenth Century

	Population at Beginning of Period (in millions)	Population at End of Period (in millions)	Mean Annual Increase	Growth Rate (percent)
1816–1846	30.0	35.4	180,000	0.55
1846–1866*	35.4	37.4	100,000	0.27
1866–1886†	36.5	37.9	70,000	0.19
1886–1901	37.9	38.4	33,000	0.08
1901–1911	38.4	39.2	80,000	0.20

* 1866: excluding Nice and Savoy.
† 1866: excluding Alsace-Lorraine.

century derives from a rapid drop in the birthrate combined with a very slow drop in the death rate. The drop in the birthrate occurred in three stages: a fairly rapid drop up to the 1850s; stagnation up to the 1870s; and a rapid drop again after 1870.

The birthrate went down considerably under the Restoration, falling from 32.9 percent in 1816–20 to 30.5 percent in 1826–30, a drop of 7.2 percent in ten years. Under the July Monarchy it went down by the same percentage in fifteen years (28.1 percent in 1841–45). In the middle of the century there is "such a break that it is as if one is dealing with two different societies" (Ch. E. Pouthas): the birthrate drops to 26.7 percent in 1846–50, a decrease of 5 percent between the two five-year periods making up the 1840s. With the exception of the two years 1870 and 1871, it remains at the level of 26.0–26.7 percent up to 1872–75. With the beginning of the 1870s, the decline resumes, at a rate similar to that under the July Monarchy up to 1881–85, and after that at a rhythm similar to that under the Restoration.

So France is characterized both by the precocity and by the steepness of the decline in its birthrate. These peculiarities result from the speed with which methods of birth control spread through the different social milieus. It has now been proven that these practices had long been known in urban communities, and in particular in small towns, as also in certain rural environments, particularly among small landowners. Birth control is associated with late marriages. But demographic behavior is quite variable: even in an area as small as the Department of Loir-et-Cher, G. Dupeux contrasts two types of canton in the early part of the nineteenth century: the purely rural regions of Perche, Beauce, and Sologne still have an eighteenth-century demographic structure, while in the valleys and small towns we already find the demographic structure characteristic of the twentieth century, with a low birthrate by which the population barely succeeds in replacing itself. The same sort of contrast is to be met with between purely rural cantons. These contrasts lead to noticeable regional differences. This is one of the most important distinctions between the regions and, according to some authors, the main cause of contrasts in growth. It is clear that zones of low demographic pressure (Aquitaine, Normandy) already contrast with zones of high pressure (Brittany, Nord, Alsace).

The death rate remained stagnant until 1830. It fell during the July Monarchy, dropping from 25.5 per thousand in 1826–30 to 22.7 per thousand in 1841–45, a drop of nearly 11 percent. It rose again and remained stable at almost 24 per thousand from 1846 to 1860; fell only slightly in the 1860s; returned to its 1841–45 level in 1872–75, and remained at that level until 1891–95. At this time the birth and death rates are equal at 22.3 per thousand. One of the most striking features is the high level of infant mortality up to 1895. Between 1816–20 and 1841–45, the infant mortality rate fell from 182 per thousand to 156 per thousand. It rose again during the Empire to a level of 179 per thousand, which is very close to the rate during the years 1826–30. From 1872 to 1895 it was between 166 and 170 per thousand.

So the break in the pattern of population growth from the middle of the 1840s onward can be explained by the sudden drop in the birthrate and the increase in the death rate at that time, while the halt in the downward trend followed by an upturn up to the beginning of the 1880s is due to the stabilization of the birthrate and the fall, followed by stabilization, of the death rate.

The trend was to a certain extent reversed in the period leading up to the First World War: from 1886 to 1901 mean annual population growth was 33,000 or 0.08 percent; from 1901 to 1911 it was 80,000 or 0.20 percent. This recovery is not due to any recovery in the birthrate; this, on the contrary, continued to fall, dropping from 24.7 per thousand in 1881–85 to 18.8 per thousand in 1911–13. The improvement in the population figures is due to a fall, at last a considerable one, in the death rate, from the 1890s onward: it fell from 23.3 per thousand in 1891–95 to 18.3 per thousand in 1911–13.

From the middle of the nineteenth century, the decline in population was partly offset by a rapid increase in immigration. A third of the increase between 1866 and 1886 is due to foreign immigration. After this date the statistics are distorted because of the 1889 law on naturalization. But even taking naturalization into account, the increase in immigration seems to have been appreciably slower between 1886 and 1906 than between 1866 and 1886: the number of foreigners entering France seems to have remained constant. Immigration did not stop: between these two dates the number of Italians rose from 264,000 to 377,000. On the other hand, the number of people from Belgium and Luxembourg fell by 210,000, dropping from 520,000 to 310,000. In the years preceding the 1914 war, there was a new spurt of immigration. This influx of immigrants is still one of the main arguments of those who try to link the slow rate of production growth to the slow rate of population growth.

National Income. Any attempt to evaluate national income in the nineteenth century in terms of current values is so full of uncertainties that it must be considered hypothetical. A. Sauvy has drawn up a set of figures using contemporary equivalents. They are very different from evaluations of national product made by the Institut de Science Economique Appliquée (ISEA) under the direction of J. Marczewski. Table 1.2 compares Sauvy's figures with estimates of national income based on Marczewski's national product series. Until 1870, Sauvy's figures are 10 years "behind" and appreciably lower than the other estimates, but the discrepancy is smaller in 1880, reversed in 1890, and disappears in 1900.

In order to calculate national income at constant prices I have made use of the set of prices drawn up by Monsieur Lévy-Leboyer (table 1.3). There are appreciable differences

Table 1.2 Two Assessments of National Income (in millions of francs current)

According to A. Sauvy		Deduced from J. Marczewski's National Product Series	
1810	6,270		
1820	7,862		
1830	8,808	1825–1830	10,575
1840	10,000	1835–1844	12,735
1850	11,412	1845–1854	15,232
1860	15,200	1855–1864	20,797
1870	18,823	1865–1874	23,667
1880	22,400	1875–1884	23,842
1890	25,000	1885–1894	23,374
1900	26,300	1894–1904	26,816
1910	33,200	1905–1913	34,711
1913	36,000		

between the rates of increase obtained from these figures and those that may be deduced from A. Sauvy's figures in terms of constant values (table 1.4). If the figures are divided up into periods of 20 years, some of the differences become less, but not all:

My Figures			Sauvy's Figures	
1825–34 to 1845–54	1.5		1830 to 1850	1.6
1845–54 to 1865–74	1.6		1850 to 1870	0.7
1865–74 to 1885–94	0.7		1870 to 1890	1.3
1885–94 to 1905–13	1.2		1890 to 1910	1.1

The main difference concerns the period 1845–54 to 1885–94 or 1850 to 1890. It disappears completely if a new grouping is made:

1825–34 to 1845–54	1.5	1830 to 1850	1.6
1845–54 to 1885–94	1.09	1850 to 1890	1
1885–94 to 1905–13	1.2	1890 to 1910	1.1

The Sauvy figures would indicate a deceleration in growth of per capita national income under the Second Empire, and an acceleration at the time of the Great Depression. But it seems more likely to me that there was a slight acceleration during the Second Empire (1.6 percent per annum instead of 1.5 percent),

Table 1.3 National Income at Constant Prices, Based on Prices of Lévy-Leboyer (in 1905–1913 francs)

	Total National Income (millions of francs)	Per Capita National Income (francs)
1825–1834	10,606	325.6
1835–1844	13,061	380.5
1845–1854	15,866	443.0
1855–1864	19,097	510.9
1865–1874	22,327	602.0
1875–1884	24,272	644.2
1885–1894	26,713	696.6
1895–1904	30,965	794.7
1905–1913	34,711	876.4

and a marked deceleration (0.7 percent) during the 1870s and 1880s. Both sets of figures show the recovery of the 1890s and 1900s as no higher than 1.2 or 1.1 percent. However, the 1.6 percent between 1900 and 1913 which can be deduced from the Sauvy figures seems to me quite acceptable.

This gives the following (very rough) periodization:

1. During the first two or three decades of the nineteenth century a rapid population growth (up 0.55 percent per annum) was accompanied by a very slow growth in per capita national income (0.5 percent).

2. During the 1830s and 1840s population growth was maintained, though it tended to decline at the end of the period: the falling-off in population growth occurred after 1846. But there was an appreciable acceleration in the increase of national income (1.5 percent from 1825–34 to 1845–54).

Table 1.4 Mean Annual Per Capita Growth Rate of National Revenue (in constant francs)

	According to ISEA Figures		According to Sauvy Figures
1825–1834 to 1835–1844	1.50	1830 to 1840	0.75
1835–1844 to 1845–1854	1.50	1840 to 1850	2.70
1845–1854 to 1855–1864	1.40	1850 to 1860	0.15
1855–1864 to 1865–1874	1.60	1860 to 1870	1.23
1865–1874 to 1875–1884	0.60	1870 to 1880	1.17
1875–1884 to 1885–1894	0.70	1880 to 1890	1.40
1885–1894 to 1895–1904	1.30	1890 to 1900	0.73
1895–1904 to 1905–1913	1.07	1900 to 1910	1.63
		1910 to 1913	1.60

3. In the 1850s and 1860s the decline in the population growth rate was not accompanied by any decline in the growth rate of per capita national income. But there was a noticeable decline in the growth rate of per capita national income in the years 1870 to 1880.

4. In the last fifteen years of the century the population of France scarcely increased at all (0.08 percent per annum from 1886 to 1901). This period corresponds to the end of the deceleration in the growth of national income and to its return to a level above 1 percent.

On the whole, the 1830s, 1840s, 1850s, and 1860s saw an increase in national income that was appreciably higher than the rate of population increase. In other words, France broke the "demographic barrier." But this economic development was accompanied by a gradual falling-off in the rate of population growth, a rate which became first stagnation and then decline. To see this as the sole cause of the falling-off in economic growth would be as absurd as to deny it any influence at all. The question needs to be examined from two points of view: did the slowdown of population growth limit the number of commercial transactions? Did it, because of lack of growth prospects, limit investment in the basic sectors, particularly in construction and in consumer goods? We can only deal with such problems through a proper analysis of such transactions and investments. Growth in per capita national income resumed at a more rapid rate in the 1890s, in other words, at a time at which stagnation had set in as far as population was concerned. But the progress that followed occurred against a demographic background that had improved because of the decrease in the mortality rate.

The Growth of Labor Forces

Total Working Population. The most obvious consequence of the slow population growth is a slower increase in available labor reserves. I have taken as the working population those who were aged from 15 to 64 years, although for a long time the real date at which people entered into active working life was much lower than 15. But 15 was the normal age at the end of the period. The percentage of those aged 15–64 as against the total population increased until 1856 (65.7 percent against 62.1 percent in 1931). After this date it remained stable. This "almost perfect structural stability on the part of the population that was of an age to work" (Toutain) explains why the development of the available labor reserve is similar to that of the total population. Here are the mean annual increases in the working-age population:

1816–46	125,000
1846–71	100,000
1872–81	80,000
1881–1911	48,000

These labor resources were gradually put to better and better use. But the uncertain nature of our sources makes it necessary to go into some methodological detail about the working population itself. The evaluation of the working population is a very uncertain matter before 1906.

There was no census in the early part of the nineteenth century. Two sets of assessments have been put forward, one set by J. C. Toutain for 1800–12 and 1840–45, and the other by Lévy-Leboyer for every ten-year period of the first half-century. These estimates are based on a backward projection of activity rates according to age as shown in the 1856 census. The census of 1851 is regarded by most commentators as exaggerated: it indicates a working population of 22,236,000 as compared with 14,216,000 in 1856. This overstatement is largely due to the fact that most of the people living on the land were counted as active. This led to an overestimate of the active agricultural population, both male and female (7,771,000 men in 1851 as against 5,146,000 in 1856; and 6,456,000 in 1851 as against 2,158,000 in 1856). But in fact the results of the 1851 census, at least as far as the men are concerned, are perhaps less erroneous than is usually thought.

After this date the census figures are clearly underestimated. E. Malinvaud has recalculated the working population in 1896, and gets the figure of 19.5 million instead of 18.9.

In these circumstances, what is one to say about earlier censuses? The figures for the working population which are derived from them show two "leaps forward," one between the census of 1872 and that of 1876 (an increase of 1.5 million) and another between the census of 1891 and that of 1896 (an increase of 2.6 million). Such differences can only be explained by changes in the methods of census-taking. It is probably to these changes that we should attribute the greater part of the "leap forward" which took place between 1891 and 1896. The 1896 census was the first to take separate account of members of the working population. The "leap forward" between 1872 and 1876, on the other hand, may be partly explained by the marked increase in the female working population which is always appreciable after wars. But here too we should allow for the possibility of a statistical distortion.

For the period 1896–1911, E. Malinvaud has not only increased the 1896 figure; he has also lowered the figures for the later censuses, so that the active population, instead of increasing by 2 million during those fifteen years, as the census figures would suggest, appears almost to have stagnated, increasing only by 500,000.

It should be observed, however, that the improvement in the census-taking methods is not without intrinsic significance. Some differences are due to erratic changes in the definition of "working" and "nonworking," but some are due to new methods of production which made the various professions more easily definable and therefore more easily identified. In other words, it is probable that the earliest censuses classified as "nonworking" people who worked only part time or intermittently and in ways not clearly defined. As censuses came to reflect the facts more clearly, they showed both a decrease in partial unemployment and increasing precision about professional status, arising out of better organization of production.

This consideration probably explains many of the differences which exist between the data as given in the censuses and those given in agricultural surveys (table 1.5). The surveys put forward much higher figures for the male agricultural working population than do the censuses. This difference

Table 1.5 Comparison of Figures on Male Agricultural Working Population (in millions)

	According to Censuses	According to Agricultural Surveys
1861	5.342	
1862		6.508
1881	5.465	
1882		6.381
1892		6.201
1896	5.675	

is easily explained by the uncertain nature of the activities pursued by a large part of the rural population. Many agricultural day laborers could be classified as part of the industrial labor force, for many rural industries used this labor part time. Moreover, many country-dwellers were classified as nonworking in the census and as working in the surveys, which included a category of "land-owning day laborers" composed of people owning just a few *ares* (one *are* equals one hundred square meters) and working irregularly. If we take these people into account, we should first of all have to increase enormously the figures previous to 1862. For on the basis of the census, J. Pautard arrives, for 1852, at a figure of 7,680,000 for the male agricultural working population, which is close to that of the census of 1851 (7,771,900). We should also have to revise entirely the figures for the other censuses. Adding together the census figures for other categories and the survey figures for male working population, we should then arrive at the figures for the working population set forth in table 1.6.

Table 1.6 Working Population Recalculated to Include Underemployed Agricultural Workers (in millions)

	Working Population Recalculated	Working Population According to Censuses
1852	16.240	13.990*
1862	15.986	14.800
1882	17.430	16.600
1892	17.456	16.300
1896	19.470	18.900

*Per Lévy-Leboyer.

These figures reveal a stagnation of the working population in the 1850s, and a slow increase from the 1860s onward. We can also deduce from them a more normal percentage of working men between 15 and 64 years of age:

1862	93.3
1882	98.4
1892	98.4
1896	102.3

instead of:

1861	83.9
1881	91.9
1891	89.7
1896	100.9

I have preferred to use the census figures, while challenging them and remembering that they are underestimated or at least that a by no means negligible part of the population which is counted as nonworking is underemployed or inappropriately employed rather than really nonworking. The gradual reduction in the difference between the levels of male participation given by the two sources reflects a gradual reduction in that part of the labor force which was incompletely employed. But we have to remember that our increases in population will be underestimated in the first part of the nineteenth century and subsequently overestimated. This "marginal" working population should really be weighted by means of a reduction factor, but such a factor is indeterminable.

Even if we were to regard it merely as a statistical illusion, the increase in the working population deduced from the censuses would reveal, through the perhaps deceptive increase in participation rates, a better utilization of labor and therefore a more intensive use of labor resources. But I am convinced that the growth in participation rates is not entirely illusory. In short, the fact that the working population increases more quickly than the population of working age can be taken to mean two things: (1) a reduction in a certain degree of chronic unemployment; and (2) a reduction in hidden unemployment.

During the early part of the century, up to the end of the 1840s, the mean annual growth of the working population was probably about 80,000, 60 percent of the increase in the population of working age. According to Lévy-Leboyer the mean annual rates of increase were as follows:

  1800–4 to 1825–29: 0.5 percent
  1825–29 to 1845–49: 0.6 percent

In fact, these figures should be increased to take into account the undervaluation of the labor force that was really active, both in agriculture, as revealed by the differences between the agricultural surveys and the censuses, and in industry.

The 1850s and 1860s seem to be characterized by a slight slackening-off in this growth, which, if we adopted the recalculated figures based on the agricultural surveys, would become almost stagnation during the 1850s, followed by a marked recovery in the 1860s. It should also be noted that if we link the census figures with those of J. C. Toutain and M. Lévy-Leboyer, we get an appreciable falling-off in the 1850s. The mean annual increase in the working population between 1845–49 and 1866 would seem to have been 76,000 per annum, a rate of 0.5 percent per annum according to the censuses. That section of the population of working age which we find in the working population rose from 60 to 76 percent. These figures should be reduced if we increase those for the working population at the end of the 1840s.

A change of direction, first discernible in the 1850s, occurred from the 1860s onward: there was a sharp check in the increase in the population of working age, but a marked ac-

Table 1.7 Increase in Working Population, According to Census Figures

	Working Population	Rate of Increase (%)
1866–1896	147,000*	0.90
1866–1876	171,000	1.09
1876–1886	60,000	0.30
1886–1896	322,000	1.19

* 1866: excluding Alsace-Lorraine (working population estimated at 1,040,000).

Table 1.8 Relation Between Number of People Aged 15–64 and the Working Population (in percent)

	Total		Men		Women	
	Census	Malinvaud	Census	Malinvaud	Census	Malinvaud
1840–1845	60.1					
1856	59.8		83.8		36.3	
1866	60.0		83.0		36.9	
1876	67.4		81.8		42.4	
1881	67.8		91.9		44.5	
1891	65.4		89.7		41.3	
1896	75.3	77.6	100.9	101.8	50.2	55.1
1906	81.4	77.0	103.8	106.2	59.5	54.6
1911	81.2	77.6	104.1	101.6	59.0	54.1

celeration in the growth of the working population (table 1.7). There were thus strong increases in the "working" proportion of the population (tables 1.8 and 1.9).

A dual paradox emerges from these figures: the period of greatest increase in the working population seems to correspond both to a period of slackening in the growth of the population of working age, and to a period of slackening in the growth of national income.

The first paradox is explained to a large extent by the considerations given above: there were mistakes, pure and simple, in the statistics, and also the censuses reflected the facts better because of an improvement in the utilization of labor which, because it was better organized, was more intensive and more continuous.

Table 1.9 Participation Rate: Relation Between Total Population and Working Population (in percent)

	Total		Men		Women	
	Census	Malinvaud	Census	Malinvaud	Census	Malinvaud
1856	39.3		54.6		24.1	
1876	43.9		60.3		27.7	
1896	49.5*		64.4		32.9	
1906	53.3*		68.2	67.0	39.0	36.0
1911	53.4*		68.6	65.5	38.7	35.5

* Malinvaud gives 51 percent for these three dates.

In order to understand the second paradox we need to break down the period 1866–96 into several subperiods, and to remember the largely artificial nature of the increase of 2.6 million in the working population between 1891 and 1896.

The first of the two ratios with which we are concerned (table 1.8) remains at a level of about 60 percent up to the 1860s, jumps to 68 percent in 1881, to 75 percent in 1896, and to 81 percent in 1906. This development results from an increase in both male and female labor, the second having increased more rapidly than the first: the proportion of men in the working population fell from 69.2 percent in 1856 to 66.4 percent in 1896 and 62.9 percent in 1906.

The second ratio (table 1.9) can be summarized as follows: 40 percent of the population of France are working in the 1850s, 44 percent in the 1870s, and 50 percent at the end of the century. We may accept that the tendency toward increase in the working population which had been evident since the beginning of the century accelerated toward the end of the period up to the early 1870s, during which the war probably affected the situation. It may also be accepted that the increase in the working population fell off between 1876 and 1891.

The "leap forward" of the years 1891–96, which varies, according to the tables used, from 1.45 to 2.6 million, is mainly attributable to statistical errors, but it is also due, probably, to a reduction in that proportion of the working population which had been difficult until then to include in the census. After this date, the revised estimates made by Malinvaud reduce the growth of the working population to 0.1 percent (33,000) per annum. His figures probably exaggerate the tendency toward stabilization.

In the period as a whole, the working population increased at an annual mean rate of 0.6 per annum during the nineteenth century. This rate reflects the gradual elimination of chronic male unemployment, the almost complete elimination of the various forms of hidden unemployment, and a more and more intense utilization of female labor. Statistically, this increase, up to the 1860s, is parallel to the increase in the population of working age. During the early part of the century, the rate of this growth gradually accelerated both on the purely statistical level and thanks to the development of activities which in fact corresponded to a kind of "hidden unemployment." We may probably allow that there was a certain deceleration in this growth in the 1850s and the beginning of the 1860s, a deceleration that was all the more marked because a greater number of people who were really underemployed were counted as working. A certain degree of acceleration seems to have occurred during the years following the 1870 war, and then there was a falling-off from the late 1870s until the early 1890s. There was then an appreciable acceleration, followed by a very slow increase which was maintained up to the First World War. In fact, from the 1860s onward, the growth of the working population becomes independent of the growth of the population of working age, while from the 1890s onward, the level reached in the latter part of the century could only be maintained through immigration.

The above considerations show the uncertainty that affects any attempt to classify the working population in the nineteenth century. Although in theory it would have been preferable to analyze separately the growth of factors in agriculture and in industry, the nature of the case obliges us to make a parallel examination of the development of the working population in the two sectors at once.

The Agricultural Working Population. As we have seen, the evolution of the agricultural working population is a controversial matter until at least 1896, as regards both men and women. The quinquennial index established by Lévy-Leboyer is based on the census figures and puts the agricultural working population at its maximum (8,800,000) in the period 1905–9, i.e., at the time of the 1906 census. The 1856 figure is 7.3 million, and the 1876 figure, which takes 89 departments into account, is 8 million, a mean annual increase of 0.3 percent per annum from 1876 to 1906. In order to eliminate the influence of variations in the evaluation of the female working population, we may consider just the male population. The maximum then occurs in 1876, with a figure of 5,750,000, and then, instead of a pattern of slow growth, we get one of slight variations around an almost constant figure: an increase of 12 percent between

1856 and 1876, though this is in fact much higher if we take Alsace-Lorraine into account.

There is a drop of 12 percent between 1876 and 1891 (though we have already pointed out the dubious nature of the figures for the 1891 census).

In 1896 there is an increase, almost reaching the figures for 1876 once more (5,675,000 instead of 5,750,000), and this increase is followed by a very slight drop of 4.7 percent up to 1911. We may wonder whether it is legitimate to apply variable percentages of female agricultural working population to figures for the male working population (see table 1.10). We can certainly allow that the departure of men forced the women left behind on the farms to do more work in the fields, but we should remember that only this consideration can justify the notion of an increase in the total agricultural working population, at least from 1876 to 1911 (see table 1.11). On the whole it seems more sensible to conclude that there was an increase up to the 1870s, the more so as the figures for these censuses are both exclusive of Alsace-Lorraine and based on a minimum estimate of the female working population. This increase seems to have been followed by a quasi-stagnation (a falling-off in the 1880s corresponding perhaps to the difficulties caused by the agricultural crisis, and a recovery in the 1890s) up to the end of the nineteenth century, whereas the early years of the twentieth century, far from being characterized, as Lévy-Leboyer's figures would indicate, by an increase in the agricultural working population, were marked by a fall: Malinvaud gives a figure of 8,350,000 in 1896 and 7,450,000 in 1913.

As I have already said, the figures for the censuses in the early and middle parts of the nineteenth century were quite different from those of the agricultural surveys. This contradiction results from the different interpretations of

Table 1.10 Proportion of Female Agricultural Working Population to Male Agricultural Population, According to Censuses (in percent)

1856	42.0	1876	38.4	1896	48.5
1861	42.0	1881	43.7	1901	48.1
1866	42.0	1886	49.8	1906	60.9
1877	36.4	1891	43.3	1911	59.9

Table 1.11 Increase in Agricultural Working Population

	Female	Total Increase
1856–1906	1,172,000	1,500,000
1872–1906	1,403,000	1,600,000
1876–1906	1,114,000	800,000

"working" and "nonworking" as regards the rural population, and from different appraisals of whether their activity was industrial or agricultural.

The Industrial Working Population. The evaluation of the industrial working population in the nineteenth century presents difficulties comparable to those which arise in evaluating the agricultural working population, but aggravated by perpetual changes of nomenclature. Up to 1896 at least, we may adopt the figures put forward by J. C. Toutain, who has reconstructed a coherent series of figures and suggested an evaluation for the early part of the nineteenth century. According to these estimates there are three different periods in the course of the century. Up to the 1840s, the industrial working population increased at a rapid rate, rising from 1.9 million in 1803–12 to 3.5 million in 1835–44, a mean annual increase of 45,700. Between the 1840s and the 1860s, the mean annual increase seems to have dropped to 32,000: according to Toutain, the industrial working population was 4.2 million in 1866.

Toutain's figures seem quite plausible: we arrive at similar results if we compare the industrial survey of 1840–45 to that of 1860–65: the first gives a figure of 1,612,000 workers, the second a figure of 1,793,000, but the authors of the survey suggest that the real figure is at least 2 million. If we apply the ratio between these two figures and the industrial working population of 1861 to the figure for 1840–45, we arrive at 3.5 million.

It is even more difficult to assess later developments. The figures for the 1872 census (3.8 million) strike one as absurd. But between 1876 and 1891 the industrial working population seems to have been more or less static (4.4 million in 1876, 4.5 million in 1891), rising to 5.6 million in 1896. Comparing the figures for 1876 with those for 1896, are we to conclude that the industrial working population showed a new acceleration in growth after the 1860s? As we have explained above, for the most part this leap forward between 1891 and 1896 is to be attributed to a change in the census methods, but this improvement in the accuracy of the censuses is also partly due to a better utilization of labor. In fact, it can be said that the industrial labor force increased at only a negligible rate during the later 1870s and the 1880s, but a new tendency toward acceleration emerged at the beginning of the 1890s. Between 1896 and 1913 the industrial working population, including the building trade, increased, according to Malinvaud, from 6 million to 6,700,000, a mean annual increase of 42,000. According to the census figures this increase would be 50,000.

The following periodization thus seems possible: up to the 1840s the annual increase is about 46,000; it then gradually decreases, to 32,000 in the 1850s and 1860s, and still lower in the 1870s and 1880s, and then from the beginning of the 1890s rises again to a rate not far from that which prevailed in the early part of the century. As we shall see, this schematization raises difficult problems when we come to compare the rural exodus with industrial growth.

Increase in Production

Agricultural Growth. The chief break in the economic history of France in the nineteenth century is probably the transition, between the 1860s and the 1880s, from agricultural growth to agricultural stagnation; even the rate of the recovery which took place in the years 1900 to 1913 was very slow compared with that of the nineteenth century. According to Lévy-Leboyer, agricultural production increased at a rate of 1.70 percent per annum from 1815 to 1840; 2.62 percent from 1840 to 1865 (excluding the years 1850–55); 0.26 percent from 1865 to 1900; and 1 percent from 1900 to 1913. These figures are rather high. In fact the rate of growth is around the level of 1.1 percent per annum from 1815–19 to 1874–78, and 0.5 percent per annum from 1874–78 to 1900–13, according to a new and as yet unpublished index worked out by Lévy-Leboyer. The rates of growth worked out by the ISEA team (in terms of mean annual increase in agricultural production) are close to these figures, and produce a similar periodization:

1825–34	to 1835–44	+1.5 percent
1835–44	to 1845–54	+0.9 percent
1845–54	to 1855–64	+1 percent
1855–64	to 1865–74	+0.6 percent
1865–74	to 1875–84	−0.3 percent
1875–84	to 1885–94	0
1885–94	to 1895–1904	+0.8 percent
1895–1904	to 1905–13	+1 percent

Jean Pautard, using the data given by the agricultural surveys of 1862 and 1892, and taking 1892 to equal 100, obtains an index of 27 in 1840, 55 in 1862, and 93 in 1882, an increase of 2.63 percent per annum from 1840 to 1882 in the French agricultural product assessed in constant value.

On the whole it seems clearly proven that the growth of agricultural production leveled off during the 1870s, and though it picked up during the years which preceded the 1914 war, it was at a rate that was low in comparison with the rest of the nineteenth century.

But this overall picture needs to be modified for different products and different regions. The increase may be described as applying to all products, while the period of stagnation and slowdown applies only to certain products, especially field crops, though this drop was partly compensated for by the continuing increase in other products, and particularly in stock raising. In fact the overall agricultural growth between 1815–19 and 1874–78 (1 percent) can be broken down into a growth of 1.1 percent for field crops raised for food, 1.5 percent for stock raising products, and 0.4 percent for raw materials. The first of these categories, where short-term production shows marked irregularities, did not show any long-term slackening, apart from the profound depression of the years 1853–56. Stock farming products showed a more sustained long-term growth (1.5 percent) with a tendency toward acceleration (1.3 percent between 1815–19 and 1861–65, and 2.3 percent between 1861–65 and 1874–78). Raw materials increased at a rate of only 0.4 percent per annum, and this can be broken down into a growth of 1.1 percent up to 1861–65 and a fall of 1.8 percent per annum after this date and up to 1874–78.

This slow differentiation among various kinds of production was maintained during the slack period. Overall growth in agricultural production continued at a rate of only 0.5 percent per annum from 1874–78 to 1909–13. This very slow increase breaks down into an almost continuous growth in stock-raising production, at a rate of 0.9 percent per annum, as the result of a slight acceleration (up 0.8 percent up to 1889–93, and up 1 percent up to 1909–13); a movement of decline in the production of field food crops, at a rate of 0.8 percent up to 1889–93, almost exactly compensated for by a movement of increase, at a rate of 0.9 percent, up to 1909–13; and finally a movement of continuous decline in production of raw materials, at a rate of 1.5 percent per annum.

Table 1.12 summarizes some of the data in real terms. This table takes partial account of the different evolution of different products: the production of potatoes certainly showed a gradual slackening in growth, but this growth never actually stopped; the production of wheat lost much of its dynamism in the 1860s; wine production reached its peak in the 1870s, showed a marked decline in the last quarter of the nineteenth

Table 1.12 Real Growth in the Production of Selected Agricultural Products

	Potatoes (millions of quintals)*	Wheat in the Grain (millions of quintals)	Wine (millions of hectoliters)	Industrial Beet (millions of quintals)
1815–1819	24.6	36.5		
1827			36.8	
1830			15.3	
1840				15.7
1861				44.3
1861–1865	87.7	76.3	49.8	
1873				77.4
1874–1878	93.6	78.7	58.7	
1889–1893	116.5	78.3	32.0	64.8
1909–1913	133.1	88.4	46.4	70.7

* 1 quintal = approximately 1 cwt.

century, returned to the level of the 1870s at the beginning of the twentieth century (an average of 56 million hectoliters from 1903 to 1907), and subsequently fell again; industrial beet experienced a spectacular boom from the 1840s to the 1870s but subsequently, apart from a few exceptional years (1900 and 1901 in particular), beet production, which was very dependent on the fate of the sugar industry, in fact stagnated. French agriculture, in reality, never stopped developing, though according to patterns which were certainly very different from those of the New World or even those of England. The "agricultural stagnation" after the 1870s results from a complex interplay of "crises" and sectoral and regional "increases," not from a general reactionary attitude in agriculture, as too many ill-informed authors still allege.

The chief productive sector in the French economy "slumped" in the 1880s. But stagnation does not necessarily mean sluggishness or ossification. Agriculture underwent a slow reconversion under conditions which became more and more difficult. But it was never entirely given over to routine and conservatism. After having been the driving force of growth in the first two-thirds of the century, it then went through a period of slow adaptation to new conditions and new markets.

Industrial Growth. Industrial growth in France during the nineteenth century and up to 1929 took place in three stages. From the 1830s, growth was steady; it accelerated until the 1860s; then it gradually slackened until the end of the century. The spurt which occurred about 1895–96 lasted some time. Stagnation reappeared between 1900 and 1905. Then began France's second great period of industrialization, which lasted until 1929. Whether this period began in 1896 rather than in 1906 is a debatable point. But it is of little importance. For the moment, we may note that "French industry went through its most rapid phase of growth in the middle of the nineteenth century. This phase was centered on the authoritarian Empire, but it began at the end of the July Monarchy" (Crouzet). So the task of industrial history is first to analyze and try to understand France's "first industrialization," and then to try to discover the factors which acted more and more as a brake from 1860 up to the beginning of the twentieth century.

There was no real "industrial revolution" or "take-off" in France in the nineteenth century, for the changes which occurred had none of the swiftness and suddenness which such terms suggest. The changes which came about were the result of a series of adjustments. The industrial growth rates which the makers of indices have discovered give us no reason to believe in a sustained acceleration in growth, and the breaks in rhythm which may be observed lead to a slackening-off rather than stagnation.

Three conclusions emerge from the work of Markovitch, Crouzet, and Lévy-Leboyer:

1. *The overall growth rate from 1815 to 1914 was a moderate one:* T. J. Markovitch suggests 2.08 percent; François Crouzet suggests an overall index of 1.6 percent and a partial index (i.e., excluding the nondynamic textile industries such as flax and hemp) of 2.97 percent. He settles finally for a probable index of 1.8 percent. Maurice Lévy-Leboyer arrives at a probably slightly overestimated figure of 2.56 percent excluding the building trade and a figure of 2.58 percent including it.

2. *On the whole this growth was fairly regular.* But all commentators agree in recognizing the existence of a *progressive deceleration*. François Crouzet's indices place it in 1854–57. His overall index gives a growth of 2.07 percent from 1829 to 1854 and of 1.46 percent from 1854 to 1905. His partial index gives a growth of 4.33 percent from 1819 to 1857, and of 2.23 percent from 1857 to 1906. He concludes that French industry went through its most rapid phase of growth in a period centered on the authoritarian Empire in the middle of the nineteenth century, that this growth began under the July Monarchy, but that, as in the case of England, the chief problem is "a precocious maturity which was reflected in the middle of the nineteenth century by a slackening-off in growth." The conclusions of Maurice Lévy-Leboyer and T. J. Markovitch are not fundamentally different from those of François Crouzet. The principal difference relates to growth rates in the early part of the nineteenth century. While Crouzet accepts an acceleration from 1829 onward and a stagnation before that

date, Lévy-Leboyer and Markovitch find the highest growth rate in the earliest years of the period and then see a kind of progressive deceleration: Markovitch's rates are 2.7 percent from 1815 to 1830, 2.5 percent from 1830 to 1845, 2.1 percent from 1850 to 1865, and 1.7 percent from 1870 to 1895. Lévy-Leboyer's rates are 2.98 percent from 1815 to 1845, 2.56 percent from 1845 to 1865, and 1.64 percent from 1865 to 1890.

The essential point is the reality of this deceleration, which in fact keeps the growth rate at a fairly steady level of over 2 percent up to the 1870s, and in the years 1875 to 1895 shows a more and more pronounced downward curve toward a sort of plateau. It is at that point that the signs of deceleration which first appeared in the 1850s and 1860s reached their greatest intensity. François Crouzet has worked the differences out exponentially in relation to the long-term trend: the differences between the two indices are almost always positive from 1843 to 1876, the maximum differences being found between 1854 and 1857.

3. *So the gradual deceleration tends, during the 1870s, to bring down the medium-term growth rate to below the average level for the century as a whole.* Recovery at a higher rate occurs either in the middle of the 1890s, or more probably from 1906 onward. Hesitation is legitimate here insofar as the crisis of the years 1901–5 was reflected by a stagnation of all the indices, interrupting for four years the strong recovery begun in 1895. François Crouzet therefore chooses to locate the real turning point in 1906, and arrives at an overall index of 1.46 percent and a partial index of 2.23 percent for 1854–1905 and at figures of 3.56 percent and 5.20 percent for 1906–13. Lévy-Leboyer prefers to believe in a recovery which gradually accelerated: 2.66 percent from 1885 to 1905 (1.93 percent excluding the building trade), and 4.42 percent from 1905 to 1913 (4.19 percent excluding the building trade). This recovery in the immediate prewar years has been brought out by the work of Malinvaud, Carre, and Dubois, who give a growth rate of 2.6 percent per annum for industrial production from 1896 to 1913. This foreshadows the growth of the 1920s. Despite the war, industrial production increased at a rate of 2.6 percent per

annum from 1913 to 1929. The periodization of French industrialization was thus as follows:

—From 1820 to 1870 industrial growth was probably about 2 percent (2.3 percent according to Malinvaud).
—A serious falling-off appeared in the 1860s and lasted until the end of the century (1.6 percent according to Malinvaud from 1870 to 1896), or, more precisely, as it seems to me, until the early years of the twentieth century.
—1906 was the beginning of a period of rapid industrialization which lasted until 1929. The rate from 1906 to 1913 (4.42 percent according to Lévy-Leboyer, 5.2 percent according to Crouzet) is found again in the 1920s, leaving the war and reconstruction out of account: the Organization for Economic Cooperation and Development (OECD) gives a growth rate of 4.7 percent for the period from 1924 to 1929.

So those are the three main periods in the history of industrialization in France: moderate growth from the 1820s to the 1870s, based on a gradual redistribution of production factors; slower and, as we shall see, difficult growth in the last quarter of the century; and accelerated growth in the years before and after the 1914–18 war.

Growth in Transport. Growth in the production of goods was accompanied by a more rapid growth in communications. Taking the 1908–12 figures as a base of 100, the overall index for transport in 1847–51 is 33, as against 35 for industry and 69 for agriculture. Although the growth rate for transportation in this period is thus similar to the industrial growth rate (1.8 percent and 1.7 percent), there were two long interruptions in this growth, one at the end of the 1870s and one at the end of the 1880s. The rate accelerated again in 1904, and continued at 2.7 percent per annum until 1913. These fluctuations are similar to those found in industrial production.

The steady growth in transportation resulted from a gradual differentiation in the use of modes of transport. The growth in traffic began well before the development of the railways, the construction of which must be seen as the inevitable answer to a situation which had reached saturation point. According to J. C. Toutain, in 1851 road transport accounted for 2,580,000,000 kilometer/tons (3,000,000,000 if 15 percent is added for the transport of animals) as against 2,000,000,000 kilometer/tons in 1830.* At this time canal transport accounted for 1,718,000,000 kilometer/tons, 57 percent of the amount accounted for by road transport if animals are included, 66.5 percent if they are excluded. At the same period the railways accounted for no more than 485,000,000 kilometer/tons.

Subsequent development can be broken down as follows. Between the beginning of the 1850s and the early 1880s, there was a railway "explosion" and rail traffic reached 10,700 million kilometer/tons in 1882. The mean annual growth rate from 1851–55 to 1879–83 is 10.8 percent. During the same period, traffic using the two other means of goods transport did not diminish but it did stagnate: in units of kilometer/tons, the figures for inland waterways rose from 34.3 to 39.2 (100 is the mean for the years 1908–12), an increase of 0.4 percent per annum, while road transport, after a slight increase in the last years of the 1850s and in the 1860s, returned at the end of the 1880s to the level of the early 1850s. The pattern of goods traffic had thus undergone a complete change (see table 1.13).

So the railways had come to be responsible for two-thirds of the goods transport in terms of volume, and one-half in terms of value, the difference being due merely to the fact that the cost of road transport had remained high.

From the beginning of the 1880s on, there was dynamic development again on the canals as well as on the railways: between 1879–83 and 1909–13 the traffic in kilometer/tons on the railways increased at a rate of 2.6 percent, and on the canals at a rate of 3.2 percent. But within this period a distinction may be made between the 1880s and 1890s on the one hand and the 1900s on the other. During the 1880s and 1890s railway traffic fell, whereas transport by canals increased at a rapid rate: between 1879–83 and 1897–1901, canal transport increased at a rate of 4.1 percent, while railway transport scarcely reached 2 percent. However, in the 1900s, the railways recovered much of the ground they had lost, growing at a rate of 3.5 percent per annum as against scarcely 2 percent for the

* A French ton = 1,000 kilograms, an English ton = 1,016 kilograms.

Table 1.13 Distribution of Goods Traffic

| | Volume (as percent of total kilometer/tons transported) | | |
	Roads	Canals	Railways
1851	52.7	36.7	10.6
1869	27.6	18.7	53.7
1882	18.0	15.0	67.0
	Turnover (as percent of total turnover) According to J. C. Toutain		
1845–1854	85.1	8.5	6.4
1875–1884	47.4	3.2	49.4

canals. Between 1882 and 1913, goods transport by road increased by 0.4 percent per annum (see table 1.14).

The somewhat anticyclical nature of the development of traffic on the waterways was not solely due to the state support which, as we shall see, was provided for inland waterways at the beginning of the 1880s. On the whole the rivalry between the two modes of transport was beneficial to the general economy.

In sum, the transformations in the structure of the French economy were less striking than those in other countries on the way to industrialization. In the working population, the percentage decline of the agricultural sector brought more gain to the tertiary sector than to the industrial sector. Table 1.15 traces this development only in an approximate manner, given the lack of certainty of the figures that we have just mentioned.

The fundamental changes in the national product appear much more striking, if different components are calculated at a constant value. We have today only very approximate esti-

Table 1.14 Distribution of Transport Among the Three Modes

| | Volume of Goods (percent of total volume) | | |
	Roads	Canals	Railways
1882	18.0	15.0	67.0
1903	12.9	20.6	66.5
1913	9.7	17.8	72.5
	Value of Goods (percent of total value)		
1875–1884	47.4	3.2	49.4
1905–1913	37.3	4.1	58.6

Table 1.15 Division of the French Working Population Among the Three Sectors (in percent)

	Agriculture	Industry	Other
1840–45	51.9	26.0	22.2
1866	49.8	27.9	22.3
1896	44.8	28.6	26.6
1906	42.7	28.2	28.1

mates of the "other" sector. In 1963 J. Marczewski proposed an estimate that took this sector's share, at a constant value, to 35.2 percent in 1852, 32.4 percent in 1892, and 31.5 percent in 1912 (in 1905–13 prices). The division of "physical product" (agriculture and industry) rests on more solid evidence. The division would then be as follows (in 1905–13 prices):

	Agriculture (percent)	Industry (percent)
1835–44	61	39
1855–64	56	44
1895–99	45	55
1905–13	40	60

The share of the industrial sector would thus go from two-fifths to three-fifths, and that of the agricultural sector from three-fifths to two-fifths, so that the share of the industrial working population in the total working population increased by scarcely 10 percent. These figures clarify, even if they are doubtless a trifle exaggerated, the propulsive role played by industry in the growth of the per capita national product.

Bibliography

Armengaud, André. *La population française au XIXème siècle.* Paris: Presses Universitaires de France, 1973.

——*Les populations de l'est aquitain au début de l'époque contemporaine.* Paris: Imprimerie Nationale, 1961.

Cameron, R. E. "Economic Growth and Stagnation in France," *The Journal of Modern History*, March 1958.

Crouzet, F. "Essai de construction d'un indice annuel de la production industrielle française au XIXème siècle," *Annales*, 25, no. 1 (1970), 56–99. Translation in *Essays in French Economic History.* Homewood,

Ill.: R. D. Irwin, 1970.

Dupeux, Georges. *Aspects de l'histoire politique et sociale du Loir et Cher.* Paris: Mouton, 1962.

Fohlen, Claude. "The Industrial Revolution in France, 1700–1914," in *The Fontana Economic History of Europe*, vol. 1, *The Emergence of Industrial Societies*, edited by C. M. Cipolla. London: Colins Fontana Books, 1973.

Landes, D. S. *The Unbound Prometheus.* London: Cambridge University Press, 1969.

Léon, P. "L'industrialisation de la France en tant que facteur de croissance économique du début du XVIIIème siècle á nos jours," in *Première conférence internationale d'histoire économique.* Paris: Mouton, 1960.

Lévy-Leboyer, M. "La croissance économique de la France au XIXème siècle, résultats préliminaires, "*Annales, Economies, Sociétés, Civilisations*, 4 (July–August 1968), 788–807.

——"La décélération de l'économie française dans la deuxième moitié du XIXème siècle," *Revue d'Histoire Economique et Sociale*, no. 4 (1971).

——"L'héritage de Simiand: Prix, profits et termes d'échange au XIXème siècle," *Revue Historique*, 243 (January–March 1971), 77–120.

Malinvaud, E., J. J. Carre, and P. Dubois. *La croissance française.* Paris: Seuil, 1972.

Marczewski, J. "Le produit physique de l'économie française de 1789 à 1913, comparaison avec la Grande Bretagne," *Cahiers de l'Institut de Science Economique Appliquée*, ser. AF, no. 4 (July 1965).

Markovitch, T. L. "L'industrie francaise de 1789 à 1964," *Cahiers de l'Institut de Science Economique Appliquée*, ser. AF, nos. 4–7 (1965–67).

Pautard, J. *Les disparités régionales dans la croissance de l'agriculture française.* Paris: Gauthier Villars, 1963.

Pouthas, C. E. *La population française pendant la première partie du XIXème siècle.* Paris: Presses Universitaires de France, 1956.

Sauvy, A. "La revenu national de la France de 1780 à 1913," *Population*, May–June 1965.

Statistique de la France: Industry. Nancy, 1873.

Statistiques industrielles, 1900–1959. Paris: Organization for Economic Cooperation and Development, 1960.

Toutain, J. C. "La population de la France de 1830 à 1965," *Cahiers de l'Institut de Science Economique Appliquée*, ser. AF, no. 3 (1963).

——"Les transports en France de 1830 à 1965," *Cahiers de l'Institut de Science Economique Appliquée*, ser. AF, no. 9 (1967).

Chapter Two: Institutional and Technical Development

France's Backwardness at the Beginning of the Nineteenth Century: The Antecedents

DURING AND AFTER the Napoleonic Wars, contemporaries had a keen sense that France was backward. The industrialism of Saint-Simon and the Anglomania of J. B. Say both give expression to this feeling of inferiority. But France wanted to follow England without imitating its excesses, and this dream of an industrialization "in the French style," avoiding excessively large concentrations of labor, dominated the whole of the nineteenth century. England was a model for others besides the intellectuals. Liévin Bauwens, who introduced textile machinery into Belgium and France, Périer, who introduced the steam engine into France, and G. Dufaud and Wendel all stayed for long periods in England, some as spies, some as experts, but all in search of a know-how which was unique. Many English industrialists came to try their fortune in France, often with success, as in the case of the Jacksons of Imphy. English workmen were much sought after by French industrialists. "They've come from Anzin to lure away my Englishmen," an ironmaster in the Ardennes laments in 1823!

During a large part of the eighteenth century, France had experienced a demographic, agricultural, and industrial growth parallel to that of England. Its foreign trade, very low in 1714, had reached the English level by about 1780. On the eve of the Revolution, France was producing less coal, nonferrous metals, ships, and cotton goods than England, but more woolens, silks, and iron. But in certain fields France's manufacturing processes were not as revolutionary as England's, chiefly because of the plentiful supply of labor in France. As far as agriculture is concerned, much stress is laid nowadays on the limited character of the changes which took place in the eighteenth century. Agricultural growth was a growth without technical upheavals. But the growing of maize in Aquitaine, buckwheat in Brittany, and potatoes had done away with famine and prepared rural France for more profound technical innovations. Because of these changes, agricultural production "did not lose the race against population" (Labrousse). In fact, the whole of French growth in the eighteenth century rested on an enormous accumulation of human labor. Against a background of "labor intensive" industry and agriculture and an Atlantic—and in particular colonial—trade, there arose a capitalism open to change.

According to Lévy-Leboyer, the economic consequences of the Revolution and the Empire were "a national disaster." The Revolution drove capital out of the country; inflation ruined those with savings, and favored speculative forms of investment at the expense of productive ones. The Revolution and the Empire ruined France's great sea trade. The revival under the Consulate was short-lived. The war and the blockade brought a new wave of bankruptcies. The policy followed under the Empire prevented French trade from adapting itself to the new conditions of international commerce, an adaptation which in any case was bound to be difficult. France's ports, whose prosperity was based on the "sugar islands," the West Indies, found it difficult to retain their position amid new trends orientated toward the American mainland. The decline of the great ports caused the collapse of regional economies which had lived off their activity.

Two generations of businessmen were ruined, one in 1793 and the other in the last years of the Empire. But the effect of the Empire was not entirely negative as far as industry was concerned. L. Bergeron·finds the first elements of a "real industrialization" under the Empire, particularly in textiles and in the chemical industry. Cotton mills using the spinning jenny were set up at Saint-Quentin, Rouen, Lille, and Paris during this period, and the growth which took place in Alsace was typically capitalistic. The first real chemical factories were built at Fos, Nanterre, and around Marseilles.

But this industrial growth was precarious. "In continental France," writes Lévy-Leboyer, "the calico trade was still 'all over the place': machinery was out of date; sources of energy were inadequate." The firms themselves were fragile, as is shown by the collapse of the industrial empire built up by Liévin Bauwens. Above all, the metallurgical industry stagnated, with regard to both production and techniques. It had not advanced since the Périer brothers introduced Watt's' steam engine in 1789. The technological gap between France and England had grown wider. This technical stagnation occurred because contacts with the outside world were few and difficult, dynamism was lacking, and the market was uncertain. Napoleonic protectionism had gradually ceased to be a spur to industry and become an instrument of war, and this was the cause of its failure.

Revolutionary legislation reinforced the tendencies of the French peasant toward individualism and strengthened his obstinate determination to possess land. It directed middle-class wealth toward the search for an income based on land, and, by maintaining a large landless rural population, increased the pressure for the retention of certain collective practices and "common" rights. In some regions there were the beginnings of a really capital-intensive agriculture, e.g., among the big stock fatteners of the Nivernais, the big farmers of the Paris Basin, the wine growers of Bordeaux and Champagne, and the producers of madder in the Vaucluse. So the Revolution and the Empire left the roots of French society, both peasant and bourgeois, as deeply rural as ever.

All in all, the backwardness of France at the beginning of the nineteenth century was as much the result of a long historical evolution as of recent events. From the beginning of the eighteenth century, French levels of consumption and technology had been lower than those in England. Insofar as the two growths could be regarded as parallel, this difference continued throughout the eighteenth century, when French growth had to do without such fundamental technological renewal as England's. The Revolution and the Empire accentuated the disparity.

France's Backwardness at the Beginning of
the Nineteenth Century: Obstacles to Growth

The most obvious expression of "French backwardness" is the technological gap, which can be broken down into two stages: first, France adopted the new methods of agricultural and industrial production to a lesser degree than did England, and then, when it did adopt them, French techniques were already old fashioned in comparison with English ones. In 1817 Great Britain produced 16 million tons of coal, while France produced only 800,000. In 1830 France used 3 million spindles for spinning cotton, while Britain used 11 million; the British used 90,000 mechanical spinning frames, the French only 5,000. "Political revolutions and wars ruined France's foundries and interrupted technical progress for a quarter of a century," writes Lévy-Leboyer. British production of cast iron increased from 85,000 to 375,000 tons between 1788 and 1814. In France and Belgium production of cast iron reached a ceiling of 175,000 tons, and these were almost entirely produced by furnaces using wood, a method no longer used in England (by the end of the Empire there were still only four furnaces using coke, all at Le Creusot). As Claude Fohlen has said, by 1830 "coal had still not won out in the two fields which properly belong to it, the steam engine and metallurgy." Up to 1835 at least, French steam-engine technology was still strongly dependent on English technology.

In addition to this technical backwardness, there was an incompleteness in France's network for circulating men, goods, and capital. The eighteenth century had created a system of roads (40,000 kilometers), bridges (400), and canals (1,000 kilometers were open in 1789), which had really unified France. But the unification of markets applied only to high-cost goods. Moreover, it had been impaired by lack of upkeep on the roads and the slowness of work on inland waterways (10 kilometers per annum) under the Revolution and the Empire. And unification of markets often ended with major roads: "Most rural communes were cut off from major communication routes," writes J. Pitié, referring to Vienne and Poitou. In the case of certain goods, these transport difficulties prevented competition in quality and price on a really national scale. They also weighed heavily on production costs. In particular they were a major obstacle to the adoption of techniques based on the use of coal or iron. The recurrent wheat crisis, which was an important factor right up to the 1860s, was largely related to transport difficulties.

All this being so, it is easy to see the limiting factors which weighed on French industry. We may distinguish three levels of activity. In the villages, consumption of industrial goods produced by the peasants themselves, and crafts using local resources (especially forests) continued to play the chief role. Higher up the scale were industries open to regional or national markets, in a context of a commercial capitalism run by the manufacturers. Higher up the scale again comes manufacturing proper, still using a very small part of the working population. Progress in the use of capitalistic techniques or techniques based on a search for higher returns are limited to markets where large orders are possible, especially from the state, and where there are large urban or foreign outlets. But most "industrial" cities in France were still really towns of craftsmen and home workers.

Probably one of the chief obstacles to real economic growth was the inadequacy, despite the institutions created by the Empire, of the monetary and banking system. Barter was still of the first importance, and in some rural areas money was not often used. One of the first conditions of growth was to include these outlying regions, which were in the majority, in the general monetary system. In order to do this it was first necessary to make a massive increase in the money supply.

Growth and the State

However, France, whose industry, when it existed, was less capital intensive and less advanced in technique than that of England, and which suffered from lack of flexibility, did possess an elite who were all in favor of industrialization. The great design for progress and happiness put forward by the *philosophes* of the eithteenth century was continued in the industrialism of Saint-Simon and the Liberals. It was during the most marked period of political reaction, the 1820s, that the Becquey Plan, the first great public works program in the nineteenth century, was drawn up. This poses questions about the institutional and technical development of the nineteenth century, which deserves the name "Age of Enlightenment" just as much as its predecessor.

But despite the spread of liberal and even ultraliberal ideas proclaimed by such French economists as Bastiat, the French government exercised guardianship and control over a considerable part of economic activity throughout the century. The chief instrument of this supervision was not local administration but the government offices in Paris. These were all-powerful as regards legislation on waterways and forests and the regulations governing fairs and markets, the use of hydraulic power, and the supervision of industrial conditions (e.g., the law of 1801 concerning insanitary factories).

The guardianship exercised by government officers in Paris is very noticeable in the transport sector. The network of national roads developed steadily at the expense of departmental roads; even the latter depended on local administration by the Ponts et Chaussées (Highways Department), which carried out instructions from Paris. At first, the great majority of railways in France were main lines—that is, they were built by permission of the administration in Paris after consultation with the Conseil d'État. A law passed in 1865 provided for branch lines, authorized by the prefect of the department concerned after consultation with the Conseil General of the department (an elected assembly consisting of one member for each canton in the department). But after the failure of the companies which built them, most of these lines were incorporated into the main network in 1883. The only local lines which remained as such were minor ones, often indirectly dependent on the main network. The same central control was exercised over the development of municipal transport services, lighting, and water, all of which were subject to regulations set by the Conseil d'État. The mining industry was governed by the law of 1810, which provided for a system of concessions and control. In the same way, authorization had to be obtained to build or enlarge iron and steel works, other factories likely to cause pollution, or water mills.

These controls were justified by considerations of public interest, such as the desire to preserve the national heritage (e.g., to preserve forests or fight pollution) or the need to retain adequate state control over the public domain (e.g., the rejection of private ownership in the transportation network). But the state had other motives too: while it wished to promote economic growth, it had to think of the possible consequences of that growth. The fear of crises which might give rise to social unrest led the state to adopt a cautious attitude on monetary policy and banking. So as not to upset vested interests too much, the state adopted a strongly protectionist policy until the 1850s, though this was modified from the 1880s onward. The same preoccupation led the state to grant subsidies for silkworm culture, for example, and, after 1870, to the merchant navy. Similarly, taxation favored small shopkeepers and businessmen, and railway rates were devised so as not to penalize customers who shipped only small amounts of goods. In general, especially from the 1870s onward, state economic policy was dominated by the desire to preserve a social order based on small and medium-sized businesses.

The Empire, learning from previous experience, created the legal framework for France's economic development in the nineteenth century. The rules established under the Empire were not modified until the 1860s. The 1808 Code of Commerce provided for three types of company: *société en nom collectif* (general partnership), *société en commandite* (limited partnership), and *société anonyme* (limited company). (As these were all special creations of French law, the English terms are only roughly equivalent.) The first type of company could be created by as few as two individuals, and all its members were subject to unlimited liability. The second type, the *société en commandite*, was a partnership contracted between one or several persons called *commandités*, who managed the business and whose liability was unlimited, and one or several persons called *commanditaires* or *associés en commandite,* who only contributed money and whose liability was limited to the amount of capital they had undertaken to provide. The capital could be divided into transferable shares. This type of arrangement provided an adequate framework for the development of most companies. It was intended to cover small and medium-sized businesses, and was only a codification of previous rules and practices. The third type of company was designed for large businesses. In order to avoid abuse and to protect private investors, this kind of company was subject to authorization in accordance with a lengthy procedure which in fact invested the power of decision in the Conseil d'État. But although the members of the Conseil d'État were eminent jurists, they knew little about business. The founding of this type of company was made difficult by the rules governing applications to do so, in particular the requirement that all capital should be paid up before the company was registered.

These rules for the creation of companies remained in force until the 1860s. What Freedeman called the "long and tortuous procedure" governing the creation of limited companies was abolished in 1863, when a law was passed allowing the creation, without authorization, of what were called *sociétés à responsabilité limitée,* which were very similar to *sociétés anonymes,* though their capital could not exceed 20 million francs. This last restriction was abolished by the law of 1867.

Until 1867, the authorization procedure was a serious obstacle to the creation of *sociétés anonymes.* The Conseil d'Etat's notion of its responsibilities was highly restrictive. "The Conseil assumed," writes Freedeman, "that it was morally responsible for the success of the enterprise." It regarded itself as the protector of the shareholders' interests, and not only did it frequently refuse authorization, but when it did grant it, surrounded this permission with a whole series of conditions concerning organization, reserves, and dividends. The procedure was an obstacle in itself. All the capital had to be paid up before anyone could file a registration for a *société anonyme.* So it is understandable that up to 1867 the *société en commandite* was the normal form of company. Thanks to it,

French legislation was in fact much more favorable to company development than was English legislation, and even more the German legislation, at the time. In France there was no "institutional obstacle" to growth, except that which exists in the mind of certain historians.

The law of 1867 was permissive to the highest degree, and subsequent legislation allowed boards of directors more rather than less liberty of action. Jurisprudence too was on the whole reasonably liberal. And the law on bankruptcy also developed in the direction of mildness: the law of 1838, nowadays judged to be so severe, was much more indulgent than previous legislation. But the decisive stage was reached with the law of 1889, which introduced the system of *liquidation judiciare*, or liquidation subject to the supervision of a court. "The bankrupt was no longer regarded as guilty, but rather as unlucky or lacking in skill." The "gradual disappearance of liability" was accompanied by a reinforcement of the rights of property owners and especially the appearance of new forms of property: the law of 1844 introduced the category of industrial property, to be applied to patents. A law of 1909, legalizing the sale and mortgaging of businesses, was the culmination of a whole century of development in this direction. Thus the commercial legislation of the nineteenth century created legal conditions propitious not only to large-scale capitalism, but also to capitalism on the level of small traders, whose rights were to be strengthened by the law of 1925 and the development of legislation on commercial property.

Liberty of contract was not total. Article 419 of the Penal Code forbade trusts, and this ban was applied with great rigor throughout the century, at least up to 1884. Before this date, most of the lawsuits brought against sales trusts were won by the plaintiffs. One example was the ban on a soda manufacturers' trust in Marseilles in 1838. Article 419 was invoked to prevent the creation of the Compagnie des Mines de la Loire in 1852. After 1884, jurisprudence on the subject became more flexible. Some trusts were still forbidden, but others were allowed, such as l'Union des Phosphates in 1890. Legal officials tended to think more and more that "natural and free" competition might be dangerous and chaotic. Striking confirmations of this tendency were the cases of the Comptoir de Longwy (1902) and of the glass consortium, the Comptoir Général de Verres et Glaces de Paris (1906). The Tribunal of Commerce recognized the traders' "right to combine their efforts . . . in order to keep down overheads and avert the ruin of their industry and trade." This ruling was upheld once and for all by the Appeal Court at Aix in 1912.

The interpretation of the law in such cases had been governed by a desire to promote competition. The state made use of other means to the same end. The 1810 law on mining provided for concessions of optimal size from the technical point of view but enough concessions to avoid monopoly. In the case of railways, concessions were used to establish a monopoly. But most public services were run on a system of short-term concessions divided among several concessionaires. In fact, just as there was an obvious contradiction between the interventionist traditions of the government and the ultraliberal economics taught by academics so there was an inconsistency between the wish to promote competition and the desire not to upset the existing state of affairs. As the financial analysis in the next chapter will show, the neutrality of the state was never anything but a theory.

Educational, Technical, and Scientific Development

One of the state's chief responsibilities was to insure the development of education. In the 1840s, the money spent on state education represented 1.2 percent of the budget. In 1868, this percentage had not changed. It rose to 2.3 percent in 1881, 3.5 percent in 1882, and 6 percent in 1913.

In 1827, three out of every five military conscripts were illiterate, and in 1836 A. d'Angeville wrote that "it is really incredible how ignorant many French people are." At that time only 49 percent of army recruits could read and write. "Educated" France lay within the triangle Geneva-Mézières-Meaux. C. Fohlen has observed that this area "covered both regions that were already industrialized and those which were in the process of becoming so." There is a fairly obvious relation between educational level and possession of craft skills. The Jura was the best-educated of the French departments. But from the 1830s on, there was rapid progress in public education. By 1886, 90 percent of conscripts could at least read. Recent studies carried out by the Études Practiques des Hautes Études (EPHE) show that there may be a link between the development of religious practice and "the way the south overtook the north in the matter of reading." These studies also show that sudden industrialization, in the form of manufacturing, could, as in the case of the department of the Nord between 1846–50 and 1856–60, bring about a leveling-off in the growth of education. The education laws of the Third Republic made it possible to reduce the illiteracy rate to 4 percent by 1911, and also to spread practical skills and values which might promote a desire for upward social mobility. Secondary education, on the other hand, remained at a very low level: by 1898 it affected only 2.9 percent of children between the ages of 10 and 19, 3.3 percent of boys between these ages. While primary education was considered "excellent" in business circles, secondary education was much criticized for being too "classically" orientated.

In fact, technical developments in the nineteenth century were still based largely on practical skills, on know-how derived from experiencing a trade and learning a "knack" rather than from the application of scientific principles. Daumas has recently shown that some of the most notable innovators in the French engineering industry in the first third of the nineteenth century were "self-educated mechanics," who either were descended, or came through practical apprenticeship, from artisan backgrounds. Men like Calla (1760–1835), Hallette of Arras, Cave (1794–1875), Cail (1804–1871) and Farcot (1798–1875) imported equipment from Britain and used these models to create new types. The nineteenth-century worker was a member of a trade rather than a technician. The importance of practical know-how is demonstrated by the survival of industrial localization in certain areas even after the resources which caused that localization had been exhausted. This is the case on the eastern edge of the Massif Central and in the Ardennes. According to Babu, the center of France had become "the home of experienced smiths who could turn out any part that you required with a power hammer," using "a whole bag of tricks of the trade." The iron-puddler, whose case has been studied by Courthéoux, typified the preeminence in nineteenth-century industrial technology of "the art and labor" of certain outstanding workmen. Engine-drivers belonged to this category. Workers and artisans with technical know-how often introduced remarkable innovations. The motorcar, at the end of the century, provides an example of this. Some of the major changes in working methods during the nineteenth century were merely the transformation of this kind of know-how into a mechanized and rationalized system.

For among the various kinds of innovation there were, to use Daumas's expression, very close links of "interaction." An innovation may be seen as a response to an appeal from other production sectors, arising out of technical pressures of economic origin. For example, obstacles to the expansion of the railways, made necessary in the 1860s and 1870s by the growth of traffic, were surmounted by means of steel rails and the use of electricity. The same thing applies generally. The motorcar, like the railways before it, gave a new impetus to innovation in the iron and steel industry, and the great innovations in the chemical industry at the end of the century arose out of the needs of the textile industry.

But the novelty of the nineteenth century resides in the gradual fusion of science and technology, in other words, in the development of applied science. It should be pointed out here that the technical gap between France and Britain at the beginning of the nineteenth century was not the same as that now separating the advanced from the underdeveloped countries. France's scientific attainments were sufficient to allow it to develop extremely fruitful connections between pure science and technology. P. Costable has shown, for example, that the publication in 1829 of a book by Coriolis on calculating the effect of machinery proved that "the possibility of subjecting machines to theory was now equally clear to scientists and technicians." Similarly, in the field of chemicals, although the treatise published by Chaptal in 1806 showed "how indifferent industry still was to the new chemical theories," the founding of the Kuhlmann company marked once and for all the penetration of chemical science into industrial technology. It is true that in other sectors this merger of technique and science, or the transformation of industrial practice into scientific theory, came about more slowly. It is only with Floris Osmond, at the end of the century, that one can really speak of a science of metallurgy.

At the same period a kind of distortion appears as between scientific and industrial chemistry. The great national technical schools played a leading role here. Although in the early part of the century graduates of the École Polytechnique tended to be scientists rather than engineers, things began to change later. Scientists wrote textbooks which put their knowledge more and more at the disposal of practical engineers and technicians. Great national bodies such as the Corps des Mines and the Corps des Ponts et Chaussées provided technical staff not only for government departments but also for big private companies. The École Centrale des Arts et Manufactures, founded privately in 1828, tried to reconcile, at a high level, theoretical knowledge and wide-ranging practical information. The various schools of arts and crafts, based on the model of the École des Arts et Métiers at Chalons-sur-Marne (founded in 1803), had the same object. In general, then, neither technical know-how, scientific knowledge, nor elementary education was lacking in France in the nineteenth century. There is some doubt, however, about how far both secondary and technical education were adapted to the needs of middle management. The French Society of Civil Engineers was continually protesting the inadequacy of the educational system in these two respects.

Bibliography

Angeville, A. d'. *Essai statistique sur la population française.* 2d ed., with an introduction by E. Leroy-Laudurie. Paris and The Hague: Mouton, 1969.
Babu, C. "L'industrie métallurgique dans la région de Sain Etienne," *Annales des Mines*, 9th ser. (1899), p. 357.
Bergeron, L. *L'épisode napoléonien.* Vol. 4 of *Nouvelle histoire de la France contemporaine.* Paris: Seuil, 1972.
——"Problèmes économiques de la France napoléonienne," *Revue d'Histoire*

Moderne et Contemporaine, special issue on *La France à l'époque napoléonienne,* July–September 1970, pp. 469–505.

Brunet, P. *Structure agraire et économie rurale des plateaux tertiaires entre Seine et Oise.* Caen: Caron, 1960.

Costabel, P. "Mécanique théorique et mécanique pratique en France dans la première moitié du XIXème siècle," in *L'aquisition des techniques par les pays non initiateurs.* Paris: Centre National de la Recherche Scientifique, 1973.

Courtheoux, J. P. "Privilèges et misères d'un métier sidérugique au XIXème siècle: Le puddleur," *Revue d'Histoire Economique et Sociale,* no. 2 (1959).

Daumas, M. "Les mécaniciens autodidactes français et l'acquisition des techniques britanniques," in *L'acquisition des techniques par les pays non initiateurs.* Paris: Center Nationale de la Recherche Scientifique, 1973.

Ententes et monopoles dans le monde: France, Les ententes profesionnelles devant la loi. Paris, Documentation Française, 1953.

Fohlen, C. "Charbon et Révolution industrielle en France, 1815–1850," in *Actes du colloque "Charbon et sciences humaines."* Paris and The Hague: Mouton, 1966.

——*Q'est ce que la révolution industrielle?* Paris: Robert Laffont, 1971.

Freedeman, C. "Joint Stock Business Organization in France," *Business History Review,* 1965, p. 184.

Labrousse, C. E., and F. Braudel. *Histoire économique et sociale de la France.* Vol 2. Paris: Presses Universitaires de France, 1970.

Leleux, F. *Liévin Bauwens, industriel gautois.* Paris: Service d'Edition et de Veute des Productions de l'Education Nationale, 1969.

Leroy-Ladurie, E. *Anthropologie du conscrit français, 1819–1836.* Paris: Mouton, 1972.

Lévy-Leboyer, M. *Les banques européennes et l'industrialisation internationale dans la première moitié du XIXème siècle.* Publications de la faculté des lettres et sciences humaines de Paris. Paris: Presses Universitaires de France, 1964.

Payen, J. *Capital et machines à vapeur au XIXème siècle: Les frères Perier et l'introduction en France de la machine à vapeur.* Paris: Mouton, 1969.

Pitié, J. *Exode rural et migration intérieure en France: L'exemple de la Vienne et du Poitou-Charentes.* Poitiers: Norois, 1971.

Ripert, G. *Aspects juridiques du capitalisme moderne.* Paris: Librairie Générale de Droit et de Jurisprudence, 1951.

Robinet, P. "Les premiers fours à puddler dans les Ardennes: Techniciens anglais et lorrains aux forges, J. N. Gudarnu," *Journal des Sociétés Savantes,* 1964.

Thuillier, A. *Economie et société nivernaise au début du XIXème siècle.* Paris: Mouton, 1974.

Thuillier, G. *Aspects de l'économie nivernaise au XIXème siècle.* Paris: Mouton, 1966.

Chapter Three: Financial Development

The Development of Institutions

MONETARY AND CREDIT problems were seen not only from the point of view of growth, but also from that of stability. The desired industrialization could take place only by means of fundamental changes in the institutions concerned with credit and in the methods available for raising capital. But trends which were liberal, and/or derived from Saint-Simon, encountered strong resistance arising from two deeply rooted attitudes on the part of the government and the ruling classes. The first was a sincere and largely justified belief in a causal relationship between a policy of lavish money issues and easy credit on the one hand, and irregularity in business cycles on the other; the second was a desire to protect savers from risky investments. The first attitude was reinforced by France's experience in earlier periods and by what was happening in contemporary England: as de Foville wrote in 1887, "crises were caused by misuse of credit and followed by bankruptcies that were all in some degree painful."

The Empire handed down to the Restoration financial institutions which, to use Billoret's expression, were "well run-in." The chief of these institutions was the Banque de France, born in 1800 out of the transformation of the Caisse des Comptes Courants, which had been founded in 1796 by a group of bankers and which already acted as a kind of special bank for Parisian bankers. The Banque de France was a bank of issue whose monopoly was limited to the Paris region until 1848. In return for the monopoly, the state was able to obtain "advances." The Bank's cash and bullion in hand acted as collateral for the paper money in circulation. The law of 1803 had defined the franc in relation to silver (5 grams) and gold (322.56 milligrams). The bank could only discount bills bearing three signatures, and bills were valid for a maximum of three months. At first the Banque de France was concerned with rediscount rather than discount. The amount of money issued was closely linked to discount policy.

After 1815 the Banque de France turned in on itself. It tried to limit the development of the regional banks which had been created, with the authorization of the Conseil d'État, to make up for the lack of branches of the central bank. The regional banks were allowed to issue money each in their own region, but not allowed to discount notes as between one town in a department and another. Such banks were set up in the three major ports of Nantes, Rouen, and Bordeaux in the years 1818–22, and in Lyons, Toulouse, Marseilles, Lille, and Orléans in the 1830s. But Dijon, unable to raise the necessary funds on the spot, was not given permission to appeal to other towns for them. From 1836 on, the bank adopted a policy of creating branches directly dependent on itself. After 1840 the state authorized no more departmental banks. The crisis of 1848 forced departmental banks into a critical position. They asked for recognition of their notes as legal tender, but as these notes were current only in the towns in which they were issued, they could not compete with the notes of the Banque de France. The demand for a legal-tender status unaccompanied by standardization of notes was in fact suicidal: and the departmental banks were absorbed by the central bank. Their disappearance established the monopoly of the Banque de France as a bank of issue, and it went on developing its branches at such a rate that by 1900 it was established in 411 different towns, thus standardizing the cost of money throughout the country. In fact, at the beginning of the twentieth century the role played by the Banque de France in the banking and monetary system was relatively much more important than that played by the Bank of England, or, to put it differently, the role of other banks was much less important than that of comparable institutions in England.

During the first part of the nineteenth century the big private merchant banks of Paris strengthened their position and developed their activities. They had been founded in the eighteenth century: by Mallet in 1723, Delessert in 1776, Perrégueaux in 1782, and Périer from Grenoble in 1792. A new generation had made its appearance under the Empire with Pillet-Will, Carrette, and Lefebvre. In the second decade of the nineteenth century and in the 1820s, still more new banks were created, often of foreign origin: these included those of the Rothschilds, Eichthal, Thurneyssen, and Fould. These had usually started out as big trading houses, attracted to Paris because of the predominant role it played in international monetary settlements. Their activities were also closely linked to those of the state. Many of these bankers were former tax collectors. But until the 1850s there was a striking contrast between the strength and international dimensions of the big merchant banks in Paris and Lyons and the fragility of the local banking network, which was isolated and without interregional links. Lévy-Leboyer writes that in many regions, around 1830, credit was still "only an empty word." In Nevers and Angers the chief sources of credit were the notaries, who lent money at usurious rates. Of course, there were banks in all the big towns, but their position was weak, as Fohlen has shown for Lille, and Léon for Grenoble. The same was true of Dijon, where the chief local bank collapsed in 1842. The intensity of the shock suffered by the local banking network at every crisis, especially in the years 1839–42, was largely due to each center's comparative isolation. Alsace, which was less isolated, held up better. Credit was not an empty word there. But on the whole, a large part of the French business community, even in Paris, was forced, either through the lack of a comprehensive banking network or because of the restrictive policy of the big banks and the Banque de France, to resort to the services of people who belonged to what Gille has called the "lower regions" of credit.

In the 1820s the banker J. Laffitte, successor to Perrégueaux, wanted to found a fund in the form of a *société anonyme,* using deposits to develop both long- and short-term credit. But the Conseil d'État refused permission. Laffitte revived his project in 1837 in the form of a *société en commandite.* The Caisse Laffitte did not have the scope its founder hoped for, but it did stimulate the development of credit. The Banque de France, as we shall see, modified its policy, and other credit establishments were founded in the 1840s.

The development of savings banks presents a strong contrast with the difficult beginnings of ordinary deposit banks. The number of passbooks rose from 121,000 in 1835 to 570,000 in 1850. On the whole, the financial structure established under the Empire "around the Treasury" survived under the Monarchy, and this virtual state monopolization of savings held back the formation of any real banking network.

The crisis of 1847 and the Revolution of 1848 marked a decisive stage in the evolution of banking institutions. The precarious edifice of the Caisses collapsed, and in the spring of 1848 most bankers both in Paris and in the provinces suspended payment, so that there was no longer any intermediary between the Banque de France and trade. It was in this way that discount branches came into being; their capital was divided between the state, the municipality, and private individuals. Moreover, the state usually granted them a loan. Seventy-seven discount branches were established. Their activities extended beyond simple discount. The branch in Paris, through seven purely private subbranches, developed advances on goods and even on stocks and shares. At the same time, the *entrepôts généraux,* or warehouses, were founded, making possible the development of deposit warrants. The discount branches were created for a period of only three years, and a decree of 1853 placed them under the jurisdiction of common law. The branch in Paris and twelve others in the provinces survived as *sociétés en commandite.* The Paris branch, the Comptoir d'Escompte de Paris, was transformed during the 1850s into a private company, though subject to certain official regulations. It started out with a capital of 4.2 million francs, which rose gradually to 80 million by 1866. It was not until 1865 that the legal status of checks was defined in France. But fact had preceded law. The late 1850s and the

1860s had seen the creation of big credit establishments destined to become the main channels for savings and the circulation of bank credit in France, thanks to the rapid development of their branches. These new establishments were the Crédit Industriel et Commercial (1859), the Crédit Lyonnais (1863), and the Société Général (1864). Other banks, such as the Société Marseillaise (1865), had a more local sphere of influence. The chief activity of these establishments was the management of demand deposits and short-term notes. But they all were concerned with long-term investment, either directly, using their own capital, or on behalf of their customers. To use Jean Bouvier's expression, they were to become "great bazaars" for investment in stocks of all kinds, French and foreign. We shall examine later the problem of their involvement in industrial affairs.

In fact, because it was largely based on English practice, the French conception of banking made a fairly clear distinction between the deposit (commercial) banks, specializing in short-term loans and the management of customers' portfolios, and the merchant banks, directed toward the promotion either of large loans or of industrial and commercial concerns, French or foreign. Banks like the Société Général belonged to both categories. But the distinction tended to become more marked. Under the Second Empire the Péreire brothers had founded a big merchant bank in the form of a *société anonyme*, the Crédit Mobilier (1852), the activities of which dominated business life under the Second Empire. It entered into liquidation in 1867 because, like other similar institutions, it had never been given permission to issue debentures. The 1870s and early 1880s saw the creation of a large number of new banks, including the Banque National de Paris et des Pays Bas in 1872. The years 1878–82 were certainly the period of the most intense speculation in France in the nineteenth century. But many of these banks, in particular the Union Général, failed between 1883 and 1886. A new wave of foundings and regroupings occurred in the years 1900–13, with the foundation of the Banque Nationale pour le Commerce et l'Industrie (1901), the Banque de l'Union Parisienne (1904), the Crédit Mobilier Français (1902), and the Société Centrale des Banques de Province (1904). The object of the founders of most of these was to set up establishments big enough to withstand large-scale international speculation. The development of deposit banks was a severe blow to regional and local banks, which had to limit their activities to unsecured credit operations. Those which managed to survive experienced a spectacular revival in the 1900s.

The Issuing of Money

In the early part of the nineteenth century, and even up to the 1860s, large areas of France were still deserts as far as money was concerned. In Picardy, "economic and social relations were based on a system of barter" (Hubscher); in the southwest, "money played only a very small part in the rural economy" (Armengaud). Guy Thuillier has shown the part that was played for a long time in regions like the Nièvre and Normandy by irregular bronze currency, both French and foreign. Such currency was estimated at 70 million francs in 1840, and was used for paying wages. So for a long time the money network in France remained compartmentalized. Those who went in for barter or used bronze coinage were not integrated into the national economy. The incorporation of these areas could only be brought about by a rapid increase in the money supply.

In describing the monetary history of France it is impossible not to refer, however briefly, to the problem of sources. We are extremely uncertain about the amount of metallic money in circulation: we know the amount that was minted, but it is difficult to estimate how much was lost. According to de Foville, in 1885 the losses amounted to half the amount of money issued in the preceding century. On the other hand, Jean Denuc estimates this loss at only 18 percent. So estimates of metallic money in circulation may easily vary by as much as half. As regards paper money, we have records of the issues of the Banque de France. Bank money is somewhat arbitrarily estimated as double the deposits in the four main banks plus the current accounts in the Banque de France. Table 3.1 presents an estimated breakdown.

Table 3.1 Estimate of Money Supply (in billions of francs)

	1814	1828	1847	1873	1885	1895	1900	1913
Metallic money								
Issues since 1785	1.5	3.2	5.1	12.1	13.9	14.1		
Reserves		0.2	0.1	0.7	2.2	3.3		
Circulation	2.0	2.7	3.8	5.9	6.0	5.5	6.7	9.0
Paper money	0.04	0.2	0.25	2.8	2.8	3.5	4.2	5.7
Bank money			0.4	1.2	2.3	3.8	5.0	12.3
Total	2.04	2.9	4.45	9.9	11.1	12.8	15.9	27.0

There were three limitations on the issue of paper money: the refusal of the Banque de France to count deposited stocks and shares as cash-in-hand, the restrictions on cash-in-hand, and the rules governing discount, which established a strict connection between issue and discount. In the early part of the nineteenth century the greater part of cash-in-hand was silver. Its gradual conversion into gold created a difficulty. When, under the Second Empire, it was the policy of the Banque de France to vary the discount rate according to the needs of the economy, the reserve ratio sometimes fell as low as 15 percent. Discount by the Banque de France was still subject to strict rules which hindered its development: there had to be three signatures, the signatories had to be approved by the bank, and they had to be resident in Paris. Notes' maturity was limited to 90 days, and virtually restricted to big businessmen and rediscounters. The discount rate remained at 4 percent from 1817 to 1852, except in 1848. Bank officials refused to countenance any kind of manipulation which, according to them, might aggravate the irregularity of business movements. This attitude was modified under the Empire, under pressure from the government. The rate then varied between 3 and 10 percent, and might be changed several times in the course of one year. Under the Third Republic rates continued to vary, but were much more stable than those of other European banks. The rate was normally 3 percent. It fell to 2 percent at the end of the 1870s, rose suddenly to 4 percent, and then fell back rapidly to 3 percent in 1882. Between 1891 and 1896 it was gradually reduced to 2 percent, rose to 3 percent again in 1899, and remained at that level until 1910. In 1913 it rose to 4 percent. The bank's policy was to maintain a high, sometimes ex-

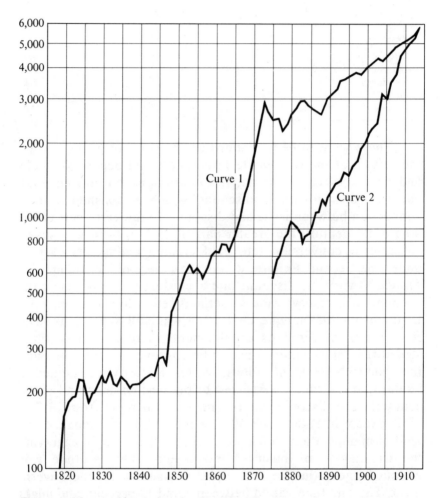

Figure 1 Money Circulation in France, 1820–1913. Curve 1: Banque de France notes in circulation (millions of francs). Curve 2: Deposits and current accounts in credit at four big banks.

SOURCES: *Annuaire statistique de la France: Résumé rétrospectif 1966*, Institut national de la statistique et des études économiques (Paris: Imprimerie Nationale, 1966), pp. 516–17; J. Denuc, "Essai de détermination de la circulation monétaire annuelle en France de 1870 à 1913," *Bulletin de la Statistique Générale de la France*, 1932, pp. 419–38.

cessively high, volume of reserves, making it possible to avoid overfrequent changes of rate (i.e., lowering the rate when reserves came in, raising the rate when they went out). In 1881 the reserve ratio fell to 52 percent; it rose again to 70 percent in 1886, and remained near, or more usually above, that level until 1910. In 1910 it fell again to 60 percent. So there was an inverse relation, though admittedly a very rough one, between the reserve ratio and the discount rate, and between the reserve ratio and the business cycle.

So the monetary history of France in the nineteenth century can be summarized as follows:

1. During the Restoration and the July Monarchy, the growth of nonmetallic money was contained, or rather severely compressed. Total circulation doubled, while the physical product increased by about 75 percent. So silver money was sufficient to satisfy the needs of growth. Most of the gold and silver used for minting was imported.

2. From 1847 to 1873 there was a parallel growth, slightly above 3 percent per annum, in the money supply and in overall product. The amount of money in circulation increased in 23 years by 120 percent. Of this increase, 38 percent was due to the growth in metallic money, 47 percent to paper money, and 15 percent to bank money. The explosion in the amount of paper money occurred mainly at the beginning and at the end of the period. The 1848 revolution was the point of departure for a monetary revolution: the value of the notes that had been issued by the Banque de France rose from 250 million francs to 650 million francs between 1848 and 1853. Between 1853 and 1864 the growth was much more moderate (to 750 million francs in 1864). A new and regular upsurge began in 1865 and increased the amount of paper money to 2.8 billion by 1873. It had thus nearly quadrupled in eight years. The decline in issues from 1874 on corresponds to a decisive turning point in the economic situation. The rapid growth in paper money was in fact either contracyclic (1849–52 or 1867–68), or corresponded to a peak in activity (1872–73). But in 1873, 60 percent of the money in circulation was still metallic money, and the Empire alone minted more coins, especially gold coins, than all previous régimes put together. These large issues were facilitated by

France's favorable balance of payments, which made it easy to buy gold and silver abroad.

3. In a third period, the growth of paper money, which fluctuated quite widely in accordance with the changes in the bank rate referred to above, up to the beginning of the 1880s (up 86 percent from 1870 to 1873; down 24 percent from 1873 to 1879; up 31 percent from 1879 to 1884; and up 10 percent from 1884 to 1888) followed a fairly regular pattern, though slow in comparison with the Second Empire period. Table 3.2 shows the comparative development of real money in circulation (in constant value) and overall product between 1873 and 1913.

In the medium term, the acceleration in the growth of the money supply corresponds to an acceleration in the growth of overall product, but the second was much less marked. In the short term, the marked deceleration in the growth of overall product between 1900 and 1905 did not cause such a strong deceleration in the growth of the money supply. On the whole, the change in the structure of and the acceleration of the increase in the money supply between 1845 and 1873 and between 1895 and 1913 are due as much to changes in the pattern of overall product as to growth of overall product. Such growth could come about only through an increase in sales

Table 3.2 Comparative Development of Real Money Supply and Overall Product, 1873–1913 (mean annual increase)

	Money	Product
1873–1885	0.8	1.3
1885–1895	1.4	1.1
1895–1900	4.3	2.6
1900–1905	3.7	0.8
1905–1913	4.3	2.4

Estimate of Real Money Supply
  (billions of francs)

1873	9.9
1885	12.8
1895	14.8
1900	17.8
1905	21.2
1913	27

areas and in the volume of transactions, which required that more money should be available. Moreover, the ratio between nominal overall income and total money stock (currency plus deposits), which shows the velocity of money circulation, fell from 2.4 in about 1870 to 1.4 in 1913. It must be supposed that liquid assets represented a much larger proportion of legacies than an analysis of inheritances would suggest (6 to 7 percent).

Savings

The increase in the amount of money in circulation and the development of paper and bank money facilitated savings. Most nineteenth-century and modern authors consider that during the whole of the nineteenth century there was a veritable "drift" of savings toward treasury and state funds in the first part of the century, and toward foreign countries at the end of the century. According to them, only the period of the Second Empire was free of this phenomenon. This alleged "sterilization" of French savings is all the more absurd since France's capacity for saving was supposed to be particularly high because of what Raffalovitch has called "the large savings made by a working population which did not spend its income, and which had reached a stationary birthrate." In fact, the rate of saving in France was no higher than that in other European countries. According to Kuznets, the average rate of saving was no higher than 4.5 percent between 1873 and 1878, 4.6 percent between 1878 and 1903, and 5.6 percent between 1903 and 1911.

The nineteenth century was characterized by what Billoret has called "long-term expansion in the financial sphere", i.e., an increase in savings in the form of stocks and shares. In 1913 the portfolio of stocks and shares amounted to 122 billion francs, while the national income was 36 billion, and the money supply 26 billion. The growth of this enormous portfolio went through the following stages: 200 million per annum from 1830 to 1850; 1,560 from 1850 to 1880; 2,000 from 1880 to 1913. It rose from 5 billion in 1830 to 122 billion in 1913. During the same period, the public debt had risen from 4.7 to 33 billion. It had expanded particularly rapidly between 1850 and 1880, rising from 5.4 billion to 21.6 billion between these two dates. The amount deposited in savings banks rose from 62 millions in 1830 to 5.8 billion in 1913.

This expansion brought about an appreciable change in the pattern of legacies: real or immovable assets grew less, movable assets increased. According to old overall estimates, immovable assets still represented 67.2 percent of assets in 1851–55, 55.8 percent in 1861–65, and 43.8 percent in 1911–15. Within the category of movable assets, the proportion of stocks and shares tended to increase. According to the same estimates, they represented 6.9 percent of total assets in 1851–55, 8.6 percent in 1871–75, 17 percent in 1881–85, 32 percent in 1891–95, and 39 percent on the eve of the 1914 war. These last two figures are greatly overestimated. According to the most recent estimates by Professor Adeline Daumard, the percentage would be 30.4 percent in 1898–99, 29.6 percent in 1906–8. These estimates also make us revise our ideas about foreign investments in French portfolios: they did not exceed 25 percent in 1898–99, i.e., 7.6 percent of total wealth, and 28.7 percent in 1906–8, i.e., 8.5 percent of the total.

The development of banking institutions took place in parallel with that of stockbroking activities linked to the distribution of stocks and shares among the public. There were close links between the two types of institution: the banks in fact promoted stockbroking activities, since one of their main roles was to invest on behalf of their clients. At the beginning of the nineteenth century most of these stocks were state securities. Decisive changes took place during the 1830s and 1840s under the influence, in particular, of railway construction. Railway shares, worth 500 francs, spread rapidly through quite a large public and always held an important place in portfolios. They familiarized the French saver with the acquisition and possession of stocks and shares.

These developments derived from variations in the value of assets and from savers' preferences in investments. The fall in the price of land and construction at the end of the nineteenth century naturally reduced the proportion which these assets represented in inheritances. The investment preferences which made the French saver develop his estate toward fixed-income securities and guaranteed-income securities (such as railway stocks) resulted from the function of savings at that period. A "saver" (*rentier*) was usually just someone who had retired, and savings fulfilled the same function then that is performed by pension funds today.

French business concerns had never overlooked the policy of appealing to external financial resources, particularly debentures. But during the early part of the nineteenth century they encountered a certain amount of difficulty in obtaining bank loans and in placing their bonds. As Gille writes, "the difficulty of obtaining long-term loans was to be one of the most obstinate plagues of the French economy in the early part of the nineteenth century." Gille cites companies like Decazeville and Alais, which were forced to raise mortgage loans during the 1830s. In the department of the Nord, Fohlen notes "a fundamental divergence between the rapid progress of industrial production and the slowness in the organization of banking." Debentures and shares of low value (usually 500 francs) began to be more widespread from the 1840s onward.

But right up to the end of the century, the bond market was almost entirely monopolized by railway companies. By their nature these stocks were quite similar to state securities. From the last years of the nineteenth century on, industrial stocks grew in volume, and this trend accelerated rapidly in the years preceding the 1914 war. H. Morsel has noted the preference of the alpine hydroelectric industries for this kind of financing. M. Gillet has made the same observation about the coal industry. Industrial capitalism was now sufficiently established in France to supply the saver with investments corresponding to his requirements.

The development of interest rates in the course of the nineteenth century reflects the tensions between the supply of savings and the need for financing. The rate fell from 1815–19 (6.27 percent) to the beginning of the 1840s (3.88 percent in 1840–44). Apart from the exceptional period of the early 1870s (the rate was 5.17 percent in 1870–74), the period 1840–80, which, as we shall see in the following chapter, was characterized by a rapid growth in basic investments (infrastructural investment), saw a fair increase in rates (4.92 percent in 1860–64), followed by a slight decline (4.13 percent in 1880–84), which subsequently accelerated (3.16 percent in 1895–99). The slackening of investment occurred at a time when the tendency to develop movable assets increased, both because of the decline in income from other assets and because of the growth of the banking network. After that, interest rates increased only slightly (3.74 percent in 1910–14). This fall in the interest rate was one of the main factors favoring the growth of investments, since of course it decreased their cost.

Bibliography

Armengaud, A. *Les populations de l'Est Aquitain au début de l'époque contemporaine.* Paris: Imprimerie Nationale, 1961.

Billoret, J. L. "Système bancaire et dynamisme économique dans un pays à monnaie stable: France (1816–1914)." Unpublished thesis, Nancy, 1969.

Bouvier, J. *Le Crédit Lyonnais de 1863 à 1889.* 2 vols. Paris: Services d'Edition et de Ventes des Productions de l'Education Nationale, 1964.

——*Un siècle de banque française.* Paris: Hachette, 1973.

Cameron, R. C. *Banking in the Early Stages of Industrialization.* London: Oxford University Press, 1967.

Daumard, A. *Les fortunes françaises au XIXème siècle.* Paris and The Hague: Mouton, 1973.

Denuc, J. "Essai de détermination de la circulation monétaire annuelle en France de 1870 à 1913, "*Bulletin de la Statistique Générale de la France,* 1932, p. 419.

Fohlen, C. "Industrie et crédit dans la région liloise," *Revue du Nord,* 1954, p. 361.

Foville, A. de. *La transformation des moyens de transport et leurs conséquences économiques et sociales.* Paris: Guillaumin, 1887.

Gille, B. *La banque et le crédit en France de 1815 à 1848.* Paris: Presses Universitaires de France, 1959.

——*La banque en France au XIXème siècle.* Geneva: Droz, 1970–73.

Gillet, M. *Les charbonnages du Nord de la France au XIXème siècle.* Paris and The Hague: Mouton, 1973.

Hubscher, R. H. "Le livre de compte d'un grande famille picarde," *Revue d'Histoire Economique et Sociale,* no. 3 (1969).

Kuznets, S. "Les différences internationales dans la formation du capital et son financement," *Economie Appliquée,* April–September, 1953.

Léon, P. *La naissance de la grande industrie en Daughiné.* Paris, Gap, 1954.

Lévy-Leboyer, M. *Les banques européennes et l'industrialisation internationale.* Paris: Presses Universitaires de France, 1964.

Morsel, H. "Les industries électrotechniques dans les Alpes du Nord de 1869 à 1921," in *L'industrialisation en Europe au XIXème siècle.* Paris: Editions du Centre National de la Recherche Scientifique, 1972.

Raffalovitch, A. "Chronique financière," *Journal des Economistes,* January 15, 1907.

Thuillier, G. "Pour une histoire monétaire de la France au XIXème siècle," *Annales, Economies, Sociétés, Civilisations,* no. 1 (1959).

Chapter Four: The Formation of Capital

THE FORMATION OF capital in the nineteenth century can be seen only by means of an index of investments, though such an index is highly uncertain. This uncertainty would be increased by any attempt to calculate an index showing the growth of net capital or an estimate of the stock of liquid capital to the point where such data would have no real credibility. But an index of investments does help us to arrive at an idea of what was happening in France. The index used here was worked out by Lévy-Leboyer and myself from various sets of data, either in real terms (e.g., steam engines, textile machinery, ships) or in monetary values (e.g., investments in railways or canals). The overall index can be broken down into three separate indices—basic (infrastructure) investment, transport material, and industrial plant or machinery—weighted according to an estimate derived from various sources—including C. Colson—of the value structure of this capital. Basic investments include building and transportation, including ports.

In 1913, Colson estimated the national capital at 302 billion, broken down as follows:

Agricultural capital: 32 percent, consisting of 26.8 percent for landed property and farm buildings and 5.2 percent for special buildings, including those connected with the raising of livestock. *Premises used for housing and professional purposes* (excluding factories): 24.5 percent.

Personal movable property: 7.7 percent.

Transport and communications: 15.3 percent.

Factories, plant machinery, industrial and commercial inventories: 9.8 percent.

Administrative premises: 6.9 percent.

Military equipment: 2.7 percent.

Gold specie: 3.8 percent.

On the basis of Colson's figures, Malinvaud has put forward a rough estimate in terms of contemporary classifications. According to Malinvaud, the fixed reproducible capital was worth 137.7 billion francs (1913), divided as follows:

Housing and administrative premises: 42.1 percent.

Productive capital: 57.9 percent, made up of
Agriculture: 6.5 percent
Industry, commerce, services: 22.1 percent
Transport and communications: 29.3 percent.

An estimate made thirty years earlier, in about 1883, would have given appreciably different percentages: the proportion of housing and transport would have been higher still.

In the long term, the curve of total investment is clearly divided into two phases: first an irregular but strong growth up to 1880–84 (2.1 percent per annum from 1815–19 to 1880–84), and then a marked deceleration which itself can be broken down into two periods—a quasi-stagnation up to the early years of the twentieth century (down 26 percent from 1882 to 1886; up 14 percent from 1886 to 1905), and a strong recovery from 1905 to 1913 (up 62 percent). The 1882 level was not reached again until 1908; in 1913 it was greatly exceeded. This new spurt foreshadowed the enormous expansion in plant and equipment in the 1920s.

In the medium term, we may break the first period down into three cycles: 1815–31, with a peak in 1825; 1831–50, with two peaks, one in 1839 and one in 1847; and 1850–71, characterized by a long period of sustained growth without any spectacular slump from 1853 to 1869 (i.e., during all the Second Empire), the growth period being preceded and followed by slack periods.

Setting aside fluctuations, we note strong growth up to 1838–42 (2.7 percent from 1820–24 to 1838–42), a slower growth of 1.4 percent from 1834–42 to 1865–69, and a very strong growth once more of 1.9 percent from 1865–69 to 1880–84.

Basic Investments

During the first main period, the overall index is dependent on the index of basic investment (2.4 percent from 1815–19 to 1880–84). There is a fairly satisfactory agreement between the index for building and the index for transportation. In France, as in the United States, we may talk of "transport building cycles" with a periodicity of 17 to 20 years. But the building index is less irregular than the transportation index. The chief disagreements between the two series occur in the 1860s, during which investments in transportation decreased after 1862, whereas growth in building was interrupted only by the war, and in the 1890s, during which investments in transportation decreased strongly up to 1897, whereas in building the lowest point was reached in 1885. After that, the two sets of figures agree again, though fluctuations in transportation are still much more marked than those in building.

Building. The long-term evolution of the building index is linked to the demand for housing. This demand depends on two demographic factors: overall population growth and population mobility. The deceleration in population growth throughout the nineteenth century resulted in a similar deceleration in the growth of construction. The steady expansion of the rural exodus up to the decade 1851–61 brought about an increase in construction up to the 1860s. The exceptional increase in building activity in the years 1878–83 clearly corresponds to the exceptional size of the exodus (821,000) in 1876–81. The long stagnation in construction from 1886 to 1906 may be explained by the decrease in the mobility of the population, and the revival of the prewar years is preceded by a renewed exodus (772,400 from 1906 to 1911).

But we must beware of thinking that the link between the

two sets of figures is always perfectly straightforward. The influence of the demographic factors is amplified by the exaggerated hopes and fears of investors. The building boom, which culminated in the early 1880s, was brought about by an increase in rents which was much more rapid than the increase in the cost of living as a whole (see table 4.1).

Between the two surveys of developed property in 1851 and 1887–89, the number of houses increased by 21 percent, and their rental value increased by 193 percent. Two-thirds of this trebling in values was due to the increase in rents, and one-third to a qualitative improvement. In fact, the increase in demand for housing was exaggerated by the overoptimistic anticipations of investors. These reached their peak in the years 1876–82, and the sudden collapse of the real estate market in 1882 was the beginning of a long period of liquidation. The explanation for these fluctuations in investment is not to be found either in the development of interest rates, or in variations in costs of construction, or in the great town planning projects: the fluctuations in building simply exaggerated the pattern of business in general.

Transportation: The Omnipotence of the Railways. Table 4.2 shows investment in transportation. The figures are my own.

Investment in roads was financed entirely by the state and local authorities. In the course of the nineteenth century these investments came to assume a dual character. The national network serving the big towns was greatly developed and

Table 4.1 A Comparison of the Increase in Rents with the Increase in the Cost of Living (1900 = 100)

Rent Index*		Retail Price Index†	
1852	56.6	1850	85.8
1862	80.3	1860	95.3
1876	88.0	1870	103.5
		1880‡	110.0
1900	100.0	1890	103.5
1908	103.4	1908	102.3

*According to *Salaires et coûts de l'existence à diverses époques jusqu'en 1910.*
†According to the Retrospective Yearbook of INSEE, 1966.
‡1880 is not a typical year. Prices were abnormally high.

Table 4.2 Investment in Transportation

	Total Investment Expenditure (Including Costs of Upkeep and Renewal) Millions of Francs (current)			Percent		
	Ports and Canals	Roads	Railways	Ports and Canals	Roads	Railways
1840–1844	62.8	164.5				
1845–1849	55.9	176.6	163.0	14.1	44.6	41.3
1850–1854	33.0	166.6	180.8	8.6	43.7	47.7
1855–1859	35.1	187.0	406.4	5.5	29.8	64.7
1860–1864	50.7	212.8	396.7	7.5	32.5	60.0
1865–1869	53.2	228.0	317.8	8.8	38.2	53.0
1870–1874	41.7	210.6	290.9	7.6	38.7	53.7
1875–1879	63.8	236.0	380.8	9.3	34.6	56.1
		Annual Means				
1880–1884	124.2	247.6	578.1	13.0	26.1	60.9
1885–1889	77.6	240.3	423.2	10.4	32.4	57.1
1890–1894	59.0	232.8	401.1	8.5	33.6	57.9
1895–1899	50.1	231.0	375.7	7.6	35.1	57.3
1900–1904	60.3	231.4	531.9	7.3	28.2	64.5
1905–1909	59.9	236.9	562.0	6.9	27.7	65.4
1910–1913	88.9	249.0	867.1	7.4	20.6	72.0
		Expenditure on New Investments				
1880–1884	105.5	46.4	396.8	19.2	8.5	72.3
1885–1889	57.9	44.0	275.3	13.3	11.7	73.0
1890–1894	38.4	43.1	241.0	11.9	13.4	74.7
1895–1899	28.8	41.6	200.0	10.7	15.4	74.0
1900–1904	37.6	45.0	342.6	8.9	10.6	80.6
1905–1909	30.4	43.8	341.2	7.3	10.5	82.1
1910–1913	66.6	43.7	595.8	9.4	6.2	84.4

improved between 1815 and 1850, though during the 1840s some of these roads were in such constant use that maintenance was difficult. Despite the development of the railways, the road network was kept up in such a way that it eventually stimulated the growth of the motorcar industry. But the great achievement of the nineteenth century was, through the laws of 1821 and 1836, the extension of secondary roads, in particular local roads at the level of the commune. By 1872 there were 330,000 kilometers of these roads, and by 1912 538,000 kilometers. They linked even the smallest hamlets to the great trade network. The self-sufficiency of the village was doomed.

Investment in canals was almost entirely financed by the state from the 1840s on. An attempt at mixed financing was made early in the twentieth century (the Baudin program of 1901), but it met with little success. The government had already been involved since 1822 (the Becquey program) in a huge project of canal construction. But the July Monarchy, which opened up 2,000 kilometers of navigable canals, did not take the trouble to maintain the navigability of rivers, except the lower Seine. By the 1840s some engineers considered that railways had made inland navigation a thing of the past. But, as one engineer put it in 1867, the water transport industry hung on for dear life, especially in the Nord. After 1860 new measures were taken to promote canals, the only real counterweight to the "monopoly of the railways": tolls were lowered in 1867 and abolished in 1880; a new impetus was given to investment, which reached a peak with the "Freycinet" plan (see figures for 1880–84 in table 4.2). France's canal network was not so much extended as given greater unity. But the scale on which the operation was carried out limited the lighterage trade to a craft level, and France preferred to ramify its railways ad infinitum rather than build big inland waterways. This sort of construction, it is true, was made costly by natural conditions, and the profitability of canal investment was doubtful. But the choice was probably a mistaken one.

As for the railways, after a few concessions were granted, such as the line from Lyons to Saint-Etienne and the network in Alsace, to local businessmen and industrialists, it quickly became evident that local capital was too dispersed to cope with the investment requirements involved. One might have thought that French tradition would then have led to a state solution of the problem. But, according to the committee which reported on the law of 1842, "The financial resources of the state are not unlimited." Yet, with a budget that increased by 24.5 percent between 1830 and 1840, expenditures on public works trebled. They doubled again between 1840 and 1847, with the budget then increasing by 16.5 percent. The only solution, therefore, was a law by which the railways were allotted to concessionaires with enough money to provide the initial outlay

and enough reputation to attract other capital. When the pro-
posal for state financing was rejected by both chambers of the
French parliament in 1838, this was the only solution. The lines
which were then conceded, in particular the Paris-Orléans and
the Paris-Rouen sections, were given to companies made up of
big bankers from Paris and Switzerland, large freight firms, and
English capitalists. The 1839 crisis forced a number of these
groups into liquidation. But in the case of the Paris-Orléans
section, the state came to the rescue of the company by
granting it a *garantie d'interêt*, i.e., by guaranteeing the interest
on the money raised to build the railway. At the time, such
measures were considered rather unsatisfactory palliatives. But
they gradually became more general.

The 1840s were a decisive period. The big banks in Paris,
and in particular the Rothschild Bank, agreed to form
companies to take on as concessions the main lines in the
French railway network. The Ministry of Public Works used
the system of competitive bidding to obtain conditions which
became more and more severe, and greatly reduced the time-
span of the concessions. Enthusiasm for railway concessions
received a check in 1847 when it became clear that the forecasts of costs and revenues upon which government conditions
has been based would not be fulfilled. Railway investment did
not pick up again until Napoleon III, who, when he came to
power, extended the concessions to 99 years. This measure was
supplemented in the 1850s when the "main lines" were built up
into virtual monopolies and guaranteed interest was extended
to all the lines which had been added to the "original"
networks. But at the beginning of the 1860s, companies were
cautious about accepting new concessions. It was then that
certain local notables and some mere speculators got together
to form companies which aimed at competing with the main
railway networks, invoking the law of 1865 on branch lines
(which substituted local for state regulation) and the law of
1867 on *sociétés anonymes* (which limited the liability of investors). Most of these new companies went bankrupt after
1875. The speculative railway lines were succeeded in 1879 by
the "electoral" railways of the Freycinet Plan. The Freycinet
Plan was financed by loans. Every little town wanted its own

railway station. The agreement of 1883, negotiated after the financial crisis of 1882 which forced the state to reduce its public works and give up financing them by means of state loans, forced the big companies, in return for the general application of guaranteed interest, to take over both the lines of the small companies and those of the Freycinet Plan, with the exception of certain lines which formed part of the state network. Most of the main lines of the network were set up in the years 1840 to 1850. They were financed without too much difficulty despite the crisis of 1847–52, and proved to be an excellent source of profit. In the years 1860–70 and up to 1883, the authorities made the companies take on lines which were not immediately remunerative in exchange for a monopoly and guaranteed interest.

There are three explanations for the decline in railway investments after 1883: first, a deliberate decrease in construction; second, a systematic policy imposed by the Ministry of Public Works, which reduced supplementary undertakings and orders for equipment with the object of reducing the amounts payable under the state guarantee; third—and it was this factor which made the Ministry of Public Works' policy possible—the large number of technical innovations which were introduced in the 1870s (among others, steel rails, bogie trucks, electric signals, and gravitational shunting). Investment in railways remained depressed until 1906, apart from the exceptional upsurge in the years 1899–1900. The building of "road railways," streetcar lines in particular, was undertaken by "strong groups" built up around a few big equipment manufacturers or public-works contractors. But the general revival of investment after 1905 is explained by the amount of work which had to be undertaken in order to cope with increases in traffic arising out of the previous policy of strict reduction of capital expenses. At this period, and since the late 1880s, the stocks of the big companies had lost much of their prestige on the Paris stock exchange, despite a brief and sudden revival in 1898–1900. It is not difficult to understand this decline. Railway shares were not included in the general revival which took place in the early 1900s.

But the big railway companies had realized handsome

profits in the early days. Between 1851 and 1867, the Compagnie du Nord distributed 323 million francs to its shareholders for an initial capital of 160 million contributed in 1847 and increased by a further 62.5 million in 1858–61. The market value increased at the same rate as the increase in dividends; in 1882 it represented 1.5 times the nominal value of the shares in the case of the Compagnie de l'Est and 5.1 times the nominal value of the shares in the case of the Compagnie du Nord. This increase in value can only be explained by the method of financing "new" lines which had been added to the first concessions. In 1882 the share capital represented only 11.7 percent of the "initial" capital (12.2 million francs), the rest having been supplied by the state (26.3 percent), and by the stock market (62 percent). Shares thus provided almost two-thirds of the financing for the construction of railways, and the success of these shares as an investment was largely due to the guaranteed interest.

But after the peak in the early 1880s the shares of the big railway companies went through a deep depression between 1884 and 1895. The companies had to cope simultaneously with a fall in their revenues due to the decrease in traffic and with an increase in charges imposed by the state under the agreement of 1883. The situation was corrected in the course of the 1890s. But, in fact, as Colson says, "the equilibrium in railway accounting had been upset." During the 1900s the increase in wages, the reduction in working hours, and the increase in the price of supplies had driven up expenses out of all proportion with the savings made possible by progress in productivity. Freight rates could not be raised, and in the case of certain companies, such as the Compagnie du Nord, guaranteed interest ended in 1914.

In the preceding chapter we examined the effect of railway investments on the development of the market in industrial products. It was chiefly by lowering transport costs that railways altered the factors of growth. Although French freight rates did not depend on cost prices but on what Jules Dupuit called in 1849 "commercial opportunities," the development of rates depended closely on that of costs, i.e., of productivity.

1. The period 1851–73 is one in which rates fell and

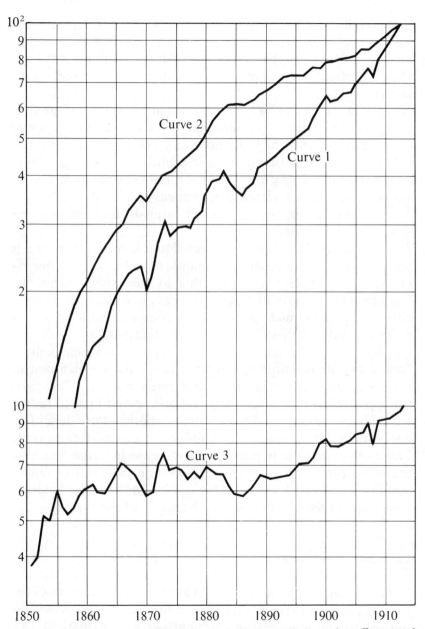

Figure 2 Productivity in the Railways. Curve 1: Index of traffic growth
(1913 = 100). Curve 2: Index of growth of factors of production (labor, energy,
and capital) (1913 = 100). Curve 3: Index of growth of overall productivity of
factors of production from 1851 to 1931 (1913 = 100).

productivity rose. According to my estimates, this rise occurred at a rate of 2.06 percent per annum. It was mainly due to an increase in capacity. During this period, technical progress was chiefly limited to locomotives; innovation in other sectors did not keep pace.

2. During the 1870s, rates remained constant and productivity dropped. The drop in productivity was due to the opening of secondary lines which did not carry much traffic, and to the difficulties which arose out of the technical disparity mentioned above. But it led those who ran the railways to go in for the various innovations already mentioned: steel rails, compound locomotives, bogie trucks, electric signals and gravitational shunting.

3. The use of these new techniques explains the rise in productivity (1.85 percent per annum) from the 1880s to the eve of the 1914 war. But it is clear that by then these techniques had reached the limit of their efficiency, and the reductions in costs which they made possible had been carried too far. The strike of 1910 gave expression to this situation.

So, on the whole, the French system was efficient: it limited distributed profits through a mechanism which restricted these once a certain level had been reached. The gains made possible by technical progress had served first, to reduce work-hours; second, to finance construction and the deficits on unprofitable lines; and third, to reduce fares and freight rates. These reductions made possible the increase in traffic which we examined earlier. We still have to examine the exact economic significance of this increase. This will be one of the subjects of a subsequent section devoted to the study of the market.

Industrial Investment

In the medium term, industrial investment went through cycles fairly similar to those we have seen in basic investments. But the cycles in industrial investment were less marked than those in basic investments up to 1885, and more marked after that date. Moreover, in the long term, industrial investment shows an element of acceleration which distinguishes it both

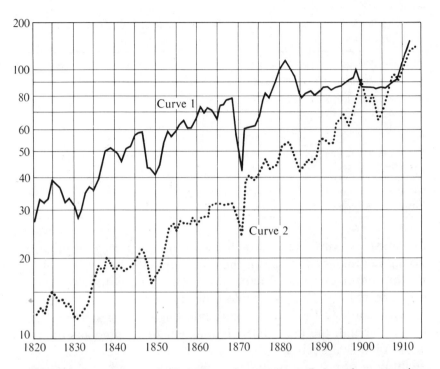

Figure 3 Index of Gross Capital Formation. Curve 1: Index of construction and public works (1908–12 = 100). Curve 2: Index of industrial equipment (1908–12 = 100).

SOURCE: F. Caron, "Investment Strategy in France," in *The Rise of Managerial Capitalism*, edited by H. Daems and H. Van der Wee (Louvain: Leuven University Press, 1974), p. 133.

from basic investments and from industrial production (see table 4.3). The curve of basic investments is convex, while that of industrial investments is concave. Thus French industry had a tendency to become more and more capital-intensive. We shall examine in more detail in chapter 7 the problems raised by a comparison between the investment and production curves. Here we shall confine ourselves to examining the methods by which enterprises were financed.

French entrepreneurs came from every kind of social milieu, but principally from among artisans, the middle-class business community, and what might be called the engineering world. In iron and steel the principal role was played by former

Table 4.3 A Comparison of Industrial Production with Industrial Investment (1908–1912 = 100)

	Industrial Production	Industrial Investment
1830–1834	12.5	12.9
1840–1844	18.1	18.4
1850–1854	23.0	21.6
1860–1864	30.4	29.1
1870–1874	33.6	34.1
1880–1884	43.2	50.1
1890–1894	52.1	58.2
1900–1904	64.4	77.3
1910–1913	95.3	110.7

iron masters converted to the new techniques, but certain of the big companies formed in the 1820s and 1830s were created by iron merchants like Boigues, men from the bourgeois business community like Schneider, or by the sons of eminent citizens who had been to the big state engineering schools. On the other hand, the great French engineering technicians of the years 1840–80, such as Calla, Farcot, and Cave, were self-taught men of peasant or craft origin. The iron and steel makers subsequently set up engineering workshops. Entrepreneurs in the textile industry often came from commercial backgrounds, though here again craft origins were also known. Many traders and commission merchants became industrialists after having been manufacturing merchants. Fohlen quotes many examples of this kind of career, including the Toulemondes and the Lemaistre Demesteres in the years 1830–40. Others, like the Agaches of Lille, went directly from trade into industry. Other industrialists in the textile sector, such as the Mequillet Noblots, came into the industry from dyeing. In fact it was quite common for someone to go from one industrial sector to another. This was the way in which the automobile industry came into being at the end of the century.

As early as the first part of the nineteenth century there are examples of local industrial bourgeoisie using the resources of their region to their own advantage, transferring their capital from one sector to another, and giving one another aid. This happened in Alsace, and in the Nivernais, where the big factories at Imphy and Fourchambault absorbed all available resources. It also happened in the department of the Nord, where the middle classes already engaged in the textile industry largely financed the beginnings of the coal industry. It happened, likewise, in Lorraine, where the iron and steel industry was born out of initiatives by iron masters from Lorraine itself or from other regions, but also by other businessmen mustering capital from all kinds of sources. Table 4.4, for example, shows a breakdown of the capital of the *société anonyme* which owned the iron works and rolling-mills at Champigneulles (according to Précheur, founded in 1872). The same thing happened, again, in the Grenoble region, where the cement, paper, and hydroelectric industries were born at different periods out of similar conditions: i.e., local initiative using local capital from various sources. And it was the same in Lyons and Paris. But these two cities played a special role in the export of capital and industry: they created new activities which were subsequently driven out by the high price of labor. Up to the 1860s, both Lyons and Paris decentralized their activities, Paris in the direction of Picardy and Champagne in the case of textiles and toward the department of the Nord in the case of iron and steel.

Up to the 1860s, company legislation, which we went into

Table 4.4 Sources of Capital for Champigneulles Ironworks, According to Précheur (1872)

	No. of Shareholders	No. of Shares
Landed proprietors	26	126
Industrialists	24	190
Attorneys, notaries, barristers	21	117
Rentiers	17	88
Wholesale dealers	16	58
Civil servants	16	69
Insurance agents	7	22
Doctors	4	10
Farmers	6	19
Bankers	1	1
Total	138	700

earlier, greatly restrained the development of *sociétés anonymes*. Between 1817 and 1867, 616 companies of this type were founded, an average of 12 per annum. Freedemann has noted that the curve denoting the number of these foundations closely follows fluctuations in the economy. Railways and canals represented 60 percent of the nominal capital, while insurance and banks made up 28 percent. It was in fact the *société en commandite* which was then the normal framework for the development of capitalism. This kind of association made it possible to use the help of relations or friends in what was usually a local context. Shares in such companies circulated among a comparatively limited group. There was a veritable explosion in the creation of companies of this kind in the 1830s. According to Freedeman, 1,106 partnerships limited by shares (*commandites par actions*) were registered by the Commercial Court of Paris alone. Two new booms occurred in the 1840s and between 1853 and 1856. From 1840 to 1859, while 14 *sociétés anonymes* were founded every year, 218 *sociétés en commandites* were founded during the period. They covered every sector of activity except insurance, which was compulsorily organized by means of *sociétés anonymes*. Although the average *société en commandite* was much smaller than the average *société anonyme*, it should be noted that most of the companies operating in the iron and steel industry adopted the *société en commandite* method. Even in the textile industry, which was famous for its family structure, the *société en commandite* played an essential role.

Since 1879, the French Statistics Bureau has regularly published the figures concerning the formation of companies. The average number of companies founded per annum between 1879 and 1883 was 4,104, and between 1909 and 1913 it was 7,151, an increase of 74 percent. The number of companies dissolved increased much less rapidly: 2,681 in 1879–83 and 3,561 in 1909–13, an increase of 33 percent. Thus the net creation of companies showed a very rapid increase, rising from 1,423 per annum in 1879–83 to 3,590 in 1909–13, an increase of 152 percent. Out of the 181,000 companies created, 120,000 (in round figures) were partnerships (*sociétés en nom collectif*); 30,600 were limited or sleeping partnerships (*sociétés en commandites simples*); and 31,200 were joint stock companies (*sociétés par actions*), of which 20,800 were *sociétés anonymes*. The *sociétés anonymes* made up 14 percent of the companies founded during the first period, and 17 percent of those founded during the second period. The share capital raised by *sociétés par actions* is known from 1889 on. The figures are as follows (annual mean, in millions of francs):

1889–93	559
1894–98	664
1899–1903	1,169
1904–8	691
1909–13	1,072

These figures bring out the importance of the last years of the nineteenth century, the years immediately before and after 1900, in the evolution of French capitalism. It was then that the share capital was assembled and the firms founded which assured the revival of French capitalism.

We have a list of the *sociétés par actions* which existed in 1898. The 6,325 companies of this type had between them a capital of 13.5 billion francs, and those of them which were quoted on the stock exchange had a capital of 12.9 billion, quoted at 14.4 billion. Industrial companies raised 22 percent of the share capital, and 34 percent of the quoted capital belonged to such companies. So it was in industry that the increase in capital was highest. Table 4.5 shows the difference between nominal and quoted values in various sectors of activity.

Up to the 1840s, the big merchant banks in Paris directed their activities chiefly toward French and foreign government bonds and the financing of international trade. There are a few cases where they took shares in industrial concerns, especially in the iron and steel industry. But not until the 1840s could one really say that these banks had an industrial policy. It was only "once the battle of the railway tenders was over" (Gille) that the Rothschilds increased their shares in iron and steel companies, in particular collaborating in the launching of new companies such as the Société de Denain-Anzin and, with other bankers, the Société des Batignolles. Under the Second Empire, the

Table 4.5 Comparison of Nominal and Quoted Value of Shares on the French Stock Exchange, Various Industrial Sectors (in millions of francs/percent)

	No. of Companies	Nominal Value of Shares	Nominal Value of Companies Quoted	Quoted Values of Companies Quoted
Mines and	366	752.2	702.5	1,731.5
quarries	14%	21.5%	24.7%	31.5%
Food	689	327.2	308.5	594.2
	26.3%	11%	10.8%	12.1%
Chemicals	496	514.6	497.1	899
	19%	17.2%	17.5%	18.2%
Metals	437	754	729.6	963.3
	16.7%	25.2%	25.6%	19.5%
Manufacturing	634	644.5	611	741.8
industries	24%	21.5%	21.4%	15.1%
Total for whole of industry	2,622	2,992.5	2,848.7	4,929.8

Crédit Mobilier of the brothers Péreire was created expressly to develop this kind of participation. As a matter of fact, the Péreires were far more interested in railways than in industrial concerns. But the kind of bank which they were trying to create—unsuccessfully, since they went bankrupt in 1867—was subsequently taken over by most of the big French merchant banks.

So, on the eve of the 1914 war, as well as having important foreign interests, the big merchant banks had shares in French industry: the Banque de Paris et des Pays-Bas and the Banque de l'Union Parisienne, the Crédit Mobilier de France, and the Banque pour le Commerce et l'Industrie (the Banque Rouvier) had interests in the iron and steel industry and in electric light companies. But from the industrial point of view, the role of the banks was never more than secondary. The real initiative had come from entrepreneurs of various origins. The big deposit banks, founded in the 1860s, at first engaged quite vigorously in the industrial sector; but after the setbacks of the years 1870–80, they seem to have drawn in their horns until the years preceding the 1914 war, when there was a revival of their industrial activity. Thus it was only at times when there was an exceptional boom in industrial investment that the deposit banks shared in the general movement.

All the works devoted to French industrial history in the nineteenth century stress the importance of self-financing. Lévy-Leboyer and Fohlen quote several instances of companies in the textile industry in the early part of the nineteenth century where the company articles made reinvestment of part of the earnings actually *compulsory*. Even if the initial capital of these companies might have been provided by bankers, the growth capital came out of their own resources. Gille makes similar observations about the iron and steel industry at the same period: "Self-financing," he writes, "was the main source of growth of liquid capital." The Decazeville company, for example, doubled the value of its capital between 1830 and 1845 by reinvesting its profits. This tendency does not seem to have lessened with the increase in the size of companies; in fact, one of the reasons for concentration was to increase the capacity for self-financing. In 1899, Babu concludes a remarkable monograph on the firms in the Saint-Étienne region as follows: "The factories of the Loire not only amortize their equipment very quickly, but they also build up large reserves, which when necessary enable them to weather a crisis or to modernize their equipment no matter how great the changes in the processes of working iron and steel." These "emergency reserves enabled such companies to look ahead to bad times without anxiety." For example, the Société Denain-Anzin decided in 1897 to build a new steel works. To do so, it set aside 85 percent of its profits. In the coal sector, Gillet says that "the extent of self-financing in the coal companies came very close to that of the self-financing in the textile companies of the Nord." The motor companies founded at the end of the nineteenth and the beginning of the twentieth century also resorted largely to self-financing. Colson, one of the best observers of his day, wrote in 1908: "Our companies devote a large part of their profits to extending their plants instead of increasing their dividends," in order to avoid "issuing new shares."

We do not possess overall figures for all this. Figures are available only after the 1890s, and even then they are not absolutely reliable. According to the contemporary economist J. Lescure, French firms put aside half of their profits as reserves. G. F. Teneul also considers that during the period 1890–1913 the retention rate was 50 percent. Between 1880 and 1913 the differences between the stock exchange capitalization of companies and their nominal capital increased markedly in the industrial sectors: the ratio rose from 1.23 to 3.13 in iron and steel works; from 1.22 to 2.33 in mechanical engineering; from 0.73 to 2.20 in naval construction; and from 1.81 to 2.5 in the chemical industries. Though no doubt they are overestimated, these figures indicate the increase in the capital value of these enterprises. Moreover, it is clear, as Jean Bouvier has shown, that the distributed profit increased much less rapidly than the overall profit.

According to Teneul, the average annual investments of firms in the period 1896–1913 amounted to 2.50 billion, of which 1.6 were provided by self-financing. For the period 1910–13, Malinvaud finds an overall self-financing rate of 80 percent.

These observations show up as particularly absurd the cynical remarks of certain authors in the 1950s who spoke of the financial market's withdrawal from company financing. The preference for internal financing stemmed primarily from the desire of entrepreneurs to preserve their independence, either because their firm was part of the family property, or because, if it was a *société en commandite* or *en nom collectif* the entrepreneur wished to maintain his personal control over his own affairs. In the case of big capitalist companies, Babu wrote, "the object was to increase capital rather than income on capital." The preference for self-financing also resulted from a desire for rational management. The "emergency reserves" of which Babu wrote in the passage quoted above were designed to deal with sudden falls in demand and technological uncertainty. The obligation to build up large reserves was always one of the conditions imposed by the Conseil d'Etat in authorizing the creation of *sociétés anonymes*.

Clearly, however, if so many precautions had to be taken it was because these prudent rules of management were not always observed. In fact, a distinction should be made between two kinds of firm, one kind which favored the retention of profits and reinvestment, and another kind which did not. The first category includes both ends of the scale of firms classified according to legal category, i.e., family firms, and joint stock companies in which management tended to be concentrated in the hands of managers whose chief object was to insure the firm's growth. On the other hand, *sociétés en commandite*, or even *sociétés anonymes*, in which the original shareholders had managed to keep control of enough of the capital to make their views felt, were often run with the object of making distributed profits as high as possible. In the coal industry of the Nord, for example, according to Gillet the distribution of large profits was the main object, and even some managers considered that they had gone too far in this direction. In the case of *sociétés en commandite* the sleeping partner often had means of bringing pressure to bear in order to obtain high distributed profits. In most of these companies there was constant tension between the sleeping partners and those who managed the business. The former would not accept the systematic reinvestment of profits unless it resulted sooner or later in substantial increases in capital, together with privileged conditions for the owners of the initial shares, so that on the whole self-financing resulted sooner or later, when the firm in question was expanding, in a distribution of profits.

It should be remembered that the transportation sector did not go in for self-financing. This was not entirely the case, for quite a large part of the maintenance costs served in fact to increase the value of the capital. But the essential rule of railway accounting was that any expenditure which increased the amount of liquid capital was an "initial" expense normally financed by loan. The railway companies did not practice industrial amortization. For them the word "amortization" merely designated the repayment of shares, usually carried out by drawing lots among a section of them. The railway companies' reserves were insignificant. But they did practice one form of reinvestment of profits by developing their "private domain," which before 1914 consisted chiefly of housing for their employees.

How did industrial self-financing develop in this way? The answer is twofold. On the one hand, there was much transformation of circulating or floating capital into fixed capital. On the other hand, despite the fall in prices and the rise in wages, industrial profits rose—though, as we shall see, not without interruption. We shall examine this second factor in chapter 8, where we shall study the mechanisms of industrial growth which combined to bring it about. For the moment it is enough to say that industrial growth could only be realized through a high rate of overall profit. The first factor—the transformation of circulating or liquid capital into fixed capital—resulted from all the financial and technical innovations which characterized the nineteenth century. It is a platitude to say that technical progress reduces the amount of liquid capital necessary to production. Commercial capitalism worked with a minimum of fixed capital, but required that a large amount of working capital be available. Similarly, the setting up of the railway system speeded up goods transport and abolished the uncertainty of delivery formerly due to frequent halts, or the vagaries of the weather, or the need to see to the maintenance of the canals: and so stocks of raw material could be reduced, and considerable capital economies made. Lastly, the development of short-term credit gave the financial management of companies much more maneuvering room. Progress in business accounting also certainly made it possible to arrive at better estimates of a company's financing capacity. The so-called cautiousness of the early French entrepreneurs seems to have been due to ignorance as often as not.

The intensity of investment after the 1890s, and particularly after 1905, explains why, despite the increase in self-financing, appeals to external resources increased considerably at the end of the nineteenth century. The issue of French

Table 4.6 Issues on the Paris Stock Exchange, According to F. Marnata

	Shares and Debentures			Shares		
	Total	Industry	Percent	Total	Industry	Percent
1892–1896	543	188	34.7	176	67.6	55.5
1897–1901	941	409	43.5	470	214.2	62.6
1902–1906	710	299	42.1	369	248.3	67.3
1907–1911	1.440	605	41.9	616	410.8	66.7

securities seems to have been equal to 6 percent of the net industrial product in 1913, as against 2.1 percent in 1896. Table 4.6 shows the issues on the Paris Stock Exchange as shown in the recent book by Mme. F. Marnata. After 1897, the industrial sector represents more than two-fifths of total issues, and two-thirds of the stock issues. The industrial sector was less able than banking and transport to resort to the bond market.

Bibliography

Aftalion, A. *Les crises générales et périodiques de surproduction.* 2 vols. Paris: Rivière, 1913.

Annuaire statistique de la France. Paris: Imprimerie Nationale, published annually since 1879.

Armengaud, A. *Les populations de l'Est aquitain au début de l'époque contemporaine.* Paris: Imprimerie Nationale, 1961.

Babu, C. "L'industrie métallurgique dans la région du Saint Etienne," *Annales des Mines,* 9th ser. (1899).

Boutin, E. "La propriété batie," in *Conférence faite à la Société de statistique de Paris.* Paris: Berger Levrault, 1891.

Caron, F. "Les commandes des Compagnies de chemin de fer en France, 1850–1914," *Revue d'Histoires de la Sidérurgie,* 3 (July–September, 1965). Translated as "French Railroad Investment, 1850–1914," in *Essays in French Economic History,* edited by R. Cameron. Homewood, Ill.: R. D. Irwin, 1970.

——"Recherches sur le capital des voies de communication en France au XIXème siècle, "in *L'industrialisation de l'Europe au XIXème siècle.* Paris: Editions du Centre National de la Recherche Scientifique, 1972.

Colson, C. *Cours d'économie politique.* 3d. ed. Paris: Gauthier Villars, 1927.

Dupuit, J. "De l'influence des péages sur l'utilité des voies de communication," *Annales des Ponts et Chaussées: Mémoires et documents,* 2d ser., vol. 17 (1849).

Fohlen, C. *Une affaire de famille au XIXème siècle: Méquillet Noblot.* Paris: A. Colin, 1955.

Freedeman, C. "Joint Stock Business Organization in France," *Business History Review,* 1965.

——*L'industrie textile au temps du Second Empire.* Paris: Plon, 1956.

Gille, B. *Histoire de la maison Rothschild des origines à 1870.* 2 vols. Geneva: Droz, 1965–67.

——*Recherches sur la formation de la grande entreprise capitaliste.* Paris: Services d'Edition et de Vente des Productions de l'Education Nationale, 1959.

Gillet, M. *Les charbonnages du Nord de la France au XIXème siècle.* Paris and The Hague: Mouton, 1973.

Landes, D. "French Entrepreneurship and Industrial Growth in the Nineteenth Century," *The Journal of Economic History,* May 1949.

Lescure, J. *L'épargne en France, 1914–1934.* Paris: Domat Montchrestien, 1936.

Malinvaud, E., J. J. Carre, and P. Dubois. *La croissance française.* Paris: Seuil, 1972.

Marnata, F. *La bourse ou le financement des investissements.* Fondation nationale des sciences politiques. Paris: A. Colin, 1973.

Precheur, C. *La Lorraine sidérurgique.* Paris, SABRI, 1959.

Teneul, G. F. *Le financement des entreprises en France depuis le fin du XIXème siècle à nos jours.* Paris: Librairie Générale de Droit et de Jurisprudence, 1961.

Chapter Five: The Development of Trade

The Growth of Consumption

THE GROWTH IN per capita national income referred to in chapter 1 resulted from a growth in industrial productivity reflected, in the long run, by a fall in prices. But these two factors, in turn, came about only because of the acceleration in demand which occurred when the whole of France and its population were incorporated into the general current of trade. Peasant incomes probably almost doubled between the 1840s and the 1880s: they may be estimated at 4,300 million francs in 1845 and 8,400 million francs in 1890. The "internal trade balance"—i.e., the ratio of the agricultural price index to the industrial price index—rose by 1.3 percent per annum between 1840 and 1882. The fall in industrial prices permitted a transfer of activity from peasant production of articles for peasant use toward industrial production of the same goods (e.g., iron tools, cotton garments, and clogs).

The growth in basic investments studied in the previous chapter was a second factor in the dynamism of demand for industrial products up to the 1880s. Combined expenditure for investments in transportation represented 8 percent of the industrial and artisan product in the years 1845–84. The railways played a particularly important role in the sectors concerned with iron and steel, the processing of metals, and construction materials. Orders represented 13–18 percent of production in the first of these sectors, 4–8 percent in the second, and 13–18 percent in the third, during the same period. But the main influence of the railways was technological: the perfecting of iron processing in the 1840s and 1850s, the introduction of the Bessemer process in the 1860s and the Gilchrist process in the 1870s, were the direct consequences of the pressure exercised by the railway companies on their suppliers. The same mechanisms came into play in other sectors, and the exploitation of the railways was a source of many innovations which spread throughout the whole technological system.

Lastly, industrial growth was to a certain extent continued to run on its own steam: it was accompanied by a redistribution of the factors of production, and in particular of labor. At the beginning of the century the big towns, like the country, were reservoirs of chronic unemployment, either partial or complete, though the workers concerned were gradually incorporated into the production process. From the 1830s onward there was a steady movement, very slow until 1860 and then very rapid, toward a rise in real wages, which until then had tended to fall. According to the figures of the French Statistics Bureau, the progression was as follows:

From 1830 to 1840: + 5.0 percent
From 1840 to 1850: + 3.5 percent
From 1850 to 1860: + 6.7 percent
From 1860 to 1870: + 9.5 percent
From 1870 to 1880: +10.7 percent

Taken as a whole, the remuneration of wage earners in trade and industry seems to have risen from 1,100 million francs (25 percent of agricultural incomes) in 1845 to 7,800 million (93 percent of agricultural incomes) in 1890.

Finally, unearned urban incomes increased markedly: we have already mentioned the increase in rents, which incidentally must have absorbed an important part of the increase in real wages. According to J. Lecaillon, the incomes of entrepreneurs in industry and trade rose from 1,400 million francs in 1845 to 2,650 million in 1890. Markovitch, using the industrial surveys of 1840–45 and 1860–65, arrives at a figure of 900 million in the case of the first survey and 2,000 million in the case of the second. The fall in the rate of return on capital, which may be observed after the early 1860s, is a consequence of the drift of capital toward savings. This movement was so marked that the amount of income distributed in this way increased considerably. Rates of profit, calculated on Paris Bourse values (1890–94 = 100), were 193.8 in 1860–64 and 112.9 in 1880–84. Interest rates fell from 4.83 percent in 1855–59 to 4.13 percent in 1880–84, and 3.49 percent in 1890–94. The amount of income distributed in this way rose from about 1,400 million in 1845 to 2,000 million in 1890.

This growth in urban incomes caused more and more people to adopt new ways of life based on the use of industrial products such as cotton goods, shoes, and household articles and the consumption of more and more varied types of food product. The mean national consumption of wine was 51 liters in 1841 and 77 liters in 1872. The mean national consumption of sugar doubled between 1840 and 1861, and tripled between 1861 and 1881, when it reached 10 kilograms per head. Mean national consumption of meat rose from 57 grams a day in 1815–24 to 102 grams a day in 1875–84.

The foundations of the growth in domestic demand were shaken in the 1880s: the rise in agricultural income was halted by a major crisis in the rural economy, which we shall examine in chapter 6. As we shall see, farm income reached its lowest level in about 1894, and did not rise again to its 1873 level until 1910. At the same time, the great enthusiasm for public works was evaporating, and building was stabilizing at a depressed level. It was only gradually that the domestic market recovered its dynamism. It may well be that the continued rise in real wages (up 20 percent from 1880 to 1890, and up 12.3 percent from 1890 to 1910)—though it was halted from 1905—was the major element in this recovery. Gradually, unearned urban and agricultural incomes overtook wages, while a new cycle of industrial investments and urban investments largely based on the use of electricity resulted, at the end of the period, in a general revival of investment.

The distribution of the national income seems to have been remarkably stable between 1890 and 1913, the only notable change apparently being a transfer of income from landed

Table 5.1 Distribution of National Income (in percent)

	1890	1913
Wages and Salaries		
(excluding agricultural wages)	42.6	43.2
Agriculture		
(excluding land rents)	23.8	23.1
Agricultural wages	9.5	
Entrepreneurs in trade and industry	11.0	11.0
Liberal professions	2.1	1.7
Income from capital	19.5	19.6
Pensions		1.4

property and real estate to income from invested capital. Table 5.1 shows the breakdown for 1890 and 1913, as far as the figures can be deduced from available sources. The proportion of income derived from capital remained stable. But whereas in 1890 that figure broke down as follows:

Ground rents	10.0 percent
Interest and dividends	8.3 percent
Business savings	0.8 percent
Foreign countries	0.4 percent,

in 1913 the breakdown was:

Stocks and shares	12.4 percent
Property	7.2 percent

It should be noted that this kind of distribution of national income was not likely to promote mass consumption. The predominance of unearned income (over 55 percent) tended to preserve a consumption pattern that varied according to social class and region despite the unification of the national market.

The Patterns of Trade

As the station master of La Chapelle remarked in 1869 (La Chapelle was the Paris goods station for the northern network), "Paris trade does not confine its operations to local speculation. It draws on the departments and on countries abroad, and also directs its goods to those places, so as to profit from every possible favorable circumstance"; thus Paris had become "the great regulating market for products such as cereals, oils and spirits." The railway had "nationalized" and even "internationalized" the markets for goods which had hitherto been exchanged chiefly within a regional framework. As Foville wrote in 1887 about cereals, "Nowadays there only has to be a rise of 1 franc on any market for the wholesale dealers within a radius of 200 or 300 kilometers, alerted by the newspapers or even by telegraph, to be ready to answer the demand." Regional differences between corn prices in nine regions of France fell from 4.61 francs in 1859 to 1.71 francs in 1878. In 1908, R. Bloch, commercial director of the Paris-Orléans line, observed that "The Paris market had become an essential stage in [the meat] trade." In 1913, re-forwarding from La Villette represented 42 percent of incoming deliveries of heavy beasts, and 47 percent, 34 percent, and 56 percent respectively of incoming deliveries of calves, sheep, and pigs.

These examples show the growing role played by Paris in wholesale trade, and more generally the importance of the changes brought about by the railways in this little-known field. The markets at Rouen and Mulhouse, and big fairs such as that at Beaucaire, disappeared. Some industrialists set up a simplified commercial system with the object of abolishing all intermediaries and relying on a network of agents. But France was a country of medium-sized enterprises not big enough to maintain a really independent commercial policy. A number of different factors, including railway rates discriminating against "grouping," hindered the formation, in France, of big freight companies like those which were set up in Germany.

Thus the commercialization of the economy and the "nationalization" of the markets brought about a confrontation among goods, and an intensified competition between regions, which had a rapid impact on some regions and which spread over the whole country as the railway system was extended. This generalized competition occurred, in fact, quite late: it dates from the years 1860–80, and was the main cause of the economic slump which followed those years. It was characterized by an almost universal process of de-industrialization. The textile industry disappeared from the department of Limousin, the metallurgical industry disappeared from Poitou, and the iron and steel industry disappeared from Berry. The cloth industry breathed its last in the centers of the south. In the departments of east-central France analyzed by Jobard, the "regression in the industrial sectors" dates from the years 1870–80. One of the causes of this regression was that the railway, by favoring the "peripheral regions" of the area, "reinforced disparities among the regions."

From the 1840s on, urbanization and the development of medium-distance transport promoted the spread of major innovations in retail trade. Department stores, the first attempts at which date from the July Monarchy, developed into a totally new instrument of sale, with Boucicaut's Bon Marché, followed by the Magasins du Louvre (1855), the Bazar de l'Hôtel de Ville (1856), the Printemps (1865), the Samaritaine (1869), and the Galéries Lafayette (1895). Fixed prices, clearly marked, the freedom to enter "without any obligation to buy," and the guarantee of quality created a new kind of relationship between customer and shopkeeper, and prices were substantially lower than those offered by small retailers. By the end of the century the Louvre and the Bon Marché had a turnover of 130 million francs.

It was then that what were known as "bazaar companies," or cheap chain stores, took on a national dimension. The first of them seem to have appeared in the region of Rheims. The success of the mutual societies founded in the 1860s in the food trade led some wholesale grocers whose position was threatened to create the "Docks Rémois" (1887), followed by the "Comptoirs Français" and the Sociéte "Goulet Turpin." The merchants of Rheims found many imitators, especially among the citizens of Saint-Étienne. By 1914 there were about 12,000 stores belonging to enterprises which worked through a number of branches. Five hundred of these stores belonged to the "Docks Rémois" and the "Comptoirs Français" alone. As Foville prophesied in 1887, "The huge store will kill the little shop." Forecasts so ominous for the maintenance of social equilibrium were held to justify a fiscal policy which favored small businesses and weighed heavily on department stores. This legislation reached its full expression in a law of 1905.

But in fact, small traders managed to find various ways of adapting themselves. The increase in the number of trading licenses issued (1.7 million in 1872, and 2.33 million in 1913) was not due exclusively, as some have maintained, to an increase in the number of wine shops and cafés, which represented scarcely a quarter of the total. The chief explanation is the development of new activities which could be carried out by small businesses: some activities which had hitherto been home based became commercial; new specialized trades appeared, such as the sale of luxury objects or that of technical supplies (e.g., photographic and electrical goods, bicycles). But above all, the development of the transportation network and the commercialization of activities in even the smallest village enabled small traders to develop their activities in a way which largely compensated for, and sometimes more than compensated for, what they lost to the department stores. Even the urban market was for from being entirely controlled by the department stores and the big bazaars. On the eve of the 1914 war, only 17 percent of the value of trade in Paris was in the hands of the department stores. In 1906, the 1,864,000 people active in the strictly commercial sector could be divided up as follows:

Sector

Food trade	33.8 percent
Wine shops and cafés	30.5 percent
Other trades	35.7 percent

Socio-Professional Category

One-man business	29.0 percent
Employers	30.8 percent
Workers and employees	40.2 percent

Of these wage-earners 68.3 percent worked in concerns employing less than 10 people, and only 10 percent worked in concerns employing over 100.

External Trade up to the 1870s

France's foreign trade showed remarkable growth during the first two-thirds of the nineteenth century. "Trade with foreign countries, which represented only 13 percent of the gross national product in 1830, appears to have reached 19 percent in 1850, 29 percent in 1860, and even 41 percent in 1870" (Lévy-Leboyer). In terms of volume, exports grew at a mean annual rate of 4.56 percent from 1815 to 1875, and this rate constantly

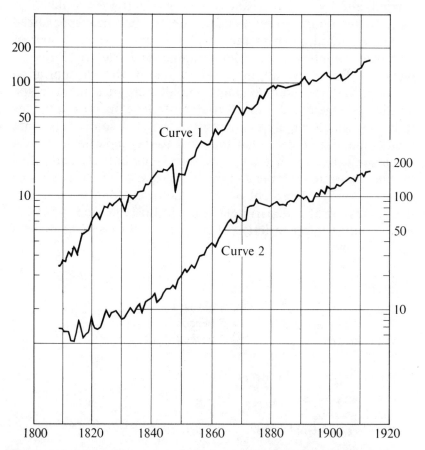

Figure 4 Volume of Imports and Exports, 1809–1913 (1890 = 100). Curve 1: Imports. Curve 2: Exports.

SOURCE: M. Lévy-Leboyer, "Croissance économique en France au XIXème siècle," *Annales, Economies, Sociétés, Civilisations,* 4 (July–August 1968), 797.

accelerated, by 3.01 percent per annum before 1840 and by 6.03 percent per annum from 1845 to 1865. Imports increased up to 1880: by 4.5 percent from 1820 to 1880, though we cannot distinguish much difference between the years before and after 1840. The roughly parallel growth of the two curves shows that France was able to establish harmony between its domestic economy and its international trade at that period, whereas in the last years of the nineteenth century this harmony disappeared. In order to understand the break it is necessary to define the bases on which the earlier expansion rested and its effect on the pattern of financial exchanges between France and the outside world.

Tariff Policy up to the Free Trade Era. Despite tendencies which were moderately protectionist at the beginning, the Restoration, under pressure from representatives elected by property-owning voters, embarked on a policy which was more and more clearly and openly protectionist and even prohibitionist. In 1817 the members of the Chambre Consultative des Arts et Manufactures of Saint-Étienne declared: "The progress of French industry is principally due to prohibition." In 1822 the Director of Customs himself said that France's object was "to buy from others as cheaply as possible and sell to them as dear as possible." So all the customs legislation of the régime pointed in the same direction: in 1816 and 1817, bans were maintained and customs duties increased; in 1819 a sliding scale for wheat was introduced, and this was revised in 1821 to make it even more favorable to producers; the laws of 1820, 1822, and 1826 established ever-increasing duties on manufactured goods. Foreign-produced sugar paid a surtax of 33 percent as against colonial sugar in 1816, and this was increased to 50 percent in 1822. In 1816, iron goods paid a duty of 16.50 francs per 100 kilograms, and this was increased in 1822 to 27.50 francs—i.e., 120 percent of the price of English iron at that period. The importation of cotton and woolen goods was prohibited. This system tended to protect French production of even raw materials such as wool.

The July Monarchy occasionally showed a tendency toward reducing customs duties and restrictions. In 1834,

Duchatel, the Minister of Trade, undertook a national survey on the subject. Most chambers of commerce agreed with the chamber of commerce of Saint-Quentin, which declared that France's whole manufacturing existence rested on import bans. The only exceptions to this opinion came from commercial circles and producers of highly elaborated finished goods, such as the silk makers of Lyons or Nicholas Koechlin. Moreover, the rigidity of the system hampered the development of centers which specialized in luxury goods using semifinished products of high quality. Producers of fine fabrics or iron goods were at the mercy of French spinners and iron and steel manufacturers who were often incapable of supplying their needs adequately. A note of 1843 observes: "There is less tax on a piece of manufactured equipment than on the material used to make it" (quoted in Lévy-Leboyer). The protection of coal and wool did not encourage the production of primary products, and the protection of machinery discouraged investment. The system did not lend itself to a complete and coherent attitude toward industrialization, and contradicted French industry's decision to concentrate on the development of highly elaborated goods. The policy of the July Monarchy was founded on an overall plan for industrialization and aimed at prolonging the commercial blockade. It saw France's industrial future in terms of a strict copy of the "English" model and stressed the idea of competition when France really needed to look for complementarity.

It was through this breach that the new régime was able to introduce a touch of liberalism: for the system of protection worked against many French producers. The law of 1836 reduced import duties on coal, substituting a very moderate form of protection which favored imports and, as a result, the industrialization of France. The same law also reduced duty on the finest cotton yarn. The law of 1841 reduced duties on woolen yarn. On the other hand, the law of 1845, in answer to protests from producers against a tariff which taxed their raw materials more than their machinery, increased the duties on manufactured goods.

So, mainly because bans were maintained, the achievement of the July Monarchy was limited. The relation between customs duties paid and the value of imports, recalculated in current value, was 22.2 percent in 1827–36 and 17.3 percent in 1837–46. But on the eve of the 1848 revolution, the move toward free trade was beginning to grow stronger. The conflict which broke out in 1847 between the big railway companies and the people that supplied them with iron and steel products foreshadowed the great arguments of the Second Empire. It was not only in intellectual circles that free trade policy grew more popular but also in business circles: the extension of the transportation network and the growth of exports gave a new impetus to free trade tendencies.

The policy of the Second Empire soon moved toward a reduction in duties on intermediate products and raw materials, with the object of reducing the cost of investments, in particular investments in railways, and also of favoring the production of finished goods. In the 1850s many reductions and exceptions were made, all in this direction. The policy inaugurated by Napoleon III's speech of January 5, 1860 provided, through treaties, a very moderate protectionist system for manufactured goods and many food products, and, through regulations, a system of exemptions from customs duty for raw materials. The value of customs duties in proportion to the value of imported goods was reduced, as follows:

1847–49	17.2 percent
1850–54	14.3 percent
1855–59	10.9 percent
1860–64	6.2 percent
1865–69	4.1 percent

Imports. The growth of imports in terms of volume was, over the long term, regular up to the 1870s: the annual mean was 4.9 percent from 1815–19 to 1875–79. There was a close interdependence between growth in imports and growth in production. Up to 1875, there was, according to Toutain, a "positive correlation between imports and the physical product, with imports anticipating production by about a year and a half." This conclusion demonstrates the principal role of imports, which was to supply the materials necessary to industry. Using foreign trade statistics (which are in current values after 1847 and in "official" values, established according to fixed scales, before 1847), we arrive at the breakdown given in table 5.2.

As the figures show, from the end of the 1830s to the end of the 1850s the proportion of manufactured goods tended to decrease. From 1839 to 1859 they increased in value by only 12 percent, whereas imports as a whole increased by 152 percent. This difference is not entirely attributable to the distortion due to the fact that official values in 1839 were overestimated. The prohibitionist protectionism worked. But in the 1860s, the supporters of free trade brought about a reversal of the situation. According to Rist, the treaty of 1860 administered a salutary shock to French industry: a marked increase in imports of manufactured and intermediate goods in 1861 and 1862 was followed by a decline in 1863–64. But the analysis needs to be carried further: the proportion of manufactured goods in imports as a whole rose from 4.1 percent in 1855–59 to 11.2 percent in 1875–79. This tendency was certainly accentuated by the loss of Alsace-Lorraine, but it is difficult not to see it also as a consequence of the treaties.

But, in the medium term, one of the chief results of the treaties and of the completion of the world transportation network was the exceptional upsurge in food imports in the 1870s: their mean annual value was 236 million francs in 1850–54, 695 million in 1865–69, and 1,225 million in 1875–79,

Table 5.2 Distribution of Imports (in percent)

	Food Products	Materials Needed for Industry	Manufactured Goods
1827–1829	27.8	63.7	8.5
1830–1834	23.1	64.2	6.7
1835–1839	20.2	71.0	8.8
1840–1844	23.2	70.1	6.7
1845–1849	27.0	67.5	5.5
1850–1854	23.4	71.6	5.0
1855–1859	28.9	67.0	4.1
1860–1864	25.3	69.3	5.4
1865–1869	23.3	69.2	7.5
1870–1874	27.2	62.4	10.4
1875–1879	30.6	58.2	11.2

the most outstanding items being cereals, livestock, and wine (see table 5.3).

Table 5.3 Mean Annual Value of Selected Food Imports (in millions of francs)

	Cereals	Livestock	Wine
1857–1866	91	65	11
1867–1876	245	137	16
1877–1886	467	170	283

The proportion of "materials needed for industry," i.e., raw materials and intermediate products such as iron and steel, reached a maximum level between 1835 and 1864 (from 67.5 percent to 71.6 percent), i.e., during the period of strongest growth in industrial production in France. Coal imports were "paralyzed by crushing customs duties" (Crouzet), at least in the case of English coal, which was much more heavily taxed than coal from Belgium. After 1834–37 this discrimination disappeared, and duties were successively reduced in 1853, 1861, and 1863. The real beginning of imports of English coal dates from 1834: the figures are 476,000 tons in 1841–45, 1,392,000 tons in 1861–65, and 3,000,000 tons in 1876–80. Imports of English coal amounted to 25 percent of total imports in 1841–45, 21 percent in 1861–65, and 35 percent in 1876–80. As Crouzet writes, "Imports of English coal increased during years of expansion and prosperity, and decreased in accordance with periods of depression." To put it more precisely, it was at the end of a cycle of expansion that imports played a decisive role, first needs being supplied by domestic production. These imports were, Crouzet notes, "a necessary condition of the industrial development which took place in the nineteenth century in the lower valleys of the Seine and the Loire," but the cost of transport, which still remained high, explains the slowness of growth in these regions.

The chief item in imports of raw materials concerned imports for the textile industry: imports of raw wool, hitherto held back by a protective tariff, exploded under the Second Empire, and rose in value from an annual mean of 52 million francs in 1847–56 to 271 million in 1867–76. Wool from Argentina made its appearance in 1855, and wool from Australia in 1858. By the end of the Empire, Australia, the Cape, and La Plata had become the chief markets. Prices of imported raw cotton fell by two-thirds between 1821 and 1845. This fall is the chief explanation of the very rapid progress in the cotton industry up to the 1840s. Its subsequent falling-off was reflected by a deceleration in the growth of imports. By 1860, France's cotton came almost entirely from America (93 percent), which explains the serious difficulties which arose out of the American Civil War. The fall in prices, which were at their lowest in 1848, was interrupted, and the 1860 level was not reached again until 1875. In other words, the conditions encountered by French industry were not favorable toward any adaptation to free trade.

The pattern followed by imports of cotton and silk yarn was much the same as that for raw wool: as Markovitch writes, "After having for a long while [up to about the middle of the nineteenth century] forced domestic production of the raw material, France wound up taking the opposite line and beginning to get supplies more and more from abroad." The value of these imports rose from 60 million francs in 1837–46 to 386 million in 1867–76.

These few examples show the decisive role played by the import of raw materials and intermediate products in France's industrial growth in the nineteenth century. France's dependence on this kind of import steadily increased, as, incidentally, did that of England. This dependence justified certain aspects of imperial policy in the early 1860s. But the policy was in total contradiction to previous policy, which had tended to build up a complete industrial system by means of protection. And one may doubt the ultimate efficiency of an economy which specialized only in the production of finished goods.

Exports. The expansion of exports was more rapid in the case of industrial products, but these had always formed the majority of exported goods: 80 percent in 1830, 70 percent in 1860, as against 20 percent and 30 percent for agricultural products. But the proportion of manufactured goods to primary and semifinished products had tended to diminish: in 1830, manufactured goods represented 69 percent of exports as against 56 percent in 1860 and 52 percent in 1873.

After the disasters of the Empire, France could play a part in world trade only by developing exports which were not in competition with those of England but complementary to them. She had no chance, and indeed no hope, of being able to achieve mass exports of modern cotton goods and cotton yarn. But might France be able to restore its trade on its old foundations, by reestablishing an export trade in colonial products imported and transformed in the mother country? It was Holland and not France, however, who managed to play this role. At the beginning of the 1840s, only 11 percent of imported sugar was refined in France and re-exported. As Lévy-Leboyer says, "This decline was serious," for it jeopardized the prosperity of the big Atlantic ports.

The really dynamic factor in French exports was the sale to a rich clientèle, especially in the English-speaking countries, of high-quality goods, usually involving a considerable proportion of hand labor. Up to 1866, textiles represented 58–60 percent of the total export of manufactured goods. This percentage subsequently diminished because of the stagnation and then fall in the value of exported silk. Silk exports, which in the 1830s and 1840s had increased much less rapidly than other textile exports, especially woolen goods, had a period of exceptional prosperity in the years 1850–60. During the decade 1867–76 they made up 25 percent of the value of manufactured goods, whereas woolen goods represented only 16.6 percent. In the years preceding this decade, several types of goods experienced remarkable growth and represented a considerable proportion of exports, but we must not expect to find among them machines (19 million francs) or tools (61 million). The goods which did prosper in this period were "fancy goods," pipes, and toys (177 million), and leather goods (115 million). In 1860, the export of manufactured goods could be broken down (in percent) as follows:

Textiles: silk	28.7
Textiles: wool	17.4
Textiles: cotton	5.5

Textiles: other	1.9
Ready-made clothing, etc.	8.1
Leather goods	8.9
Paris goods	14.5
Pharmaceuticals, etc.	4.6
Finished metals	2.3
Miscellaneous	8.1

The Balance of Payments. Up to the 1840s the trade balance varied: almost every year through 1836 it was positive, but only very slightly, and after that it was negative, sometimes markedly so, up to 1847. Exports were closely dependent on the prosperity of the rich industrialized countries. They were hampered by the protectionism of the English-speaking countries, and went through periods of deep depression linked to bad American harvests and the rising price of raw cotton. There were also sudden fluctuations in imports, due either to bad harvests in France or to more intense industrial activity which created a need for imports of both raw materials and machinery. It seemed as if France could become industrialized only by increasing its trade deficit. This deficit was not really compensated for by services income, which showed very little growth (62 million francs in 1821–25, 100 million francs in 1846–50) and remained very much below the services income in England (the French figure represented 17–19 percent of the English figure, according to the year). The chief cause of this weakness was the fact that the French fleet had not been able to develop seriously or become completely modernized, for the intermediate trade of the eighteenth century had not been restored and the imbalance between the volume of exports and the volume of imports (about a third) was unfavorable to any revival on new foundations. Income from tourism was a much more dynamic factor: it doubled between the early 1820s (25 million francs per annum) and the early 1840s.

But apparently the balance of income other than financial income was not sufficient to make possible any substantial export of capital. As for financial income, for this very reason it remained insignificant up to the beginning of the 1850s. France imported large quantities of specie during this period. These facts emerge from the figures recently published by

Lévy-Leboyer. For the two periods mentioned above, the balance of payments can apparently be broken down as follows, in terms of annual means (in millions of francs):

	1820–1836	1837–1847
Trade	+36	−76
Services	+65	+87
Tourism	+28	+53
Financial income		+6
Specie	−55	−91
Balance	+74	−21

There are big differences between these figures and those put forward in earlier studies, particularly as regards the second period. This discrepancy is due to a reevaluation of goods, in current terms, and to the fact that the later calculations are more complete than the earlier ones. (It is well known that in the early part of the nineteenth century the data concerning value supplied by official statistics were given in terms of fixed prices.) The result is a great contrast in the evaluation of the export of capital, all the more so since Lévy-Leboyer discounts the 1833 figures altogether, for the debts contracted in 1817–19 "were probably compensated for at that date by [partial] reimbursements and foreign investments." And so, whereas Rondo Cameron, who for the end of the period gives combined exports as 525 million francs, puts forward a figure for capital exports of 1,925 million in 1847, Lévy-Leboyer arrives at a figure of 107 million. But Rondo Cameron himself admits that his figures are very uncertain. Thus the early part of the nineteenth century does not seem to have been characterized by any remarkable expansion of French capital.

Yet the Paris banks played a major role in the mechanism of international settlements, for "France was the only country in Europe which offered balanced exchanges with Latin America and a positive balance with the English-speaking countries" (Lévy-Leboyer). This meant that Paris banks attracted foreign capital which they reutilized particularly for funding government debentures. Foreign stocks (Belgian, Rumanian,

Greek, Spanish) began to be funded in France in the years 1821–23, and then again in the years 1831–33, but a large proportion of the French or foreign state loans placed in Paris were in fact taken up by foreigners.

The adoption by England of a free trade policy completely changed the situation. After 1848, despite large imports of specie (an annual mean of 193.5 million francs in 1848–69), there was a large positive balance (an annual mean of 587.6 million francs in 1848–69). This improvement was largely due to growing surpluses in the trade balance. From 1848 to 1866 the mean surplus was 277 million, but the last three years of the Empire showed an adverse balance, and these deficits foreshadowed a situation which was to become the annual rule (except in 1906) from 1876 to 1913. Services income increased from an annual mean of 150 million in 1851–55 to 350 million in 1866–70. But this growth did not enable France to overcome its handicap in relation to England: France's income from services amounted to only one-fifth of the income which England derived from similar sources. Thanks to the railways, tourist income tripled between the five-year period 1846–50 and the five-year period 1866–70. Financial income increased because of the amount of reinvestment abroad. Table 5.4, which uses Lévy-Leboyer's figures, reflects this pattern of development.

Table 5.4 Balance of Payments, According to Lévy-Leboyer (mean annual revenue, in millions of francs)

	Goods	Services	Tourism	Finance	Specie	Total Balance Surplus
1848–1849	+215	+88	+71	+6	−252	+128
1850–1854	+281	+137	+124	+53	−140	+455
1855–1859	+178	+200	+155	+138	−187	+484
1860–1864	+200	+294	+184	+295	−35	+838
1865–1866	+516	+363	+209	+427	−341	+1,174
1867–1869	−192	+353	+237	+503	−421	+480

The figures in this table show the weakness of the French system: in the last years of the Empire, exports fell while imports continued to rise, and other resources, with the exception of financial income, stagnated. This fragility in the French balance of payments can be partly explained by the fact that the terms of trade deteriorated from the beginning of the 1850s to the beginning of the 1870s (whereas those of England improved from 1865 to 1873), owing to the distribution of France's imports (primary products and high-quality manufactured goods).

For French capital, the years 1850 to 1870 were the expansionist period par excellence. In 1870 the total value of the balances (surplus) reached 13.2 billion. The figure put forward by Cameron is 13.5. This capital went chiefly to southern and central Europe (probably to the extent of about 57 percent) and the Near East. In the 1850s, its primary use was to build railways and to found banks in an atmosphere of intense rivalry between the Crédit Mobilier and the Syndicat de la Haute Banque Parisienne. The Péreire brothers tried to form a great east-west network bordering the Atlantic, whereas the Haute Banque "angled its network from north to south and occupied all the areas bordering the Mediterranean." In the 1860s, this foreign penetration increased, for "not only were capital and railways exported, but also factories," especially metallurgical factories in central Europe.

External Trade, 1870–1914

Apart from a few local successes, France lost out in world competition from the 1870s onward: it was unable to maintain the share it had won during the first two-thirds of the nineteenth century. In about 1860, French exports represented nearly 60 percent of European exports, 16.5 percent of the exports of the industrialized countries, and 12.8 percent of world exports. In 1913, these percentages had fallen to 12.6 percent, 9.3 percent, and 7.2 percent, largely as a result of the quasi-stagnation in the volume of exports during the last part of the nineteenth century. Although this stagnation was followed by a revival, the rate of increase was not as high as that for world trade as a whole. France did not succeed, or succeeded only partially, in adapting itself to the new conditions of world trade. The growth of French exports was only 0.86 percent per annum from 1875 to 1895, reaching 2.74 percent from 1895 to 1913.

During the years 1870–1913, the distribution of French exports did not change appreciably. Agricultural products represented 30 percent of exports in 1860, 37 percent in 1890, and remained at a level close to 40 percent from 1865–74 to 1875–1904; the figure for 1913 was 33 percent. A different breakdown shows that manufactured goods, which represented 56 percent of exports in 1860, fell to 47 percent in 1890, and rose again to 51 percent. The remainder of the exports consisted of raw materials and semifinished goods. The peculiar nature of France's exports of manufactured goods should be stressed. They were mostly luxury goods, particularly textiles (see table 5.5).

Garments and underwear, which at the beginning of the period made up 4.3 percent of these exports, represented 4.4 percent in 1913. The other manufactured articles which were exported may be divided into two categories: the first and more important included articles made largely by hand labor, such as fashion goods and artificial flowers, leather goods, fancy goods (such as pipes and toys), books, goldsmith's work, and jewelry. But even in these categories, France encountered setbacks, as in the case of jewelry, where she met with competition from goods of lesser quality. In 1867–76, toys and other fancy articles represented 30 percent of exports; in 1909 the figure was 20 percent. On the other hand, France had managed to export some industrial articles: in 1867–76, chemical products, glass, machines, and tools represented 10 percent of her trade, whereas in 1909 they represented 13 percent. France played a

Table 5.5 Proportion of Textiles (Woolen Fabrics, Cotton and Silk Fabrics, Garments, Yarns) in the Exports of Manufactured Goods (percent)

	Total Textiles	Silk	Wool	Cotton
1867–1876	52.4	25	16.6	3.8
1877–1886	45.3	14.2	19.7	4.7
1887–1896	44.4	13.2	17.3	6.0
1897–1906	37.8	12.2	10.0	8.3
1909	34.3	10.8	6.6	10.3
1913	34.6	10.6	6.1	10.6

dominant role in the export of motorcars, and France's supremacy in this field remained unchallenged until the eve of the First World War. In the years 1900–13, France only partly managed to maintain a system of luxury exports by means of a delicate process of reconversion. The decline in the export of textiles and manufactured articles was partly compensated for by new products. But France's share in world exports of manufactured goods had steadily decreased. Up to 1870, France had been the second country in the world for the export of manufactured articles. But her share of the world market dropped from 16.2 percent in 1876–80 to 11.8 percent in 1911–13.

Lévy-Leboyer has stressed the seriousness of the indirect results of the 1870 war. The war, he writes, "caused France to lose several industrial departments, and prevented her from taking part in the last British boom of the nineteenth century, the boom of 1869–73, which enabled the English to make full use of Suez and to establish themselves in Asia." But the war was not the only obstacle to France's adaptation to the new conditions of international trade. Up to 1860, this trade had been concentrated on the North Atlantic. Between 1860 and 1875 there was a reorientation toward the Pacific, and France was late in joining in this movement.

The development of the textile industry shows the difficulty French exporters had in maintaining their markets. The kinds of goods which France had managed to export, in particular to the English-speaking world, were not suited to the new international demand of the last third of the nineteenth century, a demand concentrated on mass-produced articles designed for city dwellers.

Moreover, it is clear that France's traditional exports encountered increasingly strong competition and came up against protectionist tariffs, particularly the American tariffs of 1867 and 1892 and the German tariffs. In addition to these factors, there were changes in fashion which French industrialists now failed to keep up with as they had once done. Silk exports are a good example. In terms of volume, these exports stagnated up to the last years of the nineteenth century, dropping from a mean of 430 million francs in 1867–76 to 243 million in 1887–96. The production of silk goods expanded in Switzerland, Italy, the United States, and Germany, "where," as Poidevin writes, "the sale of silk goods from France was threatened by increasingly strong competition from the silk industries in Krefeld," where warp printing had been introduced by a Frenchman. The glove industry is an equally telling example: by about 1860 the American market was supplied entirely by French exports, apart from low-quality goods. By the beginning of the twentieth century, the demand for gloves in America had increased tenfold, but French exports had increased to cover only a third of the demand. High-quality French gloves met with competition from factory-produced imitations or goods of lower quality. Jewelry is another example, and in the field of toys and fancy goods German competition was very strong. France played a dominant role in the export of tobacco and spirits, clothing, and books. But the only category in which France's proportion of world exports increased between 1899 and 1913 was that of "modern transport vehicles," i.e., bicycles and motorcars. France was absent from the world market as far as machinery and agricultural and electrical equipment were concerned.

So the nature of France's foreign trade in 1913 was the result of three factors: the aftermath of the "luxury exports" of the years 1820–70, the aftermath of the colonial and protectionist period, and the influence of recent industrialization, though this was very slight. In 1913 60.8 percent of France's exports consisted of manufactured articles, but most of these came from the "luxury goods" tradition (silk fabrics, 6.2 percent; woolen fabrics, 3.2 percent; luxury articles, 4 percent).

France's foreign trade was chiefly orientated toward Europe, though this specialization was less marked than Germany's. England, on the other hand, directed its trade chiefly toward other continents, as can be seen from table 5.6. This table calls for some comments. First, during the 50 years it covers, England's trade was directed toward non-European markets much more than the trade of France or Germany. England remained "the workshop of the world." Second, whereas Germany's exports took on an entirely new pattern in this period, France's exports showed no important change.

Table 5.6 Distribution of Exports by Country (in percent)

	Europe	North America	South America	Asia	Africa	Oceania
1860						
France	65.1	10.2	12.0	2.4	10.1	0.1
Germany	92.3	2.1	4.0	1.4	0.2	
Austria-Hungary						
Great Britain	33.9	16.5	11.9	25.6	3.1	8.1
1880						
France	71.7	9.2	10.2	2.2	6.7	0.2
Germany	91.3	6.6	0.9	0.9	0.2	0.1
Austria-Hungary	96.1	1.1	0.6	2.0	0.2	
Great Britain	35.5	15.8	10.2	25.3	4.3	8.4
1910						
France	69.8	7.4	6.9	3.5	12.3	0.1
Germany	73.9	8.9	7.8	5.8	2.3	1.0
Austria-Hungary	85.5	3.2	1.5	6.1	2.1	0.1
Great Britain	35.0	11.6	12.5	24.4	7.4	8.6

Germany drove for the world market. For France, the proportion of non-European countries served decreased except in Asia (3.5 percent instead of 2.4 percent) and Africa (12.3 percent instead of 10.1 percent), two continents where the French colonial régimes created a protected situation for exports.

One of the things which emerges most clearly from these figures is the fact that colonial protection enabled French exports to keep going. In 1913 the colonies absorbed only 13.7 percent of France's exports, and contemporary authors were united in deploring this weakness. But the evolution of textile exports, indicated above, demonstrates the importance of this market: the weakness of woolen exports was made up for by the amount of cotton goods sent to the colonies. P. Bairoch has recently stressed "the weak penetration of French exports on foreign markets other than those with a preferential customs system favoring France." The same author, analyzing the imports of fifty different countries, shows that only in Belgium and in Haiti did imports from France exceed those from Germany and the United Kingdom; that only in Switzerland did imports from France exceed those of the United Kingdom; and that only in Egypt did imports from France exceed those from Germany. In Asia, Germany exported four to five times more than France, and in Latin America one to three times more. On the other hand, thanks to a highly preferential system, France controlled 65.5 percent of the imports of her own colonies.

Bairoch concludes that French exporters were lacking in "aggressiveness." Both before and during the 1914–18 war, contemporaries argued a great deal about this problem. In 1912 the French chambers of commerce abroad called a conference "for the defense and development of foreign trade." Several explanations were put forward, and some of them were taken up by H. Hauser in his book on German methods of expansion in 1912: the inadequacy of French methods of commercial expansion, owing to lack of initiative by entrepreneurs and to lack of enterprise by French representatives abroad, despite the founding in 1898 of the National Center for Foreign Trade; the insufficient expansion of the domestic market, partly because of demographic stagnation and partly because of a too timid domestic investment policy; and lastly, lack of connection between banking policy and export policy.

Growth in the volume of imports continued at a high level until the early 1880s (up 2.54 percent per annum from 1870 to 1875, and up 6.93 percent from 1875 to 1880). This increase was disturbing, for it occurred at a time when exports had ceased to grow. Moreover, it markedly anticipated production growth. As Toutain writes, "As production growth ran down, the increase in trade became disproportionate" (i.e., to the increase in production). The growth in imports was particularly noticeable in the case of food products. Imports of food rose from an annual mean of 695 million francs in 1865–69 to an annual mean of 1,679 million francs in 1880–84. In these circumstances, the protectionist reaction is understandable. It became irresistible when the phyloxera outbreak occurred, and the free trade party lost its chief parliamentary support, that of the representatives from the wine-growing regions. The tariff of 1892 was based on a system of "compensatory" duties, which was applied more comprehensively still in 1910. The principles on which the system was based were consistent enough: they included exemption of raw materials, the exclusion of negotiation but the establishment of a dual tariff, one maximum and the other minimum and applicable in the case of concessions. Neither the tariff of 1892 nor that of 1910 can be regarded as prohibitionist. In 1910 import duties in France represented 8 percent of the value of imports, as against 23.2 percent in the United States. The tariff of 1910 raised the duties paid on English goods to 6.3 percent of their value, and the duties paid on German goods to 8.5 percent. But this did not prevent the development of German, Belgian, and British sales at rates as high as before. Certain articles, such as wheat, were of course subjected to much heavier duties. France's agricultural protectionism hindered any decline in food prices and weighed heavily on industrial costs. As Marczewski writes, "It prevented France from adapting its agricultural and industrial structures to the needs of the world economy, and condemned France to low growth." For agricultural protection "enabled French farmers to keep their prices at a higher level than that of world prices." These comments contain a part of the truth, but they certainly overestimate the importance of the part played by protectionism, since other countries with strong protectionist policies maintained steady agricultural and industrial growth.

The growth of imports slackened off in the early 1880s until the early 1900s. After 1905, imports again increased at a more rapid rate than exports (up 4.13 percent per annum from 1905 to 1910; up 3.31 percent from 1910 to 1913). In 1890, 72 percent of France's imports were agricultural; in 1913, only 63 percent. In 1910, Méline, the chief influence behind the law of 1892, could congratulate himself that "under the shelter of protection, we have made considerable profits, and since 1892 saved 700 million in food imports" (quoted in P. Barral). Industrial imports developed more rapidly when industrialization became more intense at the end of the nineteenth century. Among industrial imports, energy rose from 16 to 18 percent, metals from 26 to 36 percent, chemical products from 12 to 13.8 percent. Metal products rose from 5 percent in 1860 to 17 percent in 1913.

The index for imported machinery developed as follows (annual means; 1910 = 100):

1870–74	7.8
1875–79	16.7
1880–84	32.6
1885–89	19.5
1890–94	26.2
1895–99	36.0
1900–4	57.4
1905–9	78.9

Imports became an instrument of industrialization. In fact, the distribution of France's imports underwent a great change between 1890 and 1900, as can be seen from table 5.7. Among the manufactured articles, worked metals and machines rose from 12.1 percent 1880 to 14.9 percent in 1890 and 29 percent in 1910.

Table 5.7 Distribution of France's Imports by Product (in percent)

	1880	1890	1910
Manufactured articles	13.9	14.4	19.0
Food products	35.2	32.1	23.6
Industrial raw materials	50.9	53.5	57.4

The Balance of Payments, 1870–1913

The trade balance (see table 5.8) showed a deficit from 1875 on, and showed this deficit steadily up to 1913, except in 1905. The deficit reached its maximum in 1880, at a billion and a half francs. It subsequently decreased, with two peaks, one in 1891 (1,134 million) and another in 1898 (928 million), until 1905, and in 1911 it reached nearly two billion francs (1,942 million). The exceptionally high deficits were all linked to a sudden increase in imports occurring just after the beginning of a period of marked or even intense domestic boom; the increase in imports was accompanied by a decrease in exports. To cope with these booms in activity, the French economy had to resort to imports, for French production was not flexible. Any increase in demand produced more imports of finished goods to meet it,

Table 5.8 Balance of Payments, According to Lévy-Leboyer (mean annual revenue, in millions of francs)

	Trade	Services	Tourism	Finance	Specie	Balance Surplus
1870–1874	−10	+400	+222	+641	−32	133.8
1875–1879	−487	+405	+244	+612	−412	362
1880–1884	−1,258	+401	+296	+610	+31	80
1885–1889	−784.8	+367	+328	+635	−35	510
1890–1894	−736	+364	+300	+669	−158	427
1895–1899	−440	+368	+307	+732	−45	922
1900–1904	−297	+415	+336	+945	−286	1,113
1905–1909	−359	+520	+435	+1,286	−487	1,395
1910–1913	−1,440	+671	+558	+1,565	−213	1,141

and more imports of intermediate products and equipment to adapt production to the new demands. In the early 1880s and the years 1900–13, the exceptionally high level of domestic investment, which alone made the import of equipment possible, raised the deficit to an intolerable level.

How could these deficits be covered? French income from services stagnated up to the beginning of the twentieth century. In the years 1895–99, it represented only 12.5 percent of English income from the same sources. Just before the 1914–18 war, the percentage had risen to 15 percent again.

The policy of subsidizing the merchant fleet was an obvious failure. The French merchant navy, which was the second in the world in 1870, was seventh in 1913. And yet, since 1881, the state had been subsidizing shipbuilding. The law of 1881 provided bonuses which had some positive effects: the tonnage of steamships rose from 277,749 in 1880 to nearly 500,000 in 1893, whereas the tonnage of sailing ships fell from 741,000 to 400,000. But the revision of the law in 1893 had harmful effects: sail navigation was subsidized more generously than steam navigation. In 1902, the steam tonnage was 550,000 and the sail tonnage 668,000. The laws of 1902 and 1906 corrected this anomaly. But the comparative decline of the French navy was now a settled thing. Between 1902 and 1913 the proportion of the French steam fleet to that of the steam fleet of the world as a whole remained the same: i.e., 4.4 percent.

The increase in revenue from tourism remained small, at least up to the beginning of the twentieth century. The balance of income other than financial was then, during quite long periods, insufficient to make up for the trade deficits. This was the case in 1878–88, and again in 1891, 1893, and 1911–13. So the surpluses in the current accounts were extremely uncertain. And financial income stagnated at about 627 million francs.

It is easy to understand why the overall balance was low from 1870 to 1895. From 1870 to 1875, the war indemnity transformed a surplus of 6 billion into a surplus of 600 million. From 1875 to 1879, 55 percent of a balance of 3.8 billion was used for the repatriation of specie. Thus, though the trade deficit did not appear until 1877 and the deficit in nonfinancial income did not appear until 1878, it was in 1871 that the balance began to deteriorate. The surpluses were at their lowest in 1880–84 (a mean of 80 million francs). From 1875 to 1894, the mean was 345 million francs (see breakdown in table 5.8). It is easy to see why financial income stagnated.

Things changed from 1895 onward, for the trade deficit decreased up to 1905, while the other items slightly increased. The sudden worsening of the deficit on the eve of the 1914 war was compensated for by the amount of financial income (1.5 billion per annum in 1910–13). From 1895 to 1913, France exported a mean of 1.1 billion in capital per annum. The figure for the combined balances increased by only 31 percent between 1870 and 1894, as against 121 percent between 1894 and 1913.

Just before the war, foreign stocks seem to have represented 14.1 percent of French wealth. This figure is probably an overestimate. Daumard suggests a figure of 7.6 percent in 1898–99, and 8.5 percent in 1906–8. Many property owners were completely ignorant of foreign stocks, which were mainly concentrated in the hands of rich investors. Foreign investments consisted of 73 percent government annuities, 12 percent debentures, and nearly 15 percent stocks and shares. The deposit banks acted as intermediaries between foreign governments and French investors. But the engagement of French banks in this way brought with it a deeper engagement of French capitalism in the economies of foreign countries. The case of Russia is typical: the involvement of the banks brought with it direct, industrial investment.

The geographical orientation of these investments underwent a great change. The favorite area for the export of capital was Eastern Europe, especially Russia, where almost 30 percent of French foreign-invested capital was placed in 1914. South America was also important, but there France played a rather secondary role in comparison with England; its role was even more modest in the "new" English-speaking countries. France maintained its presence in the Ottoman Empire and in Egypt. The French colonies received only 9 percent of the total amount of capital exported.

France's external balance was in fact precarious. It was only during the years 1895–13, and above all 1900–9, that France exported capital. During the years 1910–13, France was obliged to reduce the volume of capital exports just when other countries were exporting more and more. During the years 1905–13, these exports represented 3.6 percent of the national income. Moreover, Bouvier has noted that from 1911 on, there was a sudden increase in the proportion of French stocks issued by the Crédit Lyonnais.

Bibliography

Bairoch, P. *Commerce extérieur et développement économique de l'Europe au XIXème siècle.* Paris: Mouton, 1976.
——"La place de la France sur les marchés internationaux au XIXème siècle." Paper presented at the Deuxième congrès des historiens économistes français, 1973.
Barral, P. *Les agrariens français de Méline à Pisani.* Paris: A. Colin, 1968.
Bouvier, J., F. Furet, and M. Gillet. *Le mouvement du profit en France au XIXème siècle.* Paris: Mouton, 1965.
Cameron, R. *La France et le développement économique de l'Europe.* Paris: Le Seuil, 1971.
Caron, F. *Histoire de l'exploitation d'un grand reseau.* Paris: Mouton, 1973.
Crouzet, F. "Le charbon anglais en France au XIXème siècle," in *Charbon et sciences humaines.* Paris: Mouton, 1966.
Daumard, A. *Les fortunes françaises au XIXème siècle.* Paris: Mouton, 1973.
Foville, A. de. *La transformation des moyens de transport et leurs conséquences économiques et sociales.* Paris: Guillaumin, 1887.

Girault, R. *Emprunts russes et investissements français en Russie, 1887–1914.* Paris: A. Colin, 1973.

Hauser, H. *Les méthodes allemandes d'expansion économique.* Paris: A. Colin, 1915.

Jobard, J. P. *Les disparités régionales de croissance.* Fondation nationale des sciences politiques. Paris: A. Colin, 1971.

Lecaillon, J. "Changes in the Distribution of Incomes in the French Economy," in *The Distribution of the National Income: Proceedings of a Conference Held by the International Economic Association*, edited by J. Marchal and B. Ducros. London: Macmillan and St Martin's Press, 1968.

——*Croissance, répartition et politique des revenue.* Paris: Cujas, 1964.

Levasseur, E. *Histoire du commerce de la France*, vol. 2, *De 1789 à nos jours.* Paris: A. Rousseau, 1912.

Lévy-Leboyer, M. "La balance des paiements et l'exportation des capitaux français." Paper presented at the Deuxième congrès des historiens économistes français, 1973.

——*Les banques européennes et l'industrialisation internationale.* Paris: Presses Universitaires de France, 1964.

——"Croissance économique en France au XIXème siècle," *Annales, Economies, Sociétés, Civilisations*, 4 (July–August, 1968).

——"L'héritage de Simiand," *Revue Historique*, January–March, 1970.

Marczewski, J. "Le produit physique de l'économie française de 1789 à 1913: Comparaison avec la Grande Bretagne," *Cahiers de l'Institut de Science Economique Appliquée*, ser. AF, no. 4 (July 1965).

Markovitch, T. A. "Salaires et profits industriels en France," *Cahiers de l'Institut de Science Economique Appliquée*, ser. AF, no. 8 (1967).

Poidevin, R. *Les relations économiques et financières entre la France et l'Allemagne de 1898 à 1914.* Paris: A. Colin, 1969.

Porte, J. "La ganterie française et la concurrence internationale," *Revue Economique Internationale*, no. 1 (1908).

Rist, M. "Une expérience française de libération des échanges au XIXème siècle: le traité de 1860," *Revue d'Economie Politique*, 1956. Translation in *Essays in French Economic History*, edited by R. Cameron. Homewood, Ill.: R. D. Irwin, 1970.

Toutain, J. C. "Les structures du commerce extérieur français, 1789–1970." Paper presented at the Deuxième congrès des historiens économistes français, 1973.

Chapter Six: Agriculture

Was French Agriculture Still "Primitive" in 1840?

M. MORINEAU, HAVING analyzed the agricultural survey of 1840, concludes that "over most of France, agriculture remained stagnant, backward, and primitive." But this description is excessively severe, and the approach underlying it is debatable. France at that period could be divided up in the manner shown in table 6.1. There are three outstanding features about this distribution of land: the large amount of "arable land," two-thirds of which consisted of cereals and other farinaceous crops; the amount of land lying fallow (a quarter of the arable land); and, as a result, the small amount of artificial pasturage and fodder crops (7 percent of arable land). These figures certainly reflect the "incompleteness" of the agricultural revolution. But they do not prove complete stagnation. An exact analysis of the amount of land sown or planted with cereals between 1815 and 1835 (table 6.2) shows that, while the total area increased by 13.4 percent, the breakdown changed.

Agriculture was clearly directed toward producing as much human food as possible, thus sacrificing animal fodder at a time when the technical advance of agriculture depended largely on an increase in fodder crops and livestock. The pressure exerted by the number of people living off the soil is shown particularly clearly by the overexploitation of forests. Not only were more and more forests cleared, but customary rights and usages became abuses. As M. Chevalier writes, on the subject of the

Table 6.1 Distribution of Land in France in 1840 (in percent)

	Of Total Area	Of Cultivated Land
Arable land	49.1	64.0
Natural grassland, orchards	8.0	10.3
Vineyards	3.7	4.9
Woods and forests	16.0	20.8
Cultivated land		
(excluding pasture)	76.8	100.0
Total Area	100.0	

Table 6.2 Distribution of Land Sown or Planted with Cereals (in percent)

	1815	1835
Wheat	33.1	34.0
Mixed wheat and rye, rye, buckwheat	29.9	26.9
Barley, maize, millet, oats	29.8	30.2
Beans, peas, lentils, etc; potatoes; other grain	7.2	8.9
Total hectares*	13,835	15,691

* 1 hectare = 2.47 acres

Pyrenees around Ariège, "Nothing could hold back a population that was bent on destroying its forests." And this was not an exceptional case.

But it is plain, in spite of all this, that agriculture was not stagnant. The similarity between the yields calculated according to the 1840 census (9.5 quintals per hectare for corn, and 7.2 for rye) and the figures quoted by eighteenth-century authors is not convincing. Yields were very irregular. But in 1837 the Ministry of Agriculture published the results of the harvests of 1815–16 (bad), 1826 (good), 1832 and 1833 (good), 1830 (middling) and 1835. And if one compares years which are really comparable, a tendency toward a growth in yields is apparent, and yields are higher than those reflected in the survey of 1840 (12.18 quintals in 1826, and 13.43 quintals in 1835). For this period, Brunet quotes normal yields of 16.7 quintals per hectare in the Paris basin. And it must be remembered that land newly given over to cereals often gave poor results.

After the wheat crisis of 1817,* appreciable improvements in agricultural practice began to spread more and more rapidly. According to Guy Thuillier, it was the fall in prices between 1817 and 1828 that forced agriculture "to emerge from traditional practices and small, assured profits": it was at this period that speculation in livestock fattening began in the Nivernais. On the plateaus of the Loire Valley, decisive reduction of fallow land dates from the years 1825–35; on certain plateaus in the Paris basin, the elimination of fallow land was almost completed by 1840. The expansion of potato growing in Brittany and of maize growing in Aquitaine made it possible to keep up with population pressure.

The agricultural surveys of the early part of the nineteenth century, unlike later surveys, mention lack of labor but not lack of fertilizers. The combination of intensive agriculture with intensive stock-raising was rare and difficult. The immediate object of reducing fallow land was to insure human subsistence. The "new agriculture" certainly needed a large labor force, and population pressure was an element which favored the adoption of this new agriculture. But the great majority of historians and geographers agree that in each of the regions they have studied there was "overpopulation." One of the most recent of these historians, G. Carrier, in his book on the Beaujolais region entitles one of his sections "Shifting the Excess Population." It is clear that Carrier considers this process a necessary preliminary to the later development between 1850 and 1875, for traditional rural society was one swarming with beggars, the poor, people living on the fringe of society, and their number always increased in periods of shortage. This excess population was behind the overexploitation of the forests, which explains the survival of communal practices and accounts for the resistance to the abolition of fallow land. On the whole, it seems that the spread of new agricultural

* The crisis of 1817 was an unusually severe one, a "subsistence crisis" of the classic type encountered so frequently by the old regime. An extremely poor harvest provoked an exceptional rise in prices and near-famine conditions in some regions. Economic fluctuations disappeared only gradually, and up to 1860 "bad harvests" played an essential role in a pattern of crises, particularly in 1846–47. But irregularities in harvests tended more and more to decline. In fact, it was after the crisis of 1817 that noticeable improvements in cultivation practices spread significantly.

practices presupposed a population level below that which was general. But there was a real danger of overreducing population, if agriculture is seen not in the abstract but in terms of its real structures.

Large-scale land ownership was important: in 1826, 1 percent of the assessments on landed property amounted to 28.6 percent of the value of assessments as a whole. But large-scale land ownership was fairly localized (for example, in the Paris basin, the eastern part of central France, and certain departments of the south, such as Aude, Haute-Garonne, and Hérault). In the department of Loir-et-Cher, in about 1840, 51 percent of the total area was owned by "big landowners," defined by G. Dupeux as those owning over 100 hectares in Beauce, and over 200 hectares in Sologne. In the five Alpine departments studied by Philippe Vigier, however, assessments of more than 50 hectares represent only 25–30 percent of the total owned area. It is a pity that everyone who writes a thesis on this subject finds it necessary to adopt a different system of classification: this methodological refinement flies in the face of common sense. At all events, small and medium-sized properties are rarely absent from the land registers and often, as in the case of the Loir-et-Cher, are situated "in the areas most favored by nature." Dupeux adds that "small properties made up for their size by their quality." According to the survey of 1851, working landowners made up 35.7 percent of the rural population, and 64 percent of the total of agricultural workers. Working owners formed the great majority of the peasant population of the Alpine departments, the Massif Central, the Aquitaine basin, Alsace, the valleys of the Paris basin and of the Loire, the southern Jura, and eastern Bresse. The great majority of these owner-farmers were small and sometimes very small landowners. Large-scale properties were rarely directly exploited by their owners. A. Armengaud's observation about Aquitaine may be applied generally: "Large-scale landowning almost never coincided with large-scale farming." In Aquitaine, large estates were divided up on a sharecropping basis into *métairies* of from 25 to 40 hectares. In the Loir-et-Cher, the size of the farms caused the tax inspectors to use the term "medium-scale farming." But on the plateaus of the Paris basin, the larger agricultural enterprises were big farms exploited indirectly through tenants. Taken as a whole, indirect exploitation covered a smaller area than the properties of which it formed part, but a larger area than that covered by direct exploitation. Tenant farmers represented 23.3 percent of the total number of farmers in 1851, while sharecroppers represented 12.5 percent. There were many sharecroppers in certain central regions of France. In many areas, population pressure allowed landowners to be severe in the matter of rents.

The Rural Exodus

Thus, in certain regions, a decline in population pressure was a necessary precondition for the spread of the agricultural revolution. But the rural exodus, in combination with a low birthrate, contributed to the adoption of "extensive" methods of farming. We have two sets of figures concerning the rural exodus: one series issued by the French Statistics Bureau, and starting in 1856, and the other calculated by Maurice Lévy-Leboyer, and starting in 1801, both shown in table 6.3. As the table shows, the rural exodus—described by P. Merlin as a "continuous, slow, but massive movement which gradually became ineluctable"—increased in the 1830s and 1840s and reached a high in the 1850s which was maintained. The movement stagnated, or perhaps even regressed, after the peak in the middle of the nineteenth century. From the 1850s onward, the countryside lost 125,000 people every year (100,000 according to Lévy-Leboyer). Taking into account the decrease in the rural population, the annual surplus emigration per hundred rural inhabitants rose from 0.50 percent between 1856 and 1866 to 0.69 percent between 1906 and 1911. It reached its maximum at the time of the 1861 census. Between 1861 and 1911, the population of the French countryside fell by 3.8 million, the total exodus amounting to 5.7 million according to the French Statistics Bureau and 4.9 million according to Lévy-Leboyer. The natural growth of the rural population compensated for only a quarter or a third of the exodus.

Table 6.3 Two Sets of Figures on the Exodus from Rural Areas

Lévy-Leboyer		Statistique Générale de la France	
1801–1811	175,000		
1811–1821	69,000		
1821–1831	+82,000		
1831–1841	473,000		
1841–1851	849,000		
1851–1861	1,265,000	1856–1862	646,916
1861–1871	867,000	1861–1866	611,160
		1872–1876	417,308
		1876–1881	821,383
1872–1881	1,053,000	1872–1881	1,238,691
		1881–1886	455,534
		1886–1891	585,233
1881–1891	852,000	1881–1891	1,040,757
		1891–1896	575,816
		1896–1901	670,987
1891–1901	1,040,000	1891–1901	1,246,893
		1901–1906	556,114
		1906–1911	772,394
1901–1911	1,092,000	1901–1911	1,328,608

There is in fact a positive correlation between the level of natural population increase and the level of emigration: according to P. Merlin, "It was the surplus births which kept up the rural migrations." The "supply" regions were those which had the highest natural surpluses: Brittany, Vendée, the Center, the greater part of the Massif Central, the Northeast, the Nord, and Corsica. But regions with a low birthrate were not necessarily regions which retained their population: the exodus in such areas might be small from the national point of view, but it was very large compared with the regional population, and the effects of the exodus combined with those of the fall in the birthrate. It is instructive to compare migration in predominantly rural areas with a low birthrate with migration in predominantly rural areas with a high birthrate. I have chosen as examples Lower Normandy, the Midi-Pyrénées, Limousin, and Brittany. Lower Normandy is a region which showed an early drop in the birthrate; the drop came later in the Midi-Pyrénées; and Brittany showed a more sustained population growth than Limousin (see tables 6.4 and 6.5).

Between 1831 and 1911, the population of Brittany, which

Table 6.4 Population Movements, 1831–1911 (in thousands)

	Lower Normandy		Midi-Pyrénées		Limousin		Brittany	
	I*	II†	I	II	I	II	I	II
1831–1846	+2.3	−0.9	+11.8	−1.4	+5.9	−1.15	+11.2	+0.2
1846–1866	−1.7	−2.7	+4.5	−7.0	+3.2	−3.5	+10.7	−4.6
1872–1891	−3.3	−1.7	−1.3	−7.1	+6.6	−2.08	+14.9	−5.9
1891–1911	−4.0	−1.8	−6.8	−5.8	+4.08	−5.3	+14.8	−10.6

* I: Mean annual increase or decrease due to natural movements.
† II: Mean annual increase or decrease due to migratory movements.

Table 6.5 Regional Population, 1831–1911 (in thousands)

	Lower Normandy	Midi-Pyrénées	Limousin	Brittany
1831	1,527.8	2,448.4	845.3	2,103.8
1866	1,463.4	2,553.6	910.9	2,397.4
1872	1,397.0	2,503.6	999.8	2,345.1
1891	1,297.0	2,394.5	985.7	2,517.0
1911	1,179.8	2,140.8	960.6	2,601.0
1831–1911	−22.7%	−12.5%	+13.6%	+19.1%
Overall Balance of Migration	−142	−414.1	−234.1	−414.3
Balance of Natural Movement	−139.7	+156.3	+361.1	+964.7

had a total natural increase of 46 percent in the period, in fact increased by 19 percent, although the number of emigrants (over 400,000) represented more than two-fifths of the natural increase. In Limousin, a natural increase of 42 percent led to a final increase of 13.6 percent, emigration (234,000) being equivalent to almost two-thirds of the natural growth. The number of migrants in the Midi-Pyrénées region was equal to that in Brittany, but from 1886 on, there was a natural population decline. This development was largely due to intensity of migrations after 1846. Over the period, the population of the region was reduced by 12.5 percent, whereas the natural growth amounted to 6.3 percent of the 1831 population. The situation in Lower Normandy was the reverse of that in Brittany: the outcome there was a drop of 23 percent in the population, half of which was due to migration and half to lack of natural growth. The natural population decreased after 1846. And so the effects of the exodus varied from one region to another. In this context, we may distinguish two types of rural situation: a "Breton" type with large natural surpluses and a large amount of emigration, so that the emigration does not produce any massive depopulation of the countryside; and a "Norman" or "Southwestern" type with low natural surpluses, where migration, however slight, produces rapid and intense depopulation, favorable to the spread of "extensive" forms of agriculture.

But the rural exodus must not be confused with the agricultural exodus. The observations of P. Pinchemel on three cantons in Picardy may probably be more generally applied to other regions: in the years 1830–70, according to Pinchemel, "the agricultural sector was not the sector chiefly responsible for rural depopulation." The exodus was as much a transfer of population within the industrial sector as a transfer from agriculture to industry. The exodus also corresponded to the departure of the "marginals," those living on the fringes of society, those whom the 1852 survey describes as "journeyman landowners," driven away by the major crises of the middle of the century, and victims both of the new kind of forest management deriving from the Code of 1827* and of the spread of a new type of agriculture which abolished common land. The rural exodus reflects a sudden dispersal of the "excess population" in the 1850s, followed by a slower movement of deindustrialization from the 1860s on.

After the 1870s the movement affected chiefly the nonworking population, i.e., farmers' children rather than farmers themselves. The young women were the first to go: as the recorders of the survey of 1868 put it, "It is the daughters who go away; they take places as servants in the towns, and then settle there." At Banon, in the Basses-Alpes, out of 502 emigrants between 1836 and 1906, 409 (81 percent) left before they

---

* This code gave new life to the numerous provisions of the 1669 Colbert ordinance on the forests and subjected all those belongings to collectivities, including communal forests, to strict exploitation laws so as to safeguard and protect them against abusive and destructive "rights of usage." Its enforcement, more and more rigorous, limited the resources of village "marginals."

were 30 years old. The reason for their departure is to be found in the attraction exerted by urban incomes. Goreux has found a positive correlation between, on the one hand, the net annual rate of migration by department and by period, and, on the other hand, the difference between the level of industrial wages in the chief town of the department and the level of agricultural wages in the same department. There is also a link between the intensity of the exodus and the industrial situation. Periods of intense emigration correspond to periods when industry is booming (1856–61, 1876–81, 1896–1901, 1906–11), and periods of low emigration correspond to periods of industrial and commercial crisis (1872–76, 1881–96, 1901–6).

Growth in the Years 1840–1880

The growth in agricultural production described earlier in this chapter was the result of a sustained demand, linked both to urbanization and to the increase in real incomes, the surpluses of which led to a massive increase in the consumption of food products. The increase in demand explains why agricultural prices were maintained. There were three successive rises: in the price of cereals between 1835 and 1855, in the price of wine in the 1850s, and after that in the price of stock raising products.

Growth opportunities for agricultural production were in fact supplied as much by the development of the transportation network as by the development of local markets. Agricultural growth in the years 1840–70 was diversified regionally, in that certain kinds of specialization emerged; but at the same time, these balanced one another, so that disparities between growth rates in different regions were small. A few examples taken from studies in geography or regional history demonstrate this remarkable convergence. Agriculture in the plateaus of the Paris basin was "regenerated by the sugar beet," and turnover per hectare rose from 150–200 francs in 1840 to 400 francs in 1860. In Loir-et-Cher, between 1836 and 1861, wheat production showed a "strong and regular progress," and the quality of livestock improved. Certain vine-growing regions benefited greatly from the development of transportation. On the Côte d'Or, the productive capacity of vineyards doubled, rising from 400,000 to 800,000 hectoliters. In 1867, Jacqmin, director of the Eastern Branch of the railways, observed: "There is probably no area of Europe to which the railway has brought more well-being and even wealth than the department which used to be called Languedoc." He was thinking of the "frenzy" of vine planting, as the geographer R. Dugrand called it, which seized the region after 1850. Similarly, the need to supply the big towns with perishable goods caused graziers, fruit-growers, and market gardeners to spring up over an area much wider than before. In 1880, Paris's milk supplies were drawn from an area whose radius stretched to 100 kilometers from the capital.

Despite these specializations, mixed farming, with cereals predominating, remained the most usual type. In the three-stage system followed in the north of France, crop fodder, and then sugar beets, took the place of the fallow period. It was "roughly in the middle of the century" that this happened in the Loir-et-Cher, which has been studied by G. Dupeux. On the plateaus of the Paris basin it was after 1850 that beets took the place of fallow periods or fodder. In Brittany, potatoes, used to feed pigs, were the main element in the transformation of agriculture. In the south of France, the three-stage system took the place of a two-stage system, and crop fodder replaced fallow periods. Under the Second Empire even the "highlands of the Massif Central," which have been studied by R. Fell, witnessed attempts, often successful, to adopt systems similar to the Norfolk system (based on the substitution of crop rotation, using root crops or alfalfa, for fallow periods), and these brought about "spectacular increases in yield." In the eastern Pyrénées around Ariège (the "Pyrénées Ariègoises"), studied by M. Chevalier, it was under the July Monarchy that "the great era of artificial pasturage" occurred. Whereas, at the end of the eighteenth century, fallow land represented 30 percent of cultivated land, in 1852 it represented only 16.8 percent and in 1882 only 10.8 percent.

The "new agriculture" was a whole of which all the parts were interrelated. The Agricultural Society of Compiègne correctly described sugar beet as "the regenerator of agriculture, the real first principle of all improvements." It provided beet pulp which, like fodder crops, made it possible to increase the amount of livestock, which was a source of fertilizer as well as of income. Plants which needed weeding insured the preservation of fertilizing elements in the soil. At the same time, the spread of soil enrichers, thanks to the railways, made it possible to cultivate land hitherto underutilized. The spread of marling dates from the first part of the nineteenth century. By 1862, only twelve departments did not use this process. But it was applied only to certain kinds of land. In the years 1852–62, only 2.6 percent of arable land had been treated, and 75 percent of the land treated was in the Paris basin. As for liming, that was only just beginning in the 1870s.

Agricultural progress in the nineteenth century was achieved by means of a small amount of capital and a large amount of labor. It was directed chiefly toward increasing the productivity of the soil. The "new agriculture," as Daniel Faucher has called it, required intensive labor: "The nineteenth century," he writes, "was a weary century for the peasant." Peasant life "had lost its moments of respite." Armengaud observes that in the southwest of France, "the progressive intensification of agriculture, the more frequent use of fertilizers and soil enrichers, and above all the spread of the three-stage system, demanded more labor than in the past," and R. Dion notes that in the Loire Valley, around Berry, the abolition of fallow land "forced farmers to seek the help of a much larger labor force than before." According to the indices worked out by Lévy-Leboyer, the increase in labor and the increase in productivity were parallel up to 1879.

This progress in agricultural methods went with a transformation in the equipment used. The horse plow replaced the swing plow, the scythe replaced the sickle. It was between 1852 and 1862 that horse plows and sowing machines, and also the first horse-driven threshing machines, began to spread in Loiret-Cher. Between 1873 and 1882 tedding machines, reapers, improved mowers, and threshing machines appeared. This second and more capital-intensive stage occurred only in certain areas of large-scale farming, in particular the Paris basin. It was then that the first "technological" disparities appeared, which were to grow more marked as time went on.

Meanwhile, on the whole, agricultural growth up to the 1870s was accompanied by a decrease in regional disparities. According to Jean Pautard, the variation factor for gross product per hectare (excluding wooded lands) in the departments of France fell from 54 percent in 1852 to 46 percent in 1862 and 29 percent in 1882. According to Pautard, the departments whose growth slowed down between 1852 and 1892 were those situated north of a line drawn between Saint-Malo and Lons-le-Saulnier. The departments where production increased were those of Brittany and the Massif Central. So the old contrast between the rich northeast and the poor south was tending to grow less marked.

But this agricultural progress encountered certain limitations even before the "crisis" of the 1880s. In the first place, the demand for cereals gradually weakened. The rise in cereal prices gave way to a stagnation in the 1850s, and farmers' income could be increased only by an increase in production, though, as we have seen, production did continue to increase. The most remunerative sectors were then wine growing, sugar beets, and stock farming. But, for obvious reasons, wine-growing and sugar beet production could only be developed up to a certain point. As for animal products, production of these was developed within the mixed farming system, but not without encountering serious difficulties. Thus, on many "estates" in the Berry region of Champagne, land continued to lie fallow because, according to Gay, farmers "shrank from the expense of increasing the number of agricultural workers, and even more from the expense of buying horses to plow with." Above all, fallow land was considered indispensable for sheep-raising.

There were "areas of resistance" even in the plateaus of the Paris basin. In Brie the agricultural revolution was limited to the western part of the region because of the impermeability of the subsoil, which made extensive drainage work necessary. This work could only be undertaken in the western part of Brie because the agrarian structure, which consisted largely of small farms of about 10 hectares, made it impossible to raise the necessary capital elsewhere. In the Upper Loire Valley the introduction of sugar beets was a failure. As Dion writes, "The traditional individualism of the land of enclosed farming simply annihilated the projects of the Agricultural Society and the industrialists." In the "highlands of the Massif Central," there were many failures or partial failures, even on big estates, or at least on those which were so far from means of transport that they could not easily obtain fertilizers. R. Fell writes: "The region quickly made the transition from a balance depending on a small yield to a balance depending on intensive agriculture, but without supplying the necessary fertilizers." In the Pyrénées Ariègoises, the spread of the new methods of agriculture was limited to the lower areas known as the "pre-Pyrenees." "Nothing happened in the mountains," Chevalier writes.

Just before the great agricultural depression of the late nineteenth century, three types of region could be distinguished: regions of large-scale farming, which benefited as fully as possible from the agricultural revolution; regions which became almost exclusively specialized; and regions which, because of their isolation, the nature of their soil, or their agrarian structure, were only just beginning to change around 1880. Most of these latter regions were devoted to stock-raising, and the agricultural policy of the Third Republic, partly at least, sacrificed the future of these regions in order to safeguard that of the others.

The Years 1880–1913

The agricultural depression of the last quarter of the nineteenth century was, according to P. Barral, regarded as "a structural disequilibrium rather than a cyclical disequilibrium." We shall not repeat here the data regarding volume given earlier. But we may recall that the mean annual growth of agricultural production was 0.26 percent from 1865 to 1900; that there was a mean annual fall of 0.8 percent in the production of agricultural foodstuffs between the years 1874–78 and the years 1889–93; and that at the same time stock-raising products increased by 0.8 percent. This stagnation in production was accompanied by a general and marked drop in prices, probably equivalent to the drop in the prices of industrial products. If 1880 prices equal 100, in 1894 agricultural prices were the equivalent of 82. As P. Barral writes, "whereas, under the Empire, the value of a quintal of wheat had often exceeded 30 francs, after 1882 it dropped below 25 francs, then after a plateau slumped to 18.2 francs in 1895." "Over all, in twenty years, from 1872–79 to 1892–96, there was a drop of 33 percent." The drop in the price of potatoes was of the same order; that of animal products was, on the other hand, much less marked (7 percent for meat and butter during the same period). Jean Sirol has calculated an index, averaged out over nine years, for gross agricultural production, prices, and incomes: according to his calculations, prices fell by 37 percent between 1873 and 1894, production dropped by 11 percent, and incomes by 20 percent. According to Toutain, the final agricultural product dropped from an index number of 101 in 1865–74 to 83 in 1895–1904. The drop in net incomes was no doubt even more marked. In the department of Loir-et-Cher, net incomes, which had increased "strongly and swiftly" under the Second Empire, grew very slowly until 1885 and then fell until 1902 (by 29 percent in the case of the tenant farmer, and by 21 percent in the case of the owner farmer). But the incomes of those who lived off the rents of their land were even worse affected than the incomes of those who worked their land: in Loir-et-Cher, they dropped, during this period, by 55 percent of their nominal value and by 37 percent of their real value. This helps to explain the size of the drop in the market value of land: according to D. Zolla, the index for the market value, taking 1821 as 100, fell from 366 in 1879 to 279 in 1884.

Viewed in this way, from the standpoint of prices, the agricultural crisis emerges as one aspect of a general price drop at the end of the nineteenth century, a result of intensified international and interregional competition. We have already noted the importance of agricultural imports during the 1880s, while France was developing internal long-distance transport for such products. To this must be added a lack of dynamism in the market for vegetable products; in the case of industrial raw materials, the emergence of chemical substitutes and tropical products; and, in the case of food products, the quasi-stagnation of the population and the changes in domestic consumption described earlier. According to Toutain, annual consumption of bread per capita greatly increased up to the decade 1855–64 (213 kilograms in 1815–24 and 285 kilograms in 1855–64), then increased much more slowly (296 kilograms in 1885–94), and subsequently dropped (266 kilograms in 1905–13). It was from the 1890s onward, because of the rises in the standard of living already noted and because consumption of traditional vegetable products had reached the point of saturation, that animal products began to play a larger part in consumption. The agricultural crisis was first a cereal crisis, and it was particularly felt in regions which had remained faithful to a mixed farming system centered on cereals. Because of the stagnation of the population, animal products did not take over rapidly enough to make possible an immediate reconversion to animal and horticultural production. Moreover, the agrarian structure, as we may deduce it from the census of 1892, also worked against rapid changes. The average size of a farm had fallen from 12.5 hectares in 1862 to 11 hectares in 1892. By 1892, farms of more than 40 hectares represented 47 percent of the total area, farms of 10–40 hectares represented 30 percent, and farms of 1–10 hectares 23 percent. Of French farms, 75 percent were directly exploited by their owners and covered 53 percent of the total area, while tenant farmers worked 19 percent of the farms and represented 36 percent of the total area, and sharecroppers worked 6 percent of the farms and covered 11 percent of the total area. The phylloxera epidemic added to these general causes of depression. In 1878, a quarter of all French vineyards (650,000 hectares) were affected. Production, which had been 84 million hectoliters in 1875, dropped dramatically, and remained below 40 million hectoliters for fifteen years. The phylloxera crisis brought about the final disappearance of many local vineyards, and the market in *vins ordinaires* was monopolized by Lower Languedoc (which rapidly developed vines with high yields but of low quality) and by Algeria.

As we have seen, the chief reaction of the authorities was to impose customs duties between 1885 and 1892. Prices began to recover at the end of the 1890s. If 1880 equals 100, then according to Lévy-Leboyer agricultural prices were at 82 in 1894 and 106 in 1913. According to Sirol, the indices were 87 in 1894 and 109 in 1910. This increase followed that of industrial prices, which Sirol calls "the driving forces." The rise in agricultural incomes (index 89 in 1894 and 118 in 1910) is due largely to the dynamism of production (index 73 in 1894 and 94 in 1910) brought about by the revival of urban markets. According to G. Dupeux, in the department of Loir-et-Cher the tenant farmers' nominal income increased by 71 percent between 1900 and 1914; in the same period the owner farmers' income increased by 47 percent; while that of the proprietor living from the rents of his land increased by only 24 percent. But the effects of this recovery should not be exaggerated: growth in production during the decade leading up to the 1914 war did not exceed 1 percent per annum. Although yields increased (13.2 quintals per hectare in the case of wheat in 1909–13 as against 12.5 quintals in 1892–96), they were not outstanding, and diversification into animal products was slow and often more in the nature of an expansion. Finally, there emerged one of the chronic plagues of French agriculture: overproduction of wine, together with its corollary, a slump in prices. Production had once more attained the level it had reached in the 1870s, but quality had deteriorated and consumption flagged. The troubles of 1907 were only the first of a long series. Taken as a whole, French agriculture just before the 1914 war was still deeply affected by the consequences of the great crisis of the last quarter of the nineteenth century. Unlike the advances made at the beginning of the nineteenth century, the progress achieved since the 1890s differed markedly from one region to another, because agricultural growth now required more and more capital. So regional disparities in agricultural growth grew wider.

Bibliography

Annuaire statistique de la France: Résumé rétrospectif 1966. Institut national de la statistique et des études économiques. Paris: Imprimerie Nationale, 1966.

Armengaud, A. *Les populations de l'Est Aquitain au début de l'époque contemporaine.* Paris: Imprimerie Nationale, 1961.

Barral, P. *Les agrariens français de Méline à Pisani.* Paris: A. Colin, 1968.

Brunet, P. *Structure agraire et économie rurale des plateaux tertiaires entre Seine et Oise.* Caen: Caron, 1960.

Caron, F. *Histoire de l'exploitation d'un grand réseau: La Compagnie du chemin de fer du Nord, 1846–1937.* Paris: Mouton, 1973.

Chatelain, A. "La lente progression de la faux," *Annales, Economies, Sociétés, Civilisations,* 1956.

Chevalier, M. *La vie rurale dans les Pyrénées Ariègoises.* Paris: Librairie Médicis, 1956.

Chombart de Lauwe, J. *Bretagne et Pays de la Garonne.* Paris: Presses Universitaires de France, 1946.

Clout, H. D., and A. D. M. Phillips. "Fertilisants minéraux en France au XIXème siècle," *Etudes Rurales,* January–March 1972.

Dion, R. *Le Val de Loire.* Tours: Arrault, 1934.

Dugrand, R. *Villes et campagnes en Bas Languedoc.* Paris: Presses Universitaires de France, 1963.

Dupeux, G. *Aspects de l'histoire politique et sociale du Loir et Cher.* Paris: Mouton, 1962.

Faucher, D. "De quelques incidences en France de la Révolution agricole du XVIIIème siècle," in *Mélanges Bénévent.* Gap: Orprys, 1954.

Fel, A. *Les hautes terres du Massif Central.* Paris: Presses Universitaires de France, 1962.

Fohlen, C. "Charbon et révolution industrielle en France," in *Charbon et sciences humaines.* Paris: Mouton, 1966.

Garrier, G. *Paysans du Beaujolais et du Lyonnais, 1800–1970.* 2 vols. Grenoble: Presses Universitaires de Grenoble, 1973.

Gay, F. *La Champagne du Berry.* Bourges: Tardy, 1967.

Goraux, L. M. "Les migrations agricoles en France depuis un siècle et leurs relations avec certains facteurs économiques," *Etudes et Conjoncture,* April 1956.

Lévy-Leboyer, M. "La décélération de l'économie française dans la deuxième moitié du XIXème siècle," *Revue d'Histoire Economique et Sociale,* no. 4 (1971).

Merlin, P. *L'exode rural.* Cahiers et documents, no. 53. Paris: Institut national d'études démographiques.

Morineau, M. *Les faux semblants d'un démarrage économique: Agriculture et démographie en France au XVIIIème siècle.* Paris: A. Colin, 1971.

Pautard, J. *Les disparités régionales dans la croissance de l'agricultures française.* Paris: Gauthier Villars, 1963.

Pinchemel, P. *Structures sociales et dépopulation rurale dans les campagnes de Picardie de 1836 à 1936.* Paris: A. Colin, 1957.

Pitie, J. *Exode rural et migration intérieure en France: L'exemple de la Vienne et du Poitou-Charentes.* Poitiers: Norois, 1971.

Sirol, J. *Le rôle de l'agriculture dans les fluctuations économiques*. Paris: Sirey, 1942.

Thullier, G. "Les transformations agricoles du Nivernais de 1815 à 1840," *Revue d'Histoire Economique et Sociale*, 1956.

Toutain, J. C. "La consommation alimentaire en France de 1789 à 1964," *Cahiers de l'Institut de Science Economique Appliquée*, ser. AF, no. 11 (1971).

Viallon, J. C. "La croissance agricole en France et en Bourgogne, 1850–1970." Unpublished thesis, University of Dijon, 1975.

Vigier, P. *La seconde république dans la région alpine*. 2 vols. Paris: Presses Universitaires de France, 1963.

Zolla, D. *L'agriculture moderne*. Paris: Flammarion, 1913.

——*Etudes d'économie rurale*. Paris: Masson, 1896.

Chapter Seven: Industrialization

The Stages of Overall Industrial Growth

IT IS NOT really sensible, though most authors seem to do it, to speak as if there were just one movement of industrialization in France which developed by successive stages throughout the nineteenth century. While there is a logical connection, a continuous chain of interactions between the first innovations, which were a continuation of the English Industrial Revolution, and the innovations at the beginning of the twentieth century, this continuity is strictly technological, and the "second industrial revolution" was only a prolongation of the first, without break. But while, as Maurice Lévy-Leboyer and François Crouzet have both shown, the curve of industrial production was continuous and without any long interruption (though there was a slackening in the last third of the nineteenth century), it is clear that industrial growth factors changed profoundly between the beginning and the end of the century.

It is possible to distinguish three periods:

1. The 1830s, 1840s, 1850s, and 1860s were a period of rapid industrial growth, but this growth was highly diversified in methods of production and in the nature of the goods produced.

2. In the 1870s and 1880s, and up to about 1895, industrial growth was slower but more and more selective; investment slackened much less than industrial production.

3. In the years 1895–1913 there was another period of

rapid industrial growth with a steadily accelerating growth rate, but many new elements were introduced, and methods became more and more capitalistic.

As we have seen, the first period was characterized by sometimes sudden expansion of the market, which did not, however, become unified and homogeneous. As regards production factors, France had abundant reserves of unskilled labor that could often be used in rural home industries, but there was a comparative shortage of the kind of skilled labor that could easily be adapted to the methods of industrial production.

If, as an index of the cost of capital, we take the index of the price of heavy industrial products, weighted by the interest rate, we see that the incentive for substituting capital for labor existed through the 1860s but much less strongly then than afterward. While the index of the price of capital goods fell by an annual mean of 1.5 percent between 1815–19 and 1840–44, the index for money wages fell by 0.4 percent between 1815–19 and 1845–49. After that, nominal salaries continued to rise until the eve of the First World War, while the price of capital goods stagnated between the early 1840s and the last years of the 1850s. This plateau, which preceded a rapid fall and was caused largely by the government's customs policy, held back the adoption of production methods based on the utilization of capital.

The dualistic nature of French growth in the first two-thirds of the nineteenth century thus becomes clear. It was dualistic in the sense that highly capitalistic sectors developed alongside poorly capitalistic sectors; it was dualistic also in the sense that the same contrast could exist within one sector. According to the French Statistics Bureau, "employers" amounted to 35 percent of the total working population in 1886. T. J. Markovitch, making a systematic analysis of the two industrial surveys of 1840–45 and 1860–65, concludes that "industry" developed faster than "crafts," but he is far from concluding that the latter sector either regressed or stagnated. Between the two surveys the growth in the production of industrial goods as a whole rose to 50 percent, while the industrial product proper increased by 110.9 percent (see table 7.1).

Table 7.1 Industrial Growth Between Two Industrial Surveys, According to Markovitch (in millions of francs)

	Total Industrial Product	Industry Proper	Peasant Consumption of Own Industrial Products	Crafts
1835–1844	6,385	1,612	401	4,373
1855–1864	9,090	3,406	334	5,350
Difference	+2,705	+1,794	−067	+0,977

Thus the crafts slowed growth but did not interrupt it: their contribution to the growth of the total industrial product was close to half that of industry "proper." According to Markovitch, nearly 60 percent (to be precise, 58.9 percent) of total industrial income in about 1860–65 was produced by the work of craftsmen. But both in the crafts and in industry "proper" a considerable amount of the work was done at home. Very many industries were still organized according to the "domestic system," which, though it declined in certain sectors rapidly being industrialized, became more widespread in other sectors.

Even in actual factories labor continued to play a predominant role. The nineteenth-century factory, though it might be a system for mechanizing labor, was just as often, if not more often, a way of organizing labor which pressed into service methods used under the domestic system. This period represents a stage in the history of technology during which, while there were local breakthroughs in advanced technologies based on the use of steam and mechanization, most other activities remained dependent on hydraulic, animal, or human energy. This incomplete technical development was more marked in France than in other countries at the same period.

The industrial techniques of the mid-nineteenth century were certainly "revolutionary" compared with those of the eighteenth century, because of the use of mineral energy and the mechanization of certain operations. But even in the countries which were technically the most advanced, no coherent technological system was applied to production as a whole. Technical progress in the nineteenth century still relied largely on the craftsman's know-how, and the spread of new methods from one sector to another was much slower than it is today. Another factor which worked against the spread of new methods was the use of steam and water power, which involved concentration near the sources of energy. The lack of efficient means of distributing energy restricted the field in which it could be used.

So we may apply to the whole technological system the observations we have already made regarding railway technique: "In a world largely restricted to human and animal energy, where organization consisted largely of improvisation and trial and error, the steam engine caused a technological breakthrough. But it effects, because of this context, were not as universally beneficial as they should have been. The railway wasted human energy...the steam engine was only an exception" (Caron). The effect of the largely "manual" character of technology in France was made worse by the slow evolution of relative costs.

Lévy-Leboyer and the present author have worked out a table of figures for "industrial investment." According to these figures, industrial investment, stagnant to the beginning of the 1830s, made a leap forward in the second part of that decade. This was the "boom" of the 1830s, but growth remained small during the 1840s. There was a new leap forward in the 1850s and 1860s, as shown by the following figures (1908–12 = 100):

1840–44	18.4
1845–49	19.3
1850–54	21.6
1855–59	27.3
1860–64	29.1
1865–69	31.9

In other words, at a time when the growth of the industrial working population was slackening, the use of capital intensified. But this intensification remained partial, for new industries could call on reserves of labor set free by the decline of rural industry.

A comparison between the index of industrial production

worked out by Crouzet and the index of industrial investment worked out by Lévy-Leboyer and myself is conclusive. If we compare the fluctuations (in adjusted values) in the long-term growth of these two indices, we see that in the 1820s investments show strongly positive fluctuations: this was the era of the founding of big cotton mills and of iron and steel works on the English model. But production shows negative fluctuations. Later on, in the early 1830s, the fluctuations are negative in both cases; they are positive in both cases in the second half of the 1830s, but much less markedly so in the case of investments. The fluctuations are chiefly concentrated in the coal, iron, and steel industries, because of the early railway craze, but they are also markedly present in the textile industry (flax and cotton). In the 1840s the fluctuations are strongly positive for industrial production, while the level of investment is rather depressed. The surplus production capacity created in the 1830s was not really fully used until the 1840s. The same contrast persists during the 1850s and 1860s: fluctuations in the investment index are much less markedly positive than those in the production index during the 1850s; during the 1860s, fluctuations in investment are negative and fluctuations in production just about positive. Up to this date, the style of growth was hardly capitalistic. The growth in the amount of horsepower used in industry was really very slow (1 French horsepower = 32,549 foot-pounds per minute). Between 1843 and 1863, the amount of horsepower installed in industry increased by only 8,950 per annum. The 320,000 horsepower installed in 1869 was only one-tenth of the amount installed in 1913, and in 1878 industry had only one-fifth of the amount of power installed in the railways. In the 100,163 non-Parisian industrial establishments covered by the survey of 1861–65, the distribution of horsepower was as follows:

Water mills	60.0 percent
Windmills	8.1 percent
Horse-driven mills	0.9 percent
Steam-engines	31.0 percent

Claude Fohlen has said that in the first part of the nineteenth century "coal had not yet won out, and water power still largely predominated": this observation should be extended to the 1860s.

For the end of the July Monarchy, Clapham puts forward an estimate which corresponds to the figures of the 1861–65 census. According to Clapham, hydraulic installations still supplied double the amount of power supplied by steam engines. Fohlen also notes that the price of coal still remained an obstacle to its use.

So the increase in productivity, which according to T. J. Markovitch is characteristic of this period (a mean annual growth of 1.2 percent from 1835–44 to 1845–54; of 1.5 percent from 1845–54 to 1855–64; and of 1.6 percent from 1855–64 to 1865–74), can be accounted for both by a redistribution of industrial labor and by a capitalistic intensification of production, though in fact this was limited to certain sectors. The use of labor, hitherto based on a distinction between rural and urban labor, was called in question between the 1840s and 1860s because of the growth of the rural exodus and the slowdown of the increase in the industrial working population; another factor was an acceleration in the growth rate of the industrial population as a whole. There was a transfer of labor from rural and home work industries toward more concentrated, often urban forms of production; but neither this nor intensified investment brought about a real undermining of all the traditional methods of production. These traditional methods can be said to have stopped spreading during the 1850s, and even declined in the 1860s; in some sectors the decline took the form of a real débâcle. But certain of the old methods survived until the 1930s, sometimes because of the nature of the goods involved and sometimes because of the relative availability of the various factors of production.

During this first period, industrial prices showed an accelerated fall, then a slower fall, then stagnation: there was a swift drop at the rate of 2.5 percent per annum from 1810–1815 to 1830–35; a slower drop at the rate of 0.7 percent from 1830–35 to 1845–49; and a stagnation from 1845–49 to 1860–64. The fall in prices during the first period was general, but it was much worse in the textile industry (down 4.9 percent) than in heavy industry (down 1.4 percent), the extractive and chemical industries (down 1.3 percent), or other, miscellaneous industries (down 1.4 percent). The fall seems to have been due first to a fall in the price of raw materials: the price of imported raw materials fell by 3.6 percent per year. Moreover, there had been important increases in productivity in the textile sector, particularly cotton, whereas wages had fallen slightly. Other factors were interregional competition, especially in the textile sector, and the insecurity of the market, which brought about sudden falls every so often when industrialists would sell at whatever price they could get in order to keep their factories active during a slump.

This being so, the slowdown of the fall in industrial prices is readily explained by the slowdown of the fall in the price of raw materials, and by the stability of and subsequent rise in wages, driven upwards by an increase in agricultural prices. Progress in productivity was not sufficient to compensate for all these factors, and the establishment of a railway network did not bring about any immediate intensification of competition. On the contrary, it created shortages and bottlenecks in the production system which tended to push prices up; the railways also suddenly opened up outlets for certain producers, which the better-placed among them could exploit all the more readily because reductions in railway rates came comparatively slowly.

As we have seen, industrial growth slowed down in the 1870s, the 1880s, and the early 1890s: between 1870 and 1896 growth was up 1.6 percent per annum according to Malinvaud and 1.5 percent according to Crouzet. But unlike agricultural growth, industrial growth was not halted. The slowdown of production was not accompanied by an equivalent slowdown in the growth of industrial investment. Industrial investment even accelerated through 1883. The volume of investment decreased between 1884 and 1889, and then growth resumed. Overall, mean annual growth of investments was 3.3 percent from 1865–69 to 1880–84, as against 1.5 percent for production, and 2.4 percent from 1865–69 to 1890–94 as against 1.5 percent for production. The mean annual increase in the amount of horsepower used in industry, which was 9,500 from 1839 to 1869, was 32,800 from 1879 to 1894. A comparison of the fluctuations in real indices of industrial production (Crouzet) with those in investment indices based on the long-run exponential trend (1815–1914 = 100) gives the results presented in table 7.2.

The style of industrial growth had changed. The period 1877–83 saw the construction, in most sectors, of factories using the most modern techniques, usually very capitalistic in their methods but economical of both capital and labor.

Table 7.2 Comparison of Mean Fluctuations in Industrial Production and Industrial Investment Indices

	Investment	Production
1877–1883	+6.7	+0.5
1884–1889	−10.05	−10.1
1890–1894	−1.8	−4.6

It was a period of declining profits. The index of the profit rate, calculated by J. Denuc according to the dividends of listed companies, fell from 193.8 in 1860–64 to 98.5 in 1895–99 (1890–94 = 100). This drop is parallel to the drop in interest rates (5.87 percent in 1870–74, and 3.16 percent in 1895–99). According to Jean Bouvier, the peak for profits in the iron and steel industry occurred in 1873–84, the peak for banking in 1871–82, and the peak in the coal industry in 1870–75. The troughs occurred respectively between 1885–97, 1886–98, and 1892–98. Table 7.3 gives three examples. The profits crisis is also visible in the pattern of liabilities in bankruptcies: it rose from an average of 200 million francs in 1861–75 to 388 million in 1886–90 and 336 million in 1891–95.

In my opinion, it was the large amount of nondistributed

Table 7.3 Overall Profits of Three Companies (in millions of francs)

Chatillon-Commentry (Iron and Steel)		Comptoir d'Escompte de Paris (Banking)		Mines d'Aniche (Coal)	
1863	1.4	1849	0.29	1855	1.2
1873	6.3	1881	9.2	1873	5.1
1888	0.26	1892	3.0	1893	0.87

profits accumulated in the previous period which made possible the financing of investments in the 1870s. This created a surplus industrial production capacity which aggravated the decline in profits at a time when, as we shall see, demand was waning. The fall in profits held back investment all the more because entrepreneurs preferred internal financing.

How is the profits crisis to be interpreted?

1. Demand fell because agricultural incomes suddenly declined, external outlets stagnated after 1875, and basic investments slumped after 1883. These factors have already been studied.

2. It was not by chance that all these things happened at once. They were all due, directly or indirectly, to the intensification of competition which characterized the French economy and world economy in general after the 1860s, after the completion of transport networks and the establishment of commercial treaties. While France was adversely affected by the latter, it also suffered equally (France was probably the country worst hit) from the return to protectionism in America and Germany. So growth became selective: it presupposed an intensification of investment and an increasingly severe management of labor.

3. The increase in competition brought about a new acceleration in the fall of prices, a fall which was maintained by a strongly deflationist atmosphere. Domestic industrial prices fell from an index of 121 in 1865–69 to an index of 86 in 1895–99 (1880 = 100). Previously achieved increases in productivity, especially those of the 1870s, made such reductions possible. At the beginning of the 1870s, many industrialists had still not incorporated in their prices the drops in cost achieved more than twenty years earlier. A fall in the cost of raw materials must also be taken into account.

4. This acceleration of the long-term downward trend was accompanied by an appreciable rise in nominal salaries, which contributed both to the profits crisis and to an orientation toward more capitalistic forms of production. Table 7.4 compares the money wage index and the price of products in heavy industry.

Before the 1870s, the railways were not the only activity

Table 7.4 Comparison of the Money Wage Index and the Price of Products in Heavy Industry (1880 = 100)

	Wages	Price of Products of Heavy Industry	The Same Multiplied by Interest Rate Index
1855–1859	68.0	151.0	166
1885–1889	105.3	74.2	66
1890–1894	109.3	80.0	64

which "wasted human energy," nor were they the only one in which, in the same workshop, production methods involving a large consumption of labor coexisted with others which were comparatively more capitalistic. But the days when such contrasts were possible were beginning to be over. Thus the French entrepreneur was under pressure to substitute capital for labor at a time when the uncertainties of the market and the intensity of competition made full utilization of that capital problematical and often impossible, for in most cases the use of capital presupposes a minimum level of utilization.

The steadily-growing "disharmony" between the French economy and the international economy can only be explained by this incompleteness in the structures of French industry, the result of the factors underlying previous industrial growth.

The steady acceleration in industrial growth from the end of the nineteenth century up to the outbreak of the First World War, interrupted for a few years from 1901 to 1904, was to a certain extent autonomous: it was based on the growth of the urban market rather than on the growth of the rural market, and the dynamism of the foreign market played a less important role than it had done during the first two-thirds of the nineteenth century. With regard to the urban market, we may recall the amount of urban investment and the rise in the urban standard of living, which in fact had begun earlier.

Industrial growth varied considerably according to sector. The most active sectors—electricity, the motorcar industry, the aeronautical industry, iron and steel, electrochemistry and electrometallurgy—were either new sectors or old ones revived by the dynamism of new sectors. Table 7.5, based on François Crouzet's figures, enables us to compare the differences in growth

Table 7.5 Comparison of Growth Rates in Various Sectors, after Crouzet

	Indices			Growth Rates (percent)		
	1880	1904	1913	1880–1913	1880–1904	1904–1913
Mines	44.1	79.5	100	+2.5	+2.4	+2.5
Primary metallurgy	35.7	55.1	100	+3.1	+1.8	+6.8
Metal processing	36.9	58.2	100	+3.0	+1.9	+6.2
Chemicals	19.0	58.0	100	+5.1	+4.7	+6.2
Food industries	52.1	85.6	100	+1.9	+2.1	+1.8
Textiles (total)	66.7	75.1	100	+1.2	+0.4	+3.2
Silk, cotton, wool, jute	54.4	75.2	100	+1.8	+1.3	+3.2
Engineering industries	15.9	49.1	100	+5.7	+4.8	+8.0

between various sectors. The increasingly marked differences in the growth rates of the various sectors brought about an abnormally rapid change in the structure of the industrial working population (table 7.6).

As regards the nature of the goods produced, the structure of French industry did not undergo any fundamental change during the period. France went on directing its production toward high-quality products. Motorcars, which were later to become the most typical example of mass production, originally belonged to this category. So did aluminum. More than

Table 7.6 Distribution of the Industrial Working Population (in percent)

	1896	1913
Agricultural and food industries	7.8	7.8
Mineral fuels	2.8	3.6
Electricity, water, metal processing	0.2	0.4
Building materials	4.3	4.3
Metallurgy	1.3	1.8
Engineering industries	11.0	12.9
Chemical industries	1.2	1.6
Textiles, clothing, leather	46.5	42.4
Miscellaneous industries	11.0	10.9
Building, public works	13.9	14.3
Total	100	100

two-fifths of France's total production was in the sectors textiles, clothing, and leather, which included a high proportion of goods "made by hand" or "fashion" goods. French industry was still dualistic in structure. But now the number of capitalistic sectors was tending to grow, and similarly, within each sector, "capital intensive" methods of production were spreading.

This industrial growth was accompanied by a much lower increase in the working population, and it therefore rests on an appreciable improvement in the return on labor, which for industry as a whole showed a mean annual increase of 2 percent from 1896 to 1913. This improvement resulted chiefly from the substitution of capital for labor. The growth in industrial investment was 3.3 percent from 1890–94 to 1910–13; 3.7 percent from 1900–4 to 1910–13; and 5.2 percent from 1905–9 to 1910–13. This acceleration is parallel to the one in production. Variations in the long-term investment index are strongly positive from 1895 to 1913, except in 1897, 1904, 1905, and 1906, while variations in the production index remain negative up to 1911. The mean annual increase in the number of horsepower in industry was 73,350 from 1883 to 1903 and 141,800 from 1903 to 1913. Malinvaud has worked out the mean rate of overall investment, which was 14.9 percent from 1896 to 1913; it was 13.4 percent in 1896 and 16.8 percent in 1913. The increase was above all in industrial equipment: in 1896 this represented 30 percent of the gross formation of capital. Investment in equipment increased at a rate of 6 percent from 1896 to 1913; investment in building and public works increased at a rate of 2 percent. Between 1905 and 1913, investments in equipment more than doubled, largely because of imports. According to A. Aftalion, the index for imports of machinery rose from 30 in 1895 to 100 in 1910. In the cotton industry the number of mechanical looms doubled between 1886 and 1913. Aftalion, writing in 1903, described the irresistible onslaught of mechanization in the clothing industry, a sector naturally inclined toward manual methods: "Every time, despite its own vigorous counterattacks, domestic industry only manages to save part of its former empire."

But the relative cost of the various factors of production

was less favorable to their substitution for one another now than in the previous period. Between 1859–99 and 1910–14, the wages index showed a mean annual increase of 1.1 percent. The index of prices in heavy industry showed a mean annual increase of 1.2 percent, while the index of these prices multiplied by the index of interest rates went up by 2.3 percent. But the effect of these parallel increases in the price of capital and the price of labor may be regarded as having been offset by the high degree of technical efficiency obtained through capital expenditure.

For while, if we consider only the "physical" aspect of production, the years 1890–1900 continued the pattern embarked on in the 1870s, the later period was quite different from the earlier one from the point of view of value. True, the trend toward rising prices did not begin as early as many authors say. As far as raw materials were concerned, it began in the 1890s, but it did not really emerge clearly in most industrial sectors until the years 1905–7. In many sectors the fall in prices in 1901–4 reached a level distinctly lower than in 1891–93 or 1886–89. Nevertheless, the trend characteristic of the century as a whole was reversed.

The rise in prices was accompanied by a parallel rise in wages and a slight rise in interest rates. This period saw the launching of many new products. But it is well known that for a certain period new products can be sold at prices very much higher than their cost. Moreover, in addition to these innovations in the kinds of goods produced, this period, perhaps even more than the one immediately preceding it, and in very much the same way as the 1870s, witnessed the spread of many techniques which increased the efficiency of labor: these included the use of electric motors, which at one time were expected to bring about a revival of the "domestic system," autogenous welding, high-speed steel production, long-range transmission, and pneumatic motors.

All this brought back conditions favorable to a new rise in industrial profits, though this rise did not become really significant until the last of the prewar years. The rise was much more marked in the case of overall profits than in that of distributed profits (see table 7.7). The dividends index grew

Table 7.7 Index of Dividends and Market Value of Shares (Other Than Those of the Main Railway Companies) Quoted on the Paris Stock Exchange (1901–10 = 100)

	Dividends	Market Value
1894 to 1898	77.0	90.8
1899 to 1903	88.4	90.0
1904 to 1908	104.0	100.0
1909 to 1913	125.0	137.0

more rapidly than the market value index up to 1904–8. After that, confidence was restored and the trend was reversed. But it was the high level of distributed profits which sustained the growth of capital. The nominal capital of listed French companies rose from 3 billion francs in 1900 to 6.3 billion in 1913, and their market value rose from 5.8 to 15.1 billion. This spurt was made possible by the high level of overall profits. In his book on profit, Jean Bouvier discovers, after the lows at the end of the nineteenth century, "new peaks on the eve of 1914" for profits in iron and steel, coal, and banking. The three companies previously selected as examples (table 7.3) developed as shown in table 7.8. The levels now reached were far higher than the previous "peaks," those of the Second Empire. As space is limited, I propose to illustrate these general remarks by analyzing some examples from different sectors.

Table 7.8 Total Profits of Three Companies (in millions of francs)

Chatillon-Commentry (Iron and Steel)		Comptoir d'Escompte de Paris (Banking)		Mines d'Aniche (Coal)	
1888	0.26	1892	3.0	1893	0.87
1913	15.2	1913	18.8	1913	14.4

Examples from Different Sectors

Textiles. According to Markovitch, up to 1844 one-fifth of the value added in industry in France was supplied by the textile industry (two-fifths if clothing is included). The proportion declined later but remained still around 16 percent (30 percent if clothing is included). The growth in textiles began to flag in the 1880s. According to Crouzet, the textile growth as a whole dropped from 1.77 percent between 1831–35 and 1876–80 to 1.1 percent between 1876–80 and 1909–13. For "dynamic" fibers (wool, cotton, silk, jute) the figures are 2.3 percent and 1.78 percent. The worst period was the last twenty years of the nineteenth century (0.88 percent). As Foville wrote in 1887, "Industries like spinning and above all weaving vary enormously in their proportions, ranging from monumental factories to the humble loom of the rural weaver." But in general the "monumental factory steadily gained ground, and the humble loom survived only as its complement or because it turned out products either of very high or of very low quality."

In the French cotton industry growth was very rapid up to 1830, remained steady up to 1860 (up 2.65 percent from 1841–45 to 1856–60), and then slackened off after the crisis of the 1860s (1.9 percent between 1871–75 and 1886–90). It remained steady again at 3 percent between 1886–90 and 1911–15. The chief driving force behind this growth was the domestic market. Cotton was the first product to profit from the rise in incomes: Claude Zarka calculates that there was an elasticity of 2.44 in demand up to the 1870s. The prohibitionism of the Restoration was succeeded in 1834 by a régime designed to favor the import of high-quality goods. But according to Fohlen, from the 1850s Algeria was for some industrialists "the last refuge and only hope." The difficulties which arose after 1860 seem due more to the loss of elasticity in the domestic market, which recovered its dynamism after 1890, than to the consequences of the treaties. Cotton goods, unlike other fabrics, did not benefit from the liberal period: exports of cotton goods went to the colonies.

The reaction of supply was remarkable. The price of cotton goods fell by 2.4 percent per annum between 1810 and 1910. This fall came about in stages: down 5.54 percent between 1810 and 1845, stagnation in the years 1850–60, down 2.19 percent between 1865 and 1895, and then a new trend toward a rise. Table 7.9 shows two comparative cost structures.

Table 7.9 Distribution of Costs in the Production of Cotton Goods (in percent)

	1829 (Lévy-Leboyer)	1900 (Aftalion)
Cotton	51.0	73.2
Coal	3.2	1.9
Maintenance	1.7	3.0
Amortization of interest	15.3	10.7
Wages	28.7	9.2
Overheads		2.0

The fall in prices was due in the first place to the fall in the price of raw cotton, but the fall in cotton goods was even more rapid, except between 1876 and 1898. After 1898, the cartel of planters in the Southern states of America weighed heavily on prices. So the chief cause of the long-term fall was the increase in the productivity of labor. As early as the 1840s, cotton spinning emerged as "an already very modernized industry which was very quick to adopt the new technical discoveries" (Rolleu): it used more steam power than any other industry (244 machines). But the structures in use showed many contrasts: although Normandy was the chief textile center in France (one third of all the spindles in 1894), the industrial structure there was less capitalistic and less concentrated than Alsace, which, starting from the printed cotton goods industry, developed a spinning industry which "technically outclassed" (Lévy-Leboyer) the other regions. The same comparison holds between Normandy and the department of the Nord, where in the 1830s cotton spinning underwent a spectacular revival based on the use of the steam engine. Weaving, which was concentrated in the departments of the Haut-Rhin and the Seine Inférieure, was much more diffuse, and the domestic system still played an important role.

Between 1830 and the 1860s the number of spindles increased by 80 percent, while production increased by 200 percent. According to the Société Industrielle de Mulhouse, the annual production of a standard spindle rose from 10.65 kilograms to 18 kilograms between 1835 and 1865. The number of looms is less well known, but it doubled between 1812 and

1852. The crisis of the 1860s ruined firms which still made use of manual methods: rural hand weaving was, in Fohlen's words, "practically ruined," and in the industry as a whole there was a marked movement toward concentration, both technical and financial. The loss of Alsace-Lorraine reduced the number of spindles to 5 million, and this number remained fairly constant up to 1890; in 1913 it reached 7.7 million. And yet, during the years 1870–80, consumption of raw cotton increased by 1.9 percent, and after 1890 by 3 percent. It seems that overall productivity, calculated on the ratio between the index of gross cotton consumption and the input index (capital and labor) greatly increased in the last years of the nineteenth century (if 1880–84 = 100, 1901 = 152). This increase was backed up by modernization, whereas later growth required rapid capital expansion (1906 = 148). Mechanization was also intense in the weaving industry. It was in 1877 that the number of mechanical looms came to exceed that of hand looms (60,000 and 50,500). In 1913 there were 130,000 or 140,000 mechanical looms, but still very few automatic ones.

In 1903, A. Aftalion showed that the retreat of flax before cotton was due to the fact that cotton was more receptive to mechanization: for an equal amount of expense, cotton machinery brought about a much greater increase in productivity and functioned "with the accuracy of a mathematical problem," whereas flax was "recalcitrant" and "upset theoretical calculations." According to Zarka, elasticity in the demand for flax was 0.88 up to 1870: consumption had been increasing at an annual rate of 1.05 percent since 1830. In the 1820s, the English adopted the invention of Philippe de Girard, which satisfactorily solved the problem of spinning flax, mainly owing to the use of a very hot alkaline solution through which the fibers were passed before being stretched and twisted. But in this case protectionism worked efficiently: the industrialists of the Nord, who had come over from cotton, invested heavily in flax in the 1830s, and the flax industry continued to be characterized by advanced capitalist concentration. This renaissance reached its peak in the years 1863–66. According to Fohlen, this was the "revenge" of cotton's competitors. Sixty-six percent of the spindles were then in the department of the

Nord. It was then that the great retreat of flax began. The number of spindles fell from 623,000 in 1867 to 450,000 in 1902. Then a change in fashion brought flax back into favor: there were 577,000 spindles in 1913. These difficulties brought about greater concentration.

The pattern of growth for wool is very different from that of cotton. In the first place, wool depended much more on exports, which represented 10 percent of production under the Restoration, and 38 percent in the years 1875–84. But protectionism was as unfavorable to the woolen industry as free trade had been favorable: in the 1880s German outlets were closed up, and in the 1890s American outlets disappeared. The elasticity of domestic demand was 1.38 up to 1870. The industrialists of the woolen industry developed a remarkable commercial strategy: instead of being at the mercy of changes in fashion, they managed to dominate them.

Growth in this sector began brilliantly under the Restoration and continued up to the 1880s. Growth was localized in centers where, in the 1820s, industrialists chose and were able to invest: Sedan, Elboeuf, Louviers, Rheims, and above all Roubaix. At the end of the 1820s, the fashion for fancy fabrics was launched in Roubaix. In the 1830s the industrialists there, using the Jacquard loom, prepared, as Lévy-Leboyer says, "to take the lead in the industry." Their successes were based on the quality of the goods produced, the availability of skilful and cheap labor, and the mechanization of all sectors which could be mechanized. Between the 1840s and the 1880s, growth of capital proceeded at the same rate (2.1 percent) as growth of production. But growth varied very much within the industry: in 1883, 45 percent of the mechanical looms in France were in the Nord, and 20 percent in the department of the Marne. In the Nord, their number increased at a mean annual rate of 5.5 percent, while in the Marne it increased at 2.1 percent. Other centers, in the departments of Herault, Loir-et-Cher, the Manche, and Calvados, embarked on a hopeless decline, which had already been perceptible in the early decades of the century: the south of France, according to Lévy-Leboyer, "thought to save its industry by lowering the standard of its products." This policy was fatal. In certain centers, such as

Lodève, activity could be kept up until the 1860s only because of a monopoly on material for army uniforms. Meanwhile, the dynamic centers of the Nord, after introducing "fancy fabrics," perfected an "all-wool worsted" which swept the world market.

After the 1880s, growth and production both slackened, and the number of spindles remained the same; while hand looms, which had started their decline in the 1860s, now virtually disappeared from the scene. Exports of cloth fell in the years 1890–1900, and this fall was only partly compensated for by an increase in exports of yarn. This slower growth became more selective. Many centers, such as Fourmies, which until then had been independent, now became "jobbing" centers, working for the industrialists of Roubaix. On the eve of the First World War, the spinning industry of Roubaix and Tourcoing was made up of "huge factories with first-class equipment frequently renewed" (Aftalion), while weaving had become even more dispersed.

Growth in the silk industry was steady up to 1875. Between 1825 and 1875, the number of looms in Lyons rose from 30,000 to 120,000, and consumption of natural silk rose from 1 million kilograms to 3 million. This growth came about within a technical framework which changed little: the fashion for figured fabrics up to the 1840s and, even more, the fashion for plain materials up to the 1870s, favored the retention of the hand loom. After the rebellion of the Lyons silk-weavers in 1830, there was a development in the use of rural looms. Some of these were incorporated into factories, but "manufacturing was still a way of organizing labor and not a real instrument of industry" (Laferrere). Silk spinning, on the other hand, went through a process of industrialization in the valley of the Rhône, but was much more adversely affected than weaving by a silkworm disease after 1843, and could not adapt itself to the coarser silks from Asia. The slowdown of growth after 1860 was due to a slump in exports to the United States, which until then had been the most dynamic element in the industry's prosperity. But the glutting of the markets took a dramatic turn in 1876. The end of the fashion for heavy black silks, plus the wave of protectionism, produced a marked decline in demand. The crisis revealed the inadequacy of the commercial and industrial organization of the Lyons silk industry, "polarized by the small profits of a dual speculation in raw materials and labor costs" (Laferrere), and without contact with its retail customers. The "slow and inglorious death of the old Lyons industry of plain pure silks" made it necessary, difficult though it was, to adapt the industry to new conditions.

Growth began again in 1885. Despite the complaints of the Lyons Chamber of Commerce, which gave expression to "individual ruin rather than general catastrophe" (Gonnard), the figures prove that the level of production had risen again to that of 1871–75. The recovery was based on three innovations: one was commercial and consisted of the production of lighter, unstiffened silks; the other two were industrial and consisted of the adoption of mechanical looms and piece dyeing. The leaders of the silk industry tried to transform "a luxury industry into a mass-consumption industry," and exports recovered some of their former vigor. The number of mechanical looms rose from 7,000 in 1875 to 42,500 in 1914; in the same period, the number of hand looms dropped from 80,000 to 17,300. But the use of mechanical looms did not mean the immediate and general adoption of the big factory system. Large factories were still fairly rare, though some were built around Lyons at this period (La tour du Pin, Vizille).

In the textile industry as a whole there was a kind of vast redistribution of assets during the years 1876–95, and then again during the long crisis at the beginning of the twentieth century (1901–4). The bankruptcies of some manufacturers enabled others to build rapid fortunes and concentrate the means of production. In this sector, as in the whole of French industry, the capitalistic pattern of growth became general, though this could not lead to the establishment of such radically new structures as in Germany, for example, because of France's close dependence both on external outlets which were very special and therefore very precarious and on an uncertain and restricted domestic market. Taken as a whole, the prosperity of the textile industry during the "Belle Époque" was quite different from that of the years 1840–60: the rise in wages created a need for investment at a time when the increase in the cost of raw materials limited the prospect of profit, and when investment presupposed secure outlets which neither the precarious network of professional "ententes" nor the still limited network based on family solidarity were able to provide. Grandgeorge said in 1911 that the producers involved in the ribbon industry at Saint-Étienne produced "individually too little," and one is tempted to apply this remark to the whole of the textile sector.

Taken as a whole, textile capitalism reflects its own growth and its own market. Traditionally orientated toward high-quality goods, it had to incorporate into their manufacture the highest possible amount of know-how, and therefore of hand labor. This meant it could make do with dispersed and even domestic methods of production. But even before the years 1870–80—i.e., before the difficulties of growth which were linked to rising wages, the contraction of the domestic market, changes in fashion, and the reorientation of world markets—certain sectors, particularly cotton and wool spinning, had already adopted a more capitalistic and more concentrated structure.

Iron and Steel. Deceleration is particularly evident in the iron and steel industry: growth fell from 5.5 percent per annum between 1830–34 and 1860–64 to 2.5 percent between 1860–64 and 1879–83. These figures make the iron and steel industry a significant example, and so do the methods of production used in the industry.

The sudden irruption of English iron after the peace of 1815 almost ruined French ironworks once and for all—hence the imposition of duties which doubled the price of English iron in 1822–25. Adoption of English methods faced such natural obstacles as the inconvenient location of the deposits and the difficulty of acquiring rapidly a know-how which, as J. R. Harris has recently remarked, could not be acquired from books. As G. Dufaud has said, "Generalities are nothing—everything is in the detail." Finally, the adoption of the new methods presupposed big ideas and big markets. But the small ironmaster, who was often a simple contractor rather than a real industrialist, could not conceive big ideas while the state of transportation still gave him control of the local market.

However, in the 1820s there arose some big companies, usually *sociétés anonymes*, which tried to adopt all the English innovations, such as coke smelting, puddling, and rolling, at the same time (Terrenoire, Le Creusot, Alais, and Decazeville). This "total innovation," as B. Gille has called it, failed: all these firms except Terrenoire went bankrupt during the crisis of 1829–30. The same author regards as less artificial the other solution, which consisted of smelting with wood, as before, but using English iron. The best examples of this are Boigue's factory at Fourchambault, Marmont's factory at Chatillon, and De Wendel's at Hayange. This explains the revival and development of some old foundries. But many of them survived only because of the "difficulties of transport."

Most of the innovations of the nineteenth century derived from the spread of the use of iron. According to Landrin, iron consumption was distributed as follows between the different sectors in 1828–29: agriculture 25 percent, towns 20 percent, communications and army 12 percent, and crafts and industry 43 percent. We gave estimates earlier of the amount of iron used by the railways. The increasing use of metal girders should also be taken into account; they were general in Paris in 1855. By 1864, there were 5 metal viaducts and 122 metal bridges. Producers tried to promote the use of iron and steel, while their main customers, such as the railways, put pressure on them to supply metals of higher quality.

Small rural production of iron continued to develop up to the 1840s and was maintained to the end of the 1850s. For iron founding remained an eminently regional industry. It adopted partial innovations, such as an increase in the size of blast furnaces and the recovery of the warm gases they produced. This dynamism, and the survival it insured, enabled certain regions to acquire the metallurgical know-how that was indispensable if these regions were to be converted to other activities. The Ardennes, for example, which in 1864 had 51 iron and steel plants, including 13 blast furnaces and 40 puddling furnaces, became a center for the production of cast iron and various iron and steel products. But in most regions the iron and steel industry was associated with processing. The eastern border of the Massif Central is a typical example. The first

French blast furnace to use coke was set up at Le Creusot in 1782; the first foundry in the English style for the refining of cast iron was established at Saint-Chamond in 1820; in the second decade of the nineteenth century the Jackson brothers introduced cast steel; and in 1825 J. Holtzer founded his factory for the production of wrought steel.

This kind of activity spread rapidly: the Rives de Giers foundry was set up in 1837 by Pétin and Gaudet, two technicians who in 1841 adopted the use of the steam hammer. They produced metal tires for railway trains according to a secret process. The same symbiosis between basic metallurgy and processing also grew up at Le Creusot, which extended its activities into engineering. In the department of the Nord as in the Loire, the iron and steel industry, attracted by the abundance of coal and other local minerals, was linked to the making of cast iron.

Taken as a whole, the iron and steel industry, despite its archaisms, achieved quite high increases in productivity. But its development was based on an intensive exploitation of French ores, which began to show signs of exhaustion toward 1860. The difficulty of obtaining fuel was behind many failures. It is easy to see why industrialists systematically looked for economy in the use of fuel, and the "hot blast" innovation was immediately adopted in France as soon as it was invented in Scotland. By 1842, 117 blast furnaces used such blowers. The recovery of warm gases, first perfected in wood-burning furnaces, was subsequently adopted by the big factories. This process was linked to the installation of steam engines, which worked the blowers and the rolling mills. But the main thing was that under the pressure of price differences in the long run—the price of wood increased up to the end of the 1850s, while coal prices stagnated—coal gradually came to be substituted for wood. At the same time, between the 1830s and the 1860s, steam power triumphed over water power.

These innovations had called for exertion both in the field of investment and in the training of the labor force, within the framework of a structure which was still usually somewhat paternalist. The total capacity of the blast furnaces rose from 125,300 tons in 1826 to 1,250,000 in 1865. A comparison between the 1845 survey and that of 1865 gives the following results (in percent):

Increase in production	+150.0
Increase in number of workers	+59.0
Fall in prices (average prices weighted per ton)	−36.5
Increase in gross value of production	+93.0
Increase in net value of production	+37.0
Increase in value of plant	+280.0
Increase of capital in terms of volume	+139.0

The increase in capital thus seems to have been almost parallel to that in production, but it was the increase in capital which made it possible to raise greatly the productivity of both labor and raw materials.

The 1860s saw the beginning of the expansion of the steel industry, owing chiefly to the railways' need for stronger and more durable metals. Iron production reached its maximum in 1882. This date marks a peak in French iron and steel production, linked to the orders arising out of the Freycinet Plan. The peak was followed by a sudden drop, and it was not until 1896 that the figure for the 1882 overall production index was reached again. After 1896, growth again accelerated (up 3 percent per annum from 1889–93 to 1899–1903; up 5.8 percent from 1899–1903 to 1909–13). Growth had become much more selective as regards the quality of the goods produced. In 1913, iron production reached 400,000 tons and steel production 4,700,000. The Bessemer process, which was welcomed at first and used from the 1860s on, turned out to be unsuitable for the French steel industry, and use of the Thomas and Martin processes spread. The first of these made it possible to make steel out of the phosphorus-bearing cast iron of Lorraine; the second allowed medium-sized factories to produce high-quality goods. From the 1890s on, thanks in particular to the work of Osmond, the making of iron and steel became a science. This technical transformation brought about a complete change in the geographical and financial structures of the industry. Lorraine, with the help of capital from the region of the Loire and the Nord, made a "massive advance": by 1913, Lorraine was producing 49 percent of all the steel and 67 percent of all the cast iron produced in France, as against 3.8 percent and 35 percent respectively in 1880. In the 1890s, the region of the Nord recovered its former vigor in the basic iron and steel industry, while the region of the Loire, by a remarkable transformation, had gone over to increasingly refined products and had developed its specialization in metal processing. Although the French iron and steel industry was less dynamic than that of Germany, it had, on the eve of the First World War, reached a technical level which made it rank among the highest in Europe. It was in fact to ward off this threat of growing competition that in 1904 the German iron and steel producers, who in the last few years had won for themselves an enormous share of the world market and wanted to stabilize this situation, suggested the formation of an international cartel among steel manufacturers.

Coal. Throughout the whole nineteenth century France suffered to a certain extent from lack of coal. Under the Restoration, imports were already growing faster than production: they represented one-fifth of consumption in 1820, and the average for the years 1829–33 was 24 percent. The figure reached 35 percent in 1839–43, as a result of the reduction of customs duties in 1836. The percentage remained at 40 percent during the whole period 1849–68. It subsequently fell to 29 percent in 1894–98, and rose again to 37 percent in 1909–13. The industrialization of France depended on these imports, the major part of which came from England, which by the beginning of the twentieth century was supplying one-half. According to Crouzet, coal imports were "a necessary condition" of the industrial development of regions like the Basse Seine and the Basse Loire. In all sectors, one of the chief aims of French technology was to find economies in fuel: examples of this were the railways' adoption in the 1880s of compound locomotives and, in the iron and steel industry, techniques for the recovery of gases from blast furnaces.

Under the Restoration the production of coal doubled. In 1830 the mines of the Loire accounted for 43 percent of total production, the coalfield of the Nord for 27 percent, and the other coalfields for 30 percent. In the Loire, according to P. Guillaume, "the workings were not yet very deep and they did not require expensive equipment." Prospecting began again in the Nord at the end of the Restoration. There was a big upsurge of investment between 1836 and 1839: out of the 3 billion francs which had been invested in the coal industry of the Nord by 1842, half was invested during this period. It was no accident that a coalfield was found in 1847 in the Pas-de-Calais, and after its discovery its development was what Marcel Gillet has called "peaceful and sure." By the middle of the Second Empire, the Nord-Pas-de-Calais coalfield was producing as much as that of the Loire. After 1886, it produced over half the total French production, and on the eve of the First World War it was producing two-thirds. But the growth of French coal production as a whole underwent a steady deceleration: growth was at a rate of 5 to 6 percent up to the 1860s, then fell from 2.7 percent between 1865–74 and 1895–1904 to 1.9 percent between 1895–1904 and 1905–13. This steady decline in the growth of production was accompanied, from the 1880s on, by a parallel deceleration in the growth of productivity: while the daily output of a coal miner rose from an average of 525 kilograms in 1860–69 to 720 kilograms in 1890–99, it then leveled off. In fact, during this period the French coal industry was profiting from a privileged situation; it was a protected sector. In 1901 a cartel was established in the Nord, and the cartel fixed its own prices according to the area in which the coal was sold. It must also be remembered that natural conditions of exploitation were more difficult in France than in Germany. But it is certain that what was a "golden age" for the coal industry was, as Gillet has put it, an "awkward age" for the French economy as a whole, which was thus stinted of energy.

Bibliography

Aftalion, A. "La décadence de l'industrie linière," *Revue d'Economie Politique*, 1903.
——*Le développement de la fabrique et le travail à domicile dans l'industrie de l'habillement.* Paris: Larose et Tenin, 1903.

——*L'industrie textile pendant la guerre en France.* Paris: Presses Universitaires de France, 1920.

Bouvier, J., F. Furet, and M. Gillet. *Le movement du profit en France en XIXème siècle.* Paris: Mouton, 1965.

Bruyelle, C. "L'industrie cotonnière à Lille-Roubaix-Tourcoing," *Revue du Nord,* January–March 1954.

Caron, F. "Investment Strategy in France," in *The Rise of Managerial Capitalism,* edited by H. Daems and H. Van der Wee. Louvain: Leuven University Press, 1974.

Clapham, J. H. *Economic Development of France and Germany, 1815–1914.* 4th ed. Cambridge: Cambridge University Press, 1968.

Crouzet, F. "Le charbon anglais en France au XIXème siècle," in *Charbon et sciences humaines.* Paris: Mouton, 1966.

——"Essai de construction d'un indice annuel de la production industrielle française au XIXème siècle," *Annales, Economies, Sociétés, Civilisations,* 25, no. 10 (1970). Translation in *Essays in French Economic History,* edited by R. Cameron. Homewood, Ill.: R. D. Irwin, 1970.

Denuc, J. "Dividendes, valeurs boursières et taux de capitalisation des valeurs mobilières françaises de 1857 à 1932," *Bulletin de la Statistique Générale de la France,* 1932–33.

Falleur, G. *L'industrie lainière dans la région de Fourmies.* Paris: Presses Modernes, 1930.

Fohlen, C. "Charbon et révolution industrielle en France, 1815–1850," in *Charbon et sciences humaines.* Paris: Mouton, 1966.

Fontaine, A., et al. *La concentration des entreprises industrielles et commerciales: Conférences faites à l'Ecole des Hautes Etudes Sociales.* Paris: Alcan, 1912.

Foville, A. de. *La transformation des moyens de transport et leurs conséquences économiques et sociales.* Paris: Guillaumin, 1887.

Franchomme, J. "L'évolution démographique et économique de Roubaix de 1870 à 1900," *Revue du Nord,* April–June 1969.

Gille, B. *La sidérurgie française au XIXème siècle.* Geneva: Droz, 1968.

Gillet, M. *Les charbonnages du Nord de la France au XIXème siècle.* Paris: Mouton, 1973.

Gonnard, R. "L'industrie lyonnaise de la soie," *Revue Economique Internationale,* no. 2 (1905).

Grandgeorge, J. *L'industrie textile en France en 1911.* Commission permanente des valeurs en douane. Paris: Imprimerie Nationale, 1912.

Guillaume, P. *La Compagnie des Mines de la Loire, 1846–1854.* Paris: Presses Universitaires de France, 1965.

Houssiaux, J. *Le pouvoir de monopole.* Paris: Sirey, 1955.

Laferrere, M. *Lyon: Ville industrielle.* Paris: Presses Universitaires de France, 1960.

Léon, P. *La naissance de la grande industrie en Dauphiné.* 2 vols. Gap, 1954.

Levy, R. *Histoire économique de l'industrie cotonnière en Alsace.* Etude de sociologie descriptive. Paris: Alcan, 1912.

Lévy-Leboyer, M. *Les banques européennes et l'industrialisation internationale dans la première partie du XIXème siècle.* Paris: Presses Universitaires de France, 1964.

Malinvaud, E., J. J. Carre, and P. Dubois. *La croissance française.* Paris: Seuil, 1972.

Markovitch, T. J. "Salaires et profits industriels en France sous la Monarchie de juillet et le second empire," *Cahiers de l'Institut de Science Economique Appliquée,* ser. AF, no. 8 (1967).

Rolleu, J. "La structure de l'industrie textile en France en 1840–1844," *Revue d'Histoire des Entreprises,* no. 4 (November 1959).

Thuillier, G. *Georges Dufaud et les débuts du grand capitalisme dans la métallurgie en Nivernais au XIXème siècle.* Paris: Service d'Edition et de Ventes des Productions de l'Education Nationale, 1959.

Zarka, C. "Un example de pôle de croissance: L'industrie textile du Nord de la France, 1830–1870," *Revue Economique,* 1958.

Chapter Eight: The Structures of French Industrial Capitalism

Industrial Establishments

THE 1906 CENSUS enables us to see the structure of French industrial establishments as it had developed in a century of industrial evolution. An analysis of this structure enables us first of all to see the degree of technical concentration which French industry had reached. This depends on two different factors. The first is the national production structure, for, as A. Fontaine remarked in 1912, for each kind of production there is an optimum density for the separate plants, and this optimum density varies according to sector. The degree of concentration depends largely on the nature of the activities involved. But it also depends on the technical processes used, and so the degree of concentration tells us something about the level of technological evolution. As those who drew up the 1906 census remarked, big factories "make possible the adoption of the most advanced appliances." And although even at this period some observers were already alive to the disadvantages of exaggerated size, it is clear that the use of industrial techniques which could increase workers' productivity was reflected by a growth in the size of industrial establishments. In addition to this technical sidelight, a study of the size of the different establishments enables us to form a first approximation of the size of the firms themselves, for there were at this time few firms which had several separate installations.

From an examination of the 1906 census, two conclusions

emerge: on the one hand, small and even very small industrial establishments still played a highly important part in the French industrial structure, and on the other hand, factories, sometimes very large ones but usually what we would describe as medium-sized, occupied a place proportional to that held in French production as a whole by activities favorable to large-scale production. The number of firms which had no employees at all is very high: they formed 71 percent of all industrial establishments, and the people that ran them formed 27 percent of the total industrial working population, owners included. So there was a certain similarity between the reality and the old dream of industrialization, where labor was divided up into small independent units. Leaving this category aside and turning to employees; we find that 32 percent of these worked in establishments employing less than 10 people, 28 percent in establishments employing between 10 and 100, and 40 percent in establishments employing over 100. An average-sized business employed 45 people. The full significance of these facts only emerges when we analyze the distribution sector by sector. Then the following classification emerges:

1. Three sectors—the food, wood, and fabrics industries—were hardly industrialized at all. Their structure is shown in table 8.1. An average-sized establishment in these three sectors would employ from 4 to 6 people.

2. Building and public works, hides and leather, quarrying, and printing and kindred trades were above the national average (28 percent) in employing their workers in establishments 35 to 46 percent of which had between 11 and 100 people working for them. The average was 29. (See table 8.2.)

3. The third kind of sector is more homogeneous and brings us into the realm of industry proper. It includes textiles,

Table 8.1 Group 1 Sectors: Distribution of Employees by Size of Establishment (in percent)

Size of Establishment (No. of Employees)	Food	Fabrics	Wood
1–10	62.0	58.0	58.5
11–100	25.0	28.5	32.0
Over 100	13.0	13.5	9.5

Table 8.2 Group 2 Sectors: Distribution of Employees by Size of Establishment (in percent)

No. of Employees	Building and Public Works	Hides and Leather	Quarries	Printing and Allied Trades
1–10	47	41	28	18
11–100	40	35	46	45
Over 100	13	24	26	37
Average No.	12	18	29	47

chemicals, glassmaking, and the paper and rubber industries, all of which taken together employed 28 percent of French industrial wage earners. It was in textiles that concentration on large establishments was most marked in this category, which was characteristic of the French industrial system in the nineteenth century. (See table 8.3.)

4. The metal processing sector employed 15 percent of the total work force. The distribution of employees was different from that in the three previous categories in that it was more equally divided: 27 percent worked in establishments employing fewer than 10 people, 27 percent in establishments employing between 11 and 100, and 47 percent in establishments employing over 100. This distribution was due to the diversity of subsectors in this category, which ranged from small iron works to factories turning out large machinery; but it also reflects a certain type of organization in the French engineering industry, which might be looked into more closely.

5. Major industry is represented by mining and metallurgy. Plants employing more than 100 people accounted for 97 percent of the labor force in these sectors; plants employing

Table 8.3 Group 3 Sectors: Distribution of Employees by Size of Establishment (in percent)

No. of Employees	Glass	Chemicals	Paper	Textiles
1–10	14	11	7	9
11–100	30	36	34	22
Over 100	56	53	59	69
Over 500	20	21	20	26
Average No.	132	118	142	200

more than 500 people accounted for 86 and 80 percent, respectively, of the labor force in mining and metallurgy.

So the emphasis on comparatively small establishments is to be explained first by the production structure itself, which reflects the distribution of activities between sectors and not a deliberate intention to keep establishments small. Three considerations help us to understand the existence of these small or very small establishments. Some, as A. Fontaine has said, represented the natural and traditional domain of small-scale industry; this was so in the case of a large part of the food sector, the wood industry, and laundry. Others were the result of the survival of what Leplay has called "collective manufacture," i.e., the domestic system, which was still very much alive in the clothing industries. A. Aftalion showed in 1904 that this method of production was doomed to disappear almost entirely in the long run, and explained its survival by the fact that it produced goods either of very high or of very low quality, and that wages were kept at a very low level. But by 1906 many of these establishments, far from being a survival, were heralds of the future: this applies both to the crowd of subcontractors working, as A. Fontaine puts it, "in the wake" of large establishments, and to the growing number of repair and maintenance workshops which were taking over from the traditional artisans (e.g., electrical workshops and garages). It is intriguing that some observers rightly predicted, on the basis of contemporary evidence, that industries such as those concerned with photography, bicycles, or even motorcars would probably bring about a renaissance of the "small workshop."

Large establishments were bigger in proportion to their distance from the final product: carding was more concentrated than spinning, and spinning was more concentrated than weaving, which in turn was more concentrated than the clothing trade; paper making was more concentrated than paper processing; iron and steel making were more concentrated than metal processing. There were 574 "big establishments" employing more than 500 workers, and taken together they employed 680,000 people. They were mostly factories concerned with the manufacture of textiles (200), iron and steel (43), the processing of metals (120), and mines (66). These four sectors accounted for three-quarters of the labor employed in large establishments. They correspond to three types of industrial technology: the big factory producing semifinished products or plant and machinery, like the steel machines factory at Le Creusot; textile factories with large mechanical installations; and assembly works, modern in kind, mass-producing consumer durables. In such establishments the energy available per worker was very much higher than the average in French industry; these factories, employing 18.5 percent of industrial wage earners, had 31 percent of all the steam horsepower available. But a "normal" French factory had only between 100 and 200 workers. About 4,000 factories together employed 800,000 people divided up into units of 101–500; the average size here was 200, and this category, while employing 21.7 percent of industrial workers, used 26.6 percent of the energy available in industry. This kind of establishment was much more widely spread over the different sectors: only half belonged to the four sectors of textiles, mines, metallurgy, and metal processing. It was as if French producers were afraid of installing units of production that were too large. For the above typology of French industrial establishments is by and large an accurate reflection of the structure of French business enterprises.

Business Firms

On the eve of the First World War the structures of French capitalism reflected a long evolution during which there was tension between forces tending toward concentration in large enterprises and forces tending to maintain a system of divided and small enterprises. There seem to have been three types of sector: those in which there was wide dispersion, those dominated by a dozen or so enterprises, and those in which there was great concentration.

The first type included both traditional sectors like textiles and new sectors like motorcars. In the textile industry the nineteenth century saw a long process of concentration terminating on the eve of the war in a structure in which each subsector was dominated by one or two or three centers, each of these in turn being dominated by a fairly large group of influential family firms. At the beginning of the 1840s, the 566 cotton-spinning factories in France employed on the average 111 workers each, and 5,765 spindles. But concentration varied greatly between one region and another. The department of the Seine-Inférieure had a turnover which was 30 percent higher than that of the Haut-Rhin, and had three times as many firms. According to Fohlen, the difficulties of the 1860s hastened the process of concentration, which still continued afterward, each new crisis intensifying the process. In the department of the Nord, while in 1865 67 firms had an average of 13,200 spindles each, in 1911, in Lille, 40 had 51,500 spindles and 18 had 67,000. This concentration had come about through an increase in the size of spinning factories with more than 20,000 spindles. Cotton weaving was less concentrated. Here, in 1914, the most frequent size was something between 100 and 300 looms, and only 40 percent of the enterprises concerned combined weaving and spinning. This dispersed structure reflects a policy which tried to divide up risks in an uncertain market.

The evolution of the woolen trade was marked by the growing influence of Roubaix. Not only did Roubaix grow more rapidly than other centers, but it also dominated them commercially. For example, the industrialists at Fourmies gradually became mere jobbers working on orders for the industrialists of Roubaix. But comparatively speaking, the concentration at Roubaix remained low. In 1914 the invested capital there is estimated to have been 95 million francs, divided up among 86 enterprises. The firm with the largest capital was François Mesurel Frères, with 4 million francs. There were many family links between the different firms.

This first type of structure is in fact the "normal" one. There were 150 different firms engaged in the automobile industry, 40 firms producing gas engines, 30 producing water turbines, 30 producing small tools, and 20 producing textile machinery.

The iron and steel industry is characteristic of the second type of structure. This industry grew up during the first two-thirds of the nineteenth century and was the combined result of the internal growth of certain firms and their external growth when they reached a certain level of development. Three generations may be distinguished in the development of the big French iron and steel firms: those which came into being in the 1820s; those which were born out of the boom of the years 1835–38, especially in the north of France; and those of the 1840s. This period saw not only the birth of big new firms, but also several attempts at grouping by means of mergers or takeovers. Either small rural iron works would get together to save themselves; or, as in the case of Chatillon Commentry, a big iron works would unite with traditional blast furnaces; or, as in the case of Denain-Anzin in 1849, iron works would unite with modern blast furnaces.

This last type of concentration became common in the 1850s and 1860s: Fourchambault-Commentry and Terrenoire-Bessèges merged in 1854, and in the same year the Société de la Marine et des Chemins de Fer was founded, grouping together a series of enterprises like Pétin and Gaudet and Jackson, and incorporating all stages of iron and steel manufacture down to the making of rare machine parts. These mergers were the result of particularly rapid internal growth which had taken place beforehand as a result of the success of certain specialized products. The regrouping of old iron works and traditional blast furnaces was now doomed. In fact, concentration came about not so much through external growth as through the internal growth of the large firms. The four firms of Decazeville, Wendel, Le Creusot, and Fourchambault, which in 1840 produced 6.2 percent of the total tonnage manufactured in France, in 1869 produced 21 percent. In 1847, the seven largest firms controlled 37.5 percent of French production, and in 1860 the eight largest firms controlled 53 percent. These were the "mushroom factories" referred to by B. Gille. At the end of the Second Empire the ten leading firms accounted for 55 percent of iron and steel production, as against 13.8 percent in 1845.

This level of concentration then remained fairly stable. Later regroupings and redistribution of assets made no significant change, from the statistical point of view, in the main structures. In 1912, according to Gille, the ten leading iron and steel companies controlled 70.5 percent of the total capital in the French iron and steel industry; 10.8 percent of the total capital was controlled by the chief of these firms, the Société des Forges de la Marine et Homécourt, which was formed when the Société de la Marine took over the Homécourt factory in 1905.

This type of concentration was neither monopoly nor oligopoly, but it was characterized by the domination of a "block of about 10 very powerful companies"—an expression used by Marcel Gillet to describe the situation in the coal industry of the Nord in 1914. In this sector both the system of concessions, as defined by the law of 1910, and the legislation on cartels were used by the state to avoid too much dispersion on the one hand, and on the other, monopoly, the threat of which was represented in the north in the early nineteenth century by the Compagnie d'Anzin, and in the Loire in the middle of the century by the Compagnie des Mines de la Loire.

Some sectors were much more concentrated: these included the basic chemical industries, dominated by 5 companies themselves subject to the omnipotence of one of them, the Société de Saint Gobain. The aluminum industry consisted of 5 enterprises, but only 2 of these had any ability to influence the market.

Cartels

It is not surprising that, just before the war, the most powerful cartels were in the chemical and aluminum industries. Cartels often reflect a highly concentrated structure. That is why cartels are fewer and less powerful in France than in such countries as Germany or the United States. As J. Houssiaux has said, "Before 1914, industrial combines were exceptional, although enterprises for various reasons and for various lengths of time sometimes created common agencies." A. Aftalion has called the kind of agreements he has described in the textile industry "a simple form of cartel." These short-lived combines did not dominate the market. They were only "useful catalysts." The arrangements Gillet describes in the coal industry played a much more important role and were much more useful to those who took part in them. The cartel usually fixed the prices of coal sold by the coal industry of the Nord with reference to the prices offered by competitors in other French or foreign coalfields. In the iron and steel industry there were only four common agencies—the Comptoir de Longwy (1876), the Comptoir des Poutrelles et Aciers Thomas (1896—girders and steel), the Comptoir des Essieux (1892—axles), and the Comptoir des Tubes (1906).

All in all, French industrialists, faced with a restricted and uncertain market, adopted in most sectors a policy of dividing their risks, a strategy occasionally modified by temporary recourse to cartels.

Bibliography

Aftalion, A. *Le développement de la fabrique et le travail à domicile dans l'industrie de l'habillement.* Paris: Larose et Tenin, 1903.
——"Les Kartells dans la région du Nord de la France: Les Kartells à forme simple dans les filatures de coton et de lin, 1899–1907," *Revue Economique Internationale,* 1908.
Fohlen, C. *L'industrie textile au temps du Second Empire.* Paris: Plon, 1956.
Fontaine, A., et al. *La Concentration des entreprises industrielles et commerciales: Conférences faites à l'Ecole des Hautes Etudes Sociales.* Paris: Alcan, 1912.
Gille, B. *La sidérurgie française au XIXème siècle.* Geneva: Droz, 1968.
Gillet, M. *Les charbonnages du Nord de la France au XIXème siècle.* Paris: Mouton, 1973.
Houssiaux, J. *Le pouvoir de monopole.* Paris: Sirey, 1955.
Recensement général de 1906, vol. 2, *Etablissements industriels et commerciaux.* Paris: Imprimerie Nationale, 1908.

Part Two: The Twentieth Century

Introduction

ON THE EVE of the 1914 war, France was the second greatest financial power in the world, "the great reservoir of capital, toward which the yellow metal flowed," in the words of a writer in the *Journal des Economistes* in 1902. As the Minister of Public Works, P. Baudin, said in 1903, this glittering power was linked to a great "mediocrity" in the demographic and industrial spheres. The French population was only the fifth largest in Europe, although it had been the second largest at the beginning of the nineteenth century. French industrial production amounted to scarcely 6 percent of world industrial production, as against 9 percent in 1880. In the industrial sector, Germany surpassed and to a degree dominated France: France was producing 3.3 million tons of steel, Germany 13.0 million. German organic chemicals dominated Europe, and French firms in the field were only disguised branches of German firms. No French electrical power firm had the stature or equaled the technical capacity for innovation of the Allgemeine Elektrische Gesellschaft.

We called attention in chapter 6, however, to a quite noticeable acceleration of industrial growth in the 1900s, particularly in the metallurgical, chemical, and machine tool industries. This was a worldwide phenomenon, as readers of J. Schumpeter's *Business Cycle* know well. The new cycle of innovation, beginning at the very end of the nineteenth century and dominated by electricity, the internal combustion engine, and organic chemistry, among others, was sparked by Germany and the United States. This is well known. It would be wrong to believe that France took no part in it. Certain of France's entrepreneurs, young or old, had the wit to seize the opportunities offered to them. The proof is that many firms which were to supply the drive in French industrial life in the 1950s and 1960s were formed or found a new life in the 1890s and saw their real launching in the 1900s. This was true of the Compagnie Général d'Electricité, founded in 1898, of the great Alpine electrochemical and electrometallurgical firms, of such automobile companies as Renault and Peugeot.

In reality, French industry had entered on the path of technical modernization. Production of electricity, directly linked to industrial and urban development (even though it could appear too widely dispersed), underwent a not negligible development (from 340 million kilowatt hours in the year 1900 to 1,800 million in the year 1913). France began the exploitation of its hydroelectric reserves, particularly in the Alps: the available power went from 150,000 kilowatts in 1899 to 550,000 kilowatts in 1914. This progress was intimately linked with progress in electrochemistry and electrometallurgy. French technical skill brought the best results anywhere, in terms of productivity and cost, in certain product lines, e.g., aluminum and chlorates. In the worldwide cartels dealing with these products, France played the dominant role. In 1898–1900, the automobile industry was filled with men of whom about two-thirds came out of the ranks of small businessmen—from machine works (Peugeot), but not exclusively (Renault)—and the rest out of the ranks of artisans (Berliet) or from the aristocracy. In 1913, automobile production in France, at 45,000 vehicles, was certainly below that of the United States, but France had preserved a clear superiority in innovative design.

French industrialists have been accused of having sacrificed innovation in production methods to the constant search for new design perfections and to the continuance of a whole gamut of choices; that is why they are not truly committed to mass production. In fact, these characteristics of the French automobile industry were not peculiar to it. French industry is oriented in many instances toward producing a great variety of quality goods. That is why many industrialists thought in the 1920s that "rationalization of production" could have only a limited development in this country. The war, however, had brought out the serious defects of industrial "mediocrity" when face to face with Germany. At the same time, it had destroyed France's illusions of financial power.

Through the twentieth century, those French conscious of the true interests of the country (there were certainly as many of them under the Third and Fourth as under the Fifth Republic) sought to restore the "fallen franc" and to give the country an industrial structure which was strong and suited to its potentials. Poincaré's currency reform of 1928 lived on as a victory over the enemy; the devaluation of September 1936, however—too slight, too sluggishly accomplished—was a defeat. All those who supported the monetary action of General de Gaulle are said to have done so because they remembered the humiliations suffered under the Fourth Republic, when time and again France had to go begging for foreign aid.

Industrial design was only abandoned in the dark years of the 1930s, the Occupation, and—more recently and in a manner, we think, more apparent than real—after the death of Georges Pompidou, under the influence of antigrowth doctrines and the trauma of the crisis. Despite successful efforts since 1945, several experts brought together by Pompidou said in April 1968 that "French industry suffers from certain weaknesses built into its structures and those of our economy." The years 1969–73 marked the height of the drive for industrialization, of which the present leaders cannot in any way deny the necessity. They simply try, by giving it a greater flexibility, to adapt it to a world in crisis and to the needs of a constantly changing market.

In the first three chapters of this second part the different aspects of long-term growth will be described to bring out their continuity. Then we shall set forth a chronological study of the years 1914 to 1950, into which value judgments will be incorporated. The two last chapters will be given over to examining the evolution of the structures of French capitalism and the evolution of the behavior of state and business from 1950 to 1974. This plan results in certain repetitions, but a strictly chronological outline would not have made it possible to emphasize continuities.

Chapter Nine: Growth in France in the Twentieth Century

Problems of Periodization

"A HISTORIAN WHO wanted to pinpoint the beginning of a long acceleration in the French growth rate could probably place it just as well around 1900 as around 1950." Thus Malinvaud, Carre, and Dubois conclude their analysis of French growth rates in the twentieth century. And thus they call into question the view of French economic history put forward in studies written in the 1950s. Consciously or unconsciously, economic chroniclers, anxious to emphasize the exploits of their current hero, whether it was Jean Monnet, Pierre Mendès France, Edgar Faure, or General de Gaulle, tended to describe France's past as having been uniformly undistinguished. Some followed A. Sauvy and stressed the grave consequences of the population slump which reached its worst in the 1930s. Others described the economic system as entirely given over to a Malthusian network of corporatist-inspired combines, which though they certainly existed in the 1950s had at all costs to be traced back not to reactions to the crisis of the 1930s or to the Vichy régime, but to a sort of inherent attitude on the part of French entrepreneurs. This explanation corresponded to the view then current among some American historians that the traditional French entrepreneur was conservative rather than an "innovator."

French capitalism was described as being unfinished, French industrialization as being incomplete. Some writers placed the responsibility not on the entrepreneurs themselves but on their environment, or at least on all those social and political factors which made up traditional France: the ruling classes, of whom the entrepreneurs were just one element, trying to maintain the existing social hierarchy. According to this view, the peasants and middle classes formed a sort of alliance with the upper bourgeoisie to keep the working classes in a "ghetto," and the conditions necessary for maintaining this status quo were economic stagnation, the preservation of an archaic agriculture, and an archaic system of production and trade.

This kind of interpretation may be partly true. But clearly it cannot easily be reconciled with the periodization put forward by Malinvaud: the low level of French economic performance in 1938 or 1950 is accidental, a prolongation of the slump, which can be attributed either to human error or to the influence of sociological factors. If Malinvaud's periodization is accepted, the "French miracle" of the 1950s and 1960s no longer appears a sudden contrast with a past of stagnation or at least very slow growth.

We have already seen, especially in connection with industry, that after 1906 the growth rate accelerated. This period

Table 9.1 Annual Growth Rates of French Production (in percent)

		Malinvaud*		Vincent	
	Industry	Productive Branches	Productive Branches and Services	Agriculture	All Branches†
1896–1913	2.4	1.9	1.9	1.0	1.7
1913–1929	2.6	1.7	1.5		
1929–1938	−1.1	−0.4	−0.3	0.9	−0.5
1938–1949	0.8	0.9	1.1	0.0	1.1
1949–1963	5.3	5.0	4.6		
1949–1969	(5.3)	5.0	4.7		
1949–1962				3.3	5.1
1969–1973	6.5‡		6.6		

*From "Rapport sur les comptes de la Nation," 1973, Collection INSEE (29–30), except for 1969–73 figures.

†Agriculture, industry, commerce, transport, and postal services.

‡Comptabilité Nationale gives 7 percent.

of rapid growth based on intensive industrialization continued beyond the First World War up to 1929–30; it was followed by a period of stagnation, and then, after the disasters of the Second World War, France entered a period of strong and sustained growth. The figures in table 9.1 are those put forward by Malinvaud and L. A. Vincent.

It is interesting to break down the two periods 1896–1913 and 1913–29. According to Malinvaud's figures, the gross national product increased at a rate of 1.5 percent between 1896 and 1906 and 2.4 percent from 1906 to 1913. We may recall that according to all the indices of industrial production now published, there was a sudden acceleration between 1906 and 1913 (4.4 percent according to Lévy-Leboyer and 5.2 percent according to Crouzet). For the 1920s, L. A. Vincent breaks down the figures as follows:

	Agriculture	*All Other Branches*
1913–24	−0.4 percent	0.6 percent
1924–29	1.2 percent	2.8 percent

According to Malinvaud's figures, gross domestic production increased at an annual rate of 4.4 percent from 1922 to 1929; if 1929 equals 100, 1922 showed an index of 74 as against 76 in 1913. According to OECD figures, the annual rate of industrial growth between 1924 and 1929 was 4.7 percent.

In fact, in the 1920s, France's industrial growth rate was higher than that of the other European countries. As F. Walter wrote in 1957, French industry then "led the vanguard of European industrial progress." So everything suggests that French economic history went through a period of 25 to 30 years, including the First World War, characterized by a high growth rate despite an agricultural growth which was still fairly slow. The high rate must therefore have been due to rapid industrial growth, foreshadowing that of the 1950s and 1960s, when the new factor, in comparison with the first three decades of the twentieth century, was rapid agricultural growth. Anyhow, as Malinvaud writes, the levels of expansion achieved by France after the Second World War "scarcely exceed those which would have been reached by a continuance of the progress observed between 1896 and 1929."

In 1957, Walter described the 1930s as "an economic Sedan." It was above all an industrial Sedan: agricultural and commercial growth rates were at much the same levels as they had been in the 1920s (0.9 percent instead of 1.2 percent per annum for agriculture, and 1.2 percent instead of 1.9 percent per annum for commerce), while industry regressed to an annual rate of 1.1 percent and transport and postal services to 2.9 percent. In the 1930s agriculture, far from hampering overall growth, slowed down the decline. As we shall see, this decline itself was composed of a collapse in certain sectors compensated for by the rise of new sectors.

The growth rate of the years 1938–49 (close to 1 percent per annum) is the result of two contrary trends. If we take 1938 as 100, national income, according to the Institut National des Statistiques et des Études Économiques (INSEE), was 50 in 1944 and 109 in 1949. Table 9.2 shows the various indices.

Industrial production reached its 1938 level again in 1947, while agricultural production did not do so until 1950. The growth which started at the beginning of the 1950s is certainly a "new phenomenon," because of its length and continuity. The annual growth rate between 1896 and 1929 was 1.7 percent; between 1929 and 1963 2.1 percent; but between 1949 and 1963 it was 4.6 percent. The most recent rates only confirm this trend: during the 1960s, growth accelerated. The mean annual growth rate of gross value added was 4.5 percent from 1949 to 1959, and 6.1 percent from 1959 to 1973. Until that date there had never been a prolonged fall in production since the beginning of the 1950s. From this point of view the recent crisis creates a rupture: in fact, the gross national product increased

Table 9.2 Growth Indices, According to INSEE (1938 = 100)

	Agricultural Production	Industrial Production	National Income in Value
1944	100	38	50
1945	61	50	54
1946	76	84	83
1947	74	99	90
1948	90	113	96
1949	93	122	109

by 5.8 percent per annum from 1960 to 1972, and industrial production by 6.0 percent. In 1973 the two rates still stood at 5.8 percent and 7.1 percent, but they fell to 3.8 percent and 2.4 percent in 1974, while in 1975 the rise turned into a fall, at a rate of 1.3 percent in the case of the gross national product and of 8.3 percent in the case of industrial production. There were noticeable revivals of general activity at the end of 1975 and at the beginning of 1976. The latter was more marked and more enduring. A clear slackening appeared in general activity in the second half of 1976 and in industrial production in the third trimester of that year, both lasting into 1977. The gross domestic product rose by 5.2 percent in 1976 and 3.0 percent in 1977; the comparable figures for industrial production are 8.7 and 3.5 percent. Thus all the evidence indicates that in France, as in the industrialized nations as a whole, there is a certain middle-term slowdown in the second half of the 1970s.

This periodization does not take into account very short-term fluctuations which occasionally interrupted or slowed down growth during the 1920s (for example 1927), or even in the 1950s and 1960s (for example 1952–53), or else gave it a certain impetus in the 1930s (1937). But this periodization does reflect the trend, and prompts several historical comments:

1. In the 1920s, growth was more marked in France than in the rest of Europe. It was as much a continuation of the growth of the immediate prewar years as of the industrialist spirit of the First World War. Despite its obvious precariousness, which was demonstrated by the gravity of the slump, it seems to foreshadow the growth which came after the Second World War. So it needs to be more closely defined. To what extent was it a last spasm of a nineteenth-century type of growth, based on high quality and hand industries favored by an inflationist policy? To what extent was it a first step toward intensive industrialization, modern in style and highly capitalistic, foreshadowing the 1950s and 1960s? Is not the dualism of the years 1850–60 to be seen again in 1906–29?

2. The depression of the 1930s lasted longer and made a deeper impression in France than in the rest of Europe. But how did it vary in the different sectors? The vigor of the later recovery would be difficult to understand if the decline had

occurred on all fronts. May we not suppose that the apparent rigidity of the overall figures hides profound structural modifications? In a study of French industry in 1953, INSEE already stressed the diversity in the different sectors, some groups tending to rise and others to fall, and still others "tending to oscillate." Without denying the gravity of France's "economic Sedan," we may regard the general "catastrophe" of the 1930s as having been at the same time a new stage in the conversion of France's industrial structures.

3. France's growth in the 1950s and 1960s followed the same pattern as that of the other Western economies. In the 1950s, French growth was "average" in comparison with the other countries of the OECD, and in the 1960s it was above the OECD average (see table 9.3).

The fact that growth was general suggests that free trade policies had a directly beneficial effect on growth rates, just as

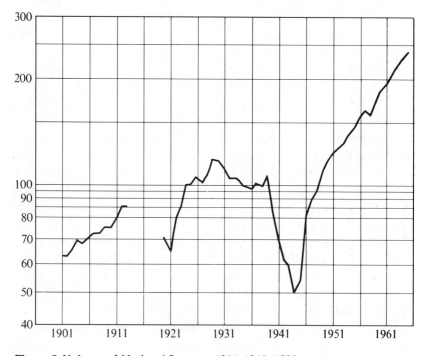

Figure 5 Volume of National Income, 1901–1965 (1938 = 100).

SOURCE: *Annuaire statistique de la France, 1966* (Paris: Imprimerie Nationale, 1966).

in the 1930s the outrageously prohibitionist policies had had a very bad effect on growth. This is confirmed by the acceleration in France's growth rate from the last years of the 1950s on. But it is clear that this liberalization was only one factor in a comprehensive economic policy.

Table 9.3 Mean Annual Growth Rates

	1949–1959 GNP	1955–1968 GDP	1959–1960 to 1970–1971 GNP	1972	1973
Canada	4.2	4.5	4.9	5.8	7.25
United States	3.3	4.0	3.9	6.1	6.00
Japan		10.2	11.1	9.6	11.00
France	4.5	5.7*	5.8	5.5	6.25
Germany	7.4	5.1	4.9	3.0	6.25
Italy	5.9	5.5	5.5	3.5	5.25
Great Britain	2.4	2.8	2.9	3.0	6.75
All these countries together		4.6	4.8	5.8	6.75

SOURCE: OECD, "La Croissance de la production, 1960–1980." Paris, 1970.
    *1959–1968.

Population and Growth

All the commentators have stressed the fact that economic evolution and demographic evolution developed in parallel. The demographic decline in France seems to have reached its lowest point in the 1930s, with a birthrate of 14.8 per 1,000 in 1935–39, though this was not exceptional at that time, France being among a group of countries where the birthrate was between 14.5 and 15.5 per thousand. The group included Austria, Belgium, Luxembourg, Norway, the United Kingdom, and Sweden as well as France. So the years between the two wars seemed to continue the previous basic trend toward a lowering of fertility: from 1870 to 1914 and from 1922 to 1939 the reproduction rate fell at a rate close to 1 percent per annum. But the fall tended to slow down rather than accelerate. In the years between the two wars, the mortality rate in France was higher than that of other countries with a similar economic structure: the rate was 15.7 per thousand in 1930–34 in France as against 10.2 in Norway and 13.2 in Belgium. That being so, population growth in the first third of the twentieth century was close to zero: in 1921 France, having lost 1.4 million people in the war and gained 1.7 million from the restoration of Alsace-Lorraine, had a population that was smaller than in 1911 because of the lack of births during the war, a loss which was not made up for by the number of immigrants (450,000). The birthrate was higher in 1920–24 than it had been in 1910–14 (19.9 as against 18.8 per thousand), and almost equal in 1925–29 (18.5 per thousand), but it collapsed in the 1930s: in 1930–34 the rate was 17.3 and in 1935–39 14.9 per thousand. As the mortality rate remained high, the population would have fallen without the influx of immigrants. The number of foreigners rose from 1 million in 1901 to 2.4 million in 1936, i.e., 5.8 percent of the total population.

The demographic recovery which occurred after the Second World War, though it really began during the war, was first and foremost the result of the birthrate's remaining relatively high:

1939–45	14.9 per thousand
1946–50	20.9 per thousand
1951–55	18.9 per thousand
1956–60	18.2 per thousand
1961–65	17.9 per thousand
1966–70	16.8 per thousand
1971	17.1 per thousand
1973	16.4 per thousand
1974	14.7 per thousand

In 1950, the fertility rate (the number of girls who might be born per generation out of 100 women aged 15–50, unaffected by the mortality rate and known to be fertile during that year), making allowances for the differing age structure, was 60 percent higher than it would have been if the trend recorded between the two wars had continued. This recovery in fertility really dates from 1935, when the rate reached its lowest level, apart from the war periods. It increased between 1935 and 1939 at a rate of 1.3 percent per annum, and in 1946–50 reached a level similar to that of the years 1895–1900 (145). It fell by 3 percent per annum from 1950 to 1953, remained stable from 1953 to 1958, and increased by 1.4 percent per annum from 1958 to 1964 (because of the rise in the marriage rate). The trend was reversed in 1964: the reproduction rate dropped by 3.3 percent per annum from 1964 to 1968, as in almost all Western European countries. But whereas in many countries, such as West Germany, Austria, Finland, Switzerland, and the Netherlands, the fall continued beyond 1968, in France, as in Italy, the United Kingdom, Norway, and Sweden the rate stabilized at its current level. The fall resumed in 1971 (3 percent in 1972, and 5 percent in 1973), and today it has reached a disturbing low. In 1974 the fertility rate was below 100. A closer study of the fertility figures points to the following conclusions:

1. Between the 1920s and the 1950s there was a great change in the size of families (see table 9.4). The difference between the couples who married at the beginning of the 1920s and those who married at the beginning of the 1950s lies chiefly in the reduction in the number of couples who had no children at all or only one child. The percentage of families with three or four children increased more than that of families with two. In the 1960s, while the first trend continued, reducing the number of couples without any children after ten years of marriage to a level close to that of physiological sterility, there were more couples with one or two children, and the proportion of couples with three children or more tended to decrease. Table 9.5 estimates the number of children produced per thousand mar-

Table 9.4 Change in Family Size between 1920s and 1950s

	Average No. of Children after 10 Years of Marriage	Percentage of Families with Number of Children as Indicated					
		0	1	2	3	4	5 or more
1920–1924	1.86	15.9	29.7	27.5	14.7	7.0	5.2
1930–1934	1.82	16.2	32.1	26.4	13.4	6.6	5.3
1940–1944	2.29	8.8	22.3	30.3	20.4	10.3	7.9
1950–1951	2.28	8.8	22.3	31.0	19.8	10.6	9.5

Table 9.5 Number of Children Per Thousand Marriages

	1950	1960
Childless	172	77
One child	203	236
Two children	214	296
Three or more	411	391

riages (couples in which the wives married under the age of 50).

Fertility in France at the beginning of the 1970s, on the whole, was above that in the neighboring European countries with the exception of Norway: the average number of offspring would be 2.47 after twenty years of marriage if the fertility level remained the same as it was in 1971. The level in France now tends to be the same as that in other European countries.

2. Occupational differences in this respect are now much less marked: the number of children after ten years of marriage for couples who got married between 1924 and 1934, and those who got married between 1940 and 1951 are given in table 9.6. These figures show the middle classes as still having the fewest children, but there is an appreciable reduction in differences between the classes.

3. Regional disparities have not disappeared. In the 1950s they continued previous tendencies; but they too have tended to decrease.

Taking the picture as a whole, the childless family has tended to disappear, the normal family is the one reduced to

Table 9.6 Average Number of Children after Ten Years of Marriage, by Occupational Group

	1920–1934	1940–1951
General average	1.80	2.30
Peasants	2.28	2.56
Employers in trade and industry	1.61	1.90
Liberal professions and higher executives	1.58	2.23
Middle management	1.40	1.95
Employees	1.56	2.04
Skilled and unskilled workers	1.85	2.40

two or three children, and occupational and regional differences have tended to grow less marked. The recent (since 1972) acceleration in the decline of fertility is a major break with previous patterns.

Mortality has been greatly reduced: it was 12 per thousand in 1960 and 10.7 per thousand in 1971. That being so, while the rate of natural population increase was 2 percent in 1921–31 and 0.5 percent in 1931–36, it was 7.5 percent in 1946–54 and 6.5 percent in both 1954–62 and 1962–68. Immigration must also be taken into account: it was interrupted between 1936 and 1946, but reached 40,000 per annum from 1946 to 1954, 155,000 from 1954 to 1961, 700,000 in 1962 (including those repatriated from Algeria), and 150,000 from 1963 to 1969. The total French population rose from 40.3 million in 1946 to 52 million in 1972, a mean annual growth rate very close to 1 percent, as against 0.2 percent between 1850 and 1910, and 0.4 percent between 1921 and 1938.

France's demographic recovery from 1942 onward contributed to her economic recovery more by its effect on demand, especially in basic investments, than by its effect on factors of production. It was only in the 1960s that the effect was felt of growth in the working population directly due to the demographic trend. Because of immigration, the population of working age increased from 26.6 million in 1920 to 28.1 million in 1930. Between 1930 and 1946 it fell to 26.7 million, almost its 1920 level. It picked up again very slowly at a rate of 0.1 percent per annum up to 1957 (27.8 million), and between 1957 and 1958 increased at a rate of 0.8 percent, mainly because of immigration, and more and more because of the rising younger generation after 1962.

The availability of what was first a stagnant and then an increased work force was reflected by various trends in the working population.

There was a long decline in the overall participation rates up to the beginning of the 1960s, followed by a stagnation:

1921	52.0 percent
1931	50.0 percent
1946	48.5 percent
1954	45.5 percent
1962	42.1 percent

1965	42.1 percent
1968	42.1 percent
1970	41.9 percent
1972	41.6 percent

This development itself results from several other tendencies: first and foremost a decline in the rate of male participation (see table 9.7), especially in old age (retirement) and in youth (school attendance). This decline suddenly accelerated after 1954. Until then the main factor had been the reduction in old age. After that there was a massive reduction in the activity of young people, as a result of wider school attendance.

Table 9.7 Male Participation Rates, by Age (in percent)

	Overall	0–14	15–24	55–64	Over 65
1921	70.0	9.0	87.0	89.0	61.0
1931	68.0	3.5	87.0	85.0	53.5
1946	66.0	2.0	81.0	81.5	48.0
1954	62.5	2.0	81.0	76.5	34.5
1968	55.0		64.0	71.5	16.0
1972	51.5		56.9	71.5	14.1
1972*	54.5		58.4	73.7	17.7

*The second figure given for 1972 includes not only those in or seeking employment but also "fringe" workers, people who worked for at least an hour during the week of the survey but do not consider themselves as "active."

The rate of female participation declined from 1921 to 1931, remained steady from 1931 to 1946, and declined again from 1946 to 1962. It was steady from 1962 to 1968, and now shows a marked upward tendency:

1921	35.5 percent
1931	33.0 percent
1946	32.0 percent
1962	27.5 percent
1968	28.0 percent
1972	29.7 percent

The decline in participation up to 1962 can be largely explained by the fact that both in the primary and in the secondary sector the percentage of women in the working population was still relatively high at the beginning of the century. Until recently, the decline in primary and secondary female activities was not compensated for by a rise in tertiary activities. The most recent surveys on employment reveal an appreciable "increase in women's contribution to economic activity." The increase in the participation rates is particularly great between the ages of 25 and 54. In 1972 the distribution of women among the different work categories was as follows:

Farmers	9.8 percent
Agricultural workers	0.5 percent
Employed in crafts and industry	1.9 percent
Shopkeepers	8.8 percent
Liberal professions and higher executives	3.6 percent
Middle management	13.6 percent
Employees	26.6 percent
Foremen	0.4 percent
Unskilled workers	21.8 percent
Domestics	12.6 percent
Others	0.4 percent

There is no exact comparison with previous situations. It may be noted however that in 1906, 43 percent of the women who were employed worked in agriculture, while in 1954 this percentage was still 36 percent. In 1906 27 percent of working women were employed in industry, and in 1954 22 percent. All this being so, the decline in female participation up to the beginning of the 1960s is due to the part played by agricultural activity in the distribution of the total working population, which explains the high percentage of women in the French working population at the beginning of the century (36 percent as against 25 percent in Great Britain, according to Malinvaud). This is partly due at least to an overestimate of female activity in this sector, which as we have said is difficult to appraise. Another factor is the importance in the French industry of the textile sector, which employed a large number of women.

So the working population evolved in the following manner (the figures are in millions):

1921	20.1
1931	20.5
1936	19.3
1946	19.4
1954	19.6
1962	19.7
1968	20.3
1971	21.2
1975	21.1

In the postwar years, it was only at the end of the 1960s that the working population reached its 1931 level again. Up to then French postwar growth had been achieved while the working population was almost stagnant. From 1949 to 1959, while the population aged 15–64 increased at a rate of 1.1 percent per annum, the working population increased at a rate of 0.1 percent. From 1955 to 1968 the mean annual natural growth in the population proceeded at a rate of 0.7 percent; that of the total population at 1.1 percent; that of the population aged 15–64 at 1 percent; that of the working population at 0.4 percent; and that of employment at a rate of 0.3 percent.

During the period 1921–73, unemployment reached high percentages only at the beginning of the 1920s (2.7 percent in 1921) and during the 1930s (5.4 percent in 1936). After the war it still remained fairly low: between 0.8 percent of the working population in 1957 (1.2 percent of wage earners) and 2.1 percent of the working population in 1968 (2.8 percent of wage earners). From 1949 to 1969 it was at an average of 1.3 percent (1.9 percent of wage earners). It was at a mean of 2 percent in 1970, 1971, and 1972. So after 1967 there was a clear upward trend in unemployment, which tended to exceed 2 percent. According to the OECD this development was probably chiefly due to "the fact that in certain branches of activity the supply of labor was inadequately adapted to the demand." In 1966 the mean monthly demand for employment was 148,000, while the mean demand for labor was 38,000 per month. In 1973 these numbers had risen to 394,000 and 252,000. They reveal the poor adaptation of supply to demand and the slow progression of unemployment even in a period of prosperity. The crisis of 1974 suddenly swelled these figures. They reached 933,000 as against 124,000 in 1976 and 1,090,000 as against 105,000 in 1977. In January 1978 the demand for employment was already very close to a million. All in all, the unemployment rate has gone from 2 percent at the beginning of the 1970s to more than 5 percent.

From the point of view of production, the stagnation of the working population up to the beginning of the 1960s was aggravated by the development within this group of "unproductive types of employment" (in financial institutions; domestic service; administration; conscripted army service). Even before the war these had increased in a slow but steady fashion, so that with this influence added to that of unemployment the percentage of productive workers fell from 87 percent in 1921 to 84 percent in 1938, the workers occupied in unproductive types of employment rising from 10.3 percent to 12.3 percent of the working population. After the war this tendency accelerated: from 1954 to 1962 their number increased at a rate of 1.2 percent, and from 1962 to 1968 at a rate of 2.3 percent. That being so, the percentage of "productive" workers fell from 83.3 percent in 1954 to 80.6 percent in 1969.

In the 1930s the reduction of activity was much more marked than the percentage of 5.4 percent of unemployed would suggest. We must also take into account underemployment: from 1930 to 1938 the index of activity really declined by one third. This is only imperfectly reflected in the statistics generally used about workhours. But for the purposes of overall analysis, we may take the indices calculated by L. A. Vincent: a drop of 14 percent from 1913 to 1929, a drop of 11 percent from 1938 to 1939, a rise of 6 percent from 1938 to 1949, and a fall of 1 percent from 1949 to 1963. This stagnation in France is in contradiction to the general evolution: in all other industrial countries there was a trend toward a reduction in working hours. This reduction did appear in France in the second half of the 1960s. From 1959 to 1971 the hours worked per week fell on an average by 0.2 percent per annum, but from

1967 to 1971 the average drop was 0.66 percent. Thus the increase in the number of people working (an average rise of 1.5 percent from 1959 to 1971 in nonagricultural branches and 1.4 percent from 1967 to 1971) was, after 1967, compensated for to the extent of 47 percent by the reduction in the working hours.

The chief fact that emerges from this analysis is that French growth after the First World War was achieved while the working and productive population stagnated and even declined during certain periods, or increased by a very small amount. So it may be supposed that growth in productivity during this period was high. But it is clear that one of the factors in this growth was the maintenance after the Second World War of relatively long working hours.

Productivity and Growth

According to L. A. Vincent the productivity of labor (output per man-hour) increased in the manner shown in table 9.8 from 1896 to 1962. Various data can be adduced concerning the evolution of productivity in the 1950s and 1960s, and all point to a mean annual growth of about 5 percent. Malinvaud's figures on Production per man-hour are given in table 9.9, and the United Nations' productivity estimates are given in table 9.10. According to OECD, the growth of production per person employed was as follows:

France (1959–68)	5.1 percent
Germany (1958–68)	4.4 percent
Great Britain (1955–68)	2.4 percent
United States (1955–68)	2.5 percent

According to INSEE, growth of apparent productivity per hour of labor in nonagricultural branches in France from 1959 to 1971 was 5 percent.

As far as industry is concerned, at least, the last years of the 1960s seem to have been marked by an acceleration of growth in productivity. In this sector, J. S. Ponsot and C.

Table 9.8 Increase in Productivity and Production of Labor, According to L. A. Vincent (in percent)

	Productivity	Production
1896–1913	+2.0	+1.7
1913–1924	+1.9	+0.6
1924–1929	+2.9	+2.8
1929–1938	+2.1	−0.5
1938–1949	+0.6	+1.1
1949–1962	+5.5	+5.1
1896–1962	+2.4	+1.9

Table 9.9 Output per Man-Hour, According to Malinvaud (mean annual rates, in percent)

	All Branches	Nonagricultural Branches
1951–1957	4.9	3.9
1957–1963	5.1	4.0
1963–1969	5.1	4.4

Table 9.10 Growth in Productivity of Labor, According to the United Nations (mean annual rates, in percent)

	1949–1959	1950–1952 to 1967–1969	1958–1960 to 1967–1969
France	4.3	4.6	4.8
Germany	5.7	5.0	4.8
United States	2.0	2.3	2.4
Great Britain	2.4	2.2	2.5

Sautter find an annual mean growth of 6.3 percent from 1959 to 1970, which rises to 10.4 percent from 1967 to 1968 and falls again to 7.2 percent from 1968 to 1970. So we may admit that there was a tendency toward accelerated growth in labor productivity, which in fact only continued a long-term trend.

There have been quite a number of econometric analyses of the growth of productivity after the Second World War. I shall confine myself here to giving the results, often divergent, of these analyses. The period before the 1950s cannot be examined in such detail. It is clear that growth in productivity is more continuous than growth in output: the 1930s were characterized by a drop of 0.5 percent in production and a growth of 2.1 percent in productivity.

This growth in productivity resulted from two factors: a transfer of large amounts of labor to highly industrialized sectors, and progress in rationalization and investment. The first will be studied in the chapter devoted to the evolution of structures. For the time being we may note that from 1906 to 1931 the number of active male workers in agriculture dropped from 5.4 to 4.4 millions. The total industrial working population during the same period rose from 6 to 7.2 million. But if one takes into account only wage earners, the figures are 3.7 and 5.44 million, i.e., an increase of 47 percent, of which only 15 percent are due to the restoration of Alsace-Lorraine. But, as we shall see in the following chapter, this increase was concentrated in certain sectors—those which were most adaptable to highly capitalistic methods of production, precisely those which best withstood the slump of the 1930s.

The first third of the twentieth century was marked by an increase in investment, more and more concentrated on the productive sectors. The overall rate of investment rose from 16.8 percent in 1913 to 20.8 percent in 1930, falling to 13.4 percent in 1938. The mean rate of growth was 16.1 percent from 1932 to 1938 as against 14.9 percent from 1896 to 1913. But the main thing is that this effort was concentrated on equipment rather than basic investment. As Malinvaud writes, "From 1906 to 1931, mechanization seems to have developed in France at a more rapid rate than in the United States and England, and at a rate close to that of Germany." Between 1906 and 1931, the total power of primary engines, including electric power stations, increased at a rate of 14 percent per year, while the power of primary engines per person employed increased at a rate of 3.2 percent and that of electric motors per person employed at a rate of 10.6 percent. Between 1906 and 1931 the number of kilowatts available per person employed in the manufacturing industries rose from 0.56 to 1.61 for wage earners as a whole, and from 0.92 to 2.01 if one takes into account only wage earners working in establishments where electric power was available. Between 1905 and 1913, investment in plant and machinery more than doubled, and it almost doubled again (up 90 percent) from 1913 to 1930.

In my opinion this increase in the availability of capital per worker was the chief cause of the increase in productivity. The methods of "rationalization," as understood in the 1920s and 1930s, presupposed intensive investment. We have already shown this in the case of the railways. But the same observation can be applied to industry as a whole. The "organization of labor" was accompanied by an increase in the amount of mechanical equipment put at the disposal of the workers.

The 1930s seem to have been characterized both by a differentiation in investment according to sector and by an overall decline in investment, which fell to a level just insuring the depreciation of the capital already invested. But here again the fall in basic investments is more marked than that in industrial equipment: the first fell by 45 percent between 1930 and 1938 (if 1913 = 100, 1930 stands at 135 and 1938 at 75), while the second fell by 33 percent (indices 184 and 123, if 1913 = 100). As we shall see, the differences among the various industrial sectors were also very marked.

The Second World War brought about the destruction of a large part of France's capital: the equivalent of 880 billion 1938 francs were destroyed, and the equivalent of 160 billion 1938 francs were lost through disinvestment. The national product in 1938 was estimated at 394 million. Out of the 880 billion francs destroyed, 393 billion represented production capital and 316 premises. If we recalculate the figures in 1954 prices, i.e., those of a year for which an estimate of the value of capital is available, we find that these losses and destructions represent 46 percent of the value of the 1944 capital. Actually, such an estimate is probably distorted by the use of inadequate price indices; but on the other hand, the extent of war losses has also probably been exaggerated.

The first French plan—the Monnet plan—gave absolute priority to reconstruction, and in particular to basic investment. It is difficult to make an accurate estimate of investment in the years 1946–48. M. Gavanier's figures are given in table 9.11.

In 1954 U.N. experts put forward estimates suggesting a rate of 21.4 percent in 1947, 19.2 percent in 1948 and 18 percent

Table 9.11 Rates of Investment from 1946 to 1948, According to M. Gavanier (in percent)

	In Current Prices	In Constant Prices (1938)
1946	15.3	21.1
1947	17.1	21.8
1948	20.2	20.4
1949	18.8	19.0

in 1949. These estimates are based on 1949 prices. So everything suggests that investment immediately after the war reached levels similar to those of the last years of the 1920s. According to official government figures, the fixed capital of companies which in 1938 represented 15.4 percent of the gross domestic product in 1949 represented only 9.3 percent in 1938.

The 1950s and 1960s have been subjected to various econometric analyses, and it may be useful to give a brief survey to show how they agree and how they differ. What the experts were looking for in the first place was an index of overall productivity, to calculate which they had first to be able to calculate an index of the growth of capital. They then tried to break down the rate of growth thus revealed into a series of quantified explanatory elements which added together made up the rate of growth. This did not preclude a search for an explanation of the growth of labor productivity alone. In either case, the first step was to define an index for the growth of capital, and this index served in the first case to measure the growth of one of the two "inputs," and in the second to provide a yardstick for the increase in one of the explanatory variables in the growth of productivity.

Data on the Growth of Capital. United Nations experts estimated the gross mean rate of investment between 1949 and 1959 at 20.1 percent and the net rate of investment at 10.2 percent. These figures are on the low side in comparison with those calculated for the fourteen other industrialized countries: the only ones that were lower were those for Belgium, the U.K., Denmark, and the United States. For the period 1959–68, the OECD puts forward a mean rate of investment, housing excluded, of 17 percent. This places France third among the countries for which the OECD calculated rates of investment at about that period (1955–68 for the other countries, and not 1959–68 as for France):

Japan	23.9 percent
Germany	18.8 percent
France	17.0 percent
Italy	14.3 percent
Great Britain	13.1 percent
United States	12.4 percent

Malinvaud, using the figures given by the French national accounts on a basis of 1956, arrives at the figures in table 9.12. So there was a tendency for investment as a whole to fall up to 1952, and for productive investment to fall up to 1954. After 1954 there was a recovery, a stabilization around the levels of 21 and 13.5 percent, then a new rise after the beginning of the 1960s. Since 1969 rates of investment have remained at a high level: the overall gross rate was 25 percent in 1969–72 and 26 percent in 1973–74.

Table 9.12 Rates of Investment at 1956 Prices, According to Malinvaud (in percent)

	Total	Productive Investment
1949	19.7	14.6
1952	17.8	11.7
1954	18.5	11.3
1957–1960	21.2	13.4
1963	22.7	14.4
1966	24.1	14.1
1969	25.0	15.0

These rates of investment correspond to high rates of increase in the volume of investment: 5.2 percent per annum from 1946 to 1951, 7 percent from 1951 to 1957, 6.5 percent from 1957 to 1963, 7 percent from 1963 to 1969, and 8.2 percent from 1969 to 1973. More recent national account figures, on the basis of 1962 prices, produce higher rates for the growth of the 1960s (see table 9.13).

Table 9.13 Growth of Investments in Terms of Volume, According to Comptabilité Nationale (in percent)

	Productive Investments	Total Investments
1959–1970	8.8*	8.7*
1959–1973	8.2*	8.4*
1966	10.2	8.9
1967	6.3	6.9
1968	6.7	6.9
1969	13.0	9.2
1970	5.6	5.2
1971	7.1	6.7
1972	9.0	7.6
1973	6.1	6.7
1974		1.3
1975		−4.3

*Annual rates.

The acceleration in the rate of growth of investments in the 1960s slowed down somewhat in 1967–68, and then in 1969 there was a "leap forward." The year 1971 again saw a high rate, though it was lower than in 1969. Many commentators admit that the 1974 crisis was introduced by this somewhat excessive growth in investment. The quasi-stagnation of 1974 and the drop in 1975 correspond to the development of the domestic product.

The rates of investment correspond to a sustained increase in the stock of capital: according to Denison, a mean annual growth rate of 4.17 percent from 1950 to 1962. Malinvaud's figures are given in table 9.14.

All in all, the rate of formation of capital accelerates throughout the period, and appears to culminate in 1969.

Total Productivity. On the basis of these figures, Denison (for the period 1950–62) and Malinvaud (for the period 1949–66) have calculated the total productivity of input for the whole of the economy. If Denison's figures are adjusted to make them comparable to those of Malinvaud (the rate of 1.24 percent per annum for the growth of inputs is corrected downward to 0.85, the contribution made to growth by improvement in the quality of labor being incorporated into the rate of growth of total

Table 9.14 Rates of Increase in Capital Stock, According to Malinvaud (in percent)

	Productive Capital	Total Capital
1949–1956	2.7	2.9
1956–1963	3.6	4.3
1949–1966	3.4	3.9
1963–1969	4.7	

productivity), growth emerges at 3.85 and 4.1 percent per annum. The first rate results from the difference between an output growth rate of 4.7 percent per annum and an input growth rate (excluding the contribution made to growth by improvement in the quality of labor) of 0.85 percent per annum. The second rate needs to be compared with a growth rate of 5.1 percent for gross domestic production. From 1913 to 1949, the growth rate of the gross domestic product seems to have been only 1.1 percent.

Denison's breakdown on the growth of total productivity is shown in table 9.15. His results emerge from arguments and calculations which Malinvaud has challenged, especially as regards economies of scale. The reader will easily find the details in Denison's book. Malinvaud is much more cautious than Denison in his quantitative estimate of the different elements of growth. Trying to break down the 5 percent per annum growth of 1951–69 he gets the results shown in table 9.16 for the productive sector alone.

The main differences between Malinvaud's calculations and Denison's concern the reduction in the age of capital. Denison does not allow it any influence: he does not sufficiently take into account the aging of capital at the beginning of the 1950s after a long period in which there was no renewal. While Malinvaud estimates at 0.6 percent the contribution made by the mobility of the working population, Denison estimates it at 0.88 percent, chiefly because he has a much higher estimate of the gains in productivity due to the exodus of farm workers. But the main cause of the difference between the two writers resides in economies of scale, to which Denison attributes a contribution of 1 percent, while Malinvaud prefers to in-

Table 9.15 Breakdown of Factors in the Productivity Analysis

Improvement in the Quality of Labor		*1.90*
Age and sex composition	0.39	
Education	0.10	
Advances of knowledge	0.76	
Changes in the lag in the application of knowledge, general efficiency, and errors and omissions	0.75	
Reduction in age of capital	0.00	
Other	0.75	
Improved Allocation of Resources		*0.95*
Contraction of agricultural inputs	0.65	
Contraction of non-agricultural self-employment	0.23	
Reduction of international trade barriers	0.07	
Economies of Scale		*1.00*
Growth of national market measured in U.S. prices	0.44	
Income elasticities	0.49	
Independent growth of local markets	0.07	
Total		*3.85*

Table 9.16 Growth in Productivity for the Productive Sector, According to Malinvaud (in percent per annum)

	1951–1969	*1913–1963*
GDP	5.0	2.1
Employment	—	−0.1
Hours of work	−0.1	−0.3
Quality of labor	0.4	0.6
Professional migration	0.6	0.3
Volume of net capital	1.1	0.5
Reduction in age of capital	0.4	—
Intensity of demand	0.1	—
Remainder	2.5	1.1

corporate it into the remainder, refusing to go beyond a maximum of 0.7 percent as a corrective.

Thus a growth rate of 5 percent per annum is explained to the extent of 0.4 percent by an improvement in the quality of labor, above all through education; 0.6 percent is explained by professional migration, which moves workers from sectors or establishments of low productivity to sectors or establishments with high productivity. The contribution of 1.1 percent made by growth in the volume of net capital combines with the effect of the reduction in the age of capital (0.4 percent). All in all, unexplained technical progress would account for 2.5 percent. As we have seen, the U.N. experts stress the fact that French investment was not exceptional, and Malinvaud even considers it "quite moderate." He explains this contradiction by the fact that productive investment formed a particularly high proportion of total investment. Moreover, after the war French equipment was so old and run-down that new investment was particularly efficient from the technical point of view. Finally, the stagnation of the working population led to investments with high capital-output ratio rather than simple extension of production capacity. This improvement, as we shall see, was the object of a systematic policy which produced numerous results: Malinvaud has analyzed the high proportion of engineers and technicians in the industrial working population (3.5 percent in 1962), expenditure on research and development, and the number of patents registered or imported. In none of these fields does he find France much more active than other industrial countries.

Two comments in conclusion:

1. The differences between Denison and Malinvaud are not mere quarrels between statisticians. Denison's analysis explains things by stressing a dual backwardness in France at the beginning of the period: a backwardness in the structures of consumption, and a backwardness in the application of labor resources ("the extent of the rural and artisan sector"); this theory is preferred to explanations relating to technical progress proper. Malinvaud, on the other hand, attributes the greater part of the changes which took place to an improvement in production techniques and management methods. Malinvaud's version makes it easier to understand why the rise in growth continued beyond the adjustment period during which, thanks to economies of scale, to the reorientation of consumption toward consumer durables, and to the rapid decline in the agricultural working population, France was

catching up on its previous backwardness. In short, the fact that France was making up a backlog may serve as explanation for the growth of the 1950s, but it cannot do so for that of the 1960s and the 1970s.

2. Perhaps Malinvaud has a tendency to minimize the effects of the growth of the stock of capital. In the 1950s, U.N. experts, analyzing the relationship between growth rates and investment rates in 22 countries, found no correlation. They did find a correlation of 0.69 when they limited their calculations to 13 industrial countries, and they concluded that an investment rate of 7 percent was necessary to maintain a constant production, and that each additional 1 percent of gross national product devoted to investment brought about an increase of 0.3 in the rate of production growth. But the correlation is far from being perfect. Nevertheless, a similar result that was reached by OECD experts for the period 1955–68 concerning the largest member countries of the OECD (the United States, Japan, France, Germany, Italy, and Great Britain): "If the rate of investment increases by, for example, 3 points, the rate of growth of the G.D.P. rises by nearly 1 point," and 85 percent of the variability in the growth rates (63 percent if Japan is excluded) can be explained statistically by the differences observed in the rates of investment. In fact, the growth of investments contributes to the growth of production not only through its direct effect on the productivity of labor, through the increased amount of equipment at the disposal of each worker, but also because "it is the means by which a large proportion of technological improvements, whether new products or new techniques, are incorporated into production."

Bibliography

Calot, G., and S. Hemery. "La fécondité diminue en France depuis quatre ans," *Economie et Statistique*, no. 1 (May 1969).

La Croissance de la Production, 1960–1980. Paris: Organization for Economic Cooperation and Development, December 1970.

Crouzet, F. "Essai de construction d'un indice annuel de la production industrielle française au XIXème siècle," *Annales*, 25, no. 1 (1970).

Translation in *Essays in French Economic History*, edited by R. Cameron. Homewood, Ill.: R. D. Irwin, 1970.

Denison, R., and J. P. Pouillier. *Why Growth Rates Differ: Postwar Experience in Nine Western Countries*. Washington, D.C.: The Brookings Institution, 1967.

Desrosieres, A. "Un découpage de l'industrie en trois secteurs," *Economie et Statistique*, no. 40 (December 1972).

Economic Growth, 1960–1970: A Mid-Decade Review of Prospects. Paris: Organization for Economic Cooperation and Development, 1970.

Enquête sur l'emploi de 1972. Collections de l'INSEE, ser. E, nos. 33–34. Paris: Institut National de la Statistique et des Etudes Economiques, November 1974.

Etudes Economiques, France. Paris: Organization for Economic Cooperation and Development, February 1973.

Fresque Historique du système productif. Collections de l'INSEE, ser. E, no. 27. Paris: Institut National de la Statistique et des Etudes Economiques, October 1974.

Guibert, et al. *La mutation industrielle de la France*. Collections de l'INSEE, ser. E, nos. 31–32. Paris: Institut National de la Statistique et des Etudes Economiques, November 1975.

Herzog, H. "Comparison des périodes d'inflation et de récession de l'économie française entre 1950 et 1965," *Etudes et Conjoncture*, March 1967.

L'industrie française en 1953. Special issue of *Etudes et Conjoncture*, 1954.

Kindelberger, C. P. *Economic Growth in France and Britain, 1851–1950*. Cambridge: Harvard University Press, 1964.

Lévy-Leboyer, M. "Croissance économique en France au XIXème siècle," *Annales, Economies, Sociétés, Civilisations*, no. 4 (July–August 1968).

Mairesse, J. *L'évaluation du capital fixe productif: Méthodes et résultats*. Collections de l'INSEE, ser. C, nos. 18–19. Paris: Institut National de la Statistique et des Etudes Economiques, 1972.

Malinvaud, E., J. J. Carre, and P. Dubois. *La croissance française*. Paris: Seuil, 1972.

Le Movement économique de la France de 1938 à 1948. Paris: Institut National de la Statistique et des Etudes Economiques, 1950.

Ponsot, J. F., and C. Sautter. "La croissance de la productivité du travail dans l'industrie s'est accélérée dès 1967, "*Economie et Statistique*, no. 13 (June 1970).

Sauvy, A. *Histoire économique de la France dans l'entre deux guerres*. Paris: Fayard, 1965–67.

Some Factors in Economic Growth in Europe during the 1950s. Geneva: United Nations, 1964.

Tableau de l'economie européenne en 1954. Geneva: United Nations, 1955. (Special study on the French economy.)

Vincent, L. A. "Evolution de la production intérieure brute en France de 1896 à 1938: Méthodes et premiers résultats," *Etudes et Conjoncture*, November 1962.

——"Population active, production et productivité dans 21 branches de l'économie française (1896–1962), "*Etudes et Conjoncture*, February 1965.

Walter, F. "Recherches sur le développement économique de la France, 1900–1955," *Cahiers de l'Institut de Science Economique Appliquée*, ser. D, no. 2 (March 1957).

Chapter Ten: Structures and Growth

Overall Data

THE OVERALL ECONOMIC growth analyzed in the preceding chapter resulted from rates of growth that were very different in different sectors. These structural changes took place rapidly in the 1920s, slowly in the 1930s, and then accelerated again in the years 1950–60, following trends already visible in the 1920s. This mobility can be examined in two ways: either by means of a study of the working population, or through an analysis of the distribution of added values.

The Working Population. Immigration and the availability of a large agricultural labor force compensated for the rigidity in working population caused by the stagnation of the population as a whole up to the 1950s. The distribution between the three sectors defined by Colin Clark, evolved in the manner set forth in table 10.1. There was a steady acceleration in the agricultural exodus. The mean rate of annual decline in the agricultural working population in 1954–62 was 3 percent, i.e., 160,000 people. The agricultural working population represented one out of two working people at the beginning of the century, one out of five in 1962. Three periods may be distinguished for the sectors which were increasing. From 1906 to 1931, the secondary sector increased slightly more quickly (14 percent) than the so-called tertiary sector. On the other hand, the periods of the slump and the war were marked by first a regression and

Table 10.1 Distribution of the Working Population, According to Clark (in percent)

	Primary Sector	Secondary Sector	Tertiary Sector
1906	43.2	29.0	26.1
1931	36.4	33.1	29.6
1946	36.0	29.5	32.5
1954	28.0	35.7	35.9
1962	21.0	39.5	39.5
1972	12.0	39.1	48.9
1975	10.1	39.1	50.8

then a stagnation in the percentage represented by the industrial working population, while the tertiary sector continued to grow (10 percent in 10 years). Later development up to the beginning of the 1960s was marked by a more rapid growth of secondary than of tertiary employments, so that in 1962 the two were equal. In the 1960s there was a much faster development of tertiary work. This was really also a continuation of a deep-seated trend which was less hampered by the slump and the war than was the trend toward growth of the industrial population. The rural exodus came to affect agricultural activity itself more and more. Above all, it affected the young men who were agricultural workers. In the three cantons in Picardy which he studied, P. Pinchemel notes that between 1911 and 1936 it was agricultural workers who left the village, whereas before it was chiefly either people who were not members of the working population or were rural artisans. Statistical analysis and sociological surveys prove that the most important reasons for leaving were economic: the difference between rural and urban salaries and the desire for stable employment. In the Loire Valley in 1934, R. Dion observed that "it was no longer, as it used to be, the victims of misfortune or those who had given up hope who formed the majority of the migrants." The exodus had entered its "terminal phase": it now affected the farmers themselves.

Value Added. Changes in the distribution of value added in terms of volume (on the basis of 1954 values) were far less marked before than after the Second World War. Between 1913 and 1929 agriculture's share in value added fell from 21.5 percent to 18.8 percent, while that of industry—including building and public works—rose from 46 to 46.7 percent. The 1930s were characterized by a revival on the part of agriculture (20.9 percent in 1938) and a decline of industry (41.4 percent in 1938). By 1949 there emerged a tendency, later to grow stronger, for agriculture to decline: the agricultural sector then represented only 17.3 percent of all values added, and industry, in the broad sense, represented 48.9 percent.

We have two sets of estimates of the distribution of value added in terms of volume in the 1950s and 1960s. Carre, Dubois, and Malinvaud have produced one for 1949, 1954, and 1963, based on 1954 prices. The other was worked out by INSEE for 1952 and 1970 on the basis of 1959 prices. While the different bases result in considerable differences in the distribution of value added, they do not alter the fundamental tendencies. Table 10.2 reproduces the two sets of figures, regrouping the first set according to the classifications used for the second. The classification of economic activity into the 11 sectors shown in the table has enabled the experts of INSEE to make comparisons which we shall use extensively in the rest of this chapter. It should also be explained why the manufacturing industries have been divided into three sectors. This division results from the analysis of 34 different criteria carried out by A. Desrosières. Desrosières distinguishes the sector of intermediate industries (iron and steel, nonferrous metals, chemicals, building materials) from the sector of equipment industries, which includes all the engineering and electrical industries, i.e., both the industries producing equipment and the industries producing consumer durables such as motorcars, household equipment, and radio and television. This classification is principally based on two criteria which factorial analysis has shown to be decisive: the destination of the product and, above all, capital intensity, i.e., the amount of equipment in relation to the amount of labor.

So France's industrial base went on widening, and the process accelerated during the 1960s. From 1952 to 1970, there was a massive increase in the proportion of value added

Table 10.2 Distribution of Values Added in Terms of Volume (in percent)

	On Basis of 1954 Prices (Malinvaud)			On Basis of 1959 Prices (INSEE)	
	1949	*1954*	*1963*	*1952*	*1972*
Agriculture	17.3	14.8	9.7	12.0	6.7
Agricultural and food industries	6.5	6.4	5.9	7.6	5.9
Energy	4.5	4.3	4.0	6.6	9.0
Intermediate industries	7.0	7.2	7.7	6.4	8.3
Equipment industries	11.9	12.6	15.1	11.4	16.1
Consumer industries	13.1	12.0	10.3	10.5	8.8
Transport and telecommunications	7.8	6.9	7.1	6.0	5.7
Building and public works	5.9	7.4	8.8	8.2	9.9
Housing services	1.5	2.7	4.4	3.3	2.8
Services	12.6	13.2	13.5	13.1	12.5
Commerce	11.9	12.5	13.5	14.9	14.3
Total	100.0	100.0	100.0	100.0	100.0
Total industry	43.0	42.5	43.0	42.5	48.1
Total of industry plus building and public works	48.9	49.9	51.8	50.7	58.0

contributed by four sectors—energy, the intermediate industries, the equipment industries, and building and public works. In three sectors there was little change: these were services, commerce, and consumer industries. Two sectors shrank enormously: agriculture and the agricultural and food industries decreased by respectively 44 percent and 22 percent. The four dynamic sectors were very closely interlinked. Highest of all came the sector dealing with industrial and domestic equipment (up 41.2 percent); it was this sector which to a large degree, through its intermediate consumption, drew energy, intermediate industry, and even building upward with it.

A comparison between the distribution of values added in constant value and the distribution of values added in current prices (see table 10.3) suggests that the differential evolution of prices was instrumental in large-scale transfers. The classification according to current values differs markedly from that which results from the distribution in terms of volume. In three quick-growing sectors there was a small growth in prices (energy, intermediate industries, equipment industries) and their contribution to current value added scarcely increased or decreased in comparison to the growth in the volume of their production: the equipment industries, where production increased at a rate of 7.4 percent per annum, increased their contribution to value added by only 10.4 percent in 20 years. In the building and public works sector there was a growth in volume and an increase in prices about 20 percent above total growth. This explains the 13 percent increase in this sector's contribution to value added. In consumer industries and trans-

Table 10.3 Distribution of Values Added in Terms of Current Price

	Values Added at Current Prices			Growth of Prices (percent)	Growth of Values Added in Volume
	1952	1972	1973	1952–1972	1952–1972
Agriculture	13.6	6.9	7.21	3.7	2.5
Agricultural and food industries	8.5	5.9	5.55	3.6	4.25
Energy	5.9	6.5	6.45	3.1	7.2
Intermediate industries	7.7	6.7	7.12	2.4	6.9
Equipment industries	12.5	13.8	13.82	2.8	7.4
Consumer industries	10.7	8.8	8.64	4.1	4.7
Housing services	2.5	5.2	5.16	10.2	4.85
Transport and telecommunications	7.7	5.7	5.65	4.3	5.2
Building and public works	10.0	11.3	10.94	5.2	6.55
Services	14.4	16.8	17.00	6.65	5.3
Commerce*	19.0	12.4	12.46	3.6*	5.35
Total	100	100	100	4.2	5.55

* The division between volume and prices is purely conventional.

port, increases in production and prices were close to the average. That being so, their contribution to value added appreciably diminished. The interplay of differential prices favored above all the services sector, where growth in terms of volume was slightly below the average, but where increases in prices were 58 percent above the average. The two "losing" sectors were agriculture and agricultural and food industries, where growth in volume and growth in prices were both below the average. All these observations serve to justify the pro-industrial slant of official French policy, since it was the industrial sectors which were both the most dynamic and the least inflationary. Prices in these sectors could be held down not only because of increased productivity but also because of the low prices of raw materials, especially energy.

The Uses of National Income

Investment. The disparities in growth between the different sectors and the consequent changes in their contribution to value added can be explained by alterations in the use of national income and in the export structure. In this connection, the figures we have are not complete until after the beginning of the 1950s. The evolution of the investment rate was examined in the preceding chapter. We shall now see what kinds of products were affected by this investment.

With the exception of the years 1926–29, during which the number of dwellings built was close to 200,000 per annum, the period 1918–52 was characterized by a serious construction shortage in France, which goes a long way toward explaining the comparative decline of the building and public works sector during the 1930s. As regards productive investments, if we take the figures in constant value put forward by J. Mairesse (on the basis of 1959 prices), we see that the proportion of the building and public works sector between 1920 and 1934 lay between 43 percent and 46 percent (43 percent in 1920–24, 46 percent from 1925–29, and 44 percent from 1930–34), mainly because of the large amount of investment in hydroelectricity. Between 1935 and 1939 it fell to 38 percent. As regards plant and machinery, in

1937 F. Battestini, analyzing the activities of industries concerned with "large-scale mechanical and electrical equipment," showed that during the 1920s the orders placed by railway companies, electrical companies, and in general by industrialists wishing "to organize their economic activity on a more rational basis" enabled turnover in this sector to exceed that of 1913 by a large margin in terms of constant value. But it fell far below this level in 1935. According to Battestini, the turnover of the large-scale equipment sector (in millions of 1928 francs) was:

1913	1,750
1926	1,660
1930	2,635
1935	1,050

Between 1952 and 1959, the number of dwellings constructed increased rapidly, rising from 90,000 per annum to 320,000. A slight drop between 1959 and 1962 (309,000) was followed by a recovery up to 1967 (422,500), by stagnation up to 1969, and by a new recovery culminating in 1972 (546,000). In 1973 the figure fell again to 500,000. As we shall see, these fluctuations were mostly linked to government policy. But the most remarkable feature of recent years has been the improvement in housing conditions: the proportion of dwellings classed as "comfortable," i.e., with an indoor lavatory and bathroom, rose from 25 percent in 1962 to 43 percent in 1968 and 61 percent in 1973. In 1959 housing represented 26.5 percent of total investment, in 1966–68 it represented 27.5 percent, and in 1973 26.2 percent. So the proportion has remained fairly stable since the beginning of the 1960s.

The nature of productive investment since the Second World War changed in favor of equipment and at the expense of construction, while at the same time the proportion of small investments increased and that of heavy investment decreased. Heavy investment is concerned with the "basic" sectors of energy, transport and telecommunications, iron and steel, and cement. Of this total, 45 percent is involved in construction, while smaller investments in other sectors account for only 20 percent of total construction investment. In terms of 1956 francs, heavy investments contributed as follows to productive investment: 56.4 percent in 1949, 45 percent in 1954, 41 percent in 1957, 45 percent again in 1959 as the result of the effort made in the public sector, and 37.5 percent in 1966. In current value, these percentages were 30 percent in 1965–67, 25 percent in 1970, and 28 percent in 1972.

Two sets of figures enable us to follow productive investment by product. The first set, by J. Mairesse, is calculated in constant value, based on 1959 prices (table 10.4). The second

Table 10.4 Breakdown of Productive Investment Expenditure, in 1959 Francs, According to Mairesse (in percent)

	Building	Equipment
1945–1949	37.0	63.0
1950–1954	33.0	67.0
1955–1959	29.4	70.6
1960–1964	28.4	71.6
1965–1969	28.7	71.3

set is based on official statistics, on the basis of 1962 prices (table 10.5). While growths in value are fairly undifferentiated in the case of the main items, the growths in volume vary much more. Productive investment in the mechanical and electrical sectors was most dynamic of all, for this kind of investment was primarily directed toward finding a way of increasing productivity.

If, in conclusion, we consider the distribution of total investment by product, we see here too a certain stability: during the 1950s, 54 to 55 percent is devoted to building, and 44 to 45 percent to the mechanical and electrical industries. A more detailed breakdown is possible for the 1960s, and is shown in table 10.6. Thus up to 1973 the growth of investment rates influenced the strong growth of building and public works and the mechanical and electrical equipment industries.

Household Consumption. Since 1950 we have been able to estimate household consumption with some accuracy. Its growth in volume progressed at a rate of 4.5 percent per annum from 1959 to 1973. But it varied considerably according to

Table 10.5 Breakdown by Sector of Productive Investment, in Current Value (in percent)

	1959	1970	1973	Annual Growth, 1959–1973	
				Volume	Value
Metal-processing	1.8	1.8	1.8	8.6	12.3
Mechanical machinery and equipment	46.7	48.0	49.1	8.9	12.9
Electrical machinery and equipment	7.6	7.6	8.0	10.0	12.9
Cars, bicycles, motorcycles	10.3	9.7	10.4	9.4	12.5
Naval and aeronautics construction	2.4	1.3	1.3	5.5	7.6
Wood, paper, and related products	0.8	0.5	0.5	5.0	8.5
Building and public works	30.4	31.1	28.9	6.9	12.1
Total	100	100	100	8.5	12.5

Table 10.6 Distribution of Investment Expenditure by Product

	1966	1969	1973
Primary metal-processing	1.1	1.3	1.2
Mechanical machinery	29.0	28.9	30.5
Electrical machinery	4.8	4.8	5.1
Cars and cycles	5.3	5.7	5.9
Naval and aeronautics construction	0.9	0.7	0.8
Wood	0.5	0.5	0.5
Building and public works	57.8	57.5	55.4
Other services	0.6	0.6	0.6

sector, following trends which were already visible in the 1950s. Food consumption increased at a rate of only 2.9 percent per annum, the rate within the sector varying from 1.8 percent for cereal products to 6.3 percent for drinks, because of the rapid growth in the consumption of mineral water and various fruit juices. Consumption in the field of clothing increased at the same rate as general growth (4.6 percent). But, as J. Niaudet writes, "It is as if the increase in incomes was used chiefly to satisfy four kinds of needs, health, housing, transport, and leisure," all in terms of "a preference for a style of living centered on the home." Expenditure on housing and the home increased in volume at an annual rate of 6.9 percent, expenditure on hygiene and pharmaceuticals increased at a rate of 8.9 percent, expenditure on transport at a rate of 8.2 percent, and expenditure on private vehicles at a rate of 10.7 percent (see table 10.7). According to V. Scardigli, director of the Centre de Recherches et de Documentation sur la Consommation (CREDOC), in a quarter of a century households had changed from a "struggle for a survival to a search for personal fulfillment" (quoted in Niaudet). This search took two main directions. First came the acquisition of durable goods, and this was linked to improvements in the home and the spread of the motorcar (see table 10.8). Before the energy crisis there were certain signs of stabilization and perhaps even saturation in this field. Especially in the towns, "demotorization" was very noticable among elderly people, while people who owned cars tended to keep the same one longer. The car market, like the market for electrical household equipment, was becoming a renewal market. On the other hand, there was no sign of

Table 10.7 Estimated Breakdown of Household Consumption, in Current Francs (in percent)

	1950	1959	1968	1973
Food and drink				
Including that consumed in restaurants and cafeterias	49.6	42.6	34.2	
Excluding that consumed in restaurants and cafeterias	48.5	37.3		26.7
Clothing	15.2	11.5	10.3	8.9
Housing and household goods	11.2	17.5	20.3	21.8
Including domestic equipment		6.6		6.5
Health care, pharmaceuticals	6.0	8.2	11.0	13.4
Transport, telecommunications	5.1	8.4	9.8	10.9
Including private vehicles	2.7	5.8	7.5	8.6
Culture, leisure	5.7	7.7	8.7	8.6
Hotels, cafes, restaurants				
Including food and drink	5.6	9.2		9.7
Excluding food and drink	4.2	4.1	5.7	
Various	3.0			

Table 10.8 Number of Appliances per Hundred Households

	1954	1972
Cars	21.0*	59
Vacuum cleaners	14.0	55
Refrigerators	7.5	83
Washing machines	8.4	60
Television sets	1.0	75

* 1953.

saturation in expenditure on hygiene and pharmaceuticals: medical consumption increased at the same rate as supply. Expenditure on leisure activities increased less rapidly than expected, but seems to have progressed swiftly in subsequent years.

Foreign Trade

The "internationalization" of the French economy has accelerated appreciably since the beginning of the 1960s. We now need to look more closely at the role played by exports in overall growth and in the growth of different sectors, and to make a brief analysis of the loss in markets represented by imports. In the 1920s, exports increased slightly faster than internal production; in the 1930s they fell much more rapidly; in the 1940s a little more rapidly; in the 1950s and 1960s they increased much faster; and this difference has had a tendency to grow. Table 10.9 gives the ratio

$$\frac{\text{export index in terms of volume}}{\text{import index in terms of volume}}$$

for different periods, and the nominal rates of increase (or decrease) of this ratio.

The trend toward internationalization was stronger during the 1920s than is indicated by the rate of 0.6 percent per annum, which was influenced by the war. J. Weiller has classified the various products in terms of their contribution to French exports during the years between the two wars. The

Table 10.9 Ratio of Exports to Import Indices (Volume) and Change Rate of Ratio

	Ratio	Rate
1896–1913	1.16	+0.8
1913–1929	1.097	+0.6
1929–1938	0.64	−4.9
1938–1949	1.063	+0.4
1949–1963	1.456	+2.7
1963–1969	1.259	+3.9

part played by food products constantly increased, rising from 12.2 percent of the total in 1913 to 15.4 percent in 1934–36. The proportion of raw materials and semi-finished goods decreased in the 1920s, increased in the 1930s (27 percent in 1913, 24.6 percent in 1928–30, and 28.4 percent in 1934–36). But among them, iron and steel products rose from 1.3 percent in 1913 to 6.9 percent in 1936, and this was not solely due to the return to France of Alsace-Lorraine. But the most interesting are manufactured products: things like cotton goods, leather, luxury and various other articles had a "regressive tendency" throughout the period, while other kinds of manufactured products expanded in the 1920s and regressed during the 1930s: these included silk goods, which fell from 7.1 percent in 1928–30 to 3.2 percent in 1934–36, woolen goods (4 percent and 1.2 percent at the same dates), and clothing. The products which increased their share in exports both in the 1920s and in the 1930s were machinery, tools and other metal articles, chemicals, and yarns. These figures are a vivid reflection of what happened between the wars: the traditional exporting industries found their outlets brilliantly expanded during the 1920s, but they were the chief victims of the shutdown of world trade during the 1930s. The new industries also suffered a good deal, but they put up a better resistance.

The reconstruction of the economy after 1945 took place in a protectionist and colonial atmosphere. Already in the 1920s, and especially in the 1930s, the colonies had played an increasing part in French exports, as they had done in English exports at the same period: the figures were 13 percent in 1913, 18.5 percent in 1928–30, and 31.9 percent in 1934–36. This same percentage—about a third—occurs again just before the collapse of the "Union Francąise" in the middle of the 1950s. But then industrial exports to the union represented only 6.6 percent of production. The products most involved were sugar (21 percent), cotton cloth (16 percent), and silk goods (14 percent). So the "colonial" element in the French economy before the Common Market should not be overestimated. The 1957 Treaty of Admission was not only accepted but also desired by the most dynamic groups of French industrialists. Davezac, chairman of the Committee of Manufacturers of Electrical Equipment, considered French industry to be "intrinsically competitive." Progress toward modernization in many sectors since 1945 was such that, according to C. Gabet, "large-scale, dynamic industry . . . was beginning to find the French market too narrow as regards capacity for accumulating capital and developing production" (quoted in Guibert et al). Most farmers too wanted this opening-up of markets, the success of which was favored, at least up to 1962, by the devaluation of 1959. For it was undoubtedly a success, even if, as we shall see, this overall judgement needs to be qualified. There were really three phases in this "internationalization": a brilliant start between 1958 and 1962, considerable difficulties between 1962 and 1970, and a new start after 1970.

Between 1959 and 1972, in all sectors, the ratio exports/production increased. But differences between sectors were marked. The evolution of these ratios reflects and partly explains changes in structure which occurred during this period: in two sectors—agriculture and the equipment industries—the ratio showed a strong increase, rising from 3.9 percent to 13.8 percent in agriculture, and from 18.5 percent to 26 percent in the equipment industries. In the other industrial sectors (agricultural and food industries, intermediate industries, and consumer industries), ratios stagnated and even regressed up to 1967–68, and subsequently increased. Overall, they rose from 6.3 percent to 10.3 percent in agricultural and food industries; from 23.4 percent to 26.7 percent in intermediate industries; and from 18.6 percent to 20 percent in consumer industries. In order to interpret the meaning of these ratios correctly, we must remember that exports increased between 1959 and 1972 at a rate of 12.2 percent per annum, while value added increased at a rate of 10.5 percent.

The "internationalization" of French sales was accompanied by a profound change in the orientation of both state and business policies. Whereas in the 1950s the French economy was directed toward trying to attain internal coherence, in the 1960s it was directed toward external competitiveness. This change explains not only the alteration in the energy policy, but also many other French choices in industrial policy during the 1960s. With the exception of sectors like computers and the arms industry proper, which are involved with military independence, the desire for self-sufficiency gave way to a desire to develop those sectors most likely to reduce the overall costs of French industry and the sectors in which French techniques were capable of rivaling foreign techniques on foreign markets or in France itself.

For, parallel to the development of exports, French producers had to face increased competition on their own markets. Sectors like services and building and public works are naturally protected from international competition. But the gradual, and after 1968 total, liberalization of industrial exchanges brought about a marked increase in imports. Between 1959 and 1972 the ratio imports/domestic production rose from 18 percent to 31 percent in the case of intermediate products, and from 7.6 percent to 21.1 percent in the case of equipment. So French producers had to call more and more on foreign producers for intermediate goods. This dependence greatly increased in the case of the chemical industries, paper, the primary processing of metal, large-scale equipment (which imported 18.3 percent of its intermediate requirements), electrical equipment (12.9 percent), and electronic equipment (15.6 percent). After the opening-up of frontiers, industries producing consumer goods were subjected to strong pressure from their competitors: their trade balance, which thanks to the colonial market had been strongly positive during the 1950s, had become negative by 1969. The ratio imports/production rose from 11 percent to 19 percent. So industrial growth was accompanied by two parallel movements: increased dependence on foreign markets both for outlets and for supplies.

Bibliography

Battestini, F. *L'industrie française du gros matériel mécanique et électrique.* Paris: Librairie Générale de Droit et de Jurisprudence, 1937.

Dion, R. *Le val de Loire.* Tours: Arrault, 1934.

Desrosieres, A. "Un découpage de l'industrie en trois secteurs," *Economie et Statistique,* no. 40 (December 1972).

Fresque historique du système productif. Collections de l'INSEE ser. E, no. 27. Paris: Institut National de la Statistique et des Etudes Economiques, October 1974.

Guibert, et al. *La mutation industrielle de la France.* Collections de l'INSEE, ser. E, no. 27. Paris: INSEE, 1974.

Herzog, P. "Comparaison des périodes d'inflation et de récession de l'économie française entre 1950 et 1965." *Etudes et Conjoncture,* March 1967.

Mairesse, J. *L'évaluation du capital fixe productif: Méthodes et résultats.* Collections de l'INSEE, ser. C, nos. 18–19. Paris: Institut National de la Statistique et des Etudes Economiques, November 1972.

Malinvaud, E., J. J. Carre, and P. Dubois. *La croissance française.* Paris: Seuil, 1972.

Niaudet, J. "L'évolution de la consommation des ménages de 1959 à 1968," *Annales du Centre de Recherches et de Documentation sur la Consommation,* nos. 2–3 (1970).

Pinchemel, P. *Structures sociales et dépopulation rurale dans les campagnes de Picardie de 1836 à 1936.* Paris: A. Colin, 1957.

Szokoloczy Syllaba, J. *Les organisations professionnelles françaises et le marché commun.* Paris: A. Colin, 1965.

Vincent, L. A. "Evolution de la production intérieure brute en France de 1896 à 1938: Méthodes et premiers résultats," *Etudes et Conjoncture,* November 1962.

Vincent, L. A. "Population active, production et productivité dans 21 branches de l'économie française (1896–1962)," *Etudes et Conjoncture,* February 1965.

Weiller, J. "Echanges extérieurs et politique commerciale de la France depuis 1870," *Cahiers de l'Institut de Science Economique Appliquée,* ser. P, nos. 16–17.

Chapter Eleven: Analysis of Some Sectors

IT IS NOT possible within the framework of this book to examine the evolution of every aspect of the French system of production. We have chosen to concentrate on four sectors: agriculture, energy, industry, and transport.

Agriculture

As F. Walter has said, between 1920 and 1929, "while French industry was making great strides, agriculture was only making good its losses." But by 1925–29, agriculture had again reached the same level of production as in 1910–13. The slump of the 1930s did not halt the growth in agricultural production and, overall, between 1920 and 1938, mean annual growth was 1.2 percent. Changes in the structure of agricultural production were small—smaller, it seems to me, than during the years leading up to the First World War. The area given over to cultivation of cereals fell from 13.5 million hectares in 1911 to 10.6 million in 1936, while fodder land rose from 15.3 million hectares to 17.2 million.

This very slow growth in production, together with the drop in the agricultural working population, means that there was an increase in agricultural productivity, and this accelerated during the slump years (1.4 percent per annum from 1913 to 1929, and 2.5 percent from 1929 to 1938). But the growth in agricultural production overall was very slight if we take into account the low technological level of French agriculture. This slowness is explained by the depressed state of world and domestic agricultural markets in the 1920s, which was reflected in a sustained deterioration in the terms of trade (stated as the ratio of industrial to agricultural prices), which reached the lowest point in 1931–35. It was the growing scarcity of agricultural labor which forced those who still remained to increase their yield. But this only compensated for the exodus itself. Some tendencies toward expansion continued, and increases in yield per hectare were fairly low (see table 11.1). Regional differences grew more marked: if you divide France into seven regions (north, west, center, east, Massif Central, southwest, south-southwest), the difference between the region with the lowest yield of wheat (the southwest in 1909–13, the Massif Central in 1929–38) and the region with the highest yield (the north) rose from 8.9 quintals to 12.3.

This disappointing development is to be explained above all by the lack of dynamism in the agricultural market. French agriculture had fallen back on a domestic market that was less and less elastic. The collapse of prices led to an extension of subsidies to cover the markets in cereals, wine, and sugar. For the first, the Popular Front created the Office National Interprofessional des Céreales, responsible for the marketing of all cereal products. Thus, while some prices were regulated—though in very different ways and to different degrees—others were entirely free. This dualism survived the war. The whole subsidy system was reorganized between 1953 and 1960, the date when the Fond d'Orientation et de Régularisation des Produits Agricoles (FORPA) was created. FORPA's job is to maintain the prices of cereals, rice, dairy products, and beef through a system of price guarantees, and it has survived the Common Market. The setting-up of the Common Market and

Table 11.1 Average Yields per Hectare for Some Agricultural Products (in quintals)

	1909–1913	1932–1936
Wheat	13.21	15.91
Potatoes	85.70	110.00
Industrial sugar beet	263.51	281.32

the establishment of a more coherent policy of agricultural prices have been the driving forces behind the progress achieved by French agriculture since the war.

The results have been remarkable. In 1948–50 the 1938 level of production was almost reached again. According to official figures, the growth in the volume of agricultural production advanced at a rate of 2.5 percent per annum between 1952 and 1972 (up 64 percent); and this growth tended to accelerate. It was much more marked for vegetable than for animal products. The difference was chiefly due to the swift growth in cereal production, which increased at a rate of 7 percent per annum, while wine production stagnated and fruit and vegetable production increased at a rate of 2 percent per annum. Productivity increased at a rate of 6 percent during the same period, owing to a large increase in the consumption of intermediate goods, which in 1949 represented 20 percent of value added as against 34 percent in 1972. Chiefly concerned were fertilizer (up 7.3 percent per annum), cattle feed, and expenditure on equipment maintenance. (To take only one example, the number of tractors rose from 30,000 in 1938 to 150,000 in 1950 and 1,300,000 in 1970.) Productive fixed capital per capita increased at a rate of 8.3 percent per annum. This growth was probably excessive in relation to the size of the farms: their smallness resulted in underemployment of capital and brought the farmers unduly into debt. It is not difficult to see why, with this increase in intermediate expenditure and capital, overall productivity increased by only 2.7 percent per annum between 1959 and 1969. But technical progress was not limited to capitalistic expansion and an increase in the consumption of intermediate products. Immediately after the war there were major changes in agricultural methods, thanks to the "fodder revolution," which resulted in the spread of cultivated grazing. By the end of the 1960s, two-thirds of the cows in France were being fertilized by means of artificial insemination. Extensive maize-growing was made possible by the adoption of hybrid maize in the 1950s.

Overall, agricultural prices increased less rapidly between 1952 and 1972 (up 3.7 percent per annum) than prices in the economy as a whole. In fact, prices increased all the more

Table 11.2 Evolution of Agricultural Accounts, 1954–1972 (in billions of francs)

	1954	1960	1972
Production	24.7	38.3	90.9
Intermediate consumption	5.2	9.8	30.7
Value added	19.5	28.5	60.2
Subsidies	0.1	0.2	1.6
Resources	19.6	28.7	61.8
Charges	4.8	6.7	16.2
Gross result	14.8	22.0	45.6

rapidly because production increased more slowly, i.e., the prices of vegetable products increased less than prices of animal products (up 3.1 percent per annum from 1944 to 1972 for vegetable products and 4.7 percent for animal products). The result of all these factors was a growth in farmers' income which was more or less the same as the increase in the income of wage earners. In fact, the gross results for farming rose from 14.8 billion francs in 1954 to 45.6 billion in 1972 (see table 11.2). It was only the decline in the number of farmers which made possible the parallel growth in the income of farmers and wage earners.

Energy

The first modernization and equipment plan, the "Monnet Plan," adopted in 1946, was a decisive turning point in the history of energy in France. Far from aiming at restoring what had gone before, the plan aimed at renovating the "infrastructures" or "key industries," to use the expressions then fashionable, so as to lay the foundations for a true industrialization of France. Energy was first among these key industries. The nationalization of coal and electricity, which we shall examine later, was justified by the needs of reconstruction. The object was to break with what was considered a "Malthusian" tradition as regards growth rate in the production of energy. But as regards choices between different sources of energy, the decisive changes did not occur until later.

The sovereignty of coal was not challenged until after the Second World War. In 1939 a group of graduates of the École Polytechnique declared that "the first object of any French energy policy must be to increase coal production." But there were many obstacles to the modernization of coal production: geological conditions were less and less favorable, and, except in Lorraine, where exploitation was more recent, the size of the workings, suitable for the techniques of the 1850s, were not adapted to the techniques of the 1920s. Yields were falling: between 1924 and 1929 productivity per hour of labor remained unchanged, while production increased by 4.1 percent. Between 1929 and 1938, productivity increased by 1.6 percent per annum, but production fell at the same rate. The Monnet Plan of 1946, which gave priority to coal, had to be revised downwards: instead of the 65 million tons aimed at in 1950, it had to be content with 52.5 million. In the four years between 1946 and 1950, France had gone from having too little coal to having too much.

In 1938, hydroelectric power represented 35.8 percent of France's electrical capacity. The first plan favored hydroelectric power, in accordance with a desire to use national sources of energy. But the bad drought of 1949 showed the disadvantages of this choice at a time when technical progress in thermal electricity, which had already been considerable between the two wars, gave the latter source an undeniable advantage as far as price was concerned. The growth of production of electricity in France had been chiefly linked to its industrial uses. In 1938 the consumption of electricity in France for domestic purposes was appreciably below what it was in other industrial states (54 kilowatt hours per capita as against 187 in Great Britain). But in 1946 a new tendency emerged: between 1946 and 1951 the production of electricity increased by an average of 10 percent per annum as against 3 percent in the 1930s.

The 1914 war had shown the necessity of working out a "national" oil policy covering both supplies of crude oil and refining. The Compagnie Française des Pétroles, founded in 1924, managed the French holding (23.75 percent) in the Iraq Petroleum Company. By 1936 oil from Iraq covered 40 percent of France's needs. An attempt was made, timid up to 1939 and very active after 1940, to discover sources of supply in France and the colonies: these efforts resulted in the discovery of the deposits at St. Marcet and Lacq in the southwest of France, and in Algerian deposits at the beginning of the 1950s. A law of 1928 strengthened the very old but hitherto ineffective legislation favoring oil refining in France itself. The 1928 law also aimed at reserving for French capital at least a part of the distribution and refining of oil. Import and refining were divided up among the different groups according to quotas fixed for three years in the case of distribution and for twenty years in the case of refining. This system amounted, in fact, to the formation of a cartel. Mainland France's refining capacity was raised from 8 million tons per annum in 1938 to 13 million in 1949. In this sector the forecasts of the first plan were exceeded.

Between 1950 and 1970, consumption of energy increased by 250 percent, and this growth tended to accelerate: annual growth was 4 percent in the 1950s and 5.3 percent in the 1960s. Between 1969 and 1972 it reached 5.8 percent. Industrial uses of energy, followed by domestic uses, tended to increase more rapidly than other applications (see table 11.3). Household consumption of energy had gradually become the most dynamic factor. The sector of consumption described as "residential and tertiary" (covering needs of households and service companies), which does not exactly correspond to the "household" sector, represented 29 percent in 1962 and nearly 37 percent in 1972 of total consumption.

Table 11.3 Total Consumption of Energy and Consumption of Electricity (in percent)

	1952		1960		1968	
	Total Energy	Electricity	Total Energy	Electricity	Total Energy	Electricity
Iron and steel	14.9	10.0	15.6	10.2	10.8	8.3
Industry	35.2	65.4	36.1	64.4	40.1	57.9
Household uses	28.6	17.4	28.9	19.1	30.1	28.3
Transport	21.3	7.2	19.3	6.3	19.0	5.5

The contrast between the 1950s and the 1960s is even more marked if one considers the energy sources used. Coal production increased up to 1958 (60 million tons). But between 1950 and 1960 the proportion contributed by coal to the total consumption of energy fell from 74 percent to 54 percent. The "Jeanneney Plan" was adopted in 1959: it aimed at making French coalfields "competitive" by gradually reducing production by closing mines which were losing too much money. Another plan, adopted in 1963 after the miners' strike, aimed at slowing down the closures, and the estimates both of this plan and the "Bettencourt Plan" of 1968 were largely exceeded: the fall in production was much stronger than they had foreseen. From 1959 to 1973 the drop in production as a whole was 57 percent. An important factor here was lack of confidence in the mining sector. Coal's share in France's energy balance sheet fell to 23 percent in 1971, and 16 percent was the figure forecast for 1975, 16.6 percent the figure realized.

The new energy policy inaugurated by the Jeanneney Plan, which was set back only briefly by the Suez War, preferred to rely on the competitiveness of the general economy, insured by supplies of cheap energy, rather than on "national" sources which would have made France independent in the matter of energy. "Security in the matter of energy," declared the Economic Council in 1959, "should not entail the insecurity of our economy as a whole in international competition." A policy based on cost comparisons and leaving out of account "supply security," as the leaders of the coal industry demanded, doomed the coal industry, where 60 percent of expenditure was on labor. It has been calculated that only a rise of 10 percent per annum in productivity could have enabled coal to compete with oil. Given the new situation in the energy market after the Yom Kippur War, it was decided to slow down the phasing-out of coal: a production of 20 million tons is forecast for 1980 instead of 13 million.

The decline of coal was the result of the continuous fall in the price of petroleum products. In 1959, a thermal unit of heavy fuel cost 1.96 centimes in 1969 prices, while a thermal unit of coal cost 1.43 centimes. In 1969 the two prices were 1.07 and 1.00. During that period techniques for using fuel oil made great progress, and that as much as the price factor accounted for the more generalized use of fuel oil. Petroleum accounted for 18 percent of primary needs in 1950, 30 percent in 1960 and 67 percent in 1973. Up to the Yom Kippur War, France, like the rest of Europe, lived in an artificial climate created by an "overabundance" of energy. In this context, French oil policy was remarkably efficient. It resulted in refining capacity which was in excess of France's own needs by 150 million tons in 1973, as against 11.5 million tons in 1950. In the 1950s, foreign groups had come to take a much larger share in both refining and distribution. The balance was restored under the Fifth Republic, by means of a stricter definition of quotas and the reorganization of the state petroleum sector through the creation in 1960 of the Union Générale des Pétroles and in December 1965 of the Entreprise de Recherches et d'Activités Pétrolières (ERAP), which included in one state company the Bureau de Récherches de Pétrole and the Régie Autonome des Pétroles. The Bureau de Récherches de Pétrole dated from 1945, and the Régie Autonome des Pétroles from 1940. In the 1950s both had organized prospecting for crude oil in France and the colonies, and they had gradually become the leaders of large groups. At the beginning of the 1960s, France, to insure supplies of crude oil, embarked on a policy of direct negotiation between states, not limited to Algeria. In this way France managed to maintain her holding of 23.75 percent of Iraq oil after its nationalization.

The quadrupling of the price of oil suddenly revealed to French public opinion the country's "dependence" in the matter of energy. The amount of primary energy imported was 49.6 percent in 1963, 66.5 percent in 1970, and 76.3 percent in 1973, as against 50 percent in Germany and 47 percent in Great Britain. The first reaction of French officials was to try to bring about a rapid development of "national" sources. But the margin for maneuver was narrow, both because of the distribution of France's energy consumption and the limited possibilities for increasing supplies from French sources (see table 11.4). As we have said before, regarding coal, it was only possible to try to slow down the decline of the mines. Among the other forms of energy, only hydroelectric and nuclear

Table 11.4 Breakdown of Energy Consumption by Source (in percent)

	1950	1960	1968	1972	1975
Solid Fuels	74.0	54.0	32.0	19.1	16.6
Petroleum products	18.0	30.0	51.0	65.0	62.1
Primary gases	0.5	3.5	6.0	8.3	10.6
Hydroelectric power	7.5	12.5	10.5	6.6 }	10.7
Nuclear power			0.5	1.9 }	
	100	100	100	100	100

power were, strictly speaking, French. French production of gas in 1972 covered only 54 percent of the country's needs. Work began in the St. Marcet deposit in 1942, and in the Lacq deposit in 1957. The distribution network of natural gas then became national. But France's domestic resources were in fact limited, and from 1967 onward she had to obtain gas from Holland and Algeria and slow down the industrial and household use of natural gas. The government has sought new sources of hydroelectricity. But reserves, in any case, are limited.

The development of nuclear power has been subjected to highly contradictory impulses at various times, because of the opposition between those who tried to set up a "national" system and those who were chiefly concerned with the problems of cost and easy exploitation. In 1969 Bertrand Goldschmidt, director of the Commisariat a l'Énergie Atomique (CEA), observed: "It was the [technical] circumstances prevailing in 1951 which determined, without possible alternative, the choice of metallic natural uranium, graphite, and gas cooling," i.e., the elements of what afterward came to be called the "French system." In 1955 the first French program was announced for the building of nuclear power stations, and cooperation between Electricité de France (EDF) and the CEA was inaugurated. The construction of four EDF power stations was decided on in 1957 in the context of the Fourth Plan, which provided for experiment with other systems beside the French system. Implementation of the plan encountered such technical difficulties that the choice of the "French system" was challenged from 1965 on, while the spectacular drop in the price of fuel oil aroused more and more substantial doubts about the "competitiveness" of nuclear power. The last years of the 1960s were marked by a veritable nuclear power crisis in France, everyone holding everyone else responsible for the various setbacks. In November 1969 it was decided to launch, during the Sixth Plan, "a program of diversification in respect of several high-power plants using enriched uranium as fuel." And when in March 1974, to overcome the energy crisis, it was decided to begin six nuclear plants in 1974 and seven in 1975, and to pursue the matter with the same vigor thereafter, all the plants involved were "light water" plants, using American patents the rights to which had been acquired by two French companies (the Compagnie Générale d'Électricité—CGE—in the case of the General Electric patent and Framatone in the case of the Westinghouse patent). So, just as she seemed about to achieve success, France abandoned a technology which she had almost succeeded in perfecting. All hopes for the future were now centered on the technique of breeder reactors, a field in which France has made considerable advances.

In all, the contribution of the energy sector to growth was decisive: energy performed better than any other sector. Between 1952 and 1972 its growth in volume was 7.2 percent per annum, while its growth in visible productivity was 8.8 percent. It was the only sector which at the turn of the sixties showed an accelerated increase in the productivity of both labor and capital. Between 1959 and 1969, productivity per hour in this sector increased at a rate of 10.1 percent per annum, and total productivity of all factors at a rate of 4.7 percent. But in 1969 the economic return on fixed assets was, at 8 percent, the lowest in all the sectors. For these exceptional performances were accompanied by a rise in prices which was much lower than the general rise (3.1 percent as against 4.3 percent). The energy sector has always been subjected either to a régime of prices imposed by the state in the case of nationalized enterprises or to a régime of regulated prices with unbridled competition in the case of "heavy" petroleum products. In both cases the result has been a drop in real value of prices. But because of these different price régimes, the problems of financing present themselves, as we shall see, in very different terms according to the subsector involved.

Industries

The Working Population. In this sector it is possible to make a comparatively accurate analysis of the evolution of the distribution of the working population, and this analysis is presented in table 11.5. Essentially, the decline in the proportion of the labor force working in the textile, clothing, and leather industries from 42.4 percent to 13 percent is compensated for by its rise in the engineering industries from 12.9 percent to 26.1 percent, in the chemical industries from 1.6 percent to 5.4 percent, and in building and public works from 14.3 percent to 25.5 percent. This trend breaks down into three phases: between 1913 and 1929 an increase of 710,000 in the number of people working in industry was the result of a fall of 550,000 in the textile-clothing-leather sector and a rise of 1,260,000 in the other sectors. In this same period there was an increase of 10.7 percent in the number of people working in industry, and an increase of 32.5 percent in the number of people working in all sectors other than textiles-clothing-leather. Between 1929 and 1949, a drop of 800,000 in the working

Table 11.5 Distribution of the Industrial Working Population, According to the Figures of L. A. Vincent and E. Malinvaud (in percent)

	1913	1929	1938	1949	1954	1968
Agricultural and food industries	7.8	7.4	9.6	9.2	8.9	8.0
Solid mineral fuels, gas	3.6	4.6	4.6	4.7	3.8	1.9
Electrictiy, water	0.4	0.8	1.1	1.2	1.3	1.5
Petroleum and motor fuel		0.3	0.5	0.6	0.7	1.0
Construction materials	4.3	4.7	4.1	3.6	3.6	3.7
Metallurgy	1.8	3.1	3.3	3.9	3.6	3.1
Engineering industries	12.8	18.9	19.1	22.0	22.6	26.1
Chemical industries	1.6	2.8	3.5	4.2	4.5	5.4
Textiles, clothing, leather	42.4	30.9	29.7	24.1	20.8	13.0
Various industries	10.9	11.4	11.5	11.1	11.0	10.8
Building, public works	14.3	15.1	12.8	15.4	19.2	25.5
Industrial working population in thousands	6,720	7,430		6,630		7,850

industrial population breaks down into a drop of 1,050,000 people in various sectors, including 700,000 in the textile-clothing-leather sector, and a rise of 250,000 in other sectors. One can see why during or at the end of this period comments were made about the "rigidity" of the structures of the working population. Between 1949 and 1968 there was a rise of 1,220,000 (18.4 percent). In fact, there was a fall of 760,000 divided between three sectors (160,000 in mineral fuels; 20,000 in metallurgy; and 580,000 in textiles-clothing-leather). The rising sectors therefore increased by nearly 2 million people (1,980,000), i.e., an increase between 1949 and 1968 of 44.4 percent. It is clear that mobility was not much greater in 1949–68 than it had been in 1913–29: the expanding sectors increased by a mean annual figure of 104,000 during the years following the Second World War, as against 78,700 between 1913 and 1929.

A more recent change in mobility has been caused chiefly by a change between the habits of parents and children. The most recent surveys made by INSEE show a tendency toward an increase in changes of activity during working life: between 1965 and 1970, 17.1 percent of the working population changed sector and 33 percent changed from one establishment to another, as against 13 percent and 20 percent between 1959 and 1965. Those who drew up the Fifth Plan declared that "professional mobility of labor" was "one of the necessary conditions for at once expanding the economy and maintaining stability."

Production. In the 1920s there were accelerated changes in the structure of industry. During this period it was the engineering industries which were most dynamic: their share in industrial value added in constant prices rose from 18 percent in 1913 to 25 percent in 1929, whereas the share of textiles, clothing, and leather fell from 40 percent to 28 percent. The engineering industries were the chief constituents of the sector which A. Desrosières has called "the equipment industries," a sector which between 1952 and 1972 showed the most rapid growth in volume. The 1920s were a dress rehearsal for the 1950s and 1960s (this evolution and its causes will be examined in detail below). During the 1930s, France's industrial decline was not uniform. In a few sectors there was steady growth between 1929 and 1939: these were the new sources of energy; rubber, which increased only slightly (1.1 percent per annum); paper and cardboard (5.1 percent per annum); and the chemical industries, which scarcely increased at all (up 0.6 percent per annum). In all other industrial sectors there was a decline in production, except in the case of the agricultural and food industries, which, thanks to the extension of pastures, were able to remain steady. The decline varied between 0.6 percent (gas) and 6.2 percent (glass, construction materials). The decline affected both the sectors which had had slow growth and those which had had swift growth in the 1920s, so that, from the industrial point of view, the 1930s had a dual significance: they confirmed the decline of "traditional" hand industries, in which entire subsectors collapsed, and they also marked a pause in France's evolution toward intensive industrialization. It is rather surprising to note that it was the most capitalistic sectors, such as metallurgy and the engineering industries, which, in this period of regression, had most difficulty in keeping up productivity. The opposite happened in the case of economies of scale (see table 11.6).

The first French plan, the "Monnet Plan," gave absolute priority to "key" or "basic" sectors: transport, energy, and iron, steel, and cement. Other industrial sectors rose quite soon to a level of activity comparable to that of the previous period; since then, however, an appreciable difference has emerged between the intermediate industries and the equipment industries on the one hand, which as early as 1949 reached and exceeded their 1929 level, and on the other hand the consumer industries, which only

Table 11.6 Comparison of Evolution of Production with Evolution of Productivity, 1929–1939, According to L. A. Vincent (in percent change per annum)

	Production	*Production per Hour*
Solid mineral fuels	−1.6	+1.6
Metal production	−4.5	−1.9
Metal processing	−4.4	−1.4
Building and public works	−4.5	+0.3
Textiles	−2.0	+3.5
Clothing	−0.9	+3.7

with difficulty reached their 1938 level at the same period (see table 11.7). This difference in evolution subsequently became more marked. The intermediate and equipment industries, with annual rates of 6.9 percent and 7.4 percent, showed appreciably

Table 11.7 Some Comparative Production Indices (1938 = 100)

	1929	1949	1952
Motorcars	107	240	406
Tractors	107	990	
Chemical industries	113	126	154
Rubber	90	155	194
Paper, cardboard	63	100	
Textiles	120	101	106
Leather	117	67	79

more growth between 1952 and 1972 than the food industries (4.25 percent) and the consumer industries (4.7 percent). This more rapid growth was accompanied by a lesser rise in prices: 2.4 percent and 2.8 percent in the intermediate and equipment industries and 3.6 percent and 4.1 percent in the food and consumer industries. From the point of view of productivity, the classification is different: the equipment industries achieved their highest level of growth in overall productivity between 1959 and 1969, with a rate of 3 percent; the intermediate and consumer industries reached a level close to this, with 2.2 percent and 2.4 percent; while the food industries had a rate of only 1.1 percent. These differences are due to three factors: the productivity per hour of labor increased much less rapidly (up 4.2 percent per annum) in the food industries than in the three others (6 to 6.4 percent per annum); on the other hand the productivity of capital consumed fell in all the industrial sectors (down 1.1 percent in the food industries, 1.3 percent in the consumer industries, and 1.8 percent in the intermediate industries), except the equipment industries (up 0.9 percent). The data in the above paragraph are set out in table 11.8.

Industry was really the chief driving force behind this momentum for growth: since productivity increased much faster than prices, "part of the surplus created through the means of production was transferred to less efficient branches"

Table 11.8 Some Data on Productivity in Various Sectors (in percent per annum)

| | Growth Rates, 1952–72 | | | |
	Agriculture and Food	Consumer	Semifinished Goods	Plant and Machinery
Production	4.5	4.7	6.9	7.4
Prices	3.6	4.1	2.4	2.8
Visible productivity of labor	4.4	6.2	6.7	5.7
Value added per unit of fixed capital	0.8	0.5	1.3	1.5
Productive fixed capital per capita	3.9	5.9	5.5	4.2
	Growth Rates, 1959–69			
Total productivity of factors	1.1	2.4	2.2	3.0
Productivity per hour of labor	4.2	6.0	6.4	6.2
Productivity of capital consumed	−1.1	−1.3	−1.8	0.9
Productivity of intermediate goods	0.5	−1.5	−0.3	0.1

(INSEE). These transfers were made in two ways: either through sales of intermediate consumer goods or through investment sales (see table 11.9). Development in service activities could only come about through an improvement in the productivity of the chief sectors producing physical goods. The INSEE experts concluded: "A picture emerges of surpluses descending from upstream (agriculture, energy, basic industries) downward (to the engineering and electrical industries)." They go on: "But obviously the recent oil crisis disturbs this picture," because the high surpluses in the energy sector were linked to low oil prices on the world markets.

Describing the main orientations of the various sectors of French industry, even as briefly as we have already done in the case of energy, would be beyond the scope of this book. Some of these orientations, because they involved choices which were not merely economic, were decided directly by the state, as in the case of nuclear energy. This happened also with aeronautics and with computers (the "computer plan" of 1966).

Table 11.9 Transfers of Surplus Among Sectors, 1959–1969 (in millions of francs 1962)

Through Sales of Intermediate Goods	
Agriculture	712
Agricultural and food industries	
Equipment industries	
Energy	4,816
Consumer industries	
Building and public works	
Intermediate industries	7,689
Services	
Commerce	
Total	13,217
Through Relative Prices on Gross Formation of Fixed Capital	
Intermediate industries	−124
Capital goods industries	−6,367
Consumer goods industries	−41
Building and public works	+553
Services	+33

But most sectors were affected by the government only indirectly, through its general economic policy, and they had to adapt themselves to the changing conditions of a market which they made more and more effort to control.

The data given in table 11.9 were overall figures. A brief breakdown follows, based largely on information supplied by Ministry of Industry and Research surveys.

1. The contribution of agricultural and food industries to value added stagnated. But this aggregate stagnation is compounded from some very different patterns. Some kinds of production were extremely dynamic, either because of foreign outlets, as in the case of white sugar, or because of an increase in home consumption, as with canning, frozen and dehydrated foods, nonalcoholic drinks, and animal foods. The increased production of animal foods was a result of developments in stock-rearing, which in its more advanced forms depended less and less on actual farming products. On the other hand, some kinds of production increased only slowly, stagnated, or regressed. Growth in production of oils and fats was limited by a leveling-off in per capita consumption, but there was a transfer in favor of domestically produced oils like sunflower

and colza. Production of pasta stagnated. Production of chocolate and sweets increased at a rate of 2.6 percent per annum from 1962 to 1973 (see table 11.10).

On the whole, this sector maintained its position by a sometimes difficult process of adaptation to the changing conditions of the market. There were major upheavals in its structure.

2. The contribution made to total value added by the intermediate industries increased by two points between 1952 and 1972, mainly because of very old sectors which made a great effort to adapt. Iron and steel underwent two "surgical operations," each of which brought about a sudden spurt. The first, immediately after the war, involved modernization and restructuring, and made possible the brilliant boom of the 1950s. The second, in July 1966, took the novel form of a contract between the state and employers in the sector. The employers, in exchange for financing facilities, undertook, by restructuring their firms, to concentrate on huge projects such as Dunkirk and Fos, so as to "achieve the best possible increase in productivity as cheaply and rapidly as possible." Production of crude steel, which had stagnated between 1964 and 1967, increased by 28 percent up to 1973. The pure oxygen process accounted for 11.2 percent of steel production in 1964 and 52 percent in 1973.

Growth in the chemical industry varied greatly. The production index for inorganic chemicals increased by 80 percent between 1955 and 1962, while that for organic chemicals tripled. Between 1962 and 1973, production in inorganic

Table 11.10 Production of Selected Goods in the Agricultural and Food Industries (in thousands of tons)

	1962	1968	1973
White sugars	1,274		2,916
Chocolate and sweets	295		393
Frozen foods		51	214
Mineral waters (thousands of liters)	1,395	2,128	2,393
Animal foods	3,310	5,680	11,187
Pasta	303	326	306

chemicals doubled, and organic chemicals increased fivefold. By then the value added contributed by inorganic chemicals was only two-thirds that of organic chemicals.

The cement industry developed at the same rate as construction: 80 percent of production went to building and 20 percent to civil engineering. Production roughly doubled every ten years. Per capita consumption of cement increased by 70 percent between 1962 (332 kg.) and 1972 (566 kg.). During this period the cement industry adopted highly automated and capitalistic methods.

3. The legacy of the nineteenth century is still to be seen in France in the large part played by "consumer industries," i.e., chiefly the textile industries. The sector as a whole did not stand up well to the internationalization of the economy. The rate at which imports were covered by exports fell from 1.26 percent in 1962 to 0.99 percent in 1972. But the pattern varied considerably according to product: while wool and cotton had very low growth, synthetic textiles, silk, and hosiery (which developed at the expense of weaving) showed sustained growth in the 1960s (see table 11.11). Hosiery and silks were driven upward by increased family consumption and high export capacity. (Silk exported an average of 35 percent of its total sales.) But this progress was achieved only through an active policy of diversification. Wool and cotton had to face competition from countries whose industries were either much more highly capitalistic or had to support much lighter labor costs.

4. The capital goods industries. This sector is mainly composed of the engineering and electrical industries. It includes basic metal processing, the engineering and electrical industries, naval construction, the aeronautics industry, and shipbuilding. Overall this sector showed strong growth, higher than that of the intermediate industries (up 7.4 percent between 1952 and 1972). Although growth in productivity of labor was only moderate in that period (up 5.7 percent), total productivity of all factors showed very strong growth (3 percent per annum from 1959 to 1969), since productivity of capital did not fall after 1964 as it did in industry as a whole. Chapter 13 will deal with the computer and aeronautics industries. Here we shall confine ourselves to some details about electrical engineering,

Table 11.11 Comparative Production Growth for Various Textiles (in thousands of tons)

	1952	1962	1973	1952–1973
Cotton and blended fabrics	182.3	223.4	198.8	0.3
Woolen fabrics	72.7	74.2	71.6	0.0
Silks	21.8	32.0	51.4	4.1
Yarns used in hosiery production	46.4	58.6	102.4*	4.0

*1972.

electronics, and the car industry. In electrical engineering, especially after the early 1960s, continual technical progress called for much more research than in most French industrial enterprises. This was the main reason why the sector developed toward the formation of two groups which were sometimes allies and sometimes rivals: the Compagnie Générale d'Electricité and the Thomson Brandt group. Between 1943 and 1973 the rate of production growth was always over 10 percent, and there was an appreciable acceleration in this growth between the late 1960s and 1974. This was due to growth in electronics, which had become the "advanced technology industry" par excellence and an export industry.

In 1953 only 20 percent of all families had a car. By 1973 the figure had risen to 63 percent. Some sociologists predicted that people would lose interest in cars, but the growth continues in France, despite the growing disapproval in some official quarters. In 1962, imports accounted for 12 percent of the domestic market in private cars. In 1972 the figure had risen to 25 percent. But in the same period French car exports rose from 26 percent to 44 percent. The exceptional dynamism of this market produced some remarkable technical results: between 1960 and 1970, production per capita increased at a mean annual rate of 6.1 percent and the investments were largely self-financed. Up to the end of the 1960s these results were achieved without large rises in sale prices. But after 1968 things changed, and to safeguard its self-financing ability the car industry was drawn, like the rest, into the inflationary movement which until then it had helped to hold back. It was also at that time that the large-scale regroupings took place which have resulted in the formation of three major groups: Renault, which produced 40.4 percent of all the private cars made in 1973, and which also controls SAVIEM and Berliet, the two largest producers of heavy vehicles; Peugeot-Citröen, formed in 1974; and Chrysler France. In 1973, Peugeot produced 21.4 percent of private cars, and Citröen, then part of the Michelin group, produced 20.6 percent. The Chrysler group produced 17.6 percent. There are also many technical agreements between these various companies for production and even sales as well as research.

Land Transport

The rate of growth in "land transport" was lower than that of gross domestic product (GDP). In 1939 it represented 3.1 percent of GDP, in 1973 only 2.6 percent. This overall development breaks down as follows: (1) Domestic travel increased in the same way as expenditure on "transport" in family consumption. In 1973 the Commission des Comptes de la Nation estimated travel in private cars at 330 billion-kilometer-passengers. This was about four times higher than the figure for public transport. (2) Transport of goods increased at a more moderate rate than production of goods and services. The development favored road transport, though less than did passenger transport. Distribution among different methods of transport is shown in table 11.12.

The reduction in rail and water transport increased markedly in the 1960s because of a strengthening tendency toward the restoration of a competitive market. The coordina-

Table 11.12 Distribution among Different Methods of Transport (in percent)

	Rail	Canals	Road		Total
			Public	Private	
1955	64.0	12.0			24.0
1959	59.8	10.6	14.9	14.7	29.6
1973	36.9	6.4	26.2	20.0	46.2

tion of transport modes imposed in the 1930s had been liberalized, though the object remained the same: to see that the transport system served the country at the lowest possible real cost. But methods had changed. The old system of regulations based on numerous prohibitions was replaced by a system of regulation through rates which were supposed to be fixed in relation to costs. This system presupposed on the one hand the abolition of restrictions on access to the road transport market (this was done, though only incompletely, by a law of 1963 and several other measures in 1973), and, on the other hand, the equalization of charges incumbent on different suppliers of transport. The latter called for a reform of the French Railways' concession. The main plan was set out in a 1967 report (known as the "Nora report" after its chief author, M. Simon Nora) on the reform of public enterprises. The report suggested that French Railways should be given greater commercial freedom by the abolition of restrictions that were the legacy of the railways' former monopoly, and that they should be compensated for losses incurred through having to maintain certain unprofitable services. The reform was carried out in two stages, in 1969 and 1971. The regulation of road transport rates proceeded in parallel with this, road rates being modeled on railway rates. But the application of these rates calls for checks and controls to which the transporters themselves do not take kindly.

According to P. Darrot the drop in rail traffic has three fundamental causes on which regulations can have no effect: (1) the drop in coal transport and the movement of heavy industry to the ports; (2) the flexibility of road transport, allowing door-to-door delivery; (3) the fact that the removal of restrictions on rail transport came too late.

Despite the low growth of traffic itself, the technical performance of French railways has been remarkable, and it is this, much more than subsidies, which has enabled them to retain a higher proportion of traffic than railways in other Western industrialized countries. The number of kilometer-units (kilometer-passengers + kilometer-tons) per hour's work was about 50 in 1938, 92 in 1952, and 207 in 1972. Between 1938 and 1972 the total consumption of energy fell from 9.2 million tons of coal-equivalent to 2.44, while traffic rose from 48.5 billion kilometer-units to 112. This progress was the result partly of electrification and partly of a reduction in the length of track (41,000 km. in 1952, of which 23,300 was single-track, as against 35,200 in 1972, 19,400 single-track).

Bibliography

Darrot, P. "La concurrence dans les transports routiers de marchandises," *Economie et Statistique*, nos. 40–41 (December 1972–January 1973).

——"Données essentielles sur l'activité des transports," *Economie et Statistique*, no. 28 (November 1971).

Desrosières, A. "Un découpage de l'industrie en trois secteurs," *Economie et Statistique*, no. 40 (December 1972).

Faure, E. "La politique française du pétrole." Unpublished thesis, Paris, 1938.

Fresque historique du système productif. Collections de l'INSEE ser. E, no. 27. Paris: Institut National de la Statistique et des Etudes Economiques, November 1975.

Huret, E. "Les entreprises de transports routiers, 1962–1967," *Economie et Statistique*, no. 12 (May 1970).

Malinvaud, E., J. J. Carre, and P. Dubois. *La croissance française*. Paris: Seuil, 1972.

Vilain, M. *La politique de l'énergie en France*. Paris: Cujas, 1969.

Vincent, L. A. "Evolution de la production intérieure brute en France de 1896 à 1938. Méthodes et premiers résultats," *Etudes et Conjoncture*, November 1962.

——"Population active, production et productivité dans 21 branches de l'économie française (1896–1962)," *Etudes et Conjoncture*, February 1965.

Wagner, C. "Vingt ans de comptes agricoles," *Economie et Statistique*, no. 50 (November 1973).

Walter, F. "Recherches sur le développement économique de la France, 1900–1955," *Cahiers de l'Institut de Science Economique Appliquée*, ser. D, no. 2 (March 1957).

Chapter Twelve: Stages of Growth and Economic Policies from 1914 to 1950

The 1914–1918 War

IT WAS NOT until the social crisis of 1917, and the fear that the "home front" might collapse, that the French leadership agreed to impose the disciplines necessary to pursue the war effort. There were two kinds of difficulty: one kind was linked to shortages, the other to financial equilibria. And the two were connected by the need for imports and the inflationary tensions caused by shortages. Only strict measures for controlling prices and movement of capital, for increasing taxes, and for managing production could contain the inflationist impulse and reduce the disequilibria. The measures taken were taken late in the day, mostly in 1917, and they were abandoned too soon after the war.

After the structural unemployment of the early months of the war, the shortage of labor was the first to become evident; it did so at the beginning of 1915 and always remained the most acute. Sixty-three percent of male workers had been called up. None of the solutions tried were more than palliatives. The substitution of capital for labor and the spread of Taylorism (the scientific organization of labor, named after its American inventor) were possible only in a limited number of sectors. In most, the shortage of labor made production impossible.

French industry on the whole was ill-adapted to the needs of war. France's iron and steel capacity was equal to only a third of German capacity, and the chemical industry produced neither the ammonia nor the nitric acid necessary in the manufacture of explosives. France had, however, developed two kinds of production, motorcars and aluminum, which were to reveal themselves as essential to the war effort.

The zone of "industrial impracticability" extended far beyond the area invaded. It covered an area responsible for the production of 74 percent of coal, 81 percent of cast iron, 63 percent of steel, 55 percent of forgings, and 76 percent of sugar, but only 25 percent of mechanical engineering. The equipment crisis broke out in the autumn of 1914 and remained acute up to January 1915. One of Joffre's officers is supposed to have said, "If we were to win another Battle of the Marne, we should be lost." But to the original shortages of coal and munitions and arms were added others, the consequences either of the general labor shortage, of import difficulties, of rising speculation, or of aspects of the new strategy: this was true particularly of the oil shortage, which became disturbing in its proportions in the spring of 1917.

"The state had no idea of the facts," wrote Delemer. The commisariat knew nothing about market prices, and the first thing needed was information: one of the first commissions was the one set up on August 6, 1914 to draw up a list of France's food resources. The state, without either sources of information or means of action, could only proceed by one improvisation after another, and it could do nothing without the help of employers' organizations. It created boards (such as the one set up to deal with chemical products on October 17, 1914), and these boards had subsidies and their own budgets; but the state also established "committees" varying in status and with responsibilities which were different and often vague. Some were simply for information gathering; others also had consultative or even decision-making and management powers. It was toward the middle of 1916 that the most efficient organizations of this kind appeared, based on collaboration between the state and employers. These were the consortia, groups of traders and industrialists attached to executive committees. By 1918 they had become part of the essential machinery of economic life.

Because of the accumulation of sometimes unexpected needs, there was, as P. Renouvin pointed out, much overlapping and duplication. By the end of 1918 there were 291 boards, committees, or commissions, of which 18 were attached to the War Ministry. But there was no fixed or clear division of responsibility. Thus, to solve the problems set from 1916 onward by the sugar shortage, there were no less than 5 commissions, with no real link between them; and there are many similar examples. However, with experience, the services established from 1917 became increasingly efficient—as, for example, the petroleum services, which administered a coherent, unified policy of purchase, distribution, control of consumption, and technology. If, as Renouvin writes, the state "on the eve of the Armistice had got to the point where, for the purposes of the war, it absorbed almost all available material resources," it had only been able to do so by building up a more and more coherent policy. Does this then mean that 1917 should be regarded as the antithesis of the liberal nineteenth century? Things are not so simple.

As early as August 1914, R. Pinot, General Secretary of the Comité des Forges (the French employers' association for heavy industry), became an "unofficial Minister of Munitions" (Poncet), for he alone could "supply the valuable information" that was necessary. At the bimonthly meeting held at the ministry with the heads of regional groups and large establishments, he was the only one with an exact knowledge of the possibilities of each individual industrialist. As A. F. Poncet has said, this "convinced liberal" thus became "a senior civil servant with a monopoly in the purchase of several kinds of raw materials, distributing them according to strict rules and making sure that commercial transactions were carried out according to definite prices." The case of metallurgy is probably an extreme example, and the actual influence of each consortium depended upon the degree of organization achieved by the employers' association of that particular sector, as was the case with the organizing committees in the Second World War.

It has been said that the war accelerated the process of industrialization. But this statement needs modifying and explaining. Sectors not directly linked with needs arising out of the conduct of the war were systematically sacrificed. Daily production of 75 mm. artillery shells rose from 10,000 at the beginning of the war to 300,000 in May 1917. According to A. Fontaine, rifle production was 290 times greater in 1918 than in 1914, and machine gun production 170 times greater. Ammunition was made by mass production from 1916 onward. By the end of the war, France was producing 30 tanks every day, as well as trucks, motorcars, and aircraft. So it was to the industry of metal processing that the war lent principal impetus. But we should not, as people did at the time, exaggerate the importance of the technical revolution which this brought about. L. C. Reboul has said that in the sphere of aviation, France only "repeated well-known types." As for production methods, the use of comparatively unskilled labor made it necessary to adopt Taylorist methods and to develop standardization, but even in a factory like that of Renault these processes had only a limited application.

The magnitude of the needs brought about a massive increase in the production of firms like Breguet, Renault, and Peugeot. France was now producing equipment which hitherto she had sought abroad, such as electric dynamos, carbon steel wire for aviation purposes, and tubes. In the field of primary metallurgy, it was enough to continue what had been begun during the years immediately before the war: four electrometallurgical factories were built, 109 Martin furnaces, 56 converters, and 11 electrical furnaces. All in all, steel production capacity increased by 40 percent in the part of France that was invaded. Companies in this area, such as Le Cruesot and the Société des Forges de la Marine et Homécourt, doubled their production.

The French chemical industry, like all the other chemical industries in the world, imitated Germany. The somewhat belated foundation of the Compagnie Nationale des Matières Colorantes et des Produits Chimiques was designed to found an industry of explosives and dyes based on various kinds of tar. It brought together a number of firms dominated by Kuhlmann's and enjoyed state aid and the support of the Banque de Paris et des Pays Bas. Traditional chemicals made a new start. The chemical production of St. Gobain's increased by 70 percent. Aluminum production, too, was stimulated, though the war only confirmed previous developments in this sector. The total hydroelectric power available in kilowatt-hours about doubled.

Other sectors were left to sink or swim. The number of people employed in building sank by 50 percent from 1914 to 1917–18. The production capacity of the textile and food industries was appreciably reduced. Agricultural production also diminished: plowed land sank from 23.6 million hectares to 21.7. In the years 1914–18, wheat production represented only 66 percent of what had been achieved in 1904–13, potatoes 72 percent, sugar beets 37 percent. This decline was due to the invasion and the devastation it caused, to the manpower shortage owing not only to the call-up of farmers but also to some intensification of the rural exodus, and also to difficulties linked to shortages of animals, tools, fertilizers, and energy.

The financing of war investments seems to have been for the most part assured by systematic self-financing, encouraged by the state. The Ministry of Munitions, "in order to encourage industrialists to invest in equipment, allowed rapid depreciation to appear in manufacturing costs," according to Jèze, who has strongly criticized State contractual arrangements: "The state's financial interests," he writes, "... were not always very well looked after by the ad hoc staff who drew up or signed the contracts." And it was never possible to compel contractors to show their account books. There is no systematic analysis of war profits, distributed or otherwise. The special tax on war profits, which applied to profits over and above those obtained during the last three years before the war, developed in the following manner:

August 1914 to December 1915	2.4 billion
1916	4.2 billion
1917	5.3 billion
1918	5.4 billion

On this basis, total profits would be 7.4 billion in 1917, 7.8 in 1918. From the few figures we have been able to derive from balance sheets we see that profits increased much less rapidly than turnover. This was the case with Renault, where the ratio of earnings to sales sank from 30.9 percent in 1914–15 to 15.7

percent in 1918. Its fixed assets was multiplied by 3.8. The net profits of the Société des Forges et Aciéries de la Marine et Homécourt were 6.8 million francs in 1914–15, 17 million in 1915–16, and 15 million in 1917–18. Those of St. Gobain were 3.4 million francs in 1914 and 22.7 million in 1916. But we must admit our ignorance. The war favored self-financing in businesses working for the government and facilitated increases of capital and the subsequent changes of structure. But it did not bring about any spectacular increase in companies' distributed profits. Overall profits seem to have increased less than turnover, and in many cases less than cost prices. If 1901–10 equals 100, the index for the stock-exchange rate of French companies was 161 in 1913, 141 in 1918, and 163 in 1919. The index of gross dividends followed the same pattern (161, 146, 167). The gross rate of capitalization remained steady. In fact it seems clear that monetary inflation eroded profits as it eroded other kinds of income, and that firms which could not or did not know how to reinvest profits immediately and continue to make use of their current investments emerged weaker rather than stronger.

The war brought about the destruction of 7.5 percent of existing buildings and a large part of France's industrial capital: it also caused the loss of 1,350,000 men. It held back growth in many sectors and directed production toward activities which were difficult to convert to peacetime purposes. Industrial production indices in 1919 were as follows (1913 = 100):

General index	57
Engineering	58
Metallurgy	29
Textiles	60
Building	16
Rubber	305
Paper	51
Leather	102

The war only confirmed certain previous tendencies in the French economy. It was not, as some people have maintained, the originator of intensive industrialization. The investment capacity it imparted to certain companies was amply compensated for, sometimes more than compensated for, by the destruction and loss due to nonmaintenance of capital.

Inflation 1914–1928

The tensions of inflation were already evident even before the end of hostilities. Up to 1916, France had the greatest difficulty in financing its external deficit; it only succeeded in doing so by realizing part of its foreign assets and entering into short-term debts. It was the United States' entry into the war which "got the Allies out of a very difficult situation" (Aftalion). The exchange rate of the franc deteriorated up to April 1916, after which the gradual change in the attitude of the United States government brought about a recovery in the value of the franc to a level fairly close to before the war; the franc was supported by loans from the U.S. Treasury. But by 1918 the franc had already begun to deteriorate in relation to other currencies such as the Swiss franc and the Swedish crown.

During the war years as a whole, export income had covered only 29 percent of import expenditure, the total deficit amounting to 64.1 billion francs, of which the invisible balance supplied only 24.3. At the end of the war, France's foreign debts amounted to 19 billion francs, and its whole system of trade depended upon American loans.

As Jèze, the best expert on financial economics at the time, wrote in 1919, "France's financial policy during the war will always be a model of what not to do." Ribot, head of the government, considered in 1914 that before "increasing the weight of taxes" it was necessary to wait for the country to be "delivered from invasion," and he did not change his mind until 1916. It was only in 1917 that a new system was adopted of income tax and tax on war profits. But despite these measures, expenditure was only covered by revenues to the extent of 16 percent between 1914 and 1918. In 1918 revenues were 6.8 billion francs and real expenditure 54.2. The deficits were financed by debt, principally short-term debt. The public debt doubled between 1913 and 1918 (rising from 31 to 62 billion), and the floating debts rose from 1.5 to 41.8 billion francs. In fact, these borrowings were only a devious means of issuing paper money. The quantity of paper money issued rose from 5.7 billion at the end of 1913 to 30.3 at the end of 1918, a multiplication by 5.3, whereas prices had multiplied by only 3.5 in 1918, and by 4.3 in 1919 as against 1914. This rise was a result both of tensions arising out of shortages and of the absence of any coherent policy of financing.

But at the beginning of 1919, tension was still very strong: while production capacities were much reduced, and there was enormous need for reconstruction investment and for production which would make up for consumption deferred during the war, there was a large amount of monetary liquidity to enable these needs to find expression. These needs for investment and consumption created a tendency to import, which far exceeded France's ability to export at a time when the country was heavily in debt.

When, in March 1919, France lost the support of Allied credits, the franc fell on the exchange markets far below the level justified by the difference between the rise in prices in France (where they had multiplied by 3.5) and the rising prices in the United States (where they had multiplied by 2). The franc fell on exchange markets until March 1920, the dollar in April of that year showing an index of 314 on a basis of July 1914 equaling 100. This deterioration was the reflection of another in the balance of payments. In 1919 the trade deficit was 23.9 billion francs, and during the first six months of 1920 it was 14.3 billion francs. The deterioration of the franc, through its influence on the price of imported goods, combined with the tensions mentioned above to bring about rising prices. No serious attempt at budgetary reform was made before the elections of 1919, when the state embarked on a policy of total compensation for war victims.

The course of events changed during 1920. The new Chamber of Deputies voted a tax reform which, according to Germain Martin, was "the greatest effort France had ever made in the course of its financial history." It was then that the tax on turnover was instituted. But the introduction of an item called "recoverable expenditure," i.e., expenditure under the reparations arrangements, cast doubt on the reality of the wish to reform, despite the effort that was being made, and served to justify pessimistic analyses of the situation. The floating debt continued to increase disturbingly, more than doubling between 1918 (41.8 billion) and 1921 (111.7). In April 1920, in order to show a desire to put things straight, an agreement was signed providing for the state to repay at a rate of 2 billion francs per annum the advances which had been obtained from the Banque de France (37.3 billion francs at the end of 1919).

But the desire to amend France's internal finances seems not to have had any noticeable effect on the exchange rate of the franc. In fact, in 1920, according to A. Aftalion, "it was the movements of prices which seemed to dictate the circulation of money." But prices depend a great deal on the level of the exchange rate.

The economic crisis which occurred in the spring of 1920 brought about a collapse in prices (index 600 in April 1920 and 358 on the average in 1921) and a recovery in the rate of the franc, justified by an improvement in the balance of payments, a certain recovery in the budget, and a fall in domestic prices. This improvement was confirmed in 1922, but was followed by a new and marked deterioration in 1923. However, the balance of current payments, in 1928 francs, showed a surplus of 4.7 billion francs in 1923, as against a deficit of 27 billion in 1920. There was a considerable relaxation in the effort to balance the budget, the Chamber refusing to accept a new turn of the screw concerning taxes. But the budget deficit was not enough to justify alarmism. The net amount of money in circulation had increased by only 11 percent between 1919 and 1924.

Despite evidence of recovery—though this certainly needed confirmation—the last months of 1923 brought an exchange crisis which continued into the early months of 1924. A. Aftalion has a "psychological" explanation for this, according to which the deterioration in the value of the franc was not to be explained by the usual "technical" reasons (the behavior of the balance of payments or a "parity" in terms of purchasing power between domestic and foreign prices). According to him, "it was the rise in the exchange rate of the dollar which determined the rise in prices." The French should not be surprised if their money lost its value when they had always declared that their financial equilibrium depended on the success of a policy which the Ruhr "adventure" branded as a failure.

The first of two operations to save the franc, initiated by Poincaré after this crisis in the spring of 1924, easily attained its goals: the fall of the franc was halted by means of certain fiscal measures and international loans. But its main consequence was the coming to power of a majority of the Left, which triggered off a new "psychological" process of mistrust, not only on the foreign money market but also in France itself among subscribers to government bonds. The crisis in public finances of 1924–25 was much more a cash crisis than a budget crisis. Between 1920 and 1925 indirect taxation doubled, direct taxation tripled, and the 1925 budget almost balanced. The recovery of France's foreign finances was confirmed. But the tendency toward improvement in the balance of payments was counteracted by a "formidable" export of capital, outweighing the excess surplus in the balance of income. The inflationary mechanisms of the time seem in fact to have been governed, as the experts of the INSEE said in 1953, more "by psychological considerations than by the mechanism of cost prices." The monetary crisis came to a head in July 1926: cost prices reached an index of 800 (1913 = 100), and the dollar was worth almost 50 francs as against 5.13 francs in 1913.

As we have said, the amount of money in circulation had increased by only 11 percent between 1919 and 1924. After that date it increased at a much more rapid rate (43 percent between 1924 and 1926), because of an unusual acceleration in the increase of the amount of bank money (up 64 percent).

Poincaré's second attempt to restore the franc followed the July 1926 crisis, and the ease with which recovery was brought about shows the importance of "psychological" factors. The new budget aimed as much at impressing public opinion as at reestablishing a balance—although it did, in fact, almost balance. Fiscal policy consisted in lightening personal taxation and increasing indirect taxation. The Banque de France was allowed to purchase gold and currency in order to try to stabilize the franc. First, the enormous mass of dated bills which acted as a permanent threat was transformed into redeemable debentures by means of a series of loans which were issued up to December 1926. The state was able to resume repayment of its debt to the Banque de France. But no attempt was made to reduce the amount of money in circulation. It was the issue of notes which enabled the Bank to buy gold and currency. As E. Moreau writes, "clearly the notes issued in exchange for gold and currency cannot be considered as another instance of inflation since they were 100 percent covered." Thus the policy of stabilizing the exchange rate was accompanied by a policy of lavish monetary issues (the amount of money in circulation in 1926 was 103 billion francs, and in 1928 it was 158 billion francs).

The recovery of the franc on the exchange market was spectacular both in scope and in speed; the pound was worth 240 francs in July and 120 francs in December. The balance of payments was still in surplus, despite the reappearance of a trade deficit and a decrease in surpluses owing to the fall of the franc. The Banque de France continued to increase its gold reserves, seeing to it that the franc did not exceed the rate it had reached at the end of 1926. Poincaré, who did not want to "impoverish the middle classes" and wished the state to "keep its promises," would have liked to return to the prewar "parity." But E. Moreau, governor of the Banque de France, and the man behind him, C. Rist, were both of the opinion that going too far in that direction might endanger the development of foreign trade and, consequently, the future of France's production. This disagreement was settled in June 1928, when the franc was stabilized at the level desired by Moreau. The law fixed gold value of the franc at a level corresponding to the prewar franc divided by 5.

In all, the period 1920–28 was characterized by what Aftalion has called the "supremacy of the exchange rate." Except for a few months in 1924, France suffered the consequences of fluctuations in the exchange rate right up to 1926. Between 1926 and 1928 France followed a policy of its own which greatly displeased its international partners, used to seeing the French put up with the effects of speculation rather than directing it. This policy combined an attempt at external stability with internal money issue, which was mostly due to an increase in bank money. France either could not or would not undertake a serious attempt at deflation. The 1928 franc was probably undervalued, but this undervaluation lasted only three years.

French Growth in the 1920s

The preceding analysis leads one to ask whether French growth in the 1920s was "inflationary." First we must examine that growth itself. As has already been said, this period continued and accentuated the evolution toward "industrialization" begun during the years preceding the 1914 war. During this period, more than ever, growth was synonymous with diversified production and intensified investment. The "rationalization" attempted, first as part of reconstruction and then as an element in the expansion of production, was not a mere matter of the organization of markets and business enterprises. Rationalization was essentially the search for a coherent strategy of investment.

Diversification. Diversification in the matter of products should be seen both as a whole and at the level of each separate sector. According to the calculations made at the beginning of the 1950s by the Organisation Européen de Coopération Économique (OECE, later to become the Organisation de Coopération et de Développement Économique and finally our present OECD), the French textile industry in 1929 reached a level similar to that of 1913, a level which it never exceeded during the 1920s. On the other hand, the metal-processing industry increased by a little over 50 percent between 1913 and 1929, and the basic metals industry increased by the same percentage between 1910 and 1929 and by 28 percent between 1913 and 1929. L. A. Vincent, comparing the indices for 1928 with those for 1913, reaches the following results: three sectors—wood, fabric processing, and building and public works—all stagnated. A second category consists of sectors with moderate growth (indices between 115 and 127): these were textiles (115), leather, the food industries, the extractive industries including coal, and the glass, gas, and iron and steel industries. A third category includes sectors with very rapid growth and indices between 140 (metal-processing and paper) and 780 (electricity). In the same class, associated with paper, come newspapers and publishing, and also chemicals, petroleums and fuels, and rubber.

It is clear that there can be no simple classification of sectors according to their growth: while growth in certain consumer industries slackened, others suddenly shot ahead. In fact, the new pattern of consumption which had emerged in the prewar years now grew clearer. It was based on the use of industrial durables. This was one of the main reasons for the dynamism in the metal-processing and chemicals sector. The other reason lay in the particular kind of investment favored at that period, which, as we shall see, was centered on equipment rather than on basic investments.

But diversification is even more apparent when we examine each sector in detail. Although this period saw coal production at its height, it also witnessed the first conscious and systematic efforts to economize on coal and find substitutes for it. Consumption of electricity increased by an average of 8.2 percent per annum between 1913 and 1929. Water power provided one third of this electricity, and consumption of coal per kilowatt produced was one-third of what it was at the beginning of the century. Electrical industries were behind many innovations in most sectors and constituted one of the chief stimulants in the capital market: in 1930–31 electricity alone absorbed 20 percent of total issues. It was also in the electricity sector that certain important combinations took place. The 1920s, as we have already seen, also saw the foundation of France's petroleum policy.

As a result of the war, "the framework of the old chemical industry broke down" (R. Berr) all over the world, France included. Every country imitated Germany and created its own organic chemical industry. The engineering and metal-processing industries benefited from the development of industrial mechanization, and from the development of motorcar production (40,000 private cars in 1920, 254,000 in 1930), which was directed more and more toward the domestic market. The large-scale equipment industry benefited from reconstruction and then from electrification. In Poincaré francs, orders in this sector amounted to 1.7 billion in 1913 and 2.6 billion in 1929. The amount of thermal power stations installed rose from 3.2 million kilowatts in 1923 to 5.6 million in 1930, and the amount of hydroelectric power from 1.3 million kilowatts to 2.3. While the building and public works sector, together with textiles, on the whole stagnated, cement production rose from 1.9 million tons in 1913 to 6.2 million in 1928, and production of artificial silk rose from 11 million kilograms to 197 million.

Investment. We should remember that this phase of industrialization was accompanied by an unprecedented amount of investment, principally concentrated on industrial plant and machinery. If 1913 equals 100, the index for investment in equipment in 1929 is 184. This capitalistic intensification was not confined to rapidly growing sectors such as chemicals, metal processing, and iron and steel. In certain slow-growing sectors like textiles, or hides and leather, the increase in available kilowatts was much superior to the increase in production. So industry as a whole, whatever its growth rate, was benefiting from more profound development, for these investments paved the way for new technologies based on the use of electricity.

Basic investment increased much less. The index calculated by J. Mairesse on the basis of 1913 as 100 reached a level of 135 in 1929. However, in the railway sector, for example, reconstruction made it possible to create a new network in the devastated areas, based on principles which presupposed much larger installations than had existed before the war. The same spirit directed reconstruction in other sectors. In the coal industry it was the "grouping together of the coalfields which had been invaded" which led reconstruction in the direction of modernization, and which subsequently prevented a fall in yields. All in all, while the rate of investment in 1929 (20 percent) equaled that of the 1950s, the pattern which had appeared at the end of the nineteenth century was confirmed: after having concentrated its efforts on basic investments, France then turned to industrial equipment.

Was the Expansion of the 1920s Inflationary? Inflation could have favored industrial growth, either by giving French exporters an advantage in foreign exchange or by giving industrialists greater possibilities of self-financing through inflationary profits.

There is no doubt that one of the main consequences of the fall of the franc within a flexible system of exchange was to favor the expansion of exports. According to J. Weiller, the "disparity" between French and United States prices (the ratio between the cost price index in France in dollars and the United States cost price index) was 0.80 in 1920, 0.91 in 1922, but 0.76 in 1926. In 1923, in terms of volume, exports were at their 1913 level, and between 1923 and 1927 they increased by 42 percent. Between 1927 and 1929, France was content to maintain its position, and exports stagnated. Export growth was due principally to "manufactured articles," which grew at a rate of 67 percent. Some contemporary economists considered that the depreciation of the franc brought about a "loss of substance," with France exporting too much in comparison with its productive capacities, or a "structural distortion," with certain sectors, such as quality textiles, being artificially favored. There is some truth in both these assertions. The depreciation of the franc did make it possible to acquire new markets in which France sometimes managed to retain its footing. It is clear, however, that the stabilization of the franc in 1928 caused France to lose certain positions, as in the case of motorcars and silk goods. In 1925, 30.5 percent of France's motorcar production was exported, while in 1930 only 8 percent was exported. The French Federation of Silk Makers observed that "when the exchange rate was very low, all the customers in the world fell on the markets at Lyons and St. Étienne." But "this formidable trade fell off as soon as the exchange rate improved, and above all after the stabilization of the franc."

The evolution of exports in the 1920s cannot be explained entirely in terms of monetary factors, however. Manufactured articles contributed a slightly larger proportion to total exports between 1913 (60.8 percent) and 1928–30 (62.8 percent). Within this category, the articles which now increased their contribution were either "traditional" ones, such as silk and woolen goods, or "new" articles such as machinery, tools, and chemicals. The articles which now contributed a lesser share included motorcars, which since the war were meeting with more and more competition from the American car industry, cotton fabrics, luxury items, and hides. Thus we see the beginnings of a modification in the distribution of French exports. The decrease in luxury items marked the decline of a system based on the export of products which were not really industrial, while the increase in new products and even, to a certain extent, in woolen goods produced by highly capitalistic methods led the way to a new export structure dominated by industrial manufactured products. This was not merely a matter of a favorable exchange rate.

Domestic inflation does not seem to have brought about a massive increase in profits which would have explained the ease with which investments were financed. In fact, there was no important change in the patterns of financing of investments as compared with 1913. Between 1913 and 1929, the net amount of fixed capital rose from 6.6 billion current francs to 54 billion. But there was no real change in the distribution among different sources of financing: 20 percent came from loans, 64 percent in 1913 and 65 percent in 1920 came from undistributed gross earnings of companies, and 16 percent in 1913 and 15 percent in 1929 from undistributed gross income of individual firms. What happened during the 1920s was an acceleration of the development characteristic of the years just before the war. The volume of issues on the Paris Stock Exchange (calculated in constant value according to a cost price index of 100, based on the mean for the years 1901–10) more than doubled. The index for the years 1919–29 was 217 in comparison with the decade 1901–10, exactly the same figure as can be derived from the index for equipment investment calculated by Mairesse. Thus, as between the two sources of financing (debt and retained earnings), the distribution remained the same. According to M. Malissen, the capital market was still "the chief source of long-term funds for companies." If we compare the index for issues with the index for investments, we see that external financing plays the principal role in 1920–22, that in 1924–26 the chief role was played by internal resources, and that this changed after 1927, so that issues resumed the chief role in 1929. So for a time inflation encouraged self-financing, while the stabilization of the franc restored the balance between the two methods of financing.

Industrial growth in the 1920s, as in the mid-nineteenth century, had a dual aspect. It was accompanied by large-scale technical changes and by a reorganization of production methods which became more and more openly capitalistic. It was based on the emergence of a mass consumer market, and on equipment investment inspired by a long-term, industrialist (even Saint-Simonian) view of France's economic future. But, as the analysis of exports has shown, the period was also characterized by the survival in some cases, and in other cases the prosperity, of certain sectors of traditional French production. This duality tended to diminish, however, and growth in highly capitalistic sectors was much stronger than that in the traditional sectors of French "quality" goods.

The 1930s

English-speaking economists still assert that French policy after the stabilization of 1928 broke the monetary solidarity which the English-speaking countries had tried to restore after the war. It is true that France had converted a large amount of currency into gold. The percentage of currency held by the Banque de France fell from 50 percent in December 1928 to 22 percent in December 1931. The Banque de France held practically no currency by December 1933. Through this policy, France is said to have created the conditions which made it necessary to suspend the convertibility of the pound in 1931. Moreover, the undervaluation of the franc aggravated the difficulties of the other industrial countries. It gave France a respite during the first years of the 1929 crisis. In France, the prosperity of the 1920s continued up to 1931, and this was due partly to the influx of capital, and in particular gold, which then was directed toward France, creating monetary abundance. These gold imports reached a peak in 1931, and the money supply reached its maximum in 1932. The franc was then a strong currency. But this situation did not last. As C. Rist wrote in 1934, France "which was still a cheap country in 1930, had become a dear country by 1931." For after the collapse of world prices came the devaluation of the pound and, soon after, that of the dollar.

Though the effects of the crisis were felt later in France than in other countries, they lasted longer. This was largely the result of economic errors, but it also reveals the precariousness of the previous expansion. By the end of 1931 France was no longer the island of prosperity lauded by the commentators. First price curves and then production and industrial profit curves fell, while indicators of unemployment rose. In 1932 the situation appeared to improve, and France seemed to be following the pattern of industrial economies as a whole. But in 1934 and 1935, France, as C. Rist wrote in 1935, "had to be content with a vegetating economy stabilized at the depressed level to which the two previous years had fallen after the great disappointment of 1933." The measures taken by the government of the Popular Front gave only a temporary impetus to activity, and in the second half of 1937 production curves stopped rising. It was not until the last months of 1938 that a real recovery was seen. So we can see why so many political leaders were overwhelmed with a feeling of helplessness, and why there emerged so many either Socialist-type or corporatist utopias, all designed to compensate for the inability of French capitalism—even French capitalism as reformed by the Popular Front—to help the country out of the slump.

The crisis was essentially an investment and a savings crisis. It manifested itself by a steep decline in industrial profits due to the fall in prices and production, and by a crisis in agricultural incomes due to overproduction and again the fall in prices. The tendency toward rising industrial profits, which had emerged at the end of the nineteenth century, continued in the 1920s. But, taking 1913 to equal 100, the index for the prices of ordinary shares in France dropped from 548 in February 1929 to 172 in November 1934. Dividends fell by 46 percent between

May 1930 and May 1933. They leveled off in 1933–34, then fell again between autumn 1934 and spring 1935. By May 1935 they had fallen by 52 percent. This drop was in fact very different in different sectors, as J. Dessirier showed in 1935. Taking 1929–30 to equal 100, the index for distributed dividends in 1934–35 was 72; the index for the "major public services" group (gas, water, electricity, mortgages) remained steady; the index for electric companies even increased by 43 percent; the index for the group of "cartelized" or "protected" sectors (sugar, naval construction, coal mines, and part of the iron and steel industry) was 67; while the index for "other sectors" was 30. France's industrial economy was certainly, as Dessirier said, in a "state of blatant disequilibrium," and it was the unprotected sectors of the economy alone which had to bear the brunt of the crisis.

The fall in profits was the result of the fall in prices and production. The index of industrial prices, if 1913 equals 100, reached 464 in 1931 and 348 in 1935, while nominal hourly wage rates decreased by only 6 percent between 1931 and 1935. Production first sagged in 1932 (down 17 percent compared with 1928). There was a slight recovery in 1933, followed by a fall, which in 1935 amounted to a decrease of 21 percent in comparison with 1929. The trouble spread from export industries to industries working for the domestic market, from luxury and semiluxury industries to consumer industries, and from consumer industries to the equipment industries. This triggered off a multiple decline in investments. Between 1929 and 1935, the volume of exports decreased by 60 percent. As C. Rist said, "the gap between the external and the internal purchasing power of the French franc" grew wider and wider, and prevented France from taking part in the recovery of the world economy after 1933. France then entered a period of "profound deflation," reinforced by government policy.

The drop in investments triggered off by the failure of the domestic market was transformed by the fall in profits into a veritable collapse. According to J. Mairesse, investments fell by 37 percent between 1930 and 1935. Company issues fell from 21.8 billion francs in 1932 to 4 billion in 1934. This fall chiefly affected the industrial sectors: issues in the electricity sector were only a third of what they had been in 1930, those in metallurgy were 5 percent, and those in chemicals 17 percent. It was this period which marked the beginning of the "disaffection" of small savers, which was to last up to the middle of the 1950s. According to M. Malissen, undistributed company profits fell from 7.4 billion francs in 1928 to 2 billion in 1934 and 1935. Self-financing was in the neighborhood of zero, and according to M. Dessirier, distributed income was largely fictional, and reached a level of 25 percent in the uncartelized sector. In certain firms this distributed profit really corresponded to a "withdrawal of investment," a "loss of substance." In 1929, 6,500 bankruptcy proceedings were opened, a figure similar to that of 1939 (6,000), while in 1935 the figure was 13,370. Bank failures, though less spectacular than in central Europe, were many (there were 670 between October 1929 and September 1937). They often affected regional banks that were very old and enjoyed a high reputation, such as the Adam bank at Boulogne-sur-Mer. Some national banks, including the Bank Nationale de Crédit, encountered grave difficulties, the result of a series of mergers between different regional banks since 1913.

In France, unemployment never rose to the levels it reached in Germany, Great Britain, or America. The number of people receiving unemployment benefits, practically nil in 1929, soared to 260,000 in 1932 and 426,000 in 1935 (the average number of unemployed at the end of the month). The lack of work was also seen in a reduction of working hours, so that the "activity index," taking 1938 to equal 100, was 152 in 1930 and 105 in 1933 (i.e., down 31 percent). The fall in activity was slightly less marked than the fall in investment, although the two declines were parallel. But the crisis affected different categories in very different ways. While unemployment was general, the real incomes of some of those who still had jobs increased, while in agriculture, as Fromont pointed out, "even in the most favorable conditions, neither the capital nor the work of the farmer and his family was remunerated; in many cases it was even worse, because their capital had been eaten into.

In 1931, agricultural prices collapsed on the French market. Wholesale prices, which in 1931 showed a factor of 5.5

as against 1913, fell to 3.25 in 1935. As we know, agricultural prices had really been falling since 1925. From 1932 on, a series of good harvests accentuated the fall. Thus the crisis in agricultural incomes must be considered one of the chief causes of the prolongation of the crisis in general.

In 1931 there was a budget deficit. The French Parliament had not managed to preserve the balance in public finances achieved in 1928. On the contrary, it had introduced many new items of expenditure which could not now be abolished. Between 1931 and 1935 revenues dropped from 50.7 to 39.5 billion francs, and expenditure from 55.7 to 50. Revenues fell because of the economic crisis, and expenditure could not be reduced proportionately because much of it had to be carried on from year to year because the state had undertaken commitments toward pensioners, civil servants, and creditors. In spite of the conversion decided on in 1932, indebtedness represented half of the 1934 revenues. But the whole economic policy of the governments which had been in power since 1932 was based on the idea, as C. Rist says, "that a vigorous cut in expenditure should be enough to bring about a fall in domestic prices which would bring French prices level with foreign ones." But this "budgetary adjustment" could not be achieved through reduction of expenditure and, even if it had been achieved, would not have been enough to reduce French prices sufficiently to stimulate the economy. Moreover, combined with an expensive money policy, it forced France into a deflation that was too severe.

This deflationist policy was not always carried out with the same degree of rigor. It reached a peak under Laval in the spring of 1935. The main feature of Laval's policy was a reduction of 10 percent in all public expenditure, including civil servants' salaries and the interest on government bonds. A similar cut was imposed on charges for public services and on rents. The price of certain goods, such as coal and bread, were compulsorily reduced. The idea was to refuse the "easy way out" offered by devaluation, which some people advocated as early as 1932, and to try to reduce prices by reducing costs. In fact, another devaluation, so soon after the devaluation of 1928, was politically impossible.

The goals of this ad hoc policy were in complete

contradiction with other more "structural" measures, most of which were designed to protect producers against the effects of the crisis. A. Sauvy has described this policy as "Malthusian," in that it tended to reduce production in certain sectors. It may also be regarded as an attempt at adaptation, similar to the attempt which the English government was making at the time, and which was justified by overproduction in certain sectors. This "structural" policy can be broken down into three main series of measures: the protectionist measures which were general throughout the world at that time; subsidies, which made the state the "savior" of certain sectors, certain work categories, and even certain types of enterprises; and the organization of markets. The first type of measure, increasing protectionism, dates from 1929, while the first quotas were established in 1931; at the same time an equalization surtax was introduced on currency transactions. In 1935 external trade depended on bilateral agreements. As for subsidies, up till 1931, the financial position allowed the government to use tax relief, but after that date the state had to come to the rescue of several companies in difficulty which were so important that they could not be allowed to collapse. The government had to refloat certain banks, in particular the Banque Nationale de Crédit. The government also had to increase its share holdings, thus extending the scope of the "mixed economy." In 1933 the Société Air-France was founded, organized on a pattern which served again in 1937 for the Société Nationale des Chemins de Fer (SNCF). It was at this period that the state acquired a majority holding in the Compagnie Générale Transatlantique. Thus it was before the Popular Front, and under governments politically oriented toward the Right, that interventionism in prices was first instituted, and that "state capitalism" gained a foothold.

Finally, while in the most concentrated sectors, such as sugar, chemicals, and iron and steel, networks of cartels regrouped or were spontaneously created, tending, as the Revue d'Économie Politique said in 1934, "toward the organized limitation of means of production with the object of halting the downward trend linked to the chaotic lack of organization in production" (see chapter 4), the state had to intervene to organize markets and thus give a certain amount of protection to producers in sectors "unprotected" by cartels because of the disperse nature of the markets. This affected first and foremost agricultural markets. After the customs measures imposed in 1927, agricultural prices continued to rise, unlike world prices, until 1931. After 1931, French agricultural prices developed in parallel with world prices, despite the isolation of the French market. An attempt was made first to control the price of corn directly (1933), then to regulate the quantities produced (1934). In 1930, measures were taken to reduce wine production and avoid inflated inventories. In industry, attempts were made to set up professional organizations, which foreshadowed and prepared the way for the corporatism of the Vichy government. The most serious of these attempts, the "Flandin-Marchandeau" project, was rejected by the Senate, sympathetic to the deep-rooted desire of French employers to preserve their individual independence vis-à-vis the state and other employers. But certain measures of this kind were taken, chiefly the *décrets-lois* (the equivalent of "orders in council") enacted by the Laval government in 1935. They affected the silk industry, the milling trade, and the shoe industry. In the case of silk, the employers who were consulted refused the proposed system. But in the shoe industry it was agreed that no factory should be expanded and no new factories built. Thus, where cartels did not come into being spontaneously, the state was powerless in most cases to impose organization on the sector concerned.

The Popular Front, which came to power in May 1936, tried to offset the crisis by manipulating the level of consumption. The leaders of the Popular Front thought an increase in demand would give investment a new start at last. A. Sauvy has often shown that this policy of suddenly increasing purchasing power could not produce the desired effects because the law reducing the working week to 40 hours, which was very strictly enforced, had taken all the elasticity out of production. Moreover, neither investment nor savings was reestablished, for France was suffering from a veritable flight of capital. And yet, between November 1936 and January 1937, it was possible briefly to hope that there would be a recovery. The Léon Blum government, despite its initial promises, had to devalue the franc by 29 percent in September 1936, fixing both a lower and a higher limit to its exchange rate and forbidding private transactions in gold; the effect of this was to prevent the return of gold which the devaluation itself should have produced.

The recovery in production and exports did not last beyond February 1937. The French economy then entered a period of a general rise in prices, accompanied by a stagnation in industrial production, despite a few fluctuations. The Popular Front had led to "stagflation." However, the rise in domestic prices continued, as did the fall of the franc on the exchange markets, and this made it possible to keep French prices below foreign prices. By May 1938 the various devaluations had brought the value of the franc down to 36 percent of its 1928 level.

At this point, production had fallen by 6 percent in relation to May 1936, investment had fallen by 11 percent, and building activity by 20 percent. The recovery of the French economy began at this period. The government of Edouard Daladier (March 1938) inaugurated an economic policy which was better defined both in its ends and in its means, and which in many ways foreshadowed postwar government planning. The measures taken between March and July 1938 were all directed toward an increase in production through the stimulation of private investment. Some measures were general, but there were several hundred others which applied to special sectors. Thus a system of interest payments was adopted to help people build their own houses, and an attempt was made to promote groupings among companies producing electricity so that they might establish equipment programs in common. "The spirit of the 1950s" is already present in this policy.

But the government, afraid of the trade unions, had drawn back from the idea of altering the law on the 40-hour week. The alteration was promulgated in November 1938, after Paul Reynaud had been made Minister of Finance on November 1st. He introduced a policy which, according to his own description, was "designed to act within the framework of liberty," his object being to "reinforce the ground floor" of the building which supports the whole edifice and is the level "at which real wealth is produced, the wealth of investment and consumption" in order to insure the strength of the "upper story," "where raw materials are transformed into arms and munitions." For all this, in addition to systematically rejecting exchange control, he "appealed to the spirit of enterprise," he "reestablished profit where the industrialist was ready to invest and take a risk." The decrees issued by Reynaud, as well as modifying the law on the 40-hour week, also provided for the easing of price controls where these existed in the noncartelized sectors, a reduction of expenditure on public works so as to finance arms expenditure, and finally a fiscal policy designed to favor investment, whether financed by loan or by self-financing. To these ad hoc measures were added others designed to stimulate the birth rate (the Code de la Famille, inspired by A. Sauvy) and give a new impetus to housing.

The recovery was spectacular. Between November and June production went up by 15 percent and inflation was halted. The movements of capital were reversed, and the expansion of exports brought down the trade deficit. It was possible to stabilize the franc at its spring 1938 level, which, once again, may be considered exaggeratedly low.

The Second World War

The Second World War was an unprecedented ordeal for France. In previous pages we have given estimates of the amount of destruction that was caused. Few French people realized how great it was at the time, and A. Sauvy was disregarded when he advised the Algiers government to tell the French people not that the enemy had looted France but that they had destroyed it. Moreover, the acceleration in technical progress which occurred in other belligerent countries did not affect France. France, totally isolated, actually regressed technically. Lastly, the war and the Occupation brought about the hyperinflation of the late 1940s. Yet Stanley Hoffmann has described the Vichy government as one of the sources of the later revival. This view corresponds to a conception of French economic history which makes too great a contrast between a totally conservative and Malthusian period before 1940 and a post-1945 period which was wholly dynamic. There is no doubt that during the Vichy period institutions and habits came into being which later on were seen to be useful in restarting France's activity. But they also increased certain "corporatist" tendencies in the economic system. While the perfecting of methods of economic observation and forecasting was an indispensable instrument in the working-out of later economic policies, it had begun under the Reynaud government, and was not specific to France alone. The strengthening of employers' associations and agricultural associations did make it possible to establish a permanent dialogue between the state and the representatives of employers and of the farming community, and this was useful, but it also dangerously increased the pressure which could be exercised by certain members of these groups. In fact, the gap between dream and reality which French governments maintained has rarely been as marked as it was under the Vichy government. The claim was that they were constructing a new, "corporatist" economic order, designed to eliminate class struggle. This corporatism was a continuation of intellectual trends seen in the crisis of the 1930s. The Charte du Travail, painfully worked out in a climate of conflicting tendencies toward trade unionism, paternalism, and state control, elicited from the employers, those chiefly affected, only "protective benevolence or polite indifference," while it produced frank hostility among the great majority of workers who belonged to unions. The real arrangements for managing and directing the French economy during the war and the Occupation were set up first of all in the early days of hostilities, then after the débâcle by the new government, which wished to prevent the occupying power from taking over the whole of France's economy without intermediaries, as it had done in the "Northern Zone."

The array of economic measures necessary for the management of a war economy was ready when war broke out: it included control of foreign trade, with various bans on exports and imports; strict control of currency exchange, the arrangements for which were ready as early as 1938; and strict control of prices and wages to prevent inflation. Another series of measures was designed to enable the state to direct production. The direction of manpower came under government control. Groups were set up for controlling imports and distribution, and these continued to function until 1945. The state defined priorities, and distributed raw materials and scarce intermediate goods among industrialists according to France's war needs.

The "organizing committees" were created on August 16, 1940 by Bichelonne, who was later to say, "It is worse for a country to lose all its strength than to choose the wrong side." He took an industrialist view characteristic of the technocrats of the 1930s. The organizing committees, armed with enormous power over business enterprises, and even with official means of compulsion, were dominated either by employers, when employers' associations were powerful in the sector concerned, or by civil servants. The committees served as instruments for applying the directives issued by the Office Central de Répartition (Central Distributing Board). In 1945 there were 231 committees actually functioning, including 129 in the industrial sector, covering 1,800,000 enterprises. Although they were largely absorbed by their immediate tasks, they introduced a method of managing the national economy founded on a cooperation between the state and the economic oligarchies which was later to be the driving force behind postwar planning.

An English historian, A. S. Milward, has given the best analysis of the methods by which the Germans exploited France. The phrase of a French Treasury official, P. Arnoult, that "the Germans seized our finances in order to buy our economy," is on the whole correct. The value of the franc in relation to the mark was fixed at an arbitrary level corresponding to an overvaluation of the mark by 50 or 63 percent, according to whether one takes the value of the dollar in June 1940 or of the pound in 1939 as a reference. The cost of the Occupation was charged to France and fixed at an extremely high figure (20 million marks per day). A clearance agreement provided that all French commerce must be transacted through Germany, and that the Banque de France had to finance deficits. Thus, when the Germans bought goods in France they did so in an undervalued currency and used advances from the

Banque de France designed to finance foreign trade. It was in this way that the Germans "bought" the French economy. The agreements made between the French and German governments concealed mechanisms for making levies which were as ruinous as any could have been under a straightforward military occupation.

But this did not stop the Germans from resorting to seizure of goods, not so much to subject France to systematic looting, but—though it often came to the same thing—to transform French industry into a sort of subcontractor of German industry. Before Stalingrad, the Germans' chief aim was to use France's economic potential to carry out their own war aims. After 1941 they followed two contradictory policies; one continued the previous system, and the other tended to make more and more onerous levies, in particular on labor. In July 1944 there were 723,000 French workers at forced labor in Germany, and at least a million French workers working for Germany in France itself. Moreover, in December 1942 the daily indemnity was raised to 25 million marks. Under the "metal plan" of 1942, levies in kind were increased. In 1944, when the German leaders were still arguing as to whether to demand additional efforts from the French system of production, or to increase the number of compulsory workers, the argument was really pointless because Germany had already taken as much from France as it was possible to take. All in all, over the whole period, payments to Germany represented half of public expenditure, 20 percent of the national income in 1941 and 1942, and 36 percent in 1943. According to A. Sauvy, 74 percent of France's iron ore production, 61 percent of iron and steel production, 64 percent of motorcars and cycles, and 34 percent of chemical products went to Germany.

These levies were the chief cause of the disequilibrium from which the French economy was suffering in 1944. In fact, two parallel economic systems functioned together under the Occupation: an economy of rationing and quotas, run by the organizing committees, the central supply committees, and national and departmental purchasing groups, which distributed products without bothering about prices because prices were fixed; and another economy in which prices operated naturally according to the law of the market. The latter was the black market, which acted as a kind of corrective to the official economy.

As we have seen from the examples of the Loiret and the Nord, the unemployment crisis which occurred at the end of 1940 was not solved until spring 1941. But one form of resistance to forced labor was declared by "employed" workers who in fact were not really working at all. The index for industrial production, taking 1938 to equal 100, fell to 72 in May 1940, 55 in May 1943, and 44 in May 1944. This overall index does not really tell us much: steel production was at an index of 82 in 1943, while textile production had been reduced to a fifth or a quarter. Building activity continued only because of the construction of the Atlantic Wall, private building having almost entirely disappeared.

This fall in production is to be explained as much, and probably more, by the largely voluntary decrease in productivity as by shortages of labor and raw materials. In 1944 it took four times as long to make a Moranne-Saulnier plane in France as it did in Germany. In agriculture, the lack of manpower, fertilizers, manure, and animal foodstuffs, together with bad weather conditions, account for a fall of 11 percent in vegetable production in 1944 as against 1934–38, and a fall of 30 percent in animal production. Rationing was only partly effective. The government did not succeed in totally controlling either production or consumption. The energy value of rations was 1,200 calories in 1943 as against 2,400 in 1938. The black market served to make up the difference, but only for those who could take advantage of it.

The dualism of the economic system, with a rationing economy on one side and a black market on the other, destroyed the unity of the price system. The wholesale price index of 135 controlled articles rose from 100 in 1938 to 300 and 222 in June 1944 for agricultural and industrial products, respectively. Within these main categories there were enormous differences according to the products concerned, and raw materials, which were better controlled, increased less than finished goods. Discrepancies were even more marked in retail prices. The prices of rents and public services did not follow the general rise. Gas increased by 25 percent and oil by 325 percent. There are equally great disparities among the few known prices on the black market. Compared with official prices, the black market prices ranged between two to three times higher (beef) and ten to thirty times higher (coal). According to INSEE, goods not subject to official pricing saw their prices multiply by an average of 8, though the figure varied between 3 and 23. So inflation began before spring 1944. The taxation of the Vichy government was far from efficient, while the enormous disparities in price changes came to be an important cause of later acceleration in inflation, because everyone naturally tried to fix his own prices at the highest level—something comparatively easy to do, since shortages, as A. Sauvy has frequently repeated, could not disappear overnight.

On the other hand, control of wages was fairly efficient. The hourly wage went up only 60 percent between 1938 and 1944, while working hours differed considerably in length from one sector to another. The most obvious consequence of the wage and price policy was a fall of at least 40 percent in real wages. This should not be forgotten if we wish to understand the social explosions which occurred after the war.

Another cause of galloping inflation was introduced, in addition to the disparity in prices. In 1943 taxes financed 32 percent of the national budget, debentures 40 percent, and loans from the Banque de France 28 percent. The public debt rose from 410 billion francs in August 1939 to 1,200 billion in 1944, a growth rate fairly close to that of wholesale prices. The amount of money in circulation quadrupled. In fact, the period is characterized by the large amount of liquidities available and by the inequality in their distribution. The increase in stocks and shares and in the price of businesses, and the increased amounts of savings deposits show that many people had enormous amounts of money available which they could not use in buying goods. The discount rate fell to 1.75 percent, while the Napoleon rose from 267 francs in August 1939 to 3,500 francs in May 1944!

Thus, all the conditions favorable to inflation were combined: an exaggeratedly large range of prices; enormous amounts of money available; a system of production largely

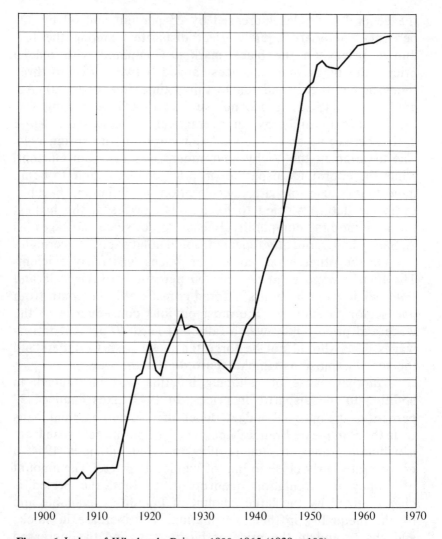

Figure 6 Index of Wholesale Prices, 1900–1965 (1938 = 100).

SOURCE: *Annuaire statistique de la France, 1966* (Paris: Imprimerie Nationale, 1966), p. 561 (A. Sauvy).

destroyed and incapable for a long time to meet the enormous potential demand; and a system of compulsory price fixing which was in fact under pressure from producers. Only firm political determination could have stopped inflation, and this determination was lacking.

Reconstruction and Inflation: 1946–1950

Before 1948 everything was sacrificed to the requirements of reconstruction. Until the early months of 1947 the great preoccupation was, as Michel Byas has pointed out, "to set things to rights again" after the destruction due to military operations and the Occupation. Rail transport and coal production had recovered their 1938 levels by the end of 1945. But gradually the idea became established that reconstruction ought to serve as an instrument for the renewal of the French economy, for catching up on the old backwardness which experts were now becoming aware of. For example, statistical data on the situation in France in 1946 showed that net industrial production per worker, in dollars, was 922 in France, 3,840 in the United States, and 1,125 in Great Britain. They also showed that in 1938 France was responsible for only 5.1 percent of world industrial production as against 7.2 percent in 1913. As we have already seen, the authors of the first plan, the Monnet Plan, believed that in order to overcome this handicap France needed to invest at all costs.

The financial market could not be relied on for financing these investments. So it was the state that took on the responsibility of transforming private liquid savings into long-term capital, controlling them by means of such institutions as the Crédit National, the Caisse des Dépôts et Consignations, and the Trésor Public. "Medium-term equipment credits" were introduced: banks could grant these to business firms, and they could be discounted with the Crédit National, the Caisse des Dépôts, and the Banque de France. The government also allocated war compensation, subsidies, long-term Treasury loans, and most important of all, credits from external debt— loans floated abroad up to 1947, and after that date loans from the Marshall Plan. The reconstruction program gave priority to "key sectors" without progress in which, according to the first plan, "no progress was possible in the economy as a whole." In particular, energy production absorbed nearly half of France's investment resources during the first plan, and in this sector first priority was given to coal. Among other industries, iron and steel and cement were given priority; they were the chief beneficiaries of credits granted by the state and, from 1948 on, by the "Fonds de Modernisation et d'Equipment" provided out of public funds. These priorities were prejudicial to the financing of investment in other sectors, which were reduced to self-financing. In this way the priorities prolonged certain shortages.

The galloping inflation France experienced at this period was to an appreciable extent the consequence of this policy of investment "at any price." It was in the spring of 1945 that the process was triggered off which was later to become uncontrollable. Some members of General de Gaulle's government had suggested the freezing of money, but the measures taken in April 1945 were limited to the mere exchange of notes in circulation (the replacement of Vichy currency). The government also set about a general tidying-up of prices and wages: the race between prices and wages had begun, all the more headlong because there was a seller's market. Attempts at government control tended only to quicken the pace. Overhasty liberalization measures, in a world where competition had been abolished, produced sudden increases which the government was forced to apply generally. In an attempt to contain the increases the state gave subsidies to agricultural products and public services which sooner or later it would have to reduce or abolish, thus producing another generalized rise. The Palais Royal Conference in April 1947 is a good illustration of the government's powerlessness: the state, instead of acting as arbiter among the various claims, recorded those of both workers' and employers' unions, which were thus added together. In May 1946 the government had granted a completely unjustified increase in agricultural prices, and was thus unable to do anything else but yield to other occupational categories.

The victims of the fixed-price system were the masses: in April 1947, after Léon Blum's successful attempt since January to keep prices stable, the purchasing power of weekly wages was only two-thirds of the 1938 level. Social unrest grew serious in the spring of 1947, when the government of the socialist Ramadier abolished food subsidies and imposed large increases in the prices of public services. The resulting conflicts culminated in the strikes of November 1947. As Jean Monnet wrote at the time, "The French economy is in danger of real dislocation. Food prices are shooting up madly. Speculative hoarding is growing more and more widespread. Even rising prices contribute to supply difficulties, because producers prefer to consume or keep their own products rather than sell them for money which is depreciating. The lowering of the worker's standard of living makes France live under the threat of strikes. Budgetary attempts to redress the balance are swept away in the flood of rising prices."

The plan put forward by René Mayer, Minister of Finance, was the first serious attempt to get the country out of this vicious circle. The plan used taxation to reduce liquidity, and above all sought to do away with the rigidity of the price fixing system. It continued the policy of abolishing subsidies which had been begun in the spring, and allowed market laws to operate; this encouraged prices to become more stable, and shortages began to disappear. The plan was a success. In the short term, industrial prices suddenly caught up with agricultural prices: between October 1947 and February 1948 they rose by 72 percent, while agricultural prices rose by only 14 percent. They then became stable. In fact, the year 1948 is a decisive turning-point in the history of inflation in France. The inflationary process begun in 1936 had gradually accelerated: between 1936 and 1938 the mean annual rise in retail prices was 15 percent, and between 1939 and 1948 it was 33 percent. Between 1948 and 1951 it was 12 percent. So 1948, thanks to the Mayer plan, showed a slowdown of inflation. Petsche, the man who succeeded Mayer in February 1949, followed in the same path of liberalization. At the end of 1949, all products were being sold at uncontrolled prices. But the good work was not carried through to its logical conclusion. The network of cartels agreed to by the state was still very strong, and when the Korean War broke out in 1950 the price system was still so rigid that it amplified the price rises resulting from the increased cost of raw materials and the increase in defense expenditure. In my view, the Mayer plan was the point of departure for a new growth, in that it opted for a liberal solution which, whatever happened, was better than the "dirigisme of privilege" which was rampant in France at that time.

Bibliography

Aftalion, A. *L'équilibre des relations économiques internationales.* Paris: Domat Montchrestien, 1937.
——"L'histoire du change en France de 1915 à 1926," *Revue d'Economie Politique*, 1930.
——"Prix, circulation et change en France de 1920 à 1924," *Revue d'Economie Politique*, 1924.
Arnoult, P. *Les finances de la France sous l'occupation allemande.* Paris: Presses Universitaires de France, 1951.
Berr, R. "Une évolution nouvelle de l'industrie chimique," *Bulletin de la Société des Ingénieurs Civils.* Account of the December 21, 1926 session.
Byas, M. *Formation du capital et reconstruction française.* Paris: A. Colin, 1952.
Delemer, A. *Le bilan de l'étatisme.* Paris: Payot, 1922.
Dessirier, J. "Secteurs 'abrités' et 'non abrités' dans le déséquilibre actuel de l'économie française," *Revue d'Economie Politique*, July–August 1935.
Ehrmann, J. *La politique du patronat français, 1936–1955.* Paris: A. Colin, 1959.
Fontaine, A. *L'industrie française pendant la guerre.* Carnegie Endowment. Paris: Presses Universitaires de France, 1925.
De la France d'avant guerre à la France d'aujourd'hui. Special issue of *Revue d'Economie Politique*, 1939.
La France économique de 1939 à 1946. Special issue of *Revue d'Economie Politique*, 1947.
La France et l'inflation. Special issue of *Etudes et Conjoncture* on the French economy, May–June, 1951.
Fridenson, P. *Histoire des usines Renault, 1898–1939.* Paris: Seuil, 1972.
Fromont, P. "L'agriculture française en 1934," *Revue d'Economie Politique*, 1935.
Germain Martin, L. *Une année de politique financière . . .* Paris: Guillemot and Lamothe, 1927.
——*Les problèmes actuels des finances publiques.* Paris: Payot, 1933.
Gruson, C. *Origines et espoirs de la planification française.* Paris: Dunod, 1968.
Hoffmann, S. *A la recherche de la France.* Paris: Seuil, 1963.
Jèze, G. *Les dépenses de guerre de la France.* Carnegie Endowment. Paris: Presses Universitaires de France, 1926.
Kuisel, R. F. *Ernest Mercier, French Technocrat.* Berkeley: University of California Press, 1967.

Mairesse, J. *L'évaluation du capital fixe productif: Méthodes et résultats.* Collections de l'INSEE, ser. C, nos. 18–19. Paris: Institut National de la Statistique des Etudes Economiques, November 1972.

Malissen, M. *L'autofinancement des sociétés en France et aux Etats Unis.* Paris: Dalloz, 1953.

Marion, M. *Histoire financière de la France depuis 1715.* Vol. 6. Paris: Rousseau et Cie, 1931.

Milward, A. S. *The New Order and the French Economy.* Oxford: Oxford University Press, 1970.

Monnet, J. "Rapport au nom de la Commission du Bilan," *Journal Officiel de la République Française,* December 13, 1947.

Moreau, E. *Souvenirs d'un gouverneur de la Banque de France, 1926–1928.* Paris: Médicis, 1954.

Petit, L. *Histoire des finances extérieures de la France pendant la guerre.* Paris: Payot, 1929.

Poncet, A. F. *La vie et l'oeuvre de Robert Pinot.* Paris: A. Colin, 1927.

Reboul, L. C. *La mobilisation industrielle,* vol. 1, *Les fabrications de guerre.* Paris: Berger Levrault, 1925.

Renouvin, P. *Les formes de gouvernement de guerre.* Carnegie Endowment. Paris: Presses Universitaires de France, 1925.

Rist, C. "L'économie française en ...," published annually in *Revue d'Economie Politique,* 1930–37.

Sauvy, A. *Histoire économique de la France entre les deux guerres.* Paris: Fayard, 1965–67.

"La situation des principales branches de l'économie nationale," *Journal Officiel de la République Française,* supplement, 1932 (report of the Conseil National Economique).

Vincent, L. A. "Evolution de la production intérieure brute en France de 1896 à 1938: Méthodes et premiers résultats," *Etudes et Conjoncture,* November 1962.

——"Population active, production et productivité dans 21 branches de l'économie francaise (1896–1962)," *Etudes et Conjoncture,* February 1965.

Weiller, J. "Echanges extérieurs et politique commerciale de la France depuis 1870," *Cahiers de l'Institut de Science Economique Appliquée,* ser. P, nos. 16 and 17.

Chapter Thirteen: Business Structures

OUR ANALYSIS OF the structures of production may be broken down as follows: to begin with we shall examine the evolution of the size of industrial establishments in terms of the number of people they employ. We shall examine both the commercial establishments and the business enterprises in this sector, for until very recently any distinction between the two would have been artificial. Second we shall examine the evolution of the size of private enterprises and try to approach the problem of the evolution of groups, private or public, in France.

Business Enterprises

The Size of Industrial Establishments. In 1954, J. M. Jeanneney, analyzing the evolution of the size of industrial establishments since the beginning of the century, spoke of the "crystallization of the French production system." More recently M. Pidier and E. Malinvaud have noted "the stability in the concentration of industrial establishments," taking into consideration only those establishments which employ more than 10 people. So the pattern here breaks down into two distinct elements: a decline in establishments employing more than 10 people, and stability in the distribution of establishments with more than 10 people. In 1906 27 percent of the working population were employed in establishments where there was no salaried employee, and in 1966 only 4 percent did so. The number of people working in establishments employing 10 and fewer people fell from 58 percent to 20 percent of the working population. The rest of the working population thus represented 42 percent of the total working population in 1906 and 80 percent in 1966. The evolution of its distribution is shown in table 13.1.

Table 13.1 Distribution of the Working Population by Size of Establishment (in percent)

No. of People Employed	1906	1931	1954	1966
11–20	12	10	8	8
21–100	28	27	28	29
101–500	31	30	31	33
Over 500	29	33	33	30

This quite varied distribution is similar to that found in Japan and Italy. These resemblances are thought to be due to "backwardness in industrial development [in these three countries] at the end of the nineteenth century, at a time when the comparative advantages of large establishments were clearer than they are today" (Didier and Nioche).

While accepting this general pattern, I should like to modify it in two ways: first by showing that if workers employed in small establishments are included, the movements were of great amplitude; and second by putting forward a periodization of the evolution based on an analysis of the distribution of supplementary workers.

The distribution of employees by size of establishment is shown in table 13.2. In the long term the fall of 60 percent in very small establishments was made up for by strongly differentiated growth in establishments of other dimensions: 15 percent in small ones, 33 percent in medium, and 40 percent in large establishments. But it is clear that three periods should be distinguished: 1906–31, 1931–54, and 1954–66. During the first period there was a marked preference for large establishments. The 1.8 million supplementary industrial employees were divided up as follows between establishments: 32 percent in

Table 13.2 Distribution of the Industrial Working Population by Size of Establishment (in percent)

No. of People Employed	1906	1931	1954	1962	1966
1–10	32.2	19.7	16.0	14.0	13.1
11–100	27.6	30.1	30.8	30.8	31.9
101–500	21.7	23.6	25.9	27.7	29.0
Over 500	18.5	26.6	27.2	27.5	26.0
Number of industrial employees (in thousands)	3,679	5,442	5,918	6,475	6,831

small ones, 26.5 percent in medium ones, and 41.5 percent in large establishments. The number of very large establishments (over 1,000 employees) rose from 215 to 395, and their average size rose from 2,228 to 2,530 employees. There is a good correlation between the size of the establishment and the ratio of capital invested to number of workers (see table 13.3). The preference for large establishments therefore seems to correspond to technological necessities.

Between 1931 and 1954 the growth in the salaried industrial population was only 475,000: a third of the new workers were employed in small establishments (with 21–100 workers), two-fifths in medium establishments, and one-fifth in large, while only 6 percent worked in very large establishments. The size of the average establishment, which doubled between 1906 and 1931, increased by only 18 percent in this period (rising from 100 to 118 workers). The number of very large establishments continued to grow (479 instead of 395), but their average size fell from 2,530 to 2,170 workers. This preference for medium-sized establishments was accentuated between 1954 and 1966.

Table 13.3 Power per 100 Employees by Size of Establishment (in kilowatts)

No. of People Employed	All Establishments	Only Those Using Machine Power
6–20	59	126
21–100	77	108
101–500	163	177
501–1000	209	216
Over 1000	360	363

It thus corresponds to a new technological pattern. For an increase of about a million in the number of industrial employees, 35 percent worked for small establishments, 45 percent for medium establishments, 20 percent in large, and only 3.3 percent in very large establishments. The highly capitalistic nature of certain new industries, the tendency toward capital intensification in all industries, and considerations of organization explain this preference.

The Legal Forms. In France a business enterprise is not a legal entity except in labor relations law. It takes the legal form of a "commercial society," as defined in the Napoleonic code of commerce. Company law has changed appreciably, but without any sudden breaks: the law of 1966 merely tidied up existing legislation. The chief novelty.dates from 1925, when the law on *sociétés à responsabilité limitée* made anonymity and nonliability "available to small traders." This law did not impose a lower limit on the amount of capital, nor did it impose any condition as to the number of people forming the company or the distribution of capital among them. This form of company was a dazzling success. The two other novelties are more recent: one was the possibility offered by the law of 1966 of organizing the *société anonyme* on the German model, i.e., with a directorate and a supervisory board instead of the *conseil d'administration* (board of directors) of 1867; the second novelty was the institution in 1967 of "economic groupings" designed to promote the creation of bodies common to several companies.

In 1969 there were 1,663,364 enterprises, as against 1,763,815 in 1961. They were distributed among the different sectors of activity as is shown in table 13.4. Out of this total, tax statistics have listed 404,908 enterprises—excluding civil companies and companies in the public sector—which are subject to the tax on real profits (see table 13.5). Other companies are subject to a system of outright taxation which, we may note in passing, is really an invitation to tax fraud.

Thus, in 1969, two-thirds of total turnover was controlled by *sociétés anonymes*, and slightly less than one-third by *sociétés à responsabilité limitée* or individual enterprises. We

Table 13.4 Distribution of Establishments among the Various Sectors

	1961		1969	
	No.	Percent	No.	Percent
Activities overseas and various	26,285	1.50	28,852	1.70
Energy	621	0.04	726	0.04
Industry	642,844	36.40	574,787	34.56
Transport and telecommunications	54,155	3.06	63,256	3.80
Commerce	889,156	50.40	832,159	50.00
Services	150,754	8.60	163,587	9.90
Total	1,763,815	100.00	1,663,367	100.00

Table 13.5 Establishments Subject to the Tax on Real Profits (in percent)

	No. of Companies	Turnover before Tax
Sociétés à responsabilité limitée	30.2	15.4
Sociétés anonymes	21.6	68.3
Sociétés en nom collectif	2.7	1.4
Sociétés en commandite simple	0.3	0.3
Sociétés en commandite par action	0.05	0.9
Sociétés cooperatives	0.5	0.9
Economic groups	0.05	0.03
Various	3.5	1.2
Individual enterprises	41.1	11.57
Total percent	100.00	100.00
Total number	404,908	1,071,835,478 f.f.

have the statistics for the companies formed up to 1964, and have extracted table 13.6. The table shows clearly the practical disappearance of *sociétés en nom collectif* to the advantage of *sociétés à responsabilité limitée,* which reflects a generalization, at all levels, of nonliability and anonymity; the decline in the spirit of enterprise in the 1930s; the explosion of capitalism among small and even very small enterprises in the years 1945–54; and the renaissance of the *sociétés anonymes* after 1955.

The Concentration of Industrial Enterprises: Up to the Beginning of the 1950s. In addition to the proliferation of small

Table 13.6 Mean Annual Number of Companies Formed

	Total	Soc. en nom collectif	Soc. à résp. limitée	Soc. anonyme
1919–1928	13,581	7,510		2,500
1926–1928			7,300	
1929–1938	9,769	1,314	6,223	1,917
1940–1944	8,460	685	6,637	817
1945–1954	23,019	1,551	17,576	923
1955–1964	13,488	1,087	8,231	3,726

companies which we have just observed, two other facts characterized the evolution of the structure of enterprises: the stability of the weight of large firms, and the relatively secondary role which mergers played in their growth. All these facts can only be understood through the development of what were called "trusts" or "Konzerns," and what we now call "groups."

Up to the beginning of the 1950s, we have no overall statistics for turnover. To analyze concentration we have to be content to use the value of the issued capital of listed companies. There were 448 of these companies in 1912, 975 in 1936, and 1,307 in 1952. Between 1911 and 1936 the value of the capital of listed companies multiplied by 5.5, while that of national income multiplied by 6.5. The concentration of assets among the top companies is given in table 13.7. To interpret this table we must take into account the growth in the number of companies included in the sample. If we take concentration as a percentage of the total working population, we get the results shown in table 13.8.

The proportion of large firms did not diminish, and we may conclude, with J. Houssiaux, that "the concentration of assets scarcely changed." An analysis of the movements which took

Table 13.7 Concentration of Assets among Top Companies, According to J. Houssiaux (in percent)

	1912	1936	1952
100 top	71	59	58
50 top	52	42	43
15 top	25	22	22

Table 13.8 Concentration as a Percentage of the Working Population

	1912	1936	1952
5 percent of firms employ	31	40	50
10 percent of firms employ	50	49	61

place within the group of the 100 top French enterprises gives the same impression of stability. Among the 100 top French enterprises in 1950, only 18 were less than 30 years old.

A few spectacular mergers took place in French industry on the eve of the First World War and in the 1920s: just before the war, important regroupings occurred in the alumina sector, which were continued in 1921 with the merger of the two main French producing companies. In 1925 the Kuhlmann company took over the Société Nationale des Matières Colorantes (dyes) which was founded during the war. In 1928 the Etablissements du Rhône and the Société Poulenc merged to form the Société Rhône-Poulenc, which is at present the chief private firm in France.

But in fact these operations were rather exceptional. On the one hand firms "chose internal growth for preference" (Houssiaux). Moreover, though the number of mergers increased, they tended to be smaller, if measured by the relation between the value of assets brought in and the value of the assets of the absorbing company (table 13.9).

The mergers of the last years of the 1920s occurred in small or medium-sized enterprises which could not by themselves maintain growth. In the 1930s, mergers tended to be rescue operations for firms in difficulties, and part of a larger pattern of reorganization of sectors.

Table 13.9 Size of Mergers, as Ratio of Assets Brought In to Assets of Absorbing Company

	No. of Mergers	Assets Ratio
1918–1926	16	27.5
1927–1931	45	13.0
1932–1938	34	24.0
1939–1944	23	10.8
1945–1950	23	8.8

As J. Denuc wrote in 1939, "instead of thousands of competing enterprises, there arose a network of holdings in enterprises which remained independent only in form, the object being a decrease in retail prices or regulation of production and prices." In 1952 the item "securities and holdings" in the balance sheet of the 100 largest French companies amounted to over 200 billion francs, while their gross assets amounted to 237 billion. These enterprises had 900 financial links, i.e., an average of 9 links per enterprise. J. Houssiaux concluded: "Despite a production structure which remains unconcentrated, most of the business in France is under the more or less direct control of the large enterprises." The iron and steel industry provides an example of this development of group structures. The regrouping operations which occurred at the end of the 1940s and brought about the creation of Sidelor, Usinor, and Lorraine-Escaut were the result of very old groupings, visible through the existence of subsidiaries common to the groups which merged. Sidelor is a continuation of what C. Precheur has called the "supergroup," Mar-Mich-Pont, i.e., a group bringing together the firms Marine et Homécourt, Micheville, and Pont à Mousson. Usinor was formed through the assets brought in by two firms of the Nord, which were connected by very ancient links: Denain/Anzin and Nord Est, which both became holding companies after transferring all their assets to Usinor. The Société Lorraine-Escaut was the result of a long and patient attempt at integration begun before the 1914 war by the Aciéries le Longwy. Chemicals showed the usual strong concentration of heavy industry, the big firms tending to be transformed into groups through the development of their shareholding network: according to Kuhlmann's balance sheet their portfolio rose from 23 to 140 million francs between 1923 and 1938, while at the same time their fixed assets rose from 167 to 199 million. The motorcar industry, on the other hand, is a typical example of a sector where the growth of big firms was carried out essentially through internal growth, noncompetitive firms simply disappearing. There were 155 motorcar manufacturers in 1924, 60 in 1932, and 31 in 1939. In 1951 the first four motorcar firms controlled 88.6 percent of the production of private vehicles (Renault: 31.8 percent; Citröen: 25.5 percent;

Peugeot: 18.5 percent; Simca, a subsidiary of Fiat: 12.8 percent). According to Houssiaux, the structure of French industry remained dispersed because of the development of networks of cartels—"kartells," as they were called at the time. Legislation forbidding cartels was modified by the law of 1926, which distinguished between good and bad cartels and authorized the first kind. This sort of link between firms relaxed during the 1920s, grew stronger in the 1930s, and was generalized under the Vichy government through the creation of the organizing committees, which in fact survived Vichy. After 1940, as a 1952 committee of inquiry observed, "all the members of one branch of industry were legally encouraged to unite to establish in common cost prices, sale prices, and profit margins to be proposed to the bodies authorizing prices." Giving evidence before the committee of inquiry, a representative of the price board declared that a large number of industrial organizations, after the abolition of the price freeze in their sector, "had replaced state control with their own control." That being so, "it was neither the market price nor the cost price which served as a basis for transactions, but the prices which were fixed by cartels." This rigid structure was the result of events since 1929 rather than any long-term preference on the part of French entrepreneurs for cartels, as most authors claimed at the beginning of the 1950s.

Since the Beginning of the 1950s. When we try to analyze the concentration of business enterprises after the beginning of the 1950s we come up against difficulties which are due not so much to the inadequacy of our sources as to their lack of homogeneity. There are two ways of tackling this. First, we can classify enterprises by category according to their size, and then analyze the distribution of value added or invested capital or turnover among these enterprises. This gives us a measure of the weight of each category within total production. Second, we can use ratios of concentration, i.e., define the part played by the most important enterprises in the deliveries in a certain sector. We are then measuring the strength of the big enterprises. The first kind of analysis can be made on the basis of the following three tables, though unfortunately they are not easily comparable with one another. The first, table 13.10

Table 13.10 Industrial Structure in 1962, All Sectors

Size of Enterprise (No. of Workers)	No. of Enter- prises	Percent Workers	Value Added	Invest- ment	Thousands of Francs Value Added per Worker	Invest- ment per Worker
0–9	88.2	16.6	10.1	6.4	12.6	1.2
10–19	4.7	5.5	4.6	3.2	17.3	2.8
20–49	4.0	10.1	8.6	6.6	17.6	2.1
50–99	1.5	8.4	7.2	5.9	17.8	2.2
100–199	0.8	9.0	8.0	6.8	18.4	2.4
200–499	0.5	11.6	11.1	10.2	19.9	2.8
500–999	0.2	8.2	8.3	8.7	20.8	3.3
Over 1,000	0.1	30.6	42.1	52.2	28.6	5.5
Totals	100	100	100	100	19.1	3.2

(1962), deals with all industrial activities in the broad sense, i.e., it includes building and public works, which are appreciably smaller in size than the other sectors, and it also includes the food sector. Tables 13.11 and 13.12, which deal with more recent years (1970 and 1971), cover a more limited field. Moreover, they exclude enterprises employing 5 or fewer workers.

In 1962, the big enterprises (employing over 500 people), of which there were 564, employed a third of the workers, and provided more than two-fifths of the value added, while carrying out over half of investments. Small enterprises (of 0–50 people) employed one-third of the labor force, provided one-

Table 13.11 Industrial Structure in 1970, Not Including Building or Agricultural and Food Industries (in percent)

Size	No. of Enterprises	Turnover	Workers	Investments
6–19	41.7	3.6	4.4	2.2
20–49	31.1	7.3	9.0	4.8
50–99	12.7	6.8	8.1	4.0
100–199	6.8	7.2	8.6	4.5
200–499	4.9	11.8	13.2	9.2
500–999	1.7	10.0	10.6	7.7
1,000–1,999	0.6	8.2	7.5	6.4
2,000 and over	0.5	45.1	38.6	61.2

Table 13.12 Industrial Structure in 1971, Not Including Building or Agricultural and Food Industries (in percent)

Size	Distribution of Workers	Distribution of Turnover	Distribution of Value Added
6–49	12.8	10.2	10.7
50–499	29.9	24.9	25.2
500–1,999	18.7	17.5	17.4
2,000 and over	38.0	45.6	46.0
Uncategorized	0.6	1.8	0.7

quarter of the value added, and were responsible for only one-sixth of investment. Medium enterprises (50–499) employed one-third of the labor force, provided one-third of value added, and were responsible for 37 percent of investments. These contrasts, which clearly differentiate three types of enterprise, are confirmed by the statistics for value added and investment per worker: for enterprises employing up to 999 people, the growth in value added per capita is fairly regular. Beyond that there is a sudden jump, but it is much more marked in the case of investments. In the category of small and medium enterprises, of from 10 to 499 employees, growth in value added from one size of enterprise to another is obtained without any appreciable increase in the investment effort. Beyond that, increase in value added per capita, though very pronounced, is only obtained through a much more rapid increase in the investment effort: there is a rise of 44 percent in value added and 96 percent in investment from enterprises with 200 workers to those with 1,000 or more.

The facts noted in connection with 1962 are even more marked in tables 13.11 and 13.12 because of the differences in the sectors covered, but also certainly because of a tendency toward concentration which declared itself in the intervening years. We can see that in 1970 the 235 enterprises of 2,000 people and over employed 38.6 percent of all workers, accounted for 45.1 percent of turnover, but were responsible for more than 60 percent of industrial investment. Enterprises of over 500 people employed 56.7 percent of workers, accounted for 63.3 percent of turnover, and were responsible for three-quarters of investment. So we can agree with INSEE on two conclusions: First, "A high concentration emerges in French industrial enterprises." Second, "French industrial enterprises are more concentrated in terms of investment than in terms of turnover, and more concentrated in terms of turnover than in terms of workers."

An analysis of the documents published by the Ministère du Développement Industriel et Scientifique (MDIS) for 1972 enables us to bring out the existence of highly concentrated sectors which are in fact the "strategic" sectors of industry. (We leave aside energy, together with the agricultural and food industries.)

Of the 33 sectors dealt with, 13 sectors, covering 48 percent of the value added, have more than 60 percent of the value added supplied by enterprises employing more than 500 people (see table 13.13).

In most of these sectors, even those which are reputed to have a dispersed structure, the big enterprises occupy a privileged position. In textiles-hosiery, 18 enterprises employ over 2,000 workers and are responsible for a quarter of the value added of the 3,308 enterprises in their sector. The 147 enterprises which employ over 500 people produce over half (51.3 percent) of the value added. In pharmaceuticals, 8 enterprises employ over 1,000 workers and contribute a quarter of the value added, and 33 employ over 500 workers and contribute half of the value added. The 16 perfumery enterprises belonging to this category also contribute close to a half of the value added.

Between 1955 and 1963 the ratios of concentration seem to have been fairly stable (table 13.14), but some sectors achieve very much higher rates (10 top—table 13.15).

The comparative stability occurred while the number of enterprises was decreasing, falling from 473,000 in 1955 to 401,000 in 1963, out of which 133,500 and 106,000 were taxed on real profits, and while an important tendency toward mergers was manifesting itself. All this being so, we conclude that during this period the growth of medium-sized enterprises was greater than that of larger enterprises, and this especially "in rapidly-expanding sectors."

The work of F. Jenny and A. P. Weber, which follows up that of J. Houssiaux, throws some light on the evolution of

Table 13.13 Ratio of Value Added of Strategic Enterprises to Total Value Added, by Size of Enterprise

	Over 500 Employees		Over 1,000 Employees		Over 2,000 Employees	
	Ratio	No. of Enterprises	Ratio	No. of Enterprises	Ratio	No. of Enterprises
Iron mines, iron and steel	96.3	33				
Aeronautics construction	92.2	18	89.1	15	78.8	7
Transport equipment	90.1	104	84.3	52	78.6	28
Glass	84.5	21				
Rubber	84.8	21	80.5	12	71.8	6
Electrical engineering	82.8	146	74.3	74	67.2	46
Nonferrous metals	82.5	10				
Inorganic chemicals	79.0	12			72.8	7
Naval construction	73.1	18	62.9	10	54.7	6
Organic chemicals	70.7	28			49.5	6
Primary steel processing	69.2	16				
Smelting works	67.6	44			40.0	6
Parachemicals	64.7	25	55.9	15	37.9	6

Table 13.14 Share in Turnover of the Big Industrial Enterprises (Excluding Building), According to E. Malinvaud (in percent)

	10 top	20 top	50 top
1955	5.8	8.3	14.3
1959	6.6	9.5	15.6
1963	6.0	9.4	15.3

concentration ratios during the 1960s. The ratio chosen by these authors is that of the share in total sales of the four first enterprises in the sector. The study covers the period 1961–69 for activities as a whole, and the period 1963–69 for just the industrial sectors, analyzed in much more detail. In 1961, 16

Table 13.15 Share in Total Sector Revenues of the Top Ten Firms (in percent)

	1955	1963
Iron and steel	61	67
Smelting works	28	35
Heavy engineering	16	14
Electrical engineering	32	31
Motorcars	66	71
Chemicals	38	36
Rubber	65	62
Cement	45	38

sectors, of which 8 were industrial, had ratios above 50 percent. The turnover of these sectors represents 11.84 percent of the total. In 1969 these highly concentrated sectors still numbered 16 and represented 10.77 percent of turnover. At the other extreme we find 50 sectors in 1961 whose concentration indices are below 20 percent. They account for 76.66 percent of the turnover. In 1969 these sectors numbered 47 and contributed 72.86 percent of the turnover. Thus, between 1961 and 1969, the weight of the highly concentrated sectors slightly decreased. Moreover, the concentration ratios increased in 47 sectors, but often in a modest fashion. There are only 7 sectors where the ratios increased by more than 10 points. These were sectors such as distribution of water (ratio 60 percent), iron and steel (55.5 percent), and general metallurgy (42.2 percent), which already had high ratios to start with. "So concentration increased in sectors which were already concentrated." Lastly, in 33 sectors the ratios decreased. In industrial activities alone, the mean ratios of concentration, weighted by turnover, rose from 20.08 percent to 22.11 percent.

F. Jenny and A. P. Weber, analyzing 238 industrial sectors at a much lower level of concentration, find that in 1963 the ratio is under 20 percent for 34 activities, covering 45.45 percent of turnover; above 50 percent for 90 activities, covering 25.78 percent of turnover. If we admit that, above 40 percent, "there is a chance of noncompetitive behavior showing itself," we must also admit that the concentration achieved then by French industry was "comparable with, if not superior to, that which was observable in West Germany, Britain, and the United States." This concentration grew appreciably more marked between 1963 and 1969. In 1969, 54 sectors accounting for 40 percent of the revenues of 238 sectors had ratios below 20 percent, and 95 sectors accounting for 27.2 percent of the same revenues had ratios above 50 percent. Ratios increased in 140 sectors and decreased in 88. The mean ratio rose from 42.28 percent to 45.08 percent, and the mean ratio weighted by turnover rose from 34.26 percent to 35.88 percent. Repeating a comparison already made by J. Bain at the beginning of the 1960s. Jenny and Weber show that French ratios were often comparable with and sometimes superior to the ratios of the United States, on a market which was, it is true, much narrower. A few factors in this comparison are given in table 13.16.

It seems possible to conclude that while, as we have said above, the 1950s and the early 1960s were a period of rapid expansion for medium-sized enterprises, the last years of the 1960s were dominated by the more rapid growth of large enterprises. There is also an acceleration in the tendency

Table 13.16 Ratios of Concentration in Selected Sectors in France Compared to Those in the United States, after Jenny and Weber (in percent)

	United States	*France*	
	1963	*1963*	*1969*
Motorcars	99	92.5	93
Locomotives	97		94
Aluminum	96		93
Sheet glass	94		90
Turbines	93		94
Lamps	92		87
Copper	78		72
Typewriters	76		61
Soaps and detergents	72		47
Spinning	68	17.7	37
Television	58		58
Synthetic rubber	57	88.7	61
Glass vessels	55		83
Steel	50		72
Textile machinery	35		52
Oil refining	34	45.8	65

toward mergers, which we shall analyze after a brief examination of commercial structures.

Commercial Enterprises. The contrast between two periods (1906–31 and 1931–44) which we have already seen in the structure of industrial establishments also exists in the case of commercial establishments: between 1906 and 1931 their number increased by only 16 percent (369,000 in 1906 and 429,500 in 1931), and a clear tendency toward concentration emerged: in 1936, 13 percent of the working commercial population was employed in establishments employing over 10 people, as against 28 percent in 1931. Between 1931 and 1954, there was a veritable explosion, particularly after the 1945 lifting of the ban on founding new businesses: their number more than doubled (1,006,500 in 1954), while the structure stabilized, and establishments of more than 10 workers employed 26 percent of the commercial working population. So this was the triumph of the small shop, which most economists, politicians, and intellectuals of all kinds lamented at the beginning of the 1950s. They are often the same people who now weep over their real or supposed disappearance.

After 1954, the evolution of commercial structures resumed: in 1966, 36 percent of the commercial working population, including the hotel trade, worked in establishments employing more than 10 people. But, as in the case of industry, the distribution of workers among the different categories of this concentrated sector remained stable between these two dates: 72 percent worked in establishments employing 11 to 100 people, and 28 percent in establishments employing more than 100. In 1966 a detailed census of the retail trade established that there were 510,000 enterprises in this sector. The great majority were individual businesses (i.e., they were not formed into companies): 97 percent in the food trade, 90 percent in trades other than the food trade. Only 11,000 of them had several branches, which employed on the average 2 to 3 workers; 330,000 enterprises employed less than 3 people, 51,000 employed more than 6, and 1,100 more than 50.

In the years between the two wars, especially in the 1930s (the decrees of October 1935), a system of legislation had been worked out which protected small traders against competition from more concentrated forms of trade such as department and chain stores. The report commissioned in 1959 from Rueff and Armand on "Obstacles to Economic Expansion" ushered in a profound change in attitude on the part of the authorities. Legislative and tax reforms gradually abolished most of the protective arrangements which had helped the small trader. As Malinvaud says, "We then saw the spread of the supermarkets and chain stores." Commercial innovation began again. New initiatives were made in a climate of political passion. Among them the Leclerc shops and the Carrefour firm were outstanding successes. Carrefour, founded in 1960, had a turnover of 4.2 billion francs in 1974, and was in the first rank of chain store enterprises. In the same year, the chief department store enterprise—the Galéries Réunies—had a turnover of 3.5 billion francs. Between 1966 and 1974 the number of discount chains rose from 5 to 292, and the number of supermarkets from 1,441 to 2,719. The evolution of shares in the market among the different forms of trade between 1969 and 1973 is given in table 13.17. Statistics allow us to distinguish three categories: (I) large-scale trading, i.e., department stores, popular stores, food chains, cooperatives, mail order firms, and the more recent supermarkets and discount chains; (II) commercial centers composed of independent shops grouped together, or a mixture of independent shops and concentrated forms of sale (a very recent development); (III) independent "traditional" trade.

Thus the dynamism of concentrated commerce has been bound up in recent years in the development of supermarkets

Table 13.17 Share in the Market Among Categories of Trading Establishment, According to *Economie et Statistique*, no. 59 (in percent)

	1969		1973	
I Concentrated trade	22.8		23.2	
Supermarkets and discount chains		3.7		9.1
II Commercial centers	2.4		6.4	
Total supermarkets, discount chains, and mixed		6.1		15.5
III Independent "traditional" trade	74.6		70.4	

and discount chains, though some of these do still include independent trading. The decline of independent commerce is not due to a decline in sales, but to "a rate of growth inferior to that in large-scale commerce." The Royer law of 1973 was designed to halt this trend by acting as a brake on large-scale trading. This law, still in force, provided that the opening of supermarkets and discount chains had to be authorized by a local commission on which representatives of small business held a majority.

Banks. In 1941 the Vichy government laid down rules about banking, following customs which had arisen in the nineteenth century. Banks proper were divided into three categories: merchant banks, deposit banks, and medium- and long-term credit banks. The third category, which was new, never came to much. The first two kinds each had a strictly defined field of activity: merchant banks could not receive deposits from anyone who did not have a stocks and shares account with them, or from firms of which they possessed no shares; deposit banks could not receive deposits of over two years. These restrictions were greatly eased by a law of 1966, and the differences between the two types of bank, though still evident, are now tending to disappear.

The evolution of the banking system was marked by the development of a public sector and by a concentration process which may be broken down into three stages:

1. The 1920s were favorable to "deconcentration" (J. Bouvier). In 1913 132 banks, and in 1929 276 banks published their balance sheets. The "big four" (Crédit Lyonnais, Société Générale, Comptoir d'Escompte, Crédit Industriel et Commercial) held 59 percent and 37 percent of deposits at those two dates.

2. The 1930s were favorable to concentration. The number of banks fell from 276 in 1929 to 187 in 1937, and the "big four" then held 45 percent of deposits: their decline had been less marked than that of the banking network as a whole. As Bouvier remarks, "This was the great holocaust of local banks, of which only a few relics remained after the Second World War."

3. The situation before the last war cannot really be compared with the situation after it. According to available statistics, there were 412 establishments in 1947 belonging to the private merchant sector, including 340 "deposit banks"; in 1972 there were 320, including 90 "deposit banks." The structure of the banking sector in 1971 is shown in table 13.18.

The only merger among the big banks was the one in 1966 between the BNCI and the Comptoir d'Escompte. The regional banks survived, but they have almost all become subsidiaries of the big banks, especially of the CIC. On the other hand, there were only 69 local banks in 1972 as against 209 in 1947. Almost all those that disappeared were absorbed into larger firms. Out of the 69 surviving local banks, 49 were affiliated. The so-called "Paris" banks apparently weathered the storm better, but they were often very specialized, and whether or not they actually belonged to banking groups, they were really only the groups' financial instruments. The same is true of most of the 42 medium- and long-term credit banks, special organs set up by the big banks to deal with real estate transactions. As M. Turin has put it, they are "captive banks." The number of merchant banks, heirs of the oldest French tradition, was stationary at around 40 from 1947 to 1958, reached 47 in 1965, and then fell to 25 in 1972. This drop was the consequence of the law of 1966, which allowed commercial banks to perform the

Table 13.18 Structure of the Banking Sector, 1971

	No.	Total b/sheet		Total Deposits	
		Billions of Francs	Percent	Billions of Francs	Percent
National banks	3	207.2	51.5	118.7	61.0
Other big banks and "Paris" banks	79	64.5	16.0	29.8	15.3
Regional banks	21	39.0	9.7	26.6	13.6
Local banks	70	4.6	1.1	3.5	1.8
Foreign deposit banks	53	39.4	9.8	6.4	3.3
Merchant banks	25	24.2	6.0	7.1	3.6
Medium and long-term credit banks	42	13.1	3.3	2.6	1.3
Others	26	10.6	2.6		
Total	319	402.6	100	194.7	100

functions of merchant banks. Many of the biggest merchant banks divided up their activities, setting up a deposit bank on the one hand and on the other a holding company playing the role of parent company to the group. For the chief purpose of a merchant bank is to develop a network of holdings, to build up a "group," just like a big industrial enterprise. Before examining banking groups in France, we need to recall the circumstances in which the "national" enterprises came into being. They too came to form groups.

Nationalization. The setting up of a big "public" sector in France does not date from the nationalizations of 1945–46. Although the state was regarded as powerless in the field of industry in the nineteenth century, certain sectors—admittedly very limited ones—were under government control. These included arsenals, tobacco and matches, and the Post Office. Before the First World War it was in the banking sector that the state was chiefly active. Since 1835 the Caisse des Dépôts, founded at the beginning of the nineteenth century, had been in charge of managing savings deposits and supporting government stocks. The Crédit Foncier, founded in 1852, did not, according to Bouvier, succeed in "finding its ultimate form" before the end of the nineteenth century, and largely failed of its original purpose.

In the interwar years there was a sudden enlargement of the public or semipublic banking sector, which took place in two stages. Immediately after the first war and in the 1920s, several privileged banking organizations were formed: these included the Crédit National, founded in 1919, and the Caisse Nationale de Crédit Agricole, founded in 1920. These two, since 1960, have won an outstanding place in the French banking system. In other sectors the development of public or semipublic enterprises was the result of necessity rather than of any desire to "socialize" the economy. In 1925 the Office National Industriel de l'Azote (nitrogen) was founded, after the failure of private groups to negotiate the acquisition of German patents. In 1930 the state acquired a holding of 35 percent in the Compagnie Française des Pétroles because of lack of enthusiasm on the part of private investors. In 1932 the slump accelerated the process. The government's acquisition of 25 percent of the stock of the Compagnie Air France was the natural consequence of the loans the state had had to make to various companies that were on the brink of bankruptcy. The Compagnie Générale Transatlantique is a similar case. In September 1931 the Banque Nationale pour le Commerce, an important bank, was advanced 2 billion francs to enable it to meet its commitments. It was eventually liquidated and re-formed under the control of the Ministry of Finance in December 1936. Even the "nationalization" of the railways in August 1937 was really the result of pressures arising out of the crisis rather than a deliberate attempt to put socialist theories into practice. A convention signed in 1921 had set up a system of financial solidarity among the various parts of the network. But the slump put an end to this. Deficits were so large that the "automatic restoration of the equilibrium" prescribed by the convention became impossible. The accumulated deficits triggered off a kind of natural process of nationalization, since it was the state which had to cover the losses. Shareholders in the companies, represented by the big merchant banks, realized that it would be best for them to sell their stock in companies which were now running at a massive loss, and which had no real hope of even breaking even in the foreseeable future. They had, in any case, had to yield all real power of decision to government auditors.

The founders of the Société Nationale des Chemins de Fer (SNCF, French Railways), in particular René Mayer, who negotiated the agreement on behalf of the companies, intended SNCF to be an enterprise independent of the state, although the government owned 51 percent of the shares. This notion of nationalized companies which were not actually run by the government was really quite close to the socialists' ideas. As early as 1919 the Confédération Générale du Travail (CGT) had adopted the idea of "industrialized" rather than "government-run" nationalization: power within such enterprises was to be shared among users, state, and staff. It was such principles that lay behind the nationalization laws of 1945–46. Some of these principles were the result of popular pressure, but most were the consequences of promises made by the Resistance, especially the Conseil National de la Résistance (CNR). The program of the CNR provided for the "return to the nation of the major nationalized means of production." The Constitution of 1946, drawn up after the event, declared that "all property and all enterprises that have acquired or shall acquire the nature of a national public service or a de facto monopoly must become the property of the community at large." The nationalizations of coal (by a law of May 11, 1946), of the Renault factories (January 1945), and of the Société Gnome et Rhone, which later formed the Société Nationale d'Etude et de Construction des Moteurs d'Aviation (SNECMA—manufacturer of aircraft engines), were all largely the result of pressure on the part of the workers concerned. On the other hand, the nationalization of the production and supply of electricity and gas (April–May 1946), the nationalization of most of the large deposit banks and insurance companies (December 1945 and April 1946), the transformation of the Compagnie des Messageries Maritimes into a mixed company, and the founding of Air France were all "cold" decisions, part of a precise and coherent program worked out during the years of the Occupation. None of the nationalizers wanted to create a government sector. They all proclaimed their desire to create enterprises run under "industrial" management but able by their very nature to take into account the general interest and in particular the general wishes of the country as defined in the plans. What most of them had in mind was the setting up of organizations more efficient economically than the capitalist enterprises they would replace, since they would no longer be run in the old Malthusian spirit of French capitalism. There is no room here to describe the way management developed in these enterprises. Suffice it to say that during the 1960s the criteria that were applied became more and more "industrial," i.e., concerned with profitability. Public opinion grew less and less willing to see these enterprises making up their deficits by means of state subsidies. But to judge the size of these deficits properly we should take into account the losses due to restrictions imposed by the state (the maintaining of suburban railway services, for example), and to the ruinous rates prescribed by the government. The 1967 report on public enterprises, known as the "Nova" report, was the first of a series of measures designed to restore some reality to their accounting and get these enterprises to achieve financial balance in exchange for greater freedom of management. Not all the inconsistencies were ironed out, and subsidies are still a heavy burden on the government budget, as we shall see.

After the nationalization movement of the Liberation came to a halt, the nationalized sector did not remain stationary, and it may today be considered as having developed in accordance with a group strategy that had a logic of its own. According to the French national accounts, public enterprises were responsible for 13.4 percent of national production in 1959 and 11.8 percent in 1969. At the same time, the number of public enterprises fell from 170 in 1957 to 118 in 1972. But this fall in numbers and percentages does not indicate a loss of influence. The number of public enterprises fell for two reasons: between 1959 and 1962, colonial enterprises disappeared; and between 1966 and 1972, public enterprises showed a trend toward concentration, especially in sectors exposed to great competition. As has been said earlier, the ERAP was formed in 1965; in 1968 the Office National Industriel l'Azote (ONIA) merged with Mines Dominiales d'Alsace (Enterprise Minière Chimique, or EMC); in 1966 the Comptoir National de l'Escompte de Paris (CNEP) and the Banque Nationale pour le Commerce et l'Industrie (BNCI) formed the Banque Nationale de Paris (BNP); and in aeronautics the various enterprises which emerged from the 1936 nationalizations were regrouped, as we shall see later, to form the Société Nationale des Industries Aeronautiques et Spaciales (SNIAS) and SNECMA. These public enterprises, then, fewer in number but more powerful, increased the number of their subsidiaries, especially those shared with private groups, so that the fall in the percentage of their contribution to national production is to a certain extent misleading. The Comptabilité Nationale classifies as "public" all enterprises in which the state holds more than 30 percent of the capital. In 1957, public enterprises had 256 subsidiaries; in 1965, 372; and in 1972, 527. If we exclude real estate assets of the public enterprises, largely used for housing staff, their industrial assets and those of their majority subsidiaries, calculated on net assets, increased at a rate of 6.2 percent per annum between 1959 and 1972, while their portfolios grew at a rate of 11 percent. M. Hani Gresh, from whom I took these figures, speaks of "an interpenetration of public and private capital," both public enterprises and private groups following a policy of "rapid external growth." Some writers have seen this as indicating a danger that the economy is being insidiously socialized.

Mergers and Groups

The Trend Toward Mergers. The state wanted to see the process of concentration accelerate. Concentration was the chief method by which the French economy adapted itself to the opening up of frontiers. The avowed object was to build up either enterprises or groups capable of standing up to international groups. The reporters for the Fifth Plan (1966–70), after observing that competition would intensify during the period covered by the plan, said that "an essential task would be to strengthen the competitiveness of the French economy by expediting . . . the creation or development of groups of international stature but with French capital, formed through technical, commercial, and financial concentration of formerly separate enterprises." They added: "In many sectors these concentrations should lead to a very small number of groups, in some rare cases even just one dominant group, and this, because of the opening up of frontiers, would not have the same disadvantages as under a protectionist régime." So a series of legislative and fiscal measures were taken—what A. P. Weber has called "an array of incentives" (Jenny and Weber). As early as 1955 decrees were issued providing for the possibility of granting various loans and bonuses. The law of July 12, 1965 provided for special tax concessions to companies that merged, and these tax advantages were increased again in 1967.

Such measures probably did no more than assist a trend which in any case would have emerged under the spur of the Common Market. It was in the name of efficiency that the presenters of the Fifth Plan hoped for the formation of monopolies or oligopolies. Such groups, they said, "would have to have enough capital at their disposal to be able to stand up to competition wherever it presented itself, to be able to invest abroad, have their own techniques and their own research centers, and, lastly, to be in a good position to negotiate agreements in a larger context with enterprises abroad." Our examination of the relation between the size of enterprises and the volume of their investment shows how fully their first argument was justified. When the Fifth Plan was being drawn up, no one seemed to doubt that only great size could make it possible to "mass-produce for sale on a wide market," because only size made it possible to mobilize the capital necessary for the adoption of cost-reducing techniques. Small enterprises could develop only through "specialization, originality, or the quality of their goods." Since then these attitudes have altered. Size is no longer considered the necessary condition of technical efficiency.

The advantages of size are not challenged, however, when it comes to research and commercial strategy, partly because of the swiftness of technical progress and partly because of the intensification of foreign competition. Research and development expenditure is highly concentrated in large firms. Firms employing over 5,000 workers were responsible for more than three-fifths of research expenditure. And research strategy is inseparable from commercial policy. As J. Echard observed of the chemicals industry, "In order to maintain one's position in a continually changing market, it is absolutely necessary to be always undertaking new research." The creation of the Common Market and the general development of international trade allowed French firms to draw up their strategies in terms of a much larger market. Also, the intensification of international competition caused a fall in profit margins, which encourages concentration through takeovers.

Statistical analysis of a sample of 1,594 enterprises recorded by the *Bulletin d'Annonces Légales Obligatoires* (which records all mergers) in 1969 enables us to distinguish three phases:

1. Between 1950 and 1958 the number of mergers was fairly small: there was an average of 61, of which 32 were in industry.

2. The first acceleration came after the signing of the Treaty of Rome: there was an annual average of 166 between 1959 and 1965, 74 of them in industry.

3. There was another acceleration after the incentive measures referred to above. Between 1966 and 1972 there was an annual mean of 213 mergers, 109 of them in industry. The trend reached its peak in 1969, with 263 transactions of this kind, 136 of them in industry.

Since then there has been an appreciable decline, more marked in industry than in other sectors. (Between 1970 and 1972 the annual mean was 191, of which 96 were in industry.)

Between 1950 and 1972, 3,176 transactions of this kind have been recorded in all. (We are speaking only of the transactions which can be traced: i.e., those carried out by *sociétés anonymes*, which are legally obliged to publish them.) For an analysis of these figures, see table 13.19.

The acceleration was accompanied by a "strong growth in the size of the enterprises taken over, and an equally strong growth in the average number of transactions carried out by the absorbing companies." In industry, the largest number of these

Table 13.19 Concentration Operations, 1950–1972, According to Jenny and Weber

	No. of enterprs. in sample	Absorbing Enterprises		Transactions		Incr. of Capital (millions of francs)	
		No.	Percent	No.	Percent	No.	Percent
Overseas and other activities	54	17	1.83	49	1.54	175.0	0.81
Energy	25	12	1.29	47	1.47	82.4	0.38
Industry	721	475	51.40	1,690	53.21	9,525.5	44.30
Transport, telecommunications	69	33	3.57	91	2.86	213.8	0.99
Commerce	187	112	12.12	404	12.72	1,915.2	8.90
Services	471	257	27.81	864	27.20	9,425.4	43.83
Indeterminate	67	18	1.95	31	0.97	164.5	0.76
Total	1,594	924	100	3,176	100		100

transactions took place in already concentrated sectors (especially iron and steel, electrical engineering, the glass industry).

But these statistics should not be thought to give a complete picture of the process of capitalistic concentration. It lumps all transactions together regardless of their legal form (takeover of a subsidiary, ordinary takeover, merger, partial bringing in of assets).* Out of 574 transactions in 1970–1972, 63 were mergers, 280 were ordinary takeovers, 149 takeovers of subsidiaries, and 82 partial bringing in of assets. Some of these transactions are really no more than the expression of a policy of group reorganization, or to put it more prosaically, disguised reevaluations of balance-sheets. The analysis of mergers is inseparable from the analysis of groups.

It would be premature to pronounce a definitive verdict on the evolution of French industrial groups in recent years. It is clear that this sort of concentration accelerated strongly after the end of the 1960s, after the big mergers regrouping the forces of previously formed smaller groups, and leading to the formation of large concerns like Péchiney-Ugine-Kuhlmann in chemicals and Creusot-Loire in iron and steel. These transactions were the culmination of a trend which had begun just after the Second World War. During the 1950s and early 1960s most big industrial firms based their strategy on the creation of subsidiaries, often shared. This was a "conquering" phase, linked to the rapid growth of the domestic market and especially to the massive penetration of a mass of technological advances (new processes and new products) which France had been deprived of during the 1930s and 1940s, when her economy stagnated and she was shut out from world markets. Chemicals are a typical example. At the end of the 1950s this sector was dominated by five groups which during recent years had created many shared subsidiaries between themselves or jointly with coal- or oil-producing companies, with the object of ensuring the development of organic chemicals in France.

---

* In the case of a merger, two independent companies form one new company; in the case of a takeover, the absorbing company acquires the corporate property of the company absorbed; in the case of a partial bringing in of assets there is a partial transfer of assets, usually accompanied by a purchase of stock in the buying company on the part of the selling company.

Two firms stood out particularly in the race: Péchiney and Rhone-Poulenc, which specialized in high-quality goods. Saint-Gobain, Ugine, and Kuhlmann were less deeply involved in organic chemicals, but not entirely out of the picture. Firms did all they could to establish themselves in as many expanding markets as possible. But at this period, diversification did not challenge the old rules of the 1920s. The only challenge of this kind came from the very rapid growth of new firms, of which the most striking example was Boussois-Souchon-Neuvesel in the glass sector. On the whole, the redistribution of assets which then took place gave production greater coherence from the technical point of view, while preserving previous relations of forces among financial and family groups.

It was chiefly because of pressure from foreign competition, and because of growing financing difficulties at a time when research and marketing costs were increasing inordinately, that the big regroupings of the 1960s took place, with the approval of the state. The object was to give French groups an international dimension. The policy of shared subsidiaries was not abandoned, but it often took on a new significance. These subsidiaries took the place of cartels, which were more difficult to keep up in the framework of the Common Market. Moreover, as de Vannoise, Hannoun, and Bouilly have noted, "the multiplication of subsidiaries shared by various groups seems to confirm the existence of a desire to limit the risks of intervening in activities or markets where success might be uncertain." These three writers have made a statistical study of the "weight" of French groups. Their first conclusions, revealed only quite recently, are derived from an analysis of the 18 most important French groups, excluding financial groups such as the banks Suez and Paribas, and excluding all foreign groups with the exception of Simca-Chrysler. This choice is a good one, since a feature of recent years has been the formation of truly industrial groups developing along quite consistent technical lines. The authors show clearly that these 18 groups "organize their activity around sectorial poles," using the word "sector" in the sense defined by Alain Desrosières, and given in chapter 11 of the present work. It may be recalled that we are concerned here with very large sectors (intermediate industries, equipment industries, consumer industries) defined mainly in terms of the nature of the product and the way the factors of production are employed. There are two "opposing" types of group within the 18 groups: on the one hand, those chiefly attached to the intermediate goods industries, and on the other hand those chiefly attached to the equipment industries. The first category includes the following groups, for which we give in each case, in parentheses, the percentage of their workers employed in the sector: Rhone-Poulenc (83), Saint-Gobain–Pont à Mousson (66), Pechiney-Ugine-Kuhlmann (94), Boussois-Souchon-Neuvesel (58), Creusot-Loire (81), Denain-Nord Est-Longwy (87), Wendel-Sidelor (99), Le Nickel (100), Ciments Lafarge (90). The second category includes the following groups: CGE (69), Renault (95), Peugeot (96), Chrysler (99), Citröen-Michelin (59), Thomson-Brandt–CSF (90), Babcock Fives (73), SNIAS-SNECMA (97). This shows strong specialization, due not only to "the amount of capital necessary for a company to establish itself in a different sector" but also to "technological, commercial and organizational obstacles," and especially to "the desire not to get involved in difficult competition with powerful competitors." In fact, we are dealing with what are almost private preserves. But within these large sectors there emerges a strong tendency toward diversification. If we break down the activities of the groups further, we see that "around the one or two sectorial poles which constitute the center of the group there is a concatenation of companies on either side favoring the expansion of the central nucleus."

Our authors, when they try to "weigh" these groups, can only do so "by default," because they do not take account of foreign companies, and certain other companies could not be identified. The workers employed by these 18 groups amounted to 10 percent of the work force in all firms taxed on real profits, and 30 percent of those employed in the equipment and intermediate goods industries. They differ from other enterprises by the size of their investments, which explains both the size of their fixed assets (41 percent of gross fixed assets in intermediate goods, and 38 percent of those in equipment goods), and the extent of their indebtedness (57 percent of the long and medium-term debts in intermediate goods, and 45 percent of those in equipment goods). This dynamism in investment is paralleled by an equal dynamism in exports (50 percent of the export turnover in intermediate goods, and 44 percent of that in equipment goods). While the figures seem to suggest a lower profitability in groups than in other enterprises, especially in the intermediary goods sector, groups are undoubtedly the main centers of decision within the various sectors which have been examined, and it may be supposed that the other enterprises depend largely on these centers, since they lack the means to establish independent policies.

Bibliography

Aszkenazy, H. *Les grandes sociétés européennes.* Brussels: Centre de Recherche et d'Information Sociopolitique, 1971.

Bain, J. *International Differences in Industrial Structure.* New Haven: Yale University Press, 1966.

Bertin, G. Y. *L'investissement étranger en France.* Paris: Presses Universitaires de France, 1963.

Bouvier, J. *Un siècle de banque française.* Paris: Hachette, 1973.

Desrosières, A. *La diversification des productions dans l'industrie française.* Collections de l'INSEE, ser. E, no. 2. Paris: Institut National de la Statistique et des Etudes Economiques, August 1969.

Didier, M., and E. Malinvaud. "La concentration de l'industrie s'est elle accentuée depuis 1900?" *Economie et Statistique,* no. 2 (1969).

Didier, M., and J. P. Nioche. *Les établissements industriels dans sept pays développés.* Collections de l'INSEE, ser. E, no. 1. Paris: Institut National de la Statistique et des Etudes Economiques, May 1969.

Echard, J. "Le processus d'innovation dans l'industrie chimique," *Revue d'Economie Politique,* 1965.

"L'evolution des structures bancaires en France: Credit Lyonnais, Rapport annuel pour l'exercice 1972," *Problèmes Economiques,* no. 1344 (October 31, 1973).

Gresh, H. "Les Entreprises publiques et la création de filiales," *Economie et Statistique,* no. 65 (1975).

Hannoun, M. "L'appareil de production des grands groupes industriels en 1972," *Economie et Statistique,* no. 87 (March 1977).

Houssiaux, J. *Le pouvoir de monopole.* Paris: Sirey, 1954.

Huret, E. "Structure des bilans et types de croissance des entreprises," *Economie et Statistique,* no. 50 (November 1973).

Jeanneney, J. M. *Forces et faiblesses de l'économie française*. Paris: A. Colin, 1959.

Jenny, F., and A. P. Weber. *Concentration et politique des structures industrielles*. Paris: Documentation Française, 1974.

——*L'entreprise et la politique de la concurrence*. Paris: Editions d'Organisation, 1976.

Loup, J. "La structure des marchés par produits," *Etudes et Conjoncture*, no. 2 (February 1969).

McArthur, J., and B. R. Scott. *L'industrie française face aux plans*. Paris: Editions d'Organisation, 1970.

Morin, F. *La structure financière du capitalisme français*. Paris: Calmann Levy, 1974.

Precheur, C. *1968: Les industries françaises à l'heure du marché commun*. Paris: Socïeté d'Edition d'Enseignement Supérieur, 1969.

Rapport sur les obstacles à l'expansion économique, présenté par un comité, présidé par MM Louis Armand et Jacques Rueff. Paris: Imprimerie Nationale, 1960.

Szokoloczy Syllaba, J. *Les organisations professionnelles françaises et le marché commun*. Paris: A. Colin, 1965.

Turin, M. "Les banques de groupe," *Entreprise*, October 12, 1973. Reprinted in *Problèmes Economiques*, no. 1344 (October 31, 1973).

Vannoise, R. de. "Etude économique et financière de 18 groupes industriels en 1972," *Economie et Statistique*, no. 87 (March 1977).

Vannoise, R. de, M. Hannoun, and D. Bouilly. "Le poids et la structure financière des grands groupes industriels en 1972. Institut National de la Statistique. Journée d'étude du Comité de Liaison des Centrales de Bilans, 9 juin 1976." Unpublished manuscript.

Weber, A. P. *Les concentrations industrielles dans la France contemporaine*. Paris: Bordas, 1971.

Chapter Fourteen: State Policy and Business Management, 1950–1973

ONE CAN ONLY explain the evolution of the French economy in the years 1950–60, which I have attempted to describe above, if one takes into account the changes which occurred in the behavior of the various economic agents involved. I shall deal here with just two kinds of agent: business and industrial enterprises, and the state. At the beginning of the 1950s the French economy could be described, to use C. Gruson's expression, as "held back by structural rigidity." This situation, which justified the experts' pessimism, forced the politicians, even those most anxious to see France develop rapidly, to moderate their ambitions. This was frequently reflected in the discussions of the Commission des Comptes. In 1954, in answer to certain criticisms, the authors of the commission's report said they had had to abandon the forecast of a high growth rate because, though such a rate was theoretically possible, "in the seclusion of the study" it "might cause violent readaptation crises in many sectors that could unleash a serious social and economic crisis in the country as a whole." The "rigidities" referred to by Gruson derived from a protective network which transformed numerous "established positions" into privileges. In the main, these protected positions were the result of commercial protectionism, which on a limited market like that of France had encouraged the setting up of cartels and "allowed the economy to hold back certain developments which would have made it fit, and to embark on methods which made it even more unfit, for international competition"; or else they arose from a sort of internal protectionism which favored the "least competitive" industries and worked by means of regulations, agreements, and direct subsidies which had grown up gradually since the beginning of the thirties. Or else, lastly, these protected positions were due to a series of measures that might be described as corporatist, enacted also during the early thirties or by the Vichy government: these tended to create closed professions and privilege. On November 13, 1959 General de Gaulle's first government set up a committee under Jacques Rueff and Louis Armand to suggest measures for "removing obstacles to expansion." It drew up a detailed list of the "rigidities affecting the economy" and the "factors militating against true costs and prices."

What I would claim here is that although an immense effort was made to get the economy working more flexibly, and in particular to increase the mobility of the factors of production and widen the field of real competition, many "rigidities" still exist. So much so that in order to understand the functioning of the French economy we have to take into account first and foremost the contrast between "exposed" sectors, to use R. Courbis' expression, and those which are not "exposed" and still enjoy certain privileges. The idea of an "exposed" sector refers to tariff policy, and we need to ponder, in the light of what was said earlier about foreign trade, on the direct and indirect consequences of the "internationalization" of the French economy. It seems to me that, apart from its measurable effects, this internationalization brought about a complete change in the methods of managing French business. But this change might also have been a result of other measures taken by the state in the fields of internal commercial legislation, of government policy on economic planning, or even of government policy on regulating the economic situation.

To examine these various factors I shall adopt a method of presentation roughly corresponding to the chronological order in which the relevant institutions came into being: planning in the French style; the opening up of frontiers, inseparable from domestic policy designed to promote competition; and the wide range of reforms voted in in the 1960s, of which the domestic policy designed to promote competition was part, and which were all aimed at restoring the mobility of the factors of production. I shall then attempt to describe how French business has modified its ways. But first it seems necessary to show the main stages in the policy of economic regulation, which belongs in the context of the history of inflation, since French governments have always had to choose between their own long-term designs and short-term constraints. They have acquired a reputation for always sacrificing stable prices to the achievement of a growth rate guaranteeing full employment. Is this reputation justified?

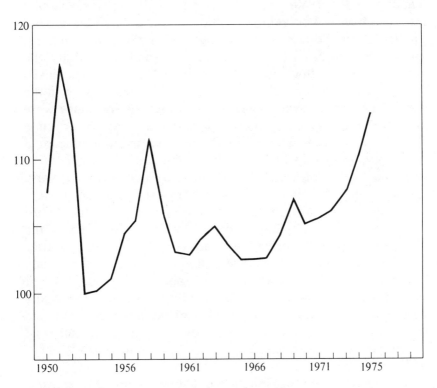

Figure 7 Price of Gross Domestic Production (previous year = 100).

SOURCE: Comptabilité Nationale.

Economic Regulation Policies

Long-Term View of Inflation. French growth over the last twenty-five years has been fairly strongly inflationary. Between 1952 and 1972 the mean annual increase in production prices was 4.2 percent per annum. Whereas, in the 1950s this was said by most experts to be the result of inherent "structural rigidities" (narrowness of the labor market, inflexibility of the incomes scale, the large part played by noncompetitive practices), the inflation of the 1960s seems rather to be a French version of a general "Western" inflation. In the last years of the sixties and the first of the seventies, the rise in international prices was as high as the rise in prices inside the OECD. The inflation of the 1960s gradually accelerated: the mean annual rate rose from 4.4 percent in 1959 to 1962 to 5.7 percent in 1967 to 1972. Alain Cotta has shown that it also changed its nature: up to 1968, prices as a whole were pushed upward by the services and building sectors, while industrial prices increased only slightly; whereas, after 1968, industrial prices shared in the general price rise. Wages rose so high that the increases were no longer covered by increased productivity, and at the same time there was an increase in the relative amount of capital necessary to sustain increases in production. Wage increases were the result of rises in nonexposed sectors (particularly services and building), and were thus transmitted to the exposed sectors. Moreover, after the beginning of the 1970s, the increase in international prices has been as high as the increase in domestic prices. Nowadays, having seen countries like Germany manage to control inflation better, we come back to explanations linking inflation in France to the "rigidity" of the French economy. This inflexibility includes the many cartels among producers, the rigidity of the incomes scale, and the retention of "established positions." A German journalist described all these things recently as amounting to an "allergy to competition."

Even admitting that inflation has some "structural" causes, one still cannot analyze it without also examining prices and the regulating policy intended to control them. The French government's powers of intervention in this field have gradually improved. There are three main methods: direct action on prices; action on currency and credit; and budgetary policy. As regards the first, several 1945 memoranda which give the administration the right to impose controlled prices on business firms have never been canceled. A first attempt at liberalization, made by René Mayer in 1948, came to nothing. In 1952, strict price controls were reintroduced. A second attempt, begun in 1957, culminated in 1963 in Valéry Giscard d'Estaing's stabilization plan. Strict regulations were then established. From 1966 on, a system of "contracts" between industry and the state attempted to introduce some flexibility into the system. But this was still a matter of controlled prices. In fact, the best way to limit price increases is to create conditions for real competition among producers. We shall examine this policy in the second part of the present chapter.

Methods of Regulation. French monetary policy made use of many different methods in the course of the 1960s. As regards refinancing, up to the early years of the decade rediscount continued to be the banks' main access to the credit of the central bank. Their ability to rediscount was limited by ceilings fixed separately for each bank. Manipulating the bank rate was, in fact, the chief instrument of monetary policy. But the banks could achieve an appreciable increase in their rediscountable effects not covered by ceilings by selling securities to the central bank and promising to repurchase them. So discount ceilings were not an efficient way of trying to limit the volume of credit. After 1960, other mechanisms were introduced. In 1960, the "treasury coefficient" was tried, to be replaced in 1967 by the system of "compulsory reserves." We cannot go into the details of these complex regulations, but they tended to lead to portfolios containing as few medium-term credits as possible. The most novel feature in comparison with previous practices, however, was the development, from the mid-sixties on, of active intervention by the Banque de France in the money market. The Banque de France's main object here was to control the movement abroad of short-term capital. From 1971 on, the Banque replaced its fixed-rate aid with aid at variable rates. This made it possible to abolish discount ceilings at the beginning of 1972. All in all, these reforms made the Banque de France's intervention much more flexible, and tended to create a genuine money market where rates might be fixed freely. But in fact the central bank never managed, before 1973, to make the big banks take their treasury situation into account in granting credit.

State intervention on credit was not restricted to refinancing: the minimum rates for bank aid to business firms and private individuals, which had long been governed by the Conseil National du Crédit, founded in 1946, were from 1966 on fixed by agreement among the banks, with the nationalized banks carrying the most weight. Both long-term rates and the interest paid on deposits have always been subject to regulation. The system of unremunerated compulsory reserves, introduced in 1967 and at first applied only to deposits, was extended in 1971 to the credits granted by banks and other financial establishments. This last method became a favorite method of controlling credit. But, in the last resort, the state could make use of even more authoritative methods, and impose a quantitative limit on the expansion of bank credit. This method was used twice: between March 1963 and June 1965, and between November 1968 and October 1970. The policy was called the "credit squeeze," and the second time it was tried was even more rigorous and selective than the first. Finally, it should be said that the French authorities have never abandoned their power to control the movements of foreign capital by means of exchange controls. Exchange regulations were gradually relaxed between 1960 and 1966 and abolished in 1967; but new measures were introduced in 1968 to limit the export of capital, and again in 1970 to control its entry into France.

Modulation of public expenditure in order to regulate the economic situation dates from the early fifties. In March 1952, in 1958, and in 1963–64, public expenditure was held down in an attempt to slow down the rise in prices. On the other hand, it was used as a pump primer in 1954–55 under Edgar Faure, whose chief object was to increase public investment, and in 1959–60 and 1962. Between 1964 and 1969 there was practically no attempt to use public markets as a means of promoting recovery. In 1969 a fund for economic action was created, but

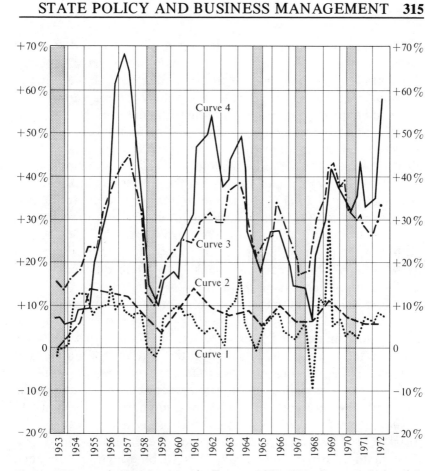

Figure 8 Economic Development in France, 1953–1972. Curve 1: Industrial production, rate of annual variation. Curve 2: Gross formation of fixed capital (nonfinancial enterprises), rate of annual variation. Curve 3: Bottlenecks—the proportion of employers who say production is hampered by lack of equipment or staff. Curve 4: Ratio of demand for labor to demand for employment (seasonally corrected).

SOURCE: Institut national de la statistique et des études économiques.

it was little used. In 1974, in a particularly serious situation, a plan for massive budgetary action was adopted, aimed at bringing about economic recovery through public investment, especially in the telecommunications sector. This strategy thus tried to be both comprehensive and selective.

The Stages of Regulation. Economic cycles may be defined in terms of various different kinds of data. They have recently been set out in a table by the Economic Review of the Banque Nationale de Paris, and include: the annual rate of variation of net fixed capital formation by nonfinancial enterprises; the ratio of jobs available to people seeking work; and the proportion of employers who, in their answers to INSEE surveys, say they are prevented from producing more by lack of equipment or labor. In this way, three cycles can be discerned in the years leading up to 1970: (1) from the third quarter of 1951 to the last quarter of 1957; (2) from the first quarter of 1958 to the second quarter of 1964; and (3) from the third quarter of 1964 to the first quarter of 1970. These were followed by a fourth cycle, with a boom which reached a peak in the third quarter of 1973 and a marked depression in 1974.

Recessions grew more and more intense. They were short in the first two cycles, longer but less marked in the third, and much more marked in the fourth. The chief variable which may explain these cycles seems to me the attitude of public and private entrepreneurs to investment. Private entrepreneurs played an increasingly important role because the public demand was growing less and less important. Decisions to invest depend on two variables: the predicted growth of the market, and the financial position of the enterprise involved. The main cause of "slackening" is to be sought in financial conditions in the general economy. These can, as they did in 1963–64, bring about a reduction in investment effort, or, as in 1958, cause entrepreneurs to raise their prices.

The stabilization policy, still in its infancy in 1950–51 according to Philippe Herzog, in fact helped to exacerbate the inflationary process. The Korean War had suddenly reactivated demand, brought about a world increase in prices of raw materials, and as a result a similar rise in costs. But there were specifically French factors aggravating the rise in prices: the methods of financing rearmament, which were sound in 1951, were no longer so in 1952; and the policy of easy credit in force up to November 1951, when René Mayer came to power, "enabled enterprises . . . to increase both production and prices without bothering about the profile of demand, while authoritarian fixing of prices and wages helped to accelerate price increases in a system which banished any real competition among producers." The downturn came during the last quarter of 1951. It was due to a quasi-stagnation of household demand and a sudden fall in private investment, the result of the measures taken to restrict credit at the end of 1951. At that point, businesses preferred to halt price rises and restrict the expansion of production and capacity instead. They were encouraged in this by the policy of Antoine Pinay. Pinay was not content with helping the movement toward the price stabilization: in 1952 the first laws were passed which were designed to break with anticompetitive practices (the law of June 20, 1952 banned price control), and the first measures were taken to give a new impetus to savings, though by questionable means (a debenture indexed on gold and exempt from death duties). Pinay's policy has been described by Gruson as "Keynesian," because it was based on the stabilization of the tax burden and to a certain extent on budgetary deficit. But at the end of 1952 this attempted return to liberalism ran into trouble: in September, the government had to go back to an authoritarian method of price fixing, and still the recession got worse.

But it was then that the "French miracle" of the fifties began—a phase of continuous expansion which lasted until the closing months of 1957. At first this growth (1954–55) took place in a context of stable prices; then, in 1956–57, in an atmosphere of inflationary imbalance. During those years, the driving force behind growth was private investment by enterprises and individuals. This recovery of investment owed much to government measures inspired by Edgar Faure, who took over the Ministry of Finance in the summer of 1953. These measures encouraged investment through their effects on taxes and credit. Energetic formation of capital on the part of business enterprises explains the increase that took place in productivity, which helped to keep prices stable. Moreover, up to the autumn of 1955, wage rises remained moderate because there was not much tension on the labor market. The strikes which took place in the summer of 1955 led to the setting up of collective bargaining procedures and a new period of wage rises.

This was enough to upset the precarious equilibrium of

prices. But the main cause of the difficulties of 1956 must be sought in the rejection of devaluation at a time when the franc was overvalued. During the preceding two years the balance of France's foreign finances had been due to the dynamism of the world economic situation and to American aid. Internal tension over wages and external tension over prices were aggravated by the financial policy of Guy Mollet, who became prime minister in January 1956; public consumption was "the main cause of the increase in demand" (up 15.4 percent in 1956), while the military drafts created tension in the labor market. In this atmosphere, business enterprises kept their investment effort at a high level.

Prices slipped in 1956 and in the first three quarters of 1957. They made a sudden leap upward at the end of 1957 and the beginning of 1958. The possibility of such an increase had been consciously accepted by Félix Gaillard's government, which came to power in June 1957. Like Faure in 1952, this government had to suspend free trade measures at a time when France was committed to the Common Market. The Gaillard government carried out a complex policy of de facto devaluation, which became official only in June 1958. At home the policy was one of budget austerity; above all there was a sudden break with vagaries in prices. The Gaillard administration, abandoning the policy of "manipulating indexes," which consisted of avoiding inevitable price rises by means of direct or indirect subsidies (in the latter case, tax remissions), unfroze prices in December 1957. At this time, strong factors tending to increase prices were bound to come into play—particularly bad harvests, although in the preceding year a system had been introduced for the indexing of agricultural prices. Price rises were very high, going far beyond a return to "true prices," an expression in vogue at the time. The policy adopted by the first governments of General de Gaulle only carried on the enlightened management of Félix Gaillard, to whose memory we ought to pay due homage.

This rise in prices caused a reduction in real incomes in 1958, and a marked recession, made worse by recession in the world as a whole. In France the recession was characterized by a big reduction in business investment, which emerged clearly between the first and second quarters of 1958. The main explanation for this was probably the financing difficulties which became apparent in the course of the year, the result of the high level of self-financing in the preceding years. The early recovery was due to the measures taken by the new government in December 1958. From the economic point of view, these measures were an extension of those taken by Félix Gaillard: the abolition of subsidies; the reorganization of public finances, though a budget deficit was retained to finance a program of public investment or "major public works," as they would have been called in the thirties; and a 15 percent devaluation on top of that of Gaillard, designed to enable France to weather the first impact of the Common Market. But foreign demand was the main cause of the recovery which took place in 1959. Investment began to make a contribution in the fourth quarter of 1959. Gruson attributes this recovery to the fact that enterprises had to "react rapidly through a major effort in the field of equipment" to "foreign competition." The effects of these two causes of expansion continued to be felt up to 1961. Excessive indebtedness on the part of French enterprises explains the slackening of their investment effort in 1962.

The initiative then passed to public expenditure, in particular the development of public enterprises, for the 1962 budget was extremely expansionist. Moreover, Michel Debré followed a policy of "easy credit." Whereas in 1960 and 1961 private consumption and investment had increased only moderately, in 1962, 1963, and 1964 they accelerated considerably. Imbalances then appeared (a 6 percent price rise during the first quarter of 1963; an even faster rise in wages; an unfavorable trade balance), and were taken all the more seriously because the memory of 1957 was fresh in everyone's minds. General de Gaulle, for whom the defense of the franc was an imperative factor in both foreign and economic policy, intervened personally with G. Pompidou and V. Giscard d'Estaing to insure that the franc was "maintained at the rate which had been fixed" by himself.

The stabilization plan of September 13, 1963 was a turning point in the use of regulation policies, for it combined traditional methods of persuasion with authoritarian measures. It inaugurated an economic policy which became more and more "empiricist." To reduce the growth of the money supply (up 18 percent in 1963 and 8 percent in 1964) Giscard d'Estaing issued a 2 billion franc debenture, introduced a severe credit squeeze, and tried to encourage saving. The measures relating to credit were part of an extensive program aimed at "reshaping the credit structure in France." His budget policy was a restrictive one. Lastly, he reintroduced the price freeze, while encouraging imports (by speeding up the reduction of customs duties) and modern methods of distribution. This severe policy was continued until the middle of 1965.

The plan of September 1963 held down prices in 1964 and brought about a "leveling off of economic activity" which according to OECD experts was characterized by a "decline in domestic consumption and in investment by private enterprises," by "a certain degree of détente on the labor market," and by a "considerable increase in stocks." Industrial production was stagnant for the greater part of 1964, but — characteristically—wages and prices continued to rise (up 6.7 percent and 3.6 percent, respectively).

Recovery began in spring 1965, thanks to an appreciable rise in exports and in household consumption. The government limited itself to what were called "accompanying" measures: the credit squeeze was ended on July 1, and prices were to some extent unfrozen. It was then that the first "stability contracts" were signed between the government and the unions. But the recovery hung fire. Investment remained slack until late 1968. The government could not adopt too "expansionist" a policy because it was introducing big reforms in credit and taxation (the generalization of value added tax), and there was a possibility that these measures might provoke reactions harmful to the stability of the franc. Moreover, the government had encouraged the various industrial sectors to "restructure," and this involved some immediate sacrifice, since firms could not pursue at one and the same time an external policy of accelerated growth and an internal policy of development through self-financing.

The recovery preceded the events of May 1968. The government, by a series of strokes in 1967, had taken measures favorable to economic revival by means of their budgetary policy and what OECD called a "very liberal credit policy" in June 1967. In January 1968 an overall plan included both fisca and social measures designed to revive investment. After the strikes of May 1968, agreements were negotiated between employers, the unions, and the government. These brought about a sudden increase in earnings (up 10.5 percent) and consequently in domestic demand. Investment soon followed, and the government of M. Couve de Murville, far from trying to moderate the recovery, as many people thought they should, anticipated it by allowing lavish credit facilities, especially to small and medium-sized businesses (June 11). This policy was strengthened by the "plan" of September 4. But by this time the government had to take into account rising prices and an acceleration in the flight of capital which had been taking place during the summer. So the measures for easy credit were accompanied by restrictive tax measures and a strict control of prices. This policy failed, ending in the monetary crisis of November 1968. On September 4, Couve de Murville had taken the risk of abolishing exchange control. But on November 23, after the newspaper *Le Monde*, making its own final contribution to speculation against the franc, had announced in its first edition that the franc had been devalued, General de Gaulle— on the advice, it is said, of Raymond Barre—grandly refused to devalue. He imposed a restrictive but fairly moderate policy: budget expenditure forecast by the September 4 plan was cut, and credit made more difficult. When Valéry Giscard d'Estaing became Minister of Finance for the second time on June 22 1969, he reinforced the credit squeeze. On August 8, 1969, he carried out a devaluation prepared in the utmost secrecy and accompanied by other measures even more clearly deflationary: tax advantages granted for investment in September 1968 were abolished, and there were big cuts in government expenditure in the last months of the year.

This policy brought about a considerable slackening of activity in early 1970. But this was soon over, largely because of the intensity of foreign demand and because in October 1970 the credit squeeze was lifted. Despite a 6 percent price rise (a rate which had provoked the "stabilization plan" in 1963), the new minister took restrictive measures only gradually and carefully in the course of 1971, but gave them up quickly at the end of the same year for fear of a rise in unemployment.

But prices were soaring, and in June 1972 Giscard d'Estaing had to return to the rigorous policy of 1963. In December he introduced a system of penalties to make banks observe the credit squeeze. The acceleration in price rises in 1973 led to a new tightening of monetary policy, and the bank rate reached 11 percent. In June 1974 a stabilization plan was launched: its chief novelty consisted in the use of fiscal measures to regulate the economy, and in the fact that the government, far from trying to favor investment as before, tried to make it slacker or more selective, for too much investment was thought to have been responsible for the inflation. But there was a sudden downturn in the economy in the last quarter of 1974, and the government had to take steps to encourage a revival: these included budgetary measures (lightening of the tax burden, government orders for investment goods), monetary measures, and a strengthening of price controls.

We may wonder whether a decisive stage in the regulation of the economy was not passed in 1969. As early as the mid-1960s it was evident that a slowdown of growth did not bring about any appreciable slowdown in price rises. At the beginning of the 1970s there was much talk of stagflation, but then it had to be admitted that unemployment and inflation were not incompatible with one another. The rise in oil prices at the end of 1973 only hastened a phenomenon that was already emerging more and more clearly from the figures. The restrictive measures adopted in 1974 did bring about a fall in the price of raw materials, but the fall was not reflected in retail prices, where the rise only slowed down from 15 percent in 1974 to 9.5 percent in 1975. The fact was that the rise in prices could be reduced only if methods of fixing incomes were changed. Price inflation was the result of income inflation, from the extraordinary rigidity in the incomes scale, and even more from the many and often unjustified privileges surviving all the attempts at "structural reform."

New State Attitudes

Planning "in the French Style". The last years of the 1940s had already been marked by the desire for expansion. But the renewed stagnation of 1952 awakened fears about France's more distant future. Malinvaud quotes an article from *Réalités* in September 1953 entitled "The Big Sleep of the French Economy," which speaks of the "slow decay of a great nation." And this was not an isolated opinion. People like A. Sauvy and M. Duverger also feared the reappearance of France's old tendencies toward "economic Malthusianism."

There is no doubt that one of the factors which enabled French businessmen to throw off their pessimism, and allowed private investment to cause the rate of investment to soar, was the launching of the Second Plan. Planning "in the French style" had won a name for itself in the 1950s, and been legitimized by the support of General de Gaulle, who, because it fitted in with his aspirations toward national unity, adopted it as a major element in his economic policy. Its nature changed considerably between the Second and the Seventh Plan: the area covered by forecasts grew larger, and the forecasts themselves became more reliable; the spirit of cooperation which lay behind the early plans was replaced by a more technocratic attitude. As regards the kind and quality of the forecasts, two major changes took place, one between the Fourth Plan (1962–65) and the Fifth (1966–70), and another between the Fifth and the Sixth (1970–75). The forecasts in the Second (1954–57), Third (1958–61) and Fourth (1962–65) Plans were purely in terms of volume. From the Fifth Plan onward there were forecasts of value. The next stage was to modify the connections between forecasts of volume and forecasts of value. In the Fifth Plan, value forecasts were only volume forecasts translated into monetary terms through theories about relative prices which made it possible to arrive at estimates of the ratio between savings and investment, and of the evolution of wages and incomes. Moreover, the transition from volume to value went only one way. This was all the more unsatisfactory because the pressure of foreign competition and the open-door economy both made forecasts more unreliable. What was needed was a model that would make it possible to take into account the interdependence between concrete variables and variables concerned with value, and which would make more allowance for what Courbis has called "the free play of attitudes on the part of agents." Thus came into being the model "Fifi"—a "physico-financial" model—which later became "Fifitof"—a "table of financial operations." It included no fewer than 1,600 equations, with 4,000 exogenous parameters.

This econometric triumph was in a way a reflection of what was now a much more "technocratic" trend in the plan. The "Commissariat au Plan" had always been very small, in terms of the number of permanent officials involved. But before the Sixth Plan a wide cooperative network had grown up, calling on an ever-increasing number of consultants. When the First Plan was being worked out there were six commissions; by the Sixth, there were about a hundred, including over four thousand participants. According to Malinvaud, most of these commissions changed from "scientific instruments for forecasting" into "arenas of confrontation among participants pursuing special interests." It was this which lay behind the new procedure employed under the Seventh Plan. Only four commissions were now set up, and the subjects of their deliberations corresponded to the current preoccupations of the government and various branches of the administration (Commission on Growth, Employment, and Financing; Commission on Foreign Trade; Commission on Social Inequalities; Commission on Town and Country Planning). The new plan, while less ambitious politically and more empiricist in its approach (it used models incorporating "uncertainty variants"), was to be a much more efficient instrument of government policy.

Some commentators, especially Americans like J. H. McArthur and B. R. Scott, both of Harvard, denied at the end of the 1960s that the plan played a major role in French growth in the fifties and sixties, alleging that the quality of its forecasts was debatable and pointing out that they always had to be revised. Moreover, they said, the decisions made by the various elements concerned, including government ministries, were "autonomous." In fact, the difference between the estimated and the real results was never as great as all that, and if decisions had to be revised on several occasions—in particular, in 1957 and 1963—it was to counter the risks of inflation. These new policies also had to take into account "imperatives" defined by the plan, particularly in the field of public investment, that were less deflationary than they would have been if there had been no plan. So we may agree with Malinvaud that the plan reduced "the dimensions of investment cycles," for investment policy as a whole had been defined with reference to objectives set out by the plan. But its scope went far beyond the public sector. As P. Masse has said, the earlier plans, by "providing an image of an expanding economy in which production was sure to find outlets," amply fulfilled their function as "reducers of uncertainty." A 1967 INSEE survey which dealt with two thousand firms shows that four-fifths of French industrial concerns were aware of the Fifth Plan's growth objective, and that two-thirds of them were familiar with the forecasts relevant to their own activity. Few were actually able to incorporate the forecasts into their own management, but some big firms were in a position to do so, and more than half the businesses employing over 5,000 people said their decisions were influenced by the plan's estimates. The investment policy of these big firms influenced that of many smaller concerns. In fact, the planning experiment enabled French capitalism to make the transition from being a closed system, in which the economy of the country could be described as a coherent and interdependent whole, to being an open system in which external pressure was a threat to overall coherence, and in which future-oriented managment became the chief consideration in each firm's development.

The Opening Up of Frontiers. It is not our concern to go over the history of the political origins of the European Coal and Steel Community or the Common Market, but one of the ideas which inspired their founders was the wish to make French producers "restructure" under pressure from foreign competition. Bjøl quotes Pierre Mendès France as saying in 1955: "One thing is certain: France cannot really put the Common Market into effect." But this was to underestimate the adaptability of many sectors of the economy. And the advocates of the EEC saw it as a way of "eliminating firms whose costs were too high" (A. Savary) and of enlarging a market "which had become too small" (G. Mollet).

As we have seen in the preceding chapter, not all French employers were against entry into the Common Market. The wish to have access to a wider market was in fact greater than fear of ruinous competition. As its founders hoped, the Common Market greatly accentuated the "internationalization" of the French economy as far as trading was concerned, so much so that one of the basic hypotheses of the Sixth Plan model, "Fifi," was the difference in behavior between firms in "protected" sectors, where prices could be fixed in terms of the firms' own self-financing requirements, and firms in "exposed" sectors, where prices were fixed by foreign competition.

It is a debatable point whether France's foreign trading results showed its economy adapting itself, as the creators of the Common Market had hoped, to foreign competition. P. Arnaud Ameller, analyzing the results of the years 1951–69, has given a severe verdict on France's performance. While France's propensity to import was not excessive in comparison with its Common Market partners, its propensity to export was inadequate. The growth in exports in the early 1960s was probably only the result of the exchange bonus arising out of the devaluation of the franc in 1958. Indeed, France "seems not only to have had a smaller share than others in the world boom, but actually to have played only a passive part in it." The 1960s were in fact characterized by a geographical reorientation of exports: exports to the franc area fell from 42 percent in 1952 to 10 percent in 1970, while exports to the EEC rose from 16 to 50 percent. This evolution presupposes a fundamental change in the nature of these exports. In 1960 French exports, compared with those of the rest of the Common Market, were relatively specialized in agricultural, semifinished, and consumer goods, but little specialized in equipment goods. But during the 1960s France's specialization in the export of equipment goods increased more than that of any another country in the Common Market. This was largely due to the fact, pointed out earlier, that France's growth was greater than that of the other industrialized countries. This had two consequences: the irregular growth of France's trading partners limited the outlets for French exports, while the dynamism of the home market tended to increase the propensity to import. The discrepancy between France's growth rate and the growth rates of her partners grew even more marked during the boom of 1969–73, and set limits to expansion of France's exports of equipment goods. But thanks to the development of car exports the export/home consumption ratio, which had stagnated since 1960, leapt from 32 percent to 42 percent. All in all, Mme Arnaud Ameller's pessimistic view is only partly justified. The breakdown of foreign trade in terms of goods is admittedly weak, and the proportion represented by equipment goods is low, but Mme Arnaud Ameller does not take sufficient account of the success of the "geographical redeployment" of French trade.

One could in fact present an overall interpretation of the last twenty years of French political history which showed it as depending mainly on the setting up of mechanisms of competition. During the first phase of the period, the devaluation of 1957–58 enabled French prices to overcome the handicap from which they had previously suffered, as was pointed out by industrialists during the discussions on the Common Market in the 1950s. At the same time, the measures taken by Félix Gaillard and Jacques Rueff reversed the trend regarding the distribution of incomes: whereas until 1957 the trend had developed in a way favorable to wages, it was now suddenly reversed at their expense. This created favorable conditions for a renaissance in self-financing and in the rate of investment. The 1960s did not, however, show an accentuation of the tendencies favorable to foreign trade, because investment was still not sufficiently selective. The measures taken to limit the pressure of wages within the framework of an overall incomes policy, and to encourage self-financing, could not properly allow for the differences between exposed and other sectors.

The great reforms of the 1960s (those concerned with the structure of business enterprises were dealt with earlier; the following section deals with those concerned with the state's more general activities) were effective only from 1968 onward. Moreover, many of them were rather disappointing in their results. In these circumstances, the devaluation of 1969 was quite a different matter from that of 1957–58. It gave France a price advantage of at least 8 percent, instead of merely doing away with a previous disadvantage. The French wage costs were probably slightly lower than those of France's partners, whereas in 1957–58 they had been distinctly higher. Lastly, the policy of "selective stimulation of supply," inaugurated in 1965, combined with the appropriate credit policy to lend the growth which took place in the period 1969–73 a quite different "style" from that of the early 1960s. The rate of household savings was high; the distribution of business incomes favored private companies rather than "individual entrepreneurs" (the proportion of private companies rose from 20 percent in 1967 to 25 percent in 1969, while that of individual entrepreneurs fell from 65 percent to 57.7 percent, a development which J. Mistral explains, adducing plausible arguments, by a swift rise in the incomes of exporting industries); and the more comfortably off private firms had access to outside financing.

International Financial Relations. There continued to be some uncertainty about the future of France's foreign trade, and this explains the weakness of the franc on the exchange markets. The hope, born in the years 1966–67, of seeing the franc become really stable, was partly disappointed. The devaluations of 1968 were the result of the overvaluation of the franc at that time. This calls for some explanation. After the period of what André de Lattre called the "destruction of reserves," between 1945 and 1947, France managed, between 1948 and 1950, to restore the balance of its external payments. This was due to the fact that at the end of 1947 René Mayer adopted a realistic, multiple rate of exchange designed to take into account the overvaluation of the pound. Between 1948 and 1950, United States aid made it possible to restore the reserves, and the trade balance improved. France was even able to liberalize its commerce (i.e., abolish quotas) to the extent of 75 percent. But, as we have seen, the consequences of the Korean War undid all this. By the second half of 1951 there was an enormous deficit in the balance of current payments, and on February 3, 1952, in the course of a very brief ministry, Edgar

Faure had to suspend the liberalization. In 1952 and 1953 balance could only be achieved thanks, again, to American aid under the "off-shore" arrangements, and to large borrowings from the European Payments Union. In 1954 and 1955 Edgar Faure adopted a policy of multiple exchange rates, with systematic aid to exports and a tax on imports. He regarded these as temporary expedients and refused, on expert advice, to carry out an official devaluation. During these years France, against the background of a world boom, had a surplus trade balance and was able to start paying off its debts—admittedly with American help—during the war in Indochina. The war ended in 1956, and at the same time a serious trade deficit reappeared. Félix Gaillard tried again to stave off devaluation in 1957, by a policy of multiple exchange rates. But domestic prices had risen so high that devaluation, too long put off, was inevitable. If 1950 equals 100, GNP prices were 151 in 1956, as against 120 in Germany and 117 in the United States.

The devaluation of December 1958 had all the characteristics of a successful "cold" devaluation. It produced not only a spectacular recovery of the trade balance but also a large influx of private capital from abroad which to a certain extent took over from previous government aid. Between 1959 and 1966 France's official reserves rose from 1,723 million dollars to 5,745, of which 5,238 were in gold. France was able to pay its foreign debts in advance. The franc strengthened on the exchange market, and in 1966 exchange control, which had been introduced twenty-five years before, was abolished.

Today, however, hopes of lasting stabilization remain unfulfilled. Although the French balance of payments was deteriorating by 1967, when the world monetary crisis occurred, France wanted to follow a policy that was independent of the other members of the Group of Ten. In March 1968 General de Gaulle dissociated himself from the measures taken in January by the government of the United States and in March by the Group of Ten which led to the creation of a dual market in gold. He refused to sign the Stockholm agreement. But the crisis of May 1968 weakened France's position and caused a considerable deterioration in the balance of payments situation. The refusal to devalue in November 1968 despite speculation against the franc was followed nine months later by a devaluation of 12.5 percent, the strong recovery in 1969 having worsened the balance-of-payments deficit.

The agreement reached at The Hague in December 1969 was the first step toward the establishment of a monetary union in Europe. It fixed an instant margin of fluctuation among European currencies, lower than the margin of fluctuation in relation to the dollar (the European monetary "snake"). After the dollar crisis in May 1971, France, whose position had undergone a marked improvement since the devaluation, had to take steps to avoid bull speculation on the franc. The agreements of December 1971, which upset the parities of the various currencies in relation to the dollar, made it necessary to revise the Hague agreements and increase the maximum of the instant margin of fluctuation. The franc remained fairly strong during the monetary crisis of June 1972, and even that of February 1973, and was able to remain within the EEC agreement, which had been revised to allow the currencies concerned to float freely but as a bloc (the snake) in relation to the dollar.

The energy crisis so threatened the equilibrium of the balance of payments that France had to leave the Community monetary agreement on January 18, 1974. It reentered it again on July 10, 1975, its balance of payments having swiftly regained its equilibrium through the "cooling" measures of 1974, which limited the growth of imports. Conversely, the recovery in the first months of 1976 brought about another disequilibrium, and in March 1976 France left the agreement again. This was a de facto devaluation made inevitable by "the desire to protect the official exchange reserves" (Report for the Seventh Plan). But "the decision to float must not exempt us from the disciplines imposed by the mechanism of fixed rates of exchange, of which these disciplines are one of the chief advantages" (from the same report). These are the disciplines of the "Barre plan" of September 1976.

In fact, it is clear, as the special committee for the Seventh Plan observes, that monetary disorder "favors the United States; does not hurt strong economies (Germany, Holland); but does not favor countries going through a crisis or those which are restructuring their industries (France)." We cannot give all the balance of payments figures here, but in tables 14.1 and 14.2 are the results of a few key years. Perpetual changes in the way the blaance is presented make it impossible to give really comparable figures.

Table 14.1 Balance of Payments, 1959–1966, According to "Profil Economique de la France" (in millions of francs)

	1953	1962	1966
Trade in goods	+2,148	+2,396	−189
Trade in services and gifts*	+1,511	+1,692	+351
Movements of long-term capital	+1,861	+1,298	+409
Miscellaneous movements	+1,921	+879	+685
General balance	+7,441	+6,265	+1,256

*"Gifts" include foreign workers' remittances plus government operations, i.e., disbursements for embassies, payments of the Fonds Européen d'orientation et de Garantie Agricole, and aid to developing countries in the form of grants (excluding loans).

Between 1960 and 1968 the trade balance "showed certain signs of weakness," and "current payments, weighed down upon by government aid expenditure and the growing amount of wages transferred by foreign workers, were always in danger of emerging as a weak point in the external situation." But entries of capital made it possible to accumulate exchange reserves. Between 1969 and 1973, thanks to the effects of

Table 14.2 Balance of Payments, 1968–1974, According to the Report on the Seventh Plan (in millions of francs)

	1968	1971	1973	1974
Goods	+434	+6,137	+3,442	−18,738
Services	+15	+3,691	+2,128	+1,583
Gifts	−4,668	−6,908	−8,572	−11,597
Long- and short-term capital	−10,949	+6,528	−219	+11,373
Adjustments	−178	+890	−441	+5,704
Total	−15,346	+10,338	−3,662	−11,675
Monetary items				
Banking sector	−2,764	+7,534	+3,971	+9,499
Public sector	+18,110	−17,872	+7,453	+2,176

devaluation, a surplus remained in the trade balance, though only a slight one. In fact, unlike Germany, France did not produce any "structural surplus." But current payments were always in surplus from 1970 to 1973, the trade balance surplus and the income from interest making up for the "structural" deficit in invisibles, due first to the transfer of wages abroad by immigrant workers and second to the deficit in certain services (insurance and transport) and to government foreign aid. The balance of movements of long-term capital, which was strongly negative in 1968, subsequently almost reached an equilibrium, as the report on the Sixth Plan had hoped. The deficit under this heading was due solely to the export of public capital. That being so, after the beginning of the 1970s France managed to keep its exchange reserves at a satisfactory level only by means of large imports of short-term capital, and this situation grew worse in 1974. In 1975 France, which is exceptionally dependent on imported energy (75 percent), had an enormous trade deficit of 20 billion francs, and a current balance of payments deficit of nearly 30 billion, whence the worsening of short-term debt. The year 1975 was brought into balance through exports to the oil-producing countries and the drop in imports owing to the slowdown in activity. But, as we have said, the recovery in 1976 brought about a deterioration. So the present problem is, how long will it take France to restore the balance of its payments on current accounts? The special committee of the Seventh Plan considers that "exceptional efforts" will be needed, but that France will not encounter major difficulties in borrowing, because it has large reserves and "its economy has shown an aptitude for growth in the past which augurs well for its solvency in the long term."

There is one aspect of the balance of payments which has been the subject of passionate discussion in recent years, and that is "direct investments and loans related to the private sector." The analysis of this item is at the heart of the political debate on the influence of the multinationals in France. Up to 1975, the amount of this kind of foreign capital entering the country was greater than the amount leaving it. The INSEE experts described France, in this respect, as a "pivot," for "the industrial countries' capital comes to be invested in France, and

France's capital goes to the countries of the Third World"
(Guibert et al.). France's direct foreign investments amounted
to 1.8 billion in 1960–63, 3 billion in 1964–67, and 11.7 billion in
1968–71. This recent boom was due to oil investment, and was
oriented chiefly toward countries other than the United States
and Europe (7.2 billion). The main capital-exporting sectors are
chemicals and nonferrous ores; in France these sectors include
groups of a multinational character such as Rhone-Poulenc and
Péchinet-Ugine-Kuhlmann. It seems likely that this export of
capital will develop in the future as an aid to the export drive.
But I shall lay most stress on the import of capital, as many
sections of French public opinion see this as a threat to
France's economic independence.

Direct investments, after increasing rather slowly since the
beginning of the 1950s, suddenly expanded after 1968. In the
1950s they had represented a growing but "tiny" proportion of
gross formation of capital. According to G. Y. Bertin, their
share amounted to 0.6 percent in 1954, 0.72 percent in 1958, and
2.48 percent in 1961. In 1962, the turnover of companies of
which 20 percent of the capital was held by foreigners
represented 8.1 percent of the total turnover of all companies.
But if one adds together direct investments and loans, France
imported 21.2 billion francs between 1962 and 1970. Taking
direct investments alone, France imported 17.5 billion francs
between 1960 and 1971, 65 percent of it between 1968 and 1971.
The United States' share in these imports was 43.3 percent, and
that of the EEC 33 percent. INSEE drew up an account of
"Foreign penetration into French industry" on January 1, 1973.
At this date, industrial enterprises of which 20 percent or more
of the capital was held by foreigners employed 18 percent of
the work force (850,000 people), carried out rather more than
25 percent of sales, and were responsible for 24 percent of
investments. Foreign interests had a majority control in 80
percent of these companies. The sectors most deeply
"penetrated" (over 30 percent) were the oil industry, electrical
engineering, chemicals, and industrial machinery. The sectors
comparatively unaffected were those dominated by nationalized enterprises, large-scale enterprises with French capital
(iron and steel, nonferrous metals, glass), or sectors where

growth was slight (textiles). These peculiarities were not found only in France.

Some commentators maintain that, thanks in particular to state aid, the American multinationals have more potential for expansion than the others. At any rate, France has not provided them with an especially favorable field of action. France's share in United States' foreign investments was 1.8 percent in 1950 and 3.3 percent in 1970, as against corresponding figures of 1.7 percent and 5.9 percent for Germany, and 5.4 percent and 15 percent for the EEC as a whole. The attitude of the state and of public opinion in France to these investments has always been changeable, a mixture of mistrust and goodwill. In the 1950s the attitude of both state and employers was one of what Bertin has called "latent" hostility. Between 1959 and 1962 the general attitude was on the whole favorable; between 1962 and 1965 it was on the whole unfavorable. Since then it has become frankly "selective." Even the reports concerning the Seventh Plan contained differing points of view. While the preparatory reports express great anxiety about the possible consequences of the French economy's becoming dominated by the multinationals, the Committee on Foreign Finances considers that foreign investment in France "has not reached a disturbing level, and places our country in a situation comparable to that of our principal European neighbors." The committee advises welcoming the creation of new enterprises rather than taking over those already in existence. But there is great fear of the effects of the "international division of labor," and to preserve France's "autonomy" the authors of the Seventh Plan ask for "control of the expansion of multinational firms" and a "redefinition of the state's contribution to the development of advanced-technology industries, and of research policy in general." Thus the multinationals are still regarded with a good deal of reserve.

The "Structural Reforms" of the 1960s, and Their Limitations. The policy encouraging the restructuring of business enterprises, examined earlier, is only one aspect of the legislative efforts which after General de Gaulle's return to power tended toward installing or restoring in France an economic system

freed of the "hindrances" and "rigidities" which had accumulated over the preceding thirty years. The measures as a
whole tended to favor competitiveness above all, and, in order
to do this, to choose a growth rate lower than the one which
would have been physically possible, this lower rate making it
possible to control both prices and the charges incumbent on
enterprises. The policy of market regulation described in the
first section of this chapter was in fact part of this design. It
was not a blindly expansionist policy systematically sacrificing
equilibrium to growth, but, on the contrary, a policy of control
over demand accompanied by reconstruction of the necessary
mechanisms to increase savings, the long-term guarantee of this
stability. We shall deal here with just three of the structural
aspects of this government action. The first concerns the
attempt to create a really competitive market; the second, a
number of measures relating to taxation and the organization of
credit, the object being to encourage saving and direct it toward
productive investment within the framework of an attempt to
restore a free and competitive financial market. The third
aspect concerns research policy and the sectorial choices involved.

The open-frontiers policy is inseparable from the policy to
promote competition between French and European producers:
the aims of the two policies are, at least in part, identical. The
relevant legislation is old, but took a long time to come into
effect. The basic decree here dates from June 30, 1945. It lays
down rules for individual practice regarding sales, and tries to
counter the undesirable effects of "cartels and established
positions." With the first aim in view, it tended to limit refusal
of sale and discrimination among buyers. Both aspects of the
text were subsequently worked out in more complete detail.
Regulations about installment sales were laid down in 1956,
about advertising in 1963, and about door-to-door selling in
1972. The financial law of July 1963 forbade resale of un-
damaged goods at a price below wholesale cost. The drive
against cartels gathered force from 1952 on. In August 1953, a
decree, quashed by the Conseil d'Etat in 1958 and immediately
revived, laid down the main lines of this policy. The government undertook not to forbid cartels which worked to "im-

prove and extend productivity, or to insure economic development through rationalization and specialization." A "Technical Committee on Cartels and Established Positions" was set up to make investigations on behalf of the prices board. But in 1958 the Rueff-Armand Committee observed that the Technical Committee "had scarcely touched cartels in France as a whole," and had merely "begun to work out the legal aspects." Since then the committee has produced no spectacular developments. F. Jenny and A. P. Weber, after analyzing its work as a whole, conclude that it fought a somewhat uncertain rearguard action and encountered great difficulty in expressing its point of view. Since 1969 its attitude has seemed to be stricter, and it has been less ready to approve cartels which claim to promote "economic progress." But it still does not deal with very many cases. Probably the cases which are dealt with reveal practices which are fairly widespread, yet the Technical Committee has clearly dealt with only a small proportion of the anticompetitive practices actually in use. If we assume that these practices concern the greater part of the market, the French economy could not be considered one of free competition. It would be a "controlled" economy, controlled either through the "production quotas" which the committee has condemned with ever-increasing energy, or through the more acceptable "wage tables" or price cartels, or by the setting up of entry barriers "aiming at maximizing profits and forbidding entry to any new competitor." The market in electric light bulbs is a typical example: here the cartel, the origins of which go back to 1943, today tends to be the instrument of the Philips monopoly, the other enterprises involved becoming more and more dependent on Philips. It is clear that cartels are now only one aspect among others of the strategy and evolution of groups, and that it is not easy to overcome the contradictions inherent in a policy which tries at one and the same time to encourage enterprises to reach the size made necessary by the desire for maximum economies of scale and to safeguard competition.

What Jean Saint Géours has called the "mythology of investment" was born in the 1950s and continued in the 1960s, but in the latter period the policy aimed at being much more selective. The fact that emerges most clearly (see table 14.3) is the reduction in the proportion of total investment represented by public investors (administration and public enterprises).

The share of public enterprises shows a marked and regular decrease, falling from 30 percent in 1949–53 to 15.7 percent in 1969–73, while that of administration rose slightly until 1964–68 and then fell. This drop has been compensated for by an appreciable increase in household investment and investment by private enterprises. This pattern of development results from deliberate choices on the part of the public authorities, choices clearly laid down under the administration of Edgar Faure and confirmed with increasing emphasis during the 1960s. Yet, even during the latter decade, public enterprises always had special sources of financing at their disposal. While they were responsible for 30 percent of investment by enterprises in these years, they used nearly 56 percent of the external resources of long-term financing available for all enterprises. They thus, according to the INSEE experts, constituted a "drain on savings resources" which may have "tended to favor more than was necessary the investments of certain public enterprises." During the 1960s one of the chief aims of the credit policy was to restore the mechanisms allowing family-budget savers to participate in the financing of enterprises. The family savings rate (ratio of gross savings to available income) did not make much progress during the 1950s (12.2 percent in 1950 and 12.9 percent in 1959), but it showed a marked increase in the 1960s, rising from a mean of 14.6 percent in 1959–63 to 15.3 percent in 1964–68 and 16.6 percent in 1969–73. This increase was welcome at a time when firms' capacity for self-financing was beginning to be affected by a reduction in profit margins. So in 1966 measures were taken to make savings more mobile: restrictions preventing deposit banks from using their resources as freely as merchant banks were lifted; banks were given more freedom in fixing rates of interest; and a mortgage market was created.

The 1966 reforms were the starting point for an unprecedented development of French credit institutions. The year 1967 saw several measures designed to promote an extension of the stock market. The Commission des Opérations en Bourse

Table 14.3 Share of Various Investors in the Gross Formation of Fixed Capital, According to Comptabil-ité Nationale (in current francs)

| | Financial Institutions | Nonfinancial Institutions | | | | | |
		Public Enterpr.	Private enterpr., not agricultural	Individual enterpr., agricultural	Families	Administration
1949–1953	0.7	29.9	38.3	8.3	13.3	9.5
1954–1958	0.9	23.7	38.4	7.4	18.5	11.1
1959–1963	1.1	22.1	42.9	5.9	16.4	11.6
1964–1968	0.9	19.9	40.6	5.2	19.8	13.6
1969–1973	1.1	15.7	45.8	4.8	19.8	12.8

(COB) was created with the object of "improving the ethical standards" of the stock market. But the latter, which had in fact made a new start in the middle of the 1950s, never recovered the role it had played before 1914. In the 1960s the proportion of issues in the French GDP was no lower than that in the other big industrial countries. On the other hand, French savers had increased their mobilizable short- and middle-term lending. While household savings was and is useful first and foremost for financing the construction drive, it also meets the need to maintain some liquid or quasi-liquid cash in the face of rising inflation. This being so, one of the chief ways of financing investment is still the transformation of short-term savings into long-term capital. Mechanisms for doing this which were introduced during the reconstruction period have in the course of time undergone considerable changes. While, during the early 1950s, the main credit base was the state or parastate institutions, later there was a drop in the part played by these institutions—in particular by the Fonds de Développement Économique et Social (FDES), successor of the Fonds du Modernisation et d'Équipement (FME)—while there was an increase in medium-term credit granted by the commercial banks, which was mobilizable with the Crédit National, the Crédit Foncier, and the Caisse des Marchés de l'Etat, and rediscountable with the Banque de France. But in 1965 these rediscount facilities were greatly reduced, and the commercial banks were led to draw more largely on their own resources. Clearly this reanimation of the financial market made possible the investment effort of the late 1960s and early 1970s.

The emergence of a tax policy designed to form part of a policy of expansion dates from the 1930s, but it was in the 1950s that this instrument took more elaborate shape. The main feature of the policy is to reduce capital costs by acting on equipment costs or levying less tax on reinvested profit than on distributed profit. In 1954 the value added tax replaced the tax on production, which had been introduced in 1936 and modified in 1948 in a way which foreshadowed the 1954 reform. In 1936 the tax was levied at the end of the production process; in 1948, the producer could deduct the taxes which had been paid on the raw materials; in 1954, the deduction could be applied to all materials added to an item. Moreover, in 1960, to expedite savings by business enterprises, a system of accelerated depreciation was applied to investments instead of the straight-line depreciation which had been applied hitherto. In other words, instead of deducting an equal sum each year, the entrepreneur could deduct larger sums in the first few years and increasingly smaller ones thereafter. Direct taxation was also used to encourage household savings: measures here included a flat-rate levy on debentures and the introduction of tax credits for owners of shares. Although such sectorial and regional tax measures have by no means fallen out of use, the present tendency of this policy is to make taxation more and more "neutral."

Similar developments took place in the field of research. The "big programs" policy of the 1960s was succeeded by a policy which according to the Direction Générale de le Recherche Scientifique et Technique (DGRST) directed its efforts toward "industry as a whole." The working out of a comprehensive research policy dates from the early 1960s. In this field, as in that of investment, a tendency toward selectivity emerged; the idea that every form of research was a contribution to "progress" was called into question, as it was in all Western countries. It seemed clear that scientific progress had to be subordinated to the needs of society and of the state, and more particularly to an "industrial policy" which in its earliest phase claimed to cover the whole technological field and at its next stage had to take into account the "international division of labor" which, according to the authors of the Seventh Plan (1976–80), was to be characteristic of the 1970s. The theory at the basis of the Seventh Plan—i.e., that the United States' technological lead would be challenged more and more by Europe and Japan—is the subject of debate. For, as Lucien Fahri, assistant director of the Société pour l'Étude du Développement Économique et Social (SEDES) remarks, commenting on the Seventh Plan, such a "multipolar" development could, in fact, only come about with the acquiesence of the United States. "France," he writes, "wanted to promote the advanced technological industries, but in order to do so it needed capital and a market the size of Europe. But as Europe could not come into being except under American influence, and as America was opposed to such a project, the project kept proving abortive." France's research policy, as well as being influenced by this "industrial" aspect, has recently, like all research policies, been subject to two other trends. In order to make research as "productive" as possible, stress has been placed on applied rather than basic research. Moreover, the preeminence of the physical sciences over the life sciences has been increasingly challenged.

The belatedness of the realization that research needed to be planned accounts for the fact that statistics on the subject before 1959 are not available. In that year the gross national expenditure on research and development amounted to 1.14 percent of the GNP. This proportion reached a maximum in 1967 (2.23 percent), and fell to 1.68 percent in 1973. Thus France's position in relation to developed countries in general is an average one. What is different about France is the part played by the state in this field, a part which grew more pronounced up to 1968 but which has since decreased, against the general background of state "disengagement." In 1963 public financing amounted to 62 percent of the total financing; in 1968, to 68 percent; and in 1971–73 to 64 percent. But a large part of private research is in fact based on direct or indirect state aid. In the state budget, research expenditure accounted for 2.46 percent in 1958, 6.22 percent in 1967, and 5.2 percent in 1969.

The distribution of this expenditure changed a great deal in the course of the 1960s. Up to about 1967 or 1968, the "big programs"—atomic, military, and aeronautic—tended to take an overwhelming slice of the pie. In 1967, the figures were 23 percent for the atomic program, 28 percent for the military program, and 6 percent for the aeronautics program. This bias was the result of the choices involved in the industrial policy of the Fifth Republic, and affected other fields besides research. Because of its desire for national independence; in order to compensate for disadvantages due to the smallness of the home market; and because a belief that some major innovation might trigger off a chain reaction in the whole technological system, the state embarked on a series of spectacular enterprises such as the Concorde program and the computer program in association with the principal enterprises involved in the sector, whether nationalized or not. These programs were accompanied by measures aimed at the restructuring of business enterprises and by direct state aid in the form of subsidies or acquisition of stock. To begin with the aeronautic industry, the six companies which had been nationalized in 1936 had been re-formed during the 1950s into two groups: Sud Aviation and Nord Aviation. These two companies, together with the Service d'Etudes et de Recherche sur les Engins Balistiques (SEREB, founded in 1959 to draw up ballistics programs), merged to form SNIAS (Société Nationale des Industriés Aéronautiques et Spaciales). In the private sector, which had been reconstructed in 1936, the two principal contractors, Dassault and Bréguet, merged in 1971. The engine sector was run by the national company , the Société Nationale d'Étude et Construction de Moteurs d'Aviation (SNECMA). The aeronautics policy of the Gaullist régime was aimed chiefly at trying to balance expanding military production with civil production. This object was not entirely achieved, and even today most of France's aeronautics activity is still military. There are many reasons why the policy did not succeed, but there is no doubt that the sales capacity of the French aeronautics industry does not match its technical level.

In the field of computers the state only gradually became aware of its responsibilities. Euphoria reigned in the early 1960s, because only a French company had been able to hold its own against IBM. The Compagnie des Machines Bull, a family company founded in 1931 to exploit the patents of F. Bull, a Norwegian engineer, had experienced outstanding growth in the 1950s, and its technical experts had managed to produce models capable of rivaling those of IBM. But the models produced in the early 1960s called for better commercial exploitation than the company could provide. There was a sudden collapse, and in 1963 Bull was in the red. The French government refused to allow a takeover by General Electric, but was obliged to accept it in July 1964. The two companies controlled by Bull and General Electric were subsequently able to develop only through General Electric's taking over more and more of the stock (66 percent in 1967). As early as 1965, the government tried to find a "French solution."

The work of the experts appointed to resolve the problem was given added impetus by President Johnson's refusal, in January 1966, to allow three big computers to be exported to France, where they were to be used for military purposes. General de Gaulle's government created a Délégation à l'Informatique—a "computer commission"—and defined the aims of its policy in a "computer plan." This was to be carried out through the Compagnie Internationale d'Informatique (CII), an association of private capital formed in April 1967 out of the computer subsidiaries of the big French electric and electronics groups, CGE and CSF, together with a few independent firms. But the state undertook to help the new company until 1972 by means of credits and through orders for work and surveys. With the help of the Délégation Générale the CII went ahead, especially in the administrative sector. State aid was not in fact halted in 1972.

Meanwhile, in 1970, General Electric—despite the fact that in 1969 it had for the first time announced a profit for its subsidiary Bull–General Electric—had transferred its holdings to another American company, Honeywell. The French government, after exploring the possibility of a European solution through bringing the CII together with Siemens and Philips, within the framework of Unidata, gave up that idea because it would have meant that the CII would have been taken over by Siemens, and agreed in 1975 to a merger between the CII and Honeywell-Bull.

The partial success of the "big programs" that were linked to General de Gaulle's industrial policy led to a revision of research policy as a whole, especially after the beginning of the Seventh Plan (1970–74). The big programs were considered too "greedy," and their "technological fallout" and "runaway effects" were challenged. It was becoming clear, moreover, that the excessive overspecialization in state expenditure on research and development was paralleled by similar overspecialization on the part of business enterprises, which in 1969 spent 7.7 billion francs on research, 22 percent of it on aerospace research. State aid accounted for 88 percent of this expenditure, as against 4.5 percent in the case of research undertaken in the chemical industries, 44 percent in electronics, and 23 percent in telecommunications. The state wanted to spread its aid more equally among the different sectors and among the different firms, and to make it depend more strictly on real risks and real successes. That being so, an attempt was made to stimulate more diversified research by means of incentive measures which provided for the sharing of both initiative and risk. As early as 1965 a procedure was introduced by which subsidies for research and development had to be repaid only in cases of success, and this procedure was used more and more widely.

It is clear how much this policy, like the investment policy, derived from the desire for "competitiveness" which arose from the opening up of frontiers and France's incorporation into the world of Western capitalism. At the same time France felt the influence of the new ideas which emerged in the United States in the early 1960s and challenged the preeminence of the physical sciences over the human and biological sciences. But this trend was suddenly checked by the energy crisis. In terms of statistics, the new trends are reflected in two ways. Within the total budget, expenditure on research (the "research package") rose from 47.4 percent to 51 percent between 1970 and 1973, and within this package the proportion of "expenditure with a social and economic object," which refers chiefly to the life sciences, rose from 5.4 percent in 1970 to 9.2 percent in 1974, while "research with an industrial object" fell from 17 percent to 16.5 percent, the big programs fell from 43.3 percent to 37.2 percent, and "basic research" rose from 34 percent to 35.6 percent.

If these facts are laid alongside those in the previous section concerning nationalized enterprises, we might ask ourselves whether France has not set out on the road toward a kind of "disguised socialization" of her economy, in which large sections of public opinion see the only hope of salvation from the spread of the multinationals. So that the reader may judge for himself we shall give two sets of statistics—on the one hand, budget figures, and on the other, the results of a recent survey by the Ministry of Finance. The evolution of the structure of the budget clearly expresses some main aspects of economic policy. Here are the principal facts.

1. The proportion of the GIP represented by the budget

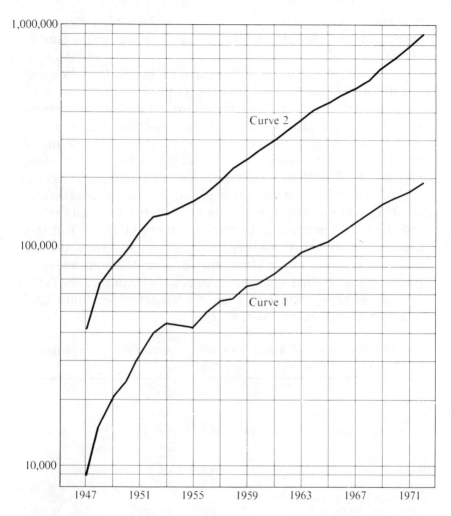

Figure 9 Growth of Budget Expenditure and Growth of Gross Domestic Product, 1947–1972. Curve 1: Overall expenditure in millions. Curve 2: GDP in millions.

SOURCE: *Evolution du budget de l'Etat*, special issue of *Statistiques et Etudes Financières*, 1974.

reached its maximum in 1953 (31.8 percent), then fell to 26.6 percent in 1955 and rose again to 28.2 percent in 1956–57. There was a sudden drop to 25.5 percent in 1958; the decline continued very slowly until 1967–68, then more swiftly (21.4 percent in 1972). The long-term trend is thus toward dis-

engagement on the part of the state, a trend which was interrupted only in 1956–57, partly because of the war effort in
Algeria.

2. "Current expenditure" increased faster than "capital
expenditure." This was due to the natural disappearance of
"war damage," to the fall in expenditure on military equipment
in the 1950s, and also, because of the "disengagement" policy
referred to above, to the growth of expenditure classed under
the heading of "treasury loans," which include, in particular,
loans by the Fonds de Développement Économique et Social
(FDES). Their share in current expenditure greatly increased in
the 1950s, and reached a maximum in 1959. It fell steeply in the
1960s (from 12 percent in 1959 to 2 percent in 1972). But this
fall was not the result of any "disengagement" from private
industry. It was rather that the practical significance of
"treasury loans" had changed between 1959 and 1972. Table
14.4 traces the evolution of France's budget expenditure, and
table 14.5 gives a breakdown of treasury loans.

Table 14.4 Distribution of Budget Expenditure, According to "Evolution du
Budget de l'Etat" (in percent)

	1953	1959	1972
Current expenditure			
Civil administration	13.6	18.8	27.0
Military expenditure	16.9	16.2	9.0
Interest on debt	3.4	5.3	2.4
Pensions	3.6	4.5	6.5
Current subsidies	17.1	24.5	30.7
Net charges on special accounts			
other than charges on loans	0.7	0.1	0.4
Total current expenditure	*55.3*	*69.4*	*76.0*
Capital expenditure			
Civil plant and equipment	3.1	6.2	9.2
Plant and equipment subsidies	0.4	0.5	2.7
Capital allowances	0	0.4	0.8
War damage	8.7	3.1	0.1
Military plant and equipment	23.9	8.7	8.0
Treasury loans	7.9	12.1	2.1
Advances	0.7	−0.4	1.1
Total capital expenditure	*44.7*	*30.6*	*24.0*
Total expenditure	100.0	100.0	100.0

Table 14.5 Treasury Loans, According to "Evolution du Budget de l'Etat"

	1959		1966		1972	
	Millions of Francs Current	*Percent*	*Millions of Francs Current*	*Percent*	*Millions of Francs Current*	*Percent*
International credits	751	9.4	284	3.7	931	18.0
Interventions in the economic sphere						
Agriculture	484	6.0	491	6.5	35	0.7
National enterprises	2,519	31.4	1,622	21.4	1,477	28.6
Housing	3,814	47.5	2,677	35.3	80	1.5
Other interventions	233	2.9	1,416	18.6	1,421	27.5
Including loans by FDES to private industry	223	2.8	1,084	14.3	1,216	23.6
Total	8,024	100	7,574	100	5,160	100

The only item in treasury loans which still had the same relative importance in 1972 as in 1959 was loans to nationalized companies. There was an appreciable increase in loans to private enterprises, but they accounted for only 0.63 percent of the total budget in 1972. Equipment subsidies and expenditure both increased in relative value, the first rising from 305 million francs in 1959 to 5,135 in 1972. The latter figure breaks down into aid for housing (49.2 percent), for aeronautics construction (30 percent), for naval construction (11.9 percent), and other subsidies (8.9 percent). The burden of aid to the aeronautics programs is clear. Among expenses on civil equipment, expenditure on education amounted to 39 percent of the total in 1959, 27 percent in 1968, and 23 percent in 1972.

Civil current expenditure could grow in relative value only because of the drop in military expenditure, which stagnated in absolute value (i.e., in fact, fell) between 1959 and 1966, then increased subsequently but more slowly than other expenditure. Expenditure on the civil services came to be more concentrated on education, rising from 42.8 percent in 1959 to 52 percent in 1968 and 50.4 percent in 1972. An increase in the proportion represented by pensions was the natural result of demographic factors. But it is important for us to examine in more detail the evolution of the allocation of "current subsidies," which is set forth in table 14.6.

All the figures in this table are the result of complex evolutions of which we cannot give a complete account. What

Table 14.6 Distribution of "Current Subsidies"

	1953	1959	1972
Aid to local collectivities	1.2	1.1	2.1
International aid	7.8	19.3	6.1
Cultural aid	4.8	5.7	10.4
Economic aid including subsidies	37.9	25.2	29.3
to nationalized companies	19.2	10.9	9.7
Housing aid	1.3	3.8	5.4
Other subsidies	15.5	4.5	4.2
Social aid	48.3	48.7	52.1
Including social security	16.3	14.2	20.0

is chiefly to be noted is that despite the oft-repeated intention of reducing them, subsidies "of an economic character," whether to nationalized companies or private enterprises, did not disappear. The steep relative drop in the 1950s illustrates one of the main lines of economic policy at that time—the return to the "natural play of market forces." Aid "in the social field" remained steady at about half the total expenditure here. An important feature is the increasingly heavy burden imposed by the social security deficit, due chiefly to the particularly high cost of health care in France, and to excessive consumption in this field. The necessary reforms are obvious, but to apply them would be to come up against extremely powerful lobbies.

3. The financing of expenditure by revenues averaged 85 percent between 1951 and 1955, and fell to 81 percent in 1956–57. Since then it has always been above 90 percent: an average of 92.3 percent from 1959 to 1964; of 96.5 percent from 1965 to 1969, despite the relapse in 1968 to 91.8 percent; and of 100 percent from 1970 to 1972. This equilibrium in public finance is one of the main arguments of those who think that speculation against the franc is not justified. A feature of the evolution of the revenue structure is the increase of tax expenditure in the 1950s, due to the gradual reduction of American aid, which after reaching a maximum of 17.8 percent of receipts in 1953, ceased in 1958. Since then tax revenues represent 92 percent of total revenues. Within these tax revenues we may note the fairly stable division between direct and indirect taxes, the former always standing at between 30 percent and 36 percent, with a maximum in 1958 of 36.3 percent. The percentage remained around 35 percent up to 1967, after which it dropped considerably, falling back to an average of 31.6 percent from 1968 to 1972.

In all, an analysis of the budget shows that while the proportion it represented of the GIP decreased, an effort was made to direct expenditure toward uses which were economically rational. Thus educational expenditure increased, and selective loans to technologically advanced sectors were preferred to subsidies designed to maintain price levels. At the same time, the government tried to use indirect taxation to encourage and even direct investment. These developments followed the growth of a body of opinion, in France and in the United States, on the need for rationalizing budget choices.

A recent study by the Ministry of Finance has attempted to measure different kinds of state aid in terms of the following categories: capital allowances; subsidies; public contracts; concerted actions and repayable advances; state loans; and loans from the Sociétés de Développement Économique Régional (SDRs) set up after 1967 and from financial institutions indirectly dependent on the state (chiefly the Crédit National). Table 14.7 shows how these different kinds of aid were distributed in 1970, according to the sectors set out in chapter two.

Capital allowances went mostly to nationalized enterprises in the energy sector; the equipment sector was the one which chiefly benefited from concerted actions and public contracts. Loans from the SDRs and the Crédit National were more widely spread. Here, too, after the early 1960s, there was a kind of "disengagement" on the part of the state: between 1963 and 1971, loans from the Fonds de Développement Economique et Social decreased at an annual rate of 4.4 percent, and subsidies increased at a rate of no more than 4.9 percent. On the other hand, loans from the Crédit National increased by 13.7 percent per annum, and public contracts by 12.4 percent. These less

Table 14.7 Distribution of State Aid by Sector, According to INSEE

	Energy	Intermediate Goods	Equipment Goods	Consumer Goods
Capital allowances and subsidies	54.8	31.8	11.2	2.2
Public contracts	2.7	7.6	83.9	5.8
Concerted actions* and repayable loans	3.0	16.7	78.2	2.1
State loans	43.0	33.2	23.3	0.5
Loans by public regional development agencies and financial institutions	1.6	41.6	26.7	30.1

*"Concerted actions" are in fact subventions granted by the Delégation Générale de la Recherche Scientifique et Technique (DGRST), founded in 1959. They finance 50 percent of the total cost of a basic research project conducted in the framework of a program recognized to be of national usefulness.

direct forms of aid were more evenly divided among the sectors than were subsidies and treasury loans. So, while there was an overall "disengagement," it was accompanied by the growth of more evenly distributed indirect aid, which meant that the state came to exercise real influence over more and more sectors and firms. State intervention spread over the whole system of production. This conclusion links up with that of my earlier section on public enterprises: the old antithesis between a heavily subsidized public sector and an independent private sector was replaced by a system in which state aid and participation were more and more widely diffused.

The Management of Private Firms

It is easier to describe the behavior of the state than to show the evolution of the management of private firms. However, great progress in our knowledge of business firms has been made in recent years, thanks largely to the creation by the Crédit National of a "Centrale des Bilans," which makes it possible to analyze the structure of the balance sheets (*bilans*) of the biggest French firms, with the help of the surveys of the Ministry for Industry and the work of the "Entreprise" section of INSEE. An attempt is being made at present to bring all this information together. But it should be noted that an analysis of balance sheets can provide only an external view of firms' policy, and cannot replace the information provided by company records, which it is to be hoped will be suitably preserved.

The changes in management which have taken place in French firms in the last thirty years derive from two factors, and may be said to correspond roughly to three main trends. The two operative factors have been described in previous chapters. From the point of view of demand, the opening up of frontiers and the changes which have come about in the behavior of consumers and of the state have helped to create an increasingly competitive climate. As we have just seen, business enterprises have tried to compensate for this intensified competition by an attempt to consolidate "established positions" through cartel networks; but these positions are much more precarious than they used to be, and can only be maintained if they are based on indisputable technological and commercial superiority. From the point of view of supply, the rising cost of labor has encouraged the development of increasingly capitalistic production, though pressure on profit margins has hampered the development of internal financing.

The three main trends which it is possible to distinguish are the following: (1) The tendency to substitute capital for labor has grown continually more marked. (2) French enterprises, while maintaining a high rate of self-financing similar to that in other European countries, have increasingly had to resort to external resources. (3) As regards manufactured goods, the trend toward diversification has prevailed more and more strongly over the old strategy of developing by means of reinvestment in the same sector of production.

The revival of private-enterprise investment in France dates from the middle of the 1950s. We have shown above how investments as a whole developed, and a previous section shows the increasingly important part played by private enterprises. E. Malinvaud has domonstrated quite clearly that the level of these investments depended chiefly on the intensity of demand. But household consumption was directed more and more toward goods which could be produced by highly capitalistic methods. This pressure from household demand was reinforced by pressure from public enterprises and authorities.

But in order that this pressure might result in a sustained movement toward investment, there had to be quite a big change in the attitude of French businessmen. They were traditionally suspicious of the possibilities of an expanding market, and had always avoided embarking on risky anticipation. That is why, as we have seen, the plans—especially the Second Plan, launched in 1953, in a period when people were hesitant and uncertain about France's future—played a crucial role: it provided entrepreneurs in the various sectors with the beginning of a vast "market survey" on a national scale. We have also seen how the employers' acceptance of the Common Market was largely due to the desire to have access to bigger markets.

As regards supply, the relative costs of capital and labor developed so that the former became the cheaper because of the rapid rise in wages and a fiscal and parafiscal policy which added to the cost of labor and lessened that of capital. The ratio of real cost of equipment to real cost of labor fell from 164 in 1949 to 152 in 1953, 64 in 1964, and 72 in 1966. That being so, in every sector, even those which had once been the least capitalistic, techniques were sought for and adopted which were economic of labor, though unusually big consumers of capital.

The financing of this massive industrial investment called for a big self-financing effort, and consequently the maintenance of a high rate of overall profit. It is plain that the old preference for internal financing was never entirely abandoned. True, there was some change in methods of financial management. Whereas at the beginning of the 1960s the level of investment was strictly dependent on the capacity for self-financing, and therefore on past profit, new attitudes began to appear in the course of the 1960s. Because the concentrations which then took place allowed the bigger companies to control the market instead of being controlled by it, and because the growth policy seemed irreversible, French firms increasingly adopted forecasting methods of management, whereby the level of investment depended on "forecast" profit instead of on the feasible rate of self-financing. Firms turned more readily to external financing. In fact, whereas in the 1950s the growth of a firm depended, as R. Goffin has said, on the "profit obtained" by a sort of "spontaneous investment," the answers to the INSEE surveys between 1958 and 1968 show, according to Vincent Thollon Pommerol, that "the entrepreneur decides on the amount of investment necessary for the proper management and the development of his business, and does all he can to reach and maintain this level of expenditure. He is only secondarily concerned with dividing his investment expenditure more or less in accordance with the various sources of financing."

During the 1950s rates of self-financing tended to fall. In nonfinancial and nonagricultural enterprises the rate fell from 96.5 percent in 1953 to 83 percent in 1959; the two years are comparable from the economic point of view. The Malinvaud school explains this by the fall in profit margins, which dropped between these two dates from 9.1 percent in the case of *sociétés anonymes* though it remained stable for other types of company. But R. Courbis suggests a reverse explanation. He writes: "The downward trend in the rate of self-financing is largely explained by a fall in the rate of self-financing *that was wished for*, given the competition on the domestic market," and, it should be added, given the improved mobility of savings. Long-term loans and new issues of stock financed 25 percent of new total fixed assets in 1953, and 40 percent in 1959. Between 1954 and 1957 the financial resources of the capital market had greatly increased (by an average of 25 percent per annum in real value), thanks first to foreign contributions and second to the increase in household savings, which grew at a rate of 6.2 percent per annum. In these circumstances, "the increase in stock issues and above all the possibilities of long-term borrowing, especially on the stock market, partly made up for the reduction of self-financing margins" (Courbis). This development increased firms' indebtedness. The ratio of total indebtedness to the total value of firms' assets rose from 17 percent in 1953 to 24 percent in 1959.

This pattern continued during the 1960s. Using information from the Comptabilité Nationale, I have calculated the rate of self-financing for private companies (see table 14.8). There was a marked fall in the rate between 1959–60 and 1962–63. The explanation is simple: it was a boom period during which investment increased faster than savings. But this time enterprises were unable to do as they had done in the period 1957–59 and raise their prices in order to restore their rates of self-financing. Foreign competition prevented this, and so, even more, did the stabilization plan of 1963. But the resources of the financial market increased less rapidly than in the 1950s (up 18 percent between 1959 and 1964). And this was why growth of investment had to be slowed down until 1967. There was again an increase in the rate of self-financing in the later 1960s, but it fell again in the early 1970s. This fall is much more marked according to the sample given by the Centrale des Bilans, and the presenters of the Seventh Plan observe that

Table 14.8 Private Companies' Rates of Self-Financing, According to the Comptabilité Nationale (in percent)

	I*	II†
1959	91.0	72.5
1960	94.3	67.0
1961	82.9	64.4
1962	76.9	61.6
1963	76.2	62.2
1964	81.4	63.9
1965	76.5	69.6
1966	81.2	68.7
1967	79.3	69.9
1968	84.3	78.7
1969	93.8	66.6
1970	86.1	63.4
1971	81.5	67.7
1972	80.5	67.4
1973	79.5	61.5

*Ratio of gross savings to gross formation of fixed capital, excluding inventory changes.

†Ratio of gross savings to gross formation of fixed capital, including inventory changes.

"industrial firms' rate of self-financing showed quite an appreciable fall during the first three years of the Sixth Plan."

We must agree with INSEE, however, that "the ratios fluctuate, according to the relevant economic situation, around a mean which remains very stable." We have already said that the whole of French government policy aimed at protecting, by tax measures among others, firms' capacity for internal financing. This is confirmed by the "Barre plan," published in September 1976. But, as table 14.9 shows, there has been a marked deterioration in the structure of firms' balance sheets.

The situation got still worse than these figures show during the first years of the Sixth Plan. According to the Centrale des Bilans, medium- and long-term debts represented 36.6 percent of net worth in 1965, 51.8 percent in 1970, and 63.5 percent in 1973. It is likely, in fact, that the real value of net worth is understated. Nevertheless, financial charges increased. In 1975, although the French companies which were among the thousand top European companies were less in debt than their Italian

Table 14.9 Evolution of the Structure of Liabilities Between 1961 and 1969, According to INSEE (in percent)

	Net work	Long- and Medium-Term Debts	Short-Term Debts
1961	44.9	12.2	42.9
1963	41.9	13.6	44.5
1969	36.0	14.1	49.9

counterparts, they were more in debt than English, Belgian, and German companies.

This heavy indebtedness of French firms seems to be largely due to a policy which aims at safeguarding the profit rate at all costs. In fact, while French companies' profit margins are low in comparison with those in other European countries, they manage to achieve a profit rate (ratio of net earnings to net worth) which is comparatively good: in 1975 it was higher than the rate achieved by German firms (9.6 as against 6.5). The profit rate has been able to maintain itself at this level only because of what business accountants call the "leverage effect" of debt. For the 564 companies studied by the Centrale des Bilans, this effect presents itself as follows between 1966 and 1972: the ratio of gross earnings to total assets fell from 10 to 8.5, but the financial leverage ratio of total debts to net worth increased from 1.35 to 1.88. This growing financial leverage ratio mitigates the fall of the ratio of return on investment (from 19.5 percent in 1966 to 17 percent in 1972), which would have been much steeper without the increasing indebtedness of companies. "The ratio of indebtedness," concludes INSEE, "plays the role of stabilizer of the rate of profitability of own capital in unfavorable periods, and the role of accelerator in favorable ones."

A feature of the evolution of profit rates since the early 1960s, after the marked increase in 1959–60, was an appreciable decrease between 1960 and 1963, followed by a stagnation (according to the Centrale des Bilans data, a fall) until 1968, more than made up for by the very strong rise in 1969. Between 1969 and 1973 there was a fall in the rates, bringing them back to the level of 1963. This evolution has been shown by Michel

Benard (of INSEE) as the resultant of three variables: (1) the productivity of capital, which increased greatly up to 1964 and has decreased since, as in most of the major Western countries; (2) the relative price of value added vis-à-vis capital, which developed in the opposite direction up to 1969; and (3) above all, the part played by profit in value added: the pattern here largely explains the "evolution of the rate of profit in terms of the economic situation." Table 14.10 traces the overall evolution of this breakdown. The figures are those put forward by C. Phéline of the Ministry of Finance, who has corrected the gross figures of the Comptabilité Nationale so as to take into account the factor "remuneration of labor" in "gross income of individual entrepreneurs."

Profit rates can only be kept up if the rise in wage costs is kept below the rise in productivity of labor, or if fiscal and other charges are lighter, because in the second case the productivity of capital diminishes, and the employer cannot control the level of prices and is subject to increasing wage pressure. In the period 1954–57, the ratio developed in favor of

Table 14.10 Corrected Percentages of Distribution of Net Nonagricultural Value Added, after C. Phéline

	Wage Costs and Social Charges	Overall Profit	Fiscal and Other Charges
1954	61.9	14.5	23.6
1957	60.4	17.0	22.6
1958	60.7	15.4	23.9
1959	59.3	18.4	22.4
1960	58.7	19.7	21.6
1961	59.9	19.3	20.9
1962	60.9	18.8	20.4
1963	61.6	18.3	20.1
1964	60.9	19.1	20.0
1965	61.7	18.7	19.7
1966	61.2	19.5	19.3
1967	61.2	19.7	19.0
1968	61.7	20.3	17.9
1969	60.1	21.8	18.1
1970	61.0	21.2	17.8
1971	61.4	20.6	18.0
1972	61.4	20.7	17.8
1973	62.0	20.2	17.8

358 THE TWENTIETH CENTURY

profit; but as the table shows the fiscal measures taken in 1958 made profits drop considerably. The situation improved between 1958 and 1960 because of the relative drop in wages and the relaxation of fiscal pressure. Between 1959 and 1964, growth in the productivity of both capital and labor, and the pursuit of a policy of reducing fiscal charges, made possible in increase in the return on both labor and capital: wage costs per unit produced increased at a rate of 5.3 percent per annum, and profit per unit produced increased at a rate of 2.4 percent per annum. Between 1964 and 1967 the profit rate became stable despite the fall in the productivity of capital, and at the cost of a check on expansion. Return on labor increased at a rate lower than that of visible hourly productivity (4.3 percent and 5 percent) and at the same rate as return on capital (4.5 percent). Between 1967 and 1969 the productivity of labor increased at an accelerated rate (6 percent) but wage costs increased even faster (6.3 percent). The chief cause of the improvement in profit is to be found in the fiscal policy introduced after the 1968 crisis (abolition of the flat rate payment on wages). Between 1969 and 1973 inflation (a rise of 5.7 percent in prices) hit profits, for wage costs rose much more and much faster than productivity of labor. The latter increased only because a high level of investment was maintained, while the rise in prices of equipment goods eased off more slowly than was the case with value added. As Phéline writes, "The combined effects of high inflation and increases in productivity were not enough, as it turned out, to make invested capital fully productive, because on the one hand of the rate of investment made necessary, and on the other hand of the pressure exerted on the profits/wages ratio by high wage claims." This being so, the crisis of 1974 may have been due to the high level of accumulation which had been maintained since 1969.

For a long while, attempts were made to establish a typology of entrepreneurs' attitudes to financing, in terms of size of firm and nature of sector. According to a survey by the Centrale des Bilans covering 400 firms between 1957 and 1967, the rate of self-financing rose up to 1960 (from 83 percent to 102 percent), fell in 1962, and went up again in 1966–67 (101 percent). In fact, M. Billaudot has shown that in the sectors

covered by the survey, big firms found self-financing easier
than the smaller ones. In the chemicals industry the big firms'
rate of self-financing was 97 percent and that of the others 63
percent. This was one reason for the move toward concentration observed in the late 1960s. There are also great
differences between sectors. In those exposed to international
competition (rubber, chemicals, iron and steel), even the big
firms had to reduce their rate of self-financing. It may be, too,
that balance-sheet structures were directly affected by changes
in demand and in the distribution of factors of production.

But in the present state of knowledge, it does not seem
worth while carrying this line of inquiry further. Eric Huret
wrote in 1973: "Sector plays only a minor part in determining
the structure of the balance sheet. This structure has little to do
with the sort of goods the firm produces. It is chiefly a
reflection of something quite different: i.e., the firm's
development policy." This assertion—a very welcome one to
the historian, because it makes the entrepreneur's *behavior* the
central explanation—is based on a factorial analysis of the
balance sheets of a sample of 287 firms, supplied by the
Centrale des Bilans.

But Huret's typology covers much more than methods of
financing, and also throws light on diversification of production.
In 1969 A. Desrosières calculated rates of specialization by
sectors (relation between deliveries of each product and
turnover of the firms which deliver them), and found that rates
fell rapidly as the firms grew larger. According to the authors of
the report on "Industry" for the Sixth Plan, small firms more
often achieved a high level of "competitiveness" when they
were "directed toward definite specialization" than when they
were "too polyvalent." Big firms, on the other hand, tend more
and more to diversify their products, even outside their original
sector. Diversification today is thus very different from what it
was in the nineteenth century, when it was limited to a firm's
original sector. This is the result, first of technological interaction, which draws the chemical industries toward textiles and
the petroleum industries toward chemicals, and, second of the
adoption of management methods based on forecasting, which
subordinate production and technology to the imperatives of

commercial strategy. Big firms, instead of limiting their activities to some particular technical field, tend to develop them as extensively as possible. Typical examples are groups like the CGE (Compagnie Générale de l'Electricité), which derived from Construction Électrique, and Saint-Gobain–Pont à Mousson, derived from glass and iron and steel, which have both expanded in the direction of building and public works. The growth of a firm no longer depends, as it used to do, on technical links, but on a commercial strategy which aims at seizing every opportunity. But firms cannot neglect technical consistency altogether.

The "commercial revolution" which took place among French firms during the 1950s and particularly during the 1960s was more a matter of method than of intensity. In 1972, French firms were still not spending more on advertising than the equivalent of 0.8 percent of the GNP. What was new was the appearance of publicity campaigns seen in terms of long-term growth of the market, and drawn up as part of an overall marketing policy. The most frequently cited example is the firm of Moulinex, which the Conseil National du Patronat Français (CNPF, the French employers' national council) put forward as a model to their members. Moulinex, which makes and sells a large range of the smaller kinds of household electrical appliance, saw its turnover rise from 1 to 20 billion francs between 1957 and 1968. This growth was based on a publicity campaign launched in 1957, with the main object not of praising the virtues of any particular articles but of "creating the brand image necessary to arouse a pre-sale demand, thus overcoming the reserves of distributors." The choice of articles was the result of detailed study of consumers' real needs. Although such campaigns were not always so spectacular, they spread. They are only an obvious aspect of a much wider strategy of business growth.

Huret puts forward a classification of the 287 firms in his sample, with growth as the main criterion. He distinguishes eight different policies divided into two main categories: policies leading to weak growth (32 percent of the sample), and policies leading to strong growth (68 percent). The sample may be subdivided as follows:

(1) Weak growth policies:

—21 firms are large-scale enterprises developing their system of participations, with rapid external and very slow internal growth. Despite high profitability, they tend to resort to bank indebtedness to finance their external growth.

—9 firms represent the culmination of the previous example, and have become holding companies.

—44 enterprises, highly capitalistic and with a high rate of self-financing, prefer profitability to growth.

—18 firms, 7 of them belonging to the textiles sector, are "on the decline and not renewing their equipment." They combine low growth with low profitability.

(2) Strong growth policies:

—70 firms resemble the 44 of the subdivision above, from the point of view of the factors of production. But they choose expansion rather than profitability, distribute few dividends, are quick to debt-finance, and because they have large investment programs, have a low rate of self-financing. They are vulnerable, and probably destined to be taken over.

—87 firms are for the most part small family businesses, not very capitalistic, not very much in debt, not very diversified.

—6 small enterprises have extremely rapid growth, are highly profitable and very little in debt. Unlike the preceding firms and unlike the "normal model" of a small firm, they practice a policy of diversification through buying into other companies.

—10 firms achieved a growth rate of 24 percent between 1963 and 1969 (as against 14 percent in the case of the 87 above). These are commercial firms.

—22 firms, including 12 belonging to the building materials sector, are in a way doomed to grow because of the highly capitalistic nature of their production. They have average growth and low profitability.

So the dilemma is as follows: in highly capitalistic sectors, profitability seems possible only through limitation of growth (the group of 44 firms). Growth can apparently be assured only at the cost of indebtedness, which involves the danger of being bought into and incorporated into a group. For firms which are not very capitalistic, it is easier to achieve reasonable profitability without undue indebtedness. It is clear, moreover, that dynamism is not exclusive to big firms. Studies like Huret's have probably helped to revise official points of view on industrial policy between the Fifth and Seventh Plans. Whereas the Fifth Plan laid chief stress on the need for concentration, the Seventh, without giving up the idea of creating huge firms capable of standing up to international competition, insisted on the need to take measures which would favor the growth of "small and average-sized firms" (i.e., according to those who drew up the report, those which employ between 6 and 499 people; in 1973 these accounted for 40 percent of industrial sales). This kind of enterprise, according to the report's authors, "are by no means a mere relic of the past, doomed to disappear," and "should not become only the subcontracting infrastructure of big firms." On the contrary, "technical progress and changes in the organization of labor often point to a reduction in the optimum size of units of production." But, as Lucien Fahri asks, is this goal really compatible with specialization of activity within the framework of an international division of labor?

Bibliography

Arnaud-Ameller, P. *La France à l'épreuve de la concurrence internationale*. Paris: A. Colin, 1972.
——*Mesures économiques et financières de décembre 1958*. Paris: A. Colin, 1967.
Bairoch, P. *Commerce extérieur et développement économique de l'Europe*. Paris: Mouton, 1976.
Bernard, M. "Rendement économique et productivité du capital fixe de 1959 à 1972," *Economie et Statistique*, no. 60 (October 1974).
Bertin, G. Y. *L'investissement étranger en France*. Paris: Presses Universitaries de France, 1963.
Billaudot, M. "Les comptes des sociétés de quelques grands secteurs industriels, 1955–1964," *Etudes et Conjoncture*, no. 9 (September 1967).
Bjøl, J. *La France devant l'Europe: La politique européenne de la IVème Republique*. Copenhagen: Munskgaard, 1966.
Boeda, M. "L'industrie, frein et moteur de l'inflation," *Economie et Statistique*, no. 77 (April 1976).
Boyer, R., and J. Mistral. "Formation du capital, prix relatifs, inflation," *Economie et Statistique*, no. 77 (April 1976).

Cotta, A. *Inflation et croissance en France depuis 1962.* Paris: Presses Universitaires de France, 1974.

Courbis, R. "Comportements financiers et développement économique," *Economie et Statistique,* no. 12 (May 1970).

—— "Tarifs publics et équilibre économique," *Economie et Statistique,* no. 30 (January 1972).

De Lattre, A. *Les finances extérieures de la France.* Paris: Presses Universitaires de France, 1959.

Echard, J. "Le processus d'innovation dans l'industrie chimique," *Revue d'Economie Politique,* 1965.

"Evolution conjoncturelle en France de 1953 à 1972," *Revue de la Banque Nationale de Paris,* July 1973.

Goffin, R. *L'autofinancement des entreprises.* Paris: Sirey, 1968.

Gruson, C. *Origine et espoirs de la planification française.* Paris: Dunod, 1968.

Guibert, et al. *La mutation industrielle de la France.* Collections de l'INSEE, ser. E, nos. 21–23. Paris: Institut National de la Statistique et des Etudes Economiques, November 1975.

Herzog, H. "Comparaison des périodes d'inflation et de récession de l'économie française entre 1950 et 1965," *Etudes et Conjoncture,* March 1967.

Huret, E. "Structure des bilans et types de croissance des entreprises," *Economie et Statistique,* no. 60 (November 1973).

Inflation, le problème actuel: Rapport du Secrétaire Général. Paris: Organization for Economic Cooperation and Development, December 1970.

Malinvaud, E., J. J. Carre, and P. Dubois. *La croissance française.* Paris: Seuil, 1972.

Mariano, A. P. *Métamorphose de l'économie française, 1963–1973.* Paris: Arthaud, 1973.

Masse, P. "Le plan ou l'antihasard," *Nouvelle Revue Française,* 1965.

Mistral, J. "Commerce extérieur et croissance française: Une mutation," *Statistiques et Etudes Financières,* no. 20 (1975).

Phéline, C. "Répartition primaire des revenus et rentabilité du capital," *Statistiques et Etudes Financières,* no. 19 (1975).

"Préparation du Vème plan: Rapport sur les principales options," *Journal Officiel de la Republique Française,* supp. no. 1251 (1964).

Problematique d'une stratégie industrielle: Premières réflexions. Etudes de politique industrielle, no. 1. Paris: Documentation Française, 1974.

Rapport de la Commission Relations économiques et financières avec l'extérieur: Préparation du VIIème plan. Paris: Documentation Française, 1976.

Saint Geour, J. *La politique économique des principaux pays industiels de l'occident.* Paris: Sirey, 1969.

Szokoloczy Syllaba, J. *Les organisations professionnelles françaises et le marché commun.* Paris: A. Colin, 1965.

Thollon Pommerol, V. "Les entreprises prévoient difficilement leurs investissements," *Economie et Statistique,* no. 54 (March 1974).

Conclusion

THE OBJECT OF this book was to show that it was possible to study the economic history of France without relying exclusively on sociological explanations. Between the size of markets and the productive structure, between the agrarian structure and the rhythm of agricultural change, between relative costs and the formation of capital, between France's position in the world in 1815 and the details of its later development, and so on and so forth, there is a series of logical relationships which can be accounted for without recourse to any psychology of nations that represents the French as ill-suited to the adoption of the capitalist system. On the whole, the French were neither more protectionist nor more corporatist than other people. Their entrepreneurs had to adapt themselves to particular geographical, historical, and demographic facts.

Throughout the ninteenth and twentieth centuries, France has remained what Andrew Shonfield has called a land where state control has been traditional. The ideologies justifying this control changed, but the permanence of the control itself is striking. Present-day technocrats trained in the *grandes écoles* obey the rules of an administrative law the principles of which go back centuries: the basic idea is that there exists, over and above particular interests, a "general interest" which the state, which alone can know what the "public welfare" is, alone has the job of defending. When the state adopts a liberal doctrine it must retain the purity of its model while at the same time correcting its imperfections. Historians are in complete disagreement with one another about the real meaning of state intervention. Was it a bad thing under the Constitutional Monarchy, as many writers claim? Was it a good thing under the Second Empire? Was the state a conservative factor under the Third Republic and an expansionary factor under the Fourth and Fifth? These are popular arguments. But they overlook the diversity of administrative action and the fundamental continuity of the inspiration behind it. When a French official wants to decentralize industry, he uses the means of action of a centralizing state. When he wants to foster the development of free enterprise, he uses the incentives of a welfare state. The opening up of frontiers has held back this gradual spread of state control through the economy, but it has also imposed aids designed to help the various sectors cope with foreign competition. It is clear that the present equilibrium between the nationalized sector and the private one is fragile, and a slight modification strengthening the former would definitely turn France into a bureaucratic system.

France's dialogue with the world economy has proceeded for the last hundred and sixty years according to the latter's rhythms. In a recent book, Paul Bairoch takes a point of view similar to mine, arguing that the free trade experiment of the 1860s was on the whole bad for the French economy: it held back innovation, and above all, by worsening the farmers' standard of living, limited the prospects of industrial growth. "The influx of agricultural products," writes Bairoch, "was the chief explanation of the failure of the French liberal experiment." The subsequent protectionist experiment was too restricted to prevent France from being subjected, in many sectors, to the pressure of foreign competition. But it became gradually stricter, and culminated in the 1930s experiment with a closed economy—though France was not alone in this. This relative closure, followed by an almost complete one, enabled French capitalism to develop, against the background of a domestic market lacking in dynamism, according to a pattern which might be described as dominated by "extended oligopolies" in capital and semi-finished goods production and by a more scattered production structure for consumer goods. The genuine degree of competition within the system varied at different times, and reached zero in the 1940s. This structure was increasingly called in question by the opening up of frontiers, and

the process of concentration accelerated as a direct consequence
of the establishment of the Common Market. Nevertheless, even
the largest French enterprises are very often still too small to
compete with the most powerful multinational enterprises in their
sectors. For this reason, the French are dubious about the
advantages of the "International Division of Labor," and dread
becoming no more than subcontractors to more powerful
economies.

Such reflections send them back to old myths. All the
political parties, from the extreme right to the extreme left, have
always declared their desire to save the "middle classes." The
"small saver," the "small shopkeeper," the "small businessman,"
the "small farmer" have been so many Davids threatened by the
Goliath of capital. The state must help and protect them. M.
Laufenburger, an eminent professor of finance, noted in 1933
that "fiscal policy in France favored the middle classes." In 1977
we see the old *patente* being replaced by a "professional tax"
chiefly distinguished by the fact that it increases to a marked
degree with the size of the business concerned. Such policies
were once regarded as the expression of an economic and social
conservatism which contributed greatly to the slowdown of
French growth. But nowadays they flaunt all the virtues of a
new-style industrialism based on the dynamism of the small
entrepreneur. For the middle class of the twentieth century is no
longer the same as that of the nineteenth. Most members of the
nineteenth-century middle class devoted the greater part of their
efforts toward saving. Monetary stability made it possible to
transfer, without risk, into investment, gains accumulated
through productive activity. But the middle class of the twentieth
century can only maintain its position by moving toward wage-
earning or by consolidating what G. Ripert has called the
"capitalism of the small shop." So the twentieth century had to
work out a legal framework and a set of tax laws fostering the
preservation and development of small and medium-sized enterprises. The foundations were laid in the 1920s, when R. Poincaré,
devaluing the franc, was afraid he might "ruin the middle
classes." The solicitude shown toward small- and medium-sized
enterprises today expresses the belief that they are a necessary
counterpoise to the concentration and multinationalization of

economic power—a manifestation of some sort of "authenticity" which is threatened by the bureaucracy of the state and of big business. That is why the reports of the Seventh Plan devote so much space to them. They react against what M. A. Adelman, in a seminar at Dijon in April 1970, called "the cult of importance." The subject of the seminar was French industry's capacity for competition, and it was noted that small enterprises were "well adapted to certain types of production," that they could be "an important instrument of innovation and diffusion of technical progress," and that big industrialized countries like Germany and the United States preserved a tight network of such enterprises. But it is clear that many of these small businesses find themselves highly dependent on the large multinational groups.

Since the middle of the 1960s French enterprises, large and small, have had to cope with stricter restraints than before. There has been an increase in the number of "exposed" sectors, and many enterprises have been able to survive only by a sort of "forward flight" or anticipation; this took the form of an unprecedented move toward concentration and investment in the years 1967–73. This being so, the 1974 crisis may be regarded as a classical overcapacity crisis, leading ultimately to a drop in the marginal profitability of capital. The rise in the price of raw materials, which created additional liquidity problems and led to a sudden cut in household consumption, worsened the present situation. There is therefore no reason why France should not be able to emerge from the present crisis.

Nor is it certain that France cannot limit inflation to a reasonable level. I have deliberately avoided attempting an overall view of French inflation, though some authors, including Sauvy, regard it as the result of a fundamental change in the behavior of the French people, who are represented as being in the grip of a kind of inflation fever. In fact, the development of inflation in France may be described as a series of waves, inflation occurring and increasing by reason of certain "rigidities" giving rise to various impulses; but these "rigidities" are not peculiar to France. The "inflation through the exchange rates" of the 1920s is not comparable to the inflation caused by growing demand of the 1930s, the inflation due to shortages and the monetary inflation of the 1940s, the inflation through demand of the late 1950s, or to the present inflation through costs. The only element all these waves of inflation have in common is the increase in the money supply; there is no study on this in France comparable to that of Milton Friedman for the United States. As regards the recent period, most analyses stress that there were "inflationary tensions" even before the rise in the cost of raw materials. Since the end of the 1960s industrial prices, which until then had acted as a brake on inflation, became an instigator of it: rising world prices exercised less pressure on French prices, and French structures themselves became less competitive. But local tensions on the labor market (especially in the engineering sector, because of the large investment effort there) caused wage increases which spread over the whole economy because of the extraordinary rigidity of the income scale in France. In these circumstances it was both necessary and possible for enterprises to finance enormous additional investments through price increases which maintained their profit margin. This alone made it possible to preserve a minimum level of self-financing and to pay the rapidly increasing financial charges. This process was accelerated to an intolerable degree by the rise in the cost of raw materials. The reason for the continued high level of inflation in 1974 and 1975, in the midst of a recession, was that this inflation was an inflation through costs.

The present uneasiness in France, aggravated by the eternal comparisons with West Germany's achievements, is reflected in the reports of the Seventh Plan; but it should not make us lose sight of the fact that France has good grounds for optimism. How many prophets of woe predicted that French industry would not survive the impact of the Common Market? The changes which have been accepted since then bear witness to the fact that although France does not enjoy what M. Boeda has called Germany's extraordinary "bonus for specialization in capital goods," it can maintain its rate of expansion at a level enabling it to meet all its commitments. All that is necessary is for France's economy to be managed with determination and with a definite object in view, as was the case between 1969 and 1973.

Bibliography

Adelman, M. A. "Rapport général," in *La capacité de concurrence de l'industrie française*, edited by Jean Chapelle et Claude Ponsard. Paris and Montreal: Bordas, 1971.

Laufenburger, H. "Fluctuations économiques et rendements fiscaux," *Revue d'Economie Politique*, 1934.

—— *L'intervention de l'Etat dan l'économie.* Paris: Pichon, 1939.

Ribert, G. *Aspects juridiques du capitalisme moderne.* Paris: Librairie Générale de Droit et de Jurisprudence, 1951.

Schonfield, A. *Modern Capitalism.* London and New York: Oxford University Press, 1965.

Index